THE DEMANDS OF CONSEQ

The Demands of Consequentialism

TIM MULGAN

CLARENDON PRESS · OXFORD

OXFORD
UNIVERSITY PRESS

Great Clarendon Street, Oxford ox2 6DP

Oxford University Press is a department of the University of Oxford.
It furthers the University's objective of excellence in research, scholarship,
and education by publishing worldwide in

Oxford New York

Auckland Cape Town Dar es Salaam Hong Kong Karachi
Kuala Lumpur Madrid Melbourne Mexico City Nairobi
New Delhi Shanghai Taipei Toronto

With offices in

Argentina Austria Brazil Chile Czech Republic France Greece
Guatemala Hungary Italy Japan Poland Singapore
South Korea Switzerland Thailand Turkey Ukraine Vietnam

Oxford is a registered trade mark of Oxford University Press
in the UK and in certain other countries

Published in the United States
by Oxford University Press Inc., New York

British Library Cataloguing in Publication Data

Data available

Library of Congress Cataloging in Publication Data

Data available

Typeset by Hope Services (Abingdon) Ltd
Printed in Great Britain
on acid-free paper by
Biddles Ltd,
King's Lynn, Norfolk

ISBN 0–19–825093–2   978–0–19–825093–7
ISBN 0–19–928697–3 (Pbk.)   978–0–19–928697–3 (Pbk.)

1 3 5 7 9 10 8 6 4 2

Preface

This book began life as my Oxford DPhil thesis. Over the ten years of writing it, I have accumulated more debts than I can hope now to adequately acknowledge.

For comments, conversations, or criticisms which have improved this book, I am grateful to Elizabeth Ashford, Margaret Bedggood, David Brink, Gillian Brock, John Broome, Tim Chappell, Colin Cheyne, John Cottingham, Roger Crisp, Ramon Das, Julia Driver, Heather Dyke, Ray Frey, Robert Goodin, Edward Harcourt, Reid Hoffman, Nils Holtug, Brad Hooker, Thomas Hurka, Frank Jackson, P. J. Kelly, Karstin Klint-Jensen, Rahul Kumar, Michael Martin, Elinor Mason, Janet McLean, Andrew Moore, Richard Mulgan, Liam Murphy, Alan Musgrave, Derek Parfit, Thomas Pedersen, Roy Perrett, Philip Pettit, Charles Pigden, Michael Smith, Peter Smith, Nick Sparks, Christine Swanton, Gwen Taylor, Roger Teichmann, Mike Thrush, Peter Unger, Peter Vallentyne, David Ward, Bernard Williams, and two anonymous readers.

I have also benefited from discussion with audiences at the Universities of Otago, Auckland, Copenhagen, Victoria, Reading, ANU, and St Andrews; at meetings of the International Society for Utilitarian Studies held in New Orleans and Winston-Salem; and at the Wolfson Philosophy Society.

For detailed feedback on innumerable drafts, and for all their support and encouragement over the years, I am particularly grateful to Brad Hooker, Andrew Moore, and Derek Parfit.

For turning my disk into a book, I am grateful for the editorial assistance of Charlotte Jenkins, Peter Momtchiloff, and Hilary Walford.

For providing a series of congenial and encouraging working environments I thank all my friends at Wolfson college, and my colleagues at the Universities of Otago and Auckland.

This book would not exist without the financial support of the British Council, the Association of Commonwealth Universities, Wolfson College Oxford, and the Universities of Otago and Auckland.

For encouraging me to spend my life writing books such as this, I thank Philip Pettit, Alan Musgrave, and, especially, my parents.

For consenting to share such a life, I am most especially grateful to Janet McLean.

All these people could have done far more good by devoting their time, energy, and money to famine relief. My hope is that this book provides some justification for such sub-optimal resource allocations.

Several sections of this book draw on material I have previously published elsewhere. I am grateful to Blackwells Publishers, Edinburgh University Press and the Johns Hopkins University Press for permission to reproduce material from the following articles: 'Slote's Satisficing Consequentialism', *Ratio*, 6 (1993), 121–34; 'Rule Consequentialism and famine', *Analysis*, 54 (1994), 187–92; 'One false virtue of Rule Consequentialism, and one new vice', *Pacific Philosophical Quarterly*, 77 (1996), 362–73; 'A Non-proportional Hybrid Moral Theory', *Utilitas* 9 (1997), 291–306; 'Two Conceptions of Benevolence', *Philosophy and Public Affairs*, 26 (1997), 1–21; and 'Ruling Out Rule Consequentialism', in B. Hooker, E. Mason, and D. E. Miller (eds.), *Morality, Rules and Consequences* (Edinburgh, Edinburgh University Press, 2000), pp. 212–21.

Contents

PART ONE

Simple Consequentialism

1

Introduction

If you are reading this, then you are very privileged. In a world of starvation, poverty, misery, and war, you have time to enjoy the luxury of philosophy. Obviously enough, so do I. One of the purposes of this book is to ask whether such behaviour is justified.

There are very many very needy people in the world. About 20 million people a year starve to death. About one billion people live in severe poverty. Gross domestic product per capita is over $20,000 in the twenty wealthiest countries, and under $250 in the poorest fifteen. Life expectancy is over 76 in Japan, virtually all of Europe, Australia, New Zealand, and the USA. It is under 50 in Afghanistan, Angola, Botswana, Chad, Ethiopia, Mozambique, Rwanda, and Somalia. In Sierra Leone, Malawi, and Uganda it is under 40.[1]

A variety of charitable agencies can alleviate these needs. No doubt governments, multinationals, and others could do far more than they do. But the question still remains: faced with such urgent needs, at least some of which I could meet at comparatively little cost to myself, how should I as an individual act?

Since the nineteenth century, one influential approach to moral questions has been Consequentialism. Consequentialists claim that the right thing to do in any situation is the act with the best consequences. (One prominent form of Consequentialism is Utilitarianism, where the value to be maximized is human happiness.) What response would Consequentialism require to the situation described in previous paragraphs? How should I spend my next dollar? Consequentialism tells me to put that dollar wherever it will do the most good. In the hands of a reputable aid agency, my dollar could save a child from a crippling illness. A few more dollars might make a substantial contribution towards a clean water supply for an entire village. Could I do anything nearly as valuable with my dollar if I kept it for myself? It is highly unlikely. Dollars do not go very far in affluent suburbs in the developed world any more.

So I should give my next dollar to charity. How should I then spend my next remaining dollar? Well, in the hands of a reputable aid agency. . . It looks

---

[1] These figures are drawn from *The Economist Pocket World in Figures 2000 edition*, pp. 86–7; quoted in Hooker, *Ideal Code, Real World*, p. 147.

as if I must keep donating till I reach the point where my own basic needs, or my ability to keep earning dollars, are in jeopardy. Most of my current activities will have to go. Nor will my sacrifice be only financial. According to Consequentialism, I should also spend my time where it will do most good. I should devote all my energies to charity work, as well as all my money.

Perhaps we would admire someone who behaved in this way. But is it plausible to claim that those of us who do not are guilty of wrongdoing; or that we have a moral obligation to devote all our resources to charity? Some advocates of Consequentialism have even suggested that our failure to do so is morally no different from murder. (On the grounds that there is no morally significant difference between killing someone and allowing him to die when one could have saved him.)

Such conclusions strike many people as absurd. This leads to the common objection that Consequentialism is unreasonably demanding, as it leaves the agent too little room (time, resources, energy) for her own projects or interests. I shall call this the Demandingness Objection. This book is an examination of Consequentialist responses to this objection. I seek to construct a Consequentialist moral theory that is not unreasonably demanding.

Our discussion will often focus on the following story.

Affluent's Tale. Affluent is an affluent citizen of a developed country, who already makes significant donations to charity. She is sitting at her desk with her cheque book. In front of her are two pamphlets: one from a reputable international aid organization, the other from her local theatre company. Affluent has enough money either to buy theatre tickets or to make a donation to the charity, but not both. Because of her love of the theatre, she buys the tickets, even though she knows that the money would have done far more good if sent to the charity.

The Demandingness Objection says that Consequentialism must condemn Affluent's behaviour, and that this is unreasonable. As the foregoing discussion makes apparent, this is no abstract tale. Allowing for minor variations— perhaps aid agencies solicit your donation by television, perhaps you prefer movies to theatre—we are all Affluent throughout much of our daily life. What Consequentialism demands of Affluent it will demand of us all. The purpose of this book is to ask what Consequentialism really does demand, and whether those demands are reasonable.

1.1. The Relevance of the book

Our discussion may seem of limited interest, as only those who are predisposed towards Consequentialism will be concerned to discover its limits. However, many other moral theories must address the same questions as Consequentialism. In particular, if we have obligations to meet the needs of others, then we are owed an explanation of the structure and limits of those obligations. Even within a Non-Consequentialist theory, obligations to aid others often take a Consequentialist form. An exploration of the limits of Consequentialism is useful to anyone interested in understanding morality.

In the remainder of this section, I explore the demands of various prominent moral and political theories and their relationship to the demands of Consequentialism. Our purpose here is to explore broad moral approaches, not to engage in detailed exegetical or analytical discussion of any particular moral theory.

1.1.1. Kantian Ethics

The basis of Kant's ethics is the search for a rational foundation for morality.[2] Only if our actions are grounded solely in rationality can they be truly free, and hence worthy of moral assessment. The test of rationality is the Categorical Imperative, under which a rational agent acts only according to maxims (or principles) that can consistently be willed as universal laws. Kant tests a maxim by asking if it would be consistent for a rational agent to desire a world where everyone obeyed that maxim. For instance, Kant argued that the maxim 'Tell lies' cannot be universally adopted, as that would be self-defeating. The point is not just that universal lying would have bad consequences. Rather, Kant is claiming that it is not possible for lying to be universal. It only makes sense to tell a lie if you expect other people to believe you. If everyone always lied, no one would ever believe anyone. There would thus be no point in lying. The very concept of lying would lose its meaning of 'deceptive presentation of falsehood intended to be accepted by others as truth'. Therefore, no rational agent will ever tell a lie, whatever the consequences.[3]

---

[2] For Kant's most accessible account of moral philosophy, see his *Groundwork of the Metaphysics of Morals*. An excellent historical introduction to contemporary themes in Kantian ethics is Schneewind, 'Autonomy, Obligation, and Virtue'. See also Korsgaard, 'Kant' and O'Neill, 'Kantian Ethics'.

[3] Korsgaard, 'The Right to Lie: Kant on Dealing with Evil'.

Kant also offers an alternative formulation of the Categorical Imperative. He argues that rational agents will always treat human beings as ends-in-themselves, and never merely as means to their own ends. Lying constitutes a classic failure to respect another as an end, as you deprive the other person of the chance to decide for himself whether or not to be used as a means to your end.

Kant's commitment to impartiality clearly rules out any foundational role for partiality or concessions to the agent's self-interest. Furthermore, Kant does include positive duties to come to the aid of others.[4] He distinguishes two types of duties: perfect and imperfect. The obligation not to lie is a perfect duty, unconditionally telling the agent exactly what to do. A perfect duty requires certain specific actions, and rules out others. By contrast, duties of benevolence are imperfect. There is no particular action the agent must perform to fulfil them. The duty to be benevolent requires us to perform *some* benevolent acts, but it does not tell us exactly which ones.

While these duties are imperfect, they still threaten to rule out devoting my resources to my own happiness. Imperfect duties do not outweigh perfect duties, but they presumably seek to fill up the space those duties leave open. Many patterns of behaviour are consistent with observance of all one's perfect duties. The crucial question for Kantians will be: at what point does a personal sacrifice in pursuit of an imperfect duty constitute a failure to treat myself, or some particular other person to whom I have a positive obligation, as an end? Only then can I refrain from aiding others.

This threatens to make Kantian ethics extremely demanding. It is hard to see how donating most of my income to charity would constitute a failure of self-respect, or otherwise violate any positive duty. (An exception would be where I have made a very demanding promise. For instance, if I promise to give all my money to you, then I do have a positive duty not to give it to charity. But then morality's demands would still be extreme.) The question determining the demands of Kantianism is also very similar to the questions raised by sophisticated Consequentialists.[5]

1.1.2. Contractualism

The classic contemporary formulation of the Contractualist account of morality is due to T. M. Scanlon: 'An act is wrong if its performance under the circumstances would be disallowed by any system of rules for the general

---

[4] McCarty, 'The Limits of Kantian Duty'.
[5] For a recent attempt to combine Kantian and Consequentialist approaches, see Cummiskey, 'Kantian Consequentialism'.

regulation of behaviour which no one could reasonably reject as a basis for informed, unforced general agreement.'[6] It certainly seems possible that this test will generate quite demanding principles. Indeed, they may be even more demanding than Consequentialism, as Contractualists often give particular priority to the worst-off individuals.

Garret Cullity, arguing from Contractualist premises, concludes that I ought to do all that I can to save other people's lives until I reach the level below which I would be giving up necessary components of my own well-being.[7] It seems reasonable for those who are starving to reject any principle permitting me to retain inessential resources rather than meeting their most basic needs.

The crucial question for Contractualist moral theory is thus: at what point do personal sacrifices deprive me of the essential components of a worthwhile life? Precisely the same question arises for Kantians and Consequentialists. Indeed, some philosophers have argued that only Utilitarian principles can pass the Contractualist test.[8] Even if this is not correct, it does seem likely that Contractualism will be every bit as demanding as Consequentialism.

Another problem for Contractualism is presented by Nagel, who argues that, in the present state of the world, it may be impossible to construct any set of principles that no one can reasonably reject. Any possible principle of aid will either make unreasonable demands on the affluent (from their point of view), or pay inadequate attention to the basic needs of the destitute (from their point of view). If the notion of reasonable rejection is at least partly determined by the agent's own perspective, then any principle will be reasonably rejected by someone.[9]

Contractualists might reply that principles of aid presuppose some background set of entitlements, guaranteeing me free use of my resources. This raises two problems. The first is that, from the fact that I own something, it does not follow that I do not have an obligation to give it away. Arguing from Contractualist premises, one might conclude that others may not force me to do so. The second problem is that, if our overall theory is Contractualist, then the property rights themselves must be given a Contractualist justification. We need a system of property rights no one can reasonably reject. Any

---

[6] Scanlon, 'Contractualism and Utilitarianism', p. 110; see also Scanlon, *What We Owe to Each Other*, p. 4. See also Brink, 'The Separateness of Persons, Distributive Norms and Moral Theory'; Nagel, *Equality and Partiality*, ch. 4; and Nagel, 'One-to-One'. See also below, Section 8.8.

[7] I owe this suggestion to Garret Cullity. For a full discussion of similar lines of argument, see Cullity, *The Demands of Morality*.

[8] Harsanyi, 'Can the Maximin Principle Serve as a Basis for Morality?'.

[9] Nagel, *Equality and Partiality*, and Nagel, 'One-to-One'. See below, Section 8.8, for further discussion of these issues.

system where property rights are very unequally distributed will be rejected by those who miss out.

Jeremy Waldron offers a similar argument in favour of universal property rights.[10] If property rights are to be justified on the basis of their contribution to human flourishing, then the only defensible system of property rights will provide every person with sufficient property to meet his basic needs and control his life. Respect for morally respectable property rights would then involve great sacrifices from those in the developed world, as a justifiable distribution of entitlements would require a great deal of redistribution in favour of the poor.

1.1.3. Common-Sense Morality

Some might conclude that extreme demands are an artefact of moral theory. We could avoid them by abandoning moral theory, and confining ourselves to the world of everyday moral intuitions. Unfortunately, problems of demandingness can also arise within the realm of Common-Sense Morality, or everyday moral intuition. In particular, many real world examples expose a tension between the following intuitively plausible principles.

The Principle of Benevolence.   When an agent is able to meet the desperate needs of an innocent stranger at negligible cost to herself, she ought to do so.

The Principle of Liveability.   It should be possible for an agent to comply with all correct moral principles and still live a worthwhile, flourishing life.[11]

In short, Common-Sense Morality includes both the thought that there are limits to the demands of morality, and the thought that the demands of morality are largely determined by the state of the world. There is obviously some tension between these two appealing ideals, especially in a world with a vast amount of unmet need.

James Fishkin has argued that any intuitively appealing principle of benevolence will place very great demands on affluent people, given the present state of the world.[12] Similarly, Garrett Cullity argues that, given our ordinary notions of kindness and justice, it is both unkind and unjust for any of us to fail to save a starving child on the other side of the world.[13] Common-Sense

---

[10] Waldron, *The Right to Private Property*, esp. ch. 12, and Brock, 'Is Redistribution to Help the Needy Unjust?', p. 57.

[11] For discussions of the demands of Common-Sense Morality, see Fishkin, *The Limits of Obligation*; Cullity, 'International Aid and the Scope of Kindness'; Kagan, *The Limits of Morality*, pp. 47–80; and Scheffler, *Human Morality*, pp. 17–28.

[12] Fishkin, *The Limits of Obligation*.

[13] Cullity, 'International Aid and the Scope of Kindness', pp. 8–10.

Morality can place great demands on agents who seek to be benevolent, kind, and just.

At the very least, defenders of Common-Sense Morality must tell us how to balance the needs of others against our own desires and projects. They must address the very same questions as Consequentialists. This is hardly surprising. The intuitive principles of Common-Sense Morality are the starting point for any moral theory. If the tension between Benevolence and Liveability is found in Common-Sense Morality itself, then we should expect similar tensions in any developed moral theory.

1.1.4. Virtue Ethics

Similar remarks apply to Virtue Ethics, often taken to be the least theoretical extension of Common-Sense Morality.[14] A plausible account of the virtues must include at least some other-regarding virtues, such as benevolence, kindness, justice, generosity, or charity. If we acknowledge the significance of such virtues, and if we live in a world where the needs of others are great, then we need some assurance that the life of virtue does not make great demands. In a world such as ours, it seems prima facie unlikely that the life of the generous person, for instance, will be a comfortable or affluent one. Sophisticated Consequentialism may provide additional resources to explore the limits of the other-regarding virtues.[15]

1.1.5. Egoism

One final moral theory is Egoism. The Egoist holds that the sole obligation of each agent is to pursue her own self-interest. It may seem obvious that such a theory has no problem with demandingness. Yet some philosophers have argued that a sophisticated form of Egoism is actually very demanding.[16] (See also the discussion in Section 1.4.2.) Moreover, Egoism faces other problems. The suggestion that we have no obligations whatsoever to others can seem extremely implausible. Indeed, many of us find Egoism every bit as alienating as Consequentialism. Every moral enquiry must begin from some undefended assumptions. This book is addressed to those who accept that the needs of others place some moral demands upon us, and for whom one

---

[14] For an introduction to contemporary Virtue Ethics, see Crisp and Slote, 'Introduction'.
[15] For recent discussions of the relationship between Consequentialism and the virtues, see Crisp, 'Utilitarianism and the Life of Virtue'; Driver, 'The Virtues and Human Nature'; and Driver, 'Monkeying with Motives'.
[16] See Brink, 'Self-Love and Altruism', and Persson, 'The Universal Basis of Egoism'.

of the central tasks of moral theory is to balance the competing requirements of the individual's own good and the interests of others. The Egoist answer seems as extreme as Consequentialism, and even less plausible.

1.1.6. Contractualist Political Theory

Moral demands also arise in the political realm. They thus pose problems for political theory as well as moral theory. This is most obvious if our political theory is itself Consequentialist. For instance, Utilitarianism is offered as an account of political as well as personal morality. The task of creating a just utilitarian society would obviously be very demanding. Non-consequentialist political theories seem less demanding. However, this appearance can be deceptive.

The most famous contemporary political Contractualist is John Rawls, who defends a very strong doctrine of liberal impartiality.[17] The basic device Rawls uses to generate his principles of justice is the Original Position, where people choose principles to govern their society. This choice is made behind a Veil of Ignorance. The choosers know *what* their society will look like if any given principle is adopted, but not *who* they will be in that society.[18] Suppose that, in a very simple society, there are two groups: the Rich and the Poor. To discover what justice requires in that society, we ask the following question: which principles of justice would a rational person choose, if he did not know whether he himself would be one of the Rich or one of the Poor?

Rawls also stipulates that the participants in the Original Position are *maximiners*. That is, when choosing under conditions of uncertainty, they choose a course of action where the worst possible outcome is at least as good as the worst possible outcome under any alternative course of action.

Although Rawls originally presents his theory as applying within an individual political community, the device of the Original Position can be applied to international political morality. The result is very demanding for citizens of the developed world. For instance, Thomas Carson argues that 'on any plausible interpretation, the original position for the law of nations will yield strongly egalitarian principles for the redistribution of wealth'.[19] Behind the veil of ignorance one would not know whether one would be living in a rich country or a poor one. A Rawlsian will then choose principles of international relations to maximize the position of those in the poor countries.

---

[17] For Rawls's original theory, see Rawls, *A Theory of Justice*. For Rawls's most recent views on international justice, see Rawls, *The Law of Peoples*.

[18] Rawls, *A Theory of Justice*, pp. 17–22.

[19] T. Carson, 'Utilitarianism and World Poverty', p. 250.

This will require great sacrifices of people in rich countries, so long as they remain at least as well off as the poor. Similarly, Charles Beitz extends Rawls's apparatus to yield a 'global maximin principle'.[20]

The question facing Rawlsians is thus: at what point will the sacrifices required of those in the developed world bring their standard of living below that of the world's poorest people? Once again, this comes very close to the question asked by sophisticated Consequentialists. Indeed, the resulting theory may be even more demanding than Consequentialism, as the main difference is that Rawls gives greater weight to the interests of the worse off. As many commentators have observed, if we were to replace Rawls's maximin with maximization of expected utility, then we might end up with Utilitarianism.[21]

Rawls might reply that the principles of justice apply only to institutions, not to individuals. They thus cannot place demands on individuals, beyond the requirement to obey the dictates of just institutions. In a world of just institutions, deprivation and poverty could be solved by a modest level of general taxation. The demands on affluent individuals would thus be slight.

The main problem with this reply is that we do not live in a world of just institutions. If our political theory is to offer us relevant advice, then we must move to an impure theory, and ask what individuals should do in a world without just institutions. Two obvious alternatives present themselves. (1) Individuals have an obligation to seek to bring just institutions into existence. (2) Individuals have an obligation to pursue the goals a just institution would pursue. If just institutions would include a welfare state, then in the absence of such institutions individuals must engage in personal charity. These obligations obviously threaten to become very demanding, and we are owed an account of their limits.[22]

1.1.7. Libertarianism

The central Libertarian idea is that people have absolute, inviolable property rights. Everybody owns themselves, together with whatever they justly acquire, whatever is justly transferred to them by a previous owner, and whatever they produce using their own labour.[23] All politically enforceable rights follow from these property rights. I can *justly* do whatever I want with

---

[20] Beitz, *Political Theory and International Relations*, quoted in Fishkin, 'Obligations beyond Borders', p. 11.

[21] Harsanyi, 'Can the Maximin Principle Serve as a Basis for Morality?'.

[22] Murphy, 'Institutions and the Demands of Justice'.

[23] This view goes back to Locke. The most prominent modern exponent is Robert Nozick (see his *Anarchy, State, and Utopia*).

anything I own, so long as I do not actively interfere with anything that you own. If I own all my money, I can do whatever I want with it. It might be *desirable* for me to give some money to the poor. Perhaps I would be a better person if I did. However, justice requires that I be allowed to refrain from giving money to the poor, if I so choose.

Another crucial feature of Libertarianism is what Nozick calls the 'Lockean proviso'.[24] This is a limitation on just acquisition, whereby you can acquire something only if you leave 'as much and as good for others'. You cannot justly acquire the last portion of some particular resource, as this would leave nothing for others. However, as Nozick himself realizes, the original Lockean proviso will not work for limited resources, as it would imply that no one could justly acquire anything. For instance, as land is a scarce resource, no one can leave as much land available for others. So no one could ever justly acquire land. Nozick thus reinterprets the proviso as follows: an acquisition is just if and only if it leaves other people *no worse off* than they would have been if the acquisition had not taken place.

It may seem obvious that Libertarians can avoid the problem of demandingness altogether, as their theory appears to generate no positive obligations whatsoever. So long as I do not interfere with other people's exercise of their property rights, I have done all that justice requires of me. Unfortunately, things are not so simple. In the first place, justice is not the whole of morality. Indeed, Libertarians often stress the fact that their theory is merely an account of politically enforceable rights. We do have other moral obligations, but they are not politically enforceable. Libertarian negative rights must be supplemented by an account of our positive moral duties. We cannot assume in advance that this account is less demanding than other theories of benevolence.

A second problem is internal to the notion of Libertarian property rights. Such rights arise only as a result of a just process of acquisition, creation, or transfer. They are thus constrained by the requirements of justice in acquisition, in particular by the Lockean proviso. Furthermore, as Gillian Brock has argued, these 'constraints on legitimate initial acquisition play a *permanent* role in maintaining the legitimacy of property rights'.[25] I must exercise my property rights consistently with the proviso grounding those rights. Under the Lockean proviso, as Nozick interprets it, 'whether or not an initial acquisition is justified depends importantly on the scarcity of resources relative to

---

[24] For discussions of the Lockean proviso, see Nozick, *Anarchy, State, and Utopia*, pp. 175–82; Wolff, *Robert Nozick: Property, Justice, and the Minimal State*, pp. 107–12; and Kymlicka, *Contemporary Political Philosophy*, pp. 110–18.

[25] Brock, 'Is Redistribution to Help the Needy Unjust?', p. 53.

those who need them'.[26] If my acquisition would leave others without sufficient resources to meet their basic needs, then I cannot acquire full property
rights. I may well be entitled to some reward for my efforts, but whether the
appropriate reward is a full property right depends largely on the situation of
others. Suppose I initially acquire a water hole when they are abundant.
Subsequently, all the other water holes dry up. It would now be inconsistent
with the Lockean proviso for me to acquire a water hole. I can no longer prevent others from using my water hole, as the condition that legitimized my
initial acquisition (namely, the abundance of water holes) no longer applies.
The Lockean proviso may thus oblige me to redistribute in times of scarcity.
Brock concludes that redistribution to meet the needs of others 'is frequently
a necessary condition for our retaining any defensible property rights at all',
even on a Libertarian account of those rights.[27]

To determine whether I can spend my money on myself rather than meeting the needs of others, even Libertarians must balance my preferences
against those needs. The resulting theory of property rights may be very
demanding. As we saw earlier, this result is not peculiar to Libertarianism.
Some element of distributive justice may be an essential feature of any
acceptable account of property rights. In practice, the difference between
Libertarian and Contractualist accounts of property rights may not be as significant as is often supposed. (See Section 1.1.2.)

Our treatment of moral and political theory has hardly been exhaustive.
However, I trust it has been sufficient to demonstrate that the issues
addressed in this book should be of interest to all moral theorists, and not
merely to Consequentialists. Every theory needs an account of the structure
and limits of the demands of morality, especially in relation to the needs of
others. Different moral theories are also more similar than is commonly
thought. They all suffer from similar tensions, and must all address the same
questions.

1.2. Arguments in Favour of Consequentialism

Another reason to explore the resources of Consequentialism is the considerable appeal of the Consequentialist approach. In this section I highlight
that appeal by briefly sketching the main arguments in favour of Consequentialism.

The simplest way to motivate Consequentialism is to see it as developing
the thought that morality or moral action should be concerned with making

---

[26] Ibid. 55.   [27] Ibid. 58.

the world a better place. At the extreme, this argument takes Consequentialism to be true by definition. This seems to have been the view of Moore, who argued that 'x is right' simply means 'x best promotes the good'.[28] A more modest formulation is that, while it is possible to imagine Non-Consequentialist moral theories, the most rational way to respond to any value is to promote it.[29] For instance, if we believe that happiness is valuable, then it is rational to seek to maximize the amount of happiness in the world. Consequentialism is thus the most rational moral theory, as it always tells us to promote value. We might support this conclusion using an analogy between moral rationality and individual rationality. On many views of the latter, it is rational for an agent to seek to maximize her own expected utility. By analogy, a moral theory should tell us how a rational agent would behave if she attached equal weight to the well-being of all agents. That is, if she were completely impartial. Consequentialism is the answer to this question.[30]

Similarly, we might see Consequentialism as a natural account of the central moral values of impartiality and equality. On the face of it, Consequentialism treats all agents perfectly equally, and is thus perfectly impartial.[31] Consequentialism thus competes with Kantian and Contractualist accounts of impartiality or equality.

A final argument in favour of Consequentialism appeals to the theoretical virtue of simplicity. If we accept that promotion is sometimes a rational response to value, then the simplest moral theory will recommend promotion as a universal response to value.[32]

None of these arguments is conclusive. Indeed, they are all highly controversial. Consequentialist accounts of rationality, impartiality, equality, and simplicity have all been challenged, as has the underlying assumption that an acceptable moral theory must be rational, impartial, or simple. Many of these debates will surface again as we explore various Consequentialist solutions. The purpose of this section has merely been to establish that the Consequentialist approach is worthy of full exploration.

---

[28] Quoted in Holbrook, 'Consequentialism: The Philosophical Dog that does not Bark', pp. 107–8.

[29] The terminology here is borrowed from Philip Pettit, as is the general argument (Pettit, 'Consequentialism', pp. 230–3). See also Scheffler, *The Rejection of Consequentialism*, p. 123.

[30] Scheffler, 'Agent-Centred Restrictions, Rationality and the Virtues', p. 414.

[31] Crisp, 'Utilitarianism and the Life of Virtue', pp. 139–40, and Scheffler, *Human Morality*, pp. 108–9.

[32] Pettit, 'Consequentialism', pp. 236–40.

1.3. Related Objections to Consequentialism

The Demandingness Objection is often linked to several other common objections to Consequentialism. In this section I distinguish these objections and explore their interconnections.

1.3.1. The Integrity Objection

Another common objection to Consequentialism is the 'integrity' or 'alienation' objection. The classic formulation is due to Bernard Williams: 'how can a man, as a utilitarian agent, come to regard as one satisfaction among others, and a dispensable one, a project or attitude round which he has built his life. . .'[33]

Williams suggests that, by requiring every agent to take no more account of her own welfare than of the welfare of others, Consequentialism undermines the *integrity* of the agent's life. The Consequentialist agent must view every life from the outside, seeing it only in terms of the value it adds to the overall value of the universe. We might refer to this as the impersonal value of a life. The charge is that Consequentialism requires us to view our lives only from the impersonal perspective. Williams suggests that no agent can view her own life in this way and flourish.

Peter Railton expresses a similar objection in terms of *alienation*, which 'can be characterized . . . as a kind of estrangement . . . resulting in some sort of loss'.[34] By requiring us always to adopt the impersonal perspective, Utilitarianism threatens to alienate us from our own lives. If, following Susan Wolf, we define a meaningful life as a life 'of active engagement in projects of worth',[35] then we might object that no agent who followed Consequentialist moral theory could live a meaningful life, as she would be unable to identify with her own projects.

It is important not to be misled by the term 'integrity'. This does not refer to a separable valuable component of a good life, or to moral uprightness. Rather, Williams speaks of the integrity of a human life in the same way that we might speak of the integrity of a work of art.[36] The integrity of a life is its wholeness, unity, or shape.

---

[33] Smart and Williams, *Utilitarianism: For and Against*, p. 116. For an overview of the debate surrounding this objection, see Crisp, *Mill: On Utilitarianism*, pp. 135–53.

[34] Railton, 'Alienation, Consequentialism and Morality', p. 134. Railton acknowledges that this characterization is 'very rough', but it is sufficient for our present purposes.

[35] Wolf, 'Happiness and Meaning: Two Aspects of the Good Life', p. 209.

[36] This analogy is drawn from Crisp, *Mill: On Utilitarianism*, p. 136.

The Integrity Objection is logically distinct from the Demandingness Objection. A moral theory could violate integrity without making any strong demands in the ordinary sense. For instance, we might imagine a theory, let us call it Impartial Spectatorism, requiring agents to view the world from the impersonal perspective at all times, but with no obligation to act in the world. Alternatively, a moral theory could be very demanding without violating anyone's integrity. For instance, a theory telling agents to devote their lives to a religious vocation might foster highly unified integral lives, while making great demands on each agent's resources (although this degree of religious devotion might itself become alienating).

Despite their distinctness, however, the two objections are closely related. In the first place, the violation of integrity is a striking *example* of the unreasonable demands of Consequentialism. A naive Consequentialist might argue that his theory only requires Affluent to give up money, which is not a vital component of human flourishing. A Marxian Consequentialist might even suggest that Affluent is better off without the distractions of consumer society. Opponents of Consequentialism will reply that Consequentialism not only requires Affluent to sacrifice resources she could have devoted to her own projects, it also requires her to be prepared to abandon those projects immediately should they cease to be her most effective way of maximizing the impersonal good.

This is a very significant point. The force of the Demandingness Objection is a function, not only of the number of demands a given theory makes, but also of the moral significance of each demand to the individual agent. Some components or aspects of well-being may be more significant than others. For instance, we may judge the demand that I give up my freedom more harshly than the demand that I relinquish most of my worldly possessions, even though the latter leaves me worse off than the former. (I explore such possibilities at some length in the final part of this book.)

Alternatively, the notion of integrity might provide not only an example of the unreasonableness of Consequentialism, but also an *explanation* of that unreasonableness. Why does Consequentialism make such demands? Because it ignores the moral significance of integrity. Consequentialism makes extreme demands because it requires us always to view the world from the impersonal perspective, and ignore our own personal point of view. This is unreasonable because, unless we are allowed to view the world from a perspective granting special weight to our own concerns, we cannot live recognizably human lives.

1.3.2. *Separateness of Persons*

Another common objection to Consequentialism is that it 'ignores the separateness of persons'.[37] In other words, Consequentialism pays insufficient attention to the fact that each person has a separate and unique life to live. For instance, traditional Utilitarianism seeks to maximize the sum total of hedonic units. It is uninterested in how these units are combined into lives, and is thus willing to sacrifice one person's life to provide a small amount of happiness to a large enough number of people. Because it ignores questions regarding the distribution of utility across lives, Utilitarianism permits unacceptable levels of uncompensated sacrifice, and pays inadequate regard to the separateness of persons.

Taken to the extreme, this objection would rule out all redistribution and all obligations to come to the aid of others. After all, uncompensated sacrifice occurs whenever a moral principle requires one agent to give something up to further the interests of another.[38] Such an extreme position does not seem plausible. The complaint against Consequentialism cannot be simply that it requires the agent to balance her own needs against those of others. Every plausible moral theory involves some such balancing. Rather, the objection is presumably that Consequentialism offers an inaccurate account of this balance. The complaint is not that Consequentialism makes demands, but that it makes too many demands, or the wrong demands.

The integrity and separateness objections are clearly related. Part of what it is to see one's life as an integrated whole is precisely to see it as distinct from the lives of others. The two notions are thus two sides of the same coin. If Consequentialism ignores one, then it is not surprising that it overlooks the other.

At this point we need to ask two questions: (1) how should agents balance their own interests against those of others, and (2) how might Consequentialism balance them? Until we have answered these questions, we cannot assume that Consequentialists cannot provide an adequate account of the balance between the agent's own interests and the impersonal good. The main task of this book is to seek answers to these two questions, and to demonstrate that the Consequentialist solution is acceptable.

Once again, we can see this complaint as providing a striking *example* of the unreasonable demands of Consequentialism. Consequentialism requires the agent to ignore the fact that her life is separate from the lives of others.

---

[37] This phrase appears to originate with John Rawls (see his *A Theory of Justice*, p. 27). For evaluations of the objection, see Raz, *The Morality of Freedom*, pp. 271–87; Brink, 'The Separateness of Persons, Distributive Norms and Moral Theory'; and Brink, 'Self-Love and Altruism'.

[38] Ibid. 154.

The notion of separateness also *explains* the failure of Consequentialism. Consequentialism demands too much because it ignores the separateness of persons. Lacking an adequate theory of human nature, Consequentialism cannot even see why its demands are unreasonable. It places unreasonable demands on moral agents simply because it does not understand what moral agents are like.

This line of argument suggests two further questions. Can one acquire an adequate understanding of humanity, morality, and agency and still be a Consequentialist? If so, what form will one's Consequentialism take? This book seeks to motivate an affirmative answer to the first question by exploring several possible answers to the second.

1.3.3. The Transcendental Objection

A more basic objection to Consequentialism is that, because it ignores the separateness of persons, it fails to count as a moral theory at all. Adequate moral theorizing must proceed from the standpoint of practical reason, which requires certain assumptions about human agency. These assumptions are inconsistent with Consequentialism. For instance, Christine Korsgaard's defence of the Kantian concept of the person might become an attack on Consequentialism in general, if it can be shown that Consequentialism cannot accommodate any substantive notion of personal identity and agency.[39] (Korsgaard's argument is outlined in Section 1.4.2.) John Cottingham raises a similar objection when he argues that 'any ethic which requires people to be agents . . . must on pain of absurdity permit agent-related partialism'.[40] If Consequentialism forbids such partialism, then it cannot be taken seriously as a moral theory.

In some ways this is a deeper objection than the others we have considered, as it denies the very idea of a Consequentialist moral theory. However, the Consequentialist response will be the same. If we can show that Consequentialists need not ignore the separateness of persons, or any other central feature of agency, then we will have dissolved the transcendental objection. We must ask how someone viewing the world from the standpoint of practical reason might construct a Consequentialist moral theory.

---

[39] Korsgaard, 'Personal Identity and the Unity of Agency'.
[40] Cottingham, 'Partiality, Favouritism and Morality', p. 365.

1.4. Methodology, Metaphysics, and Meta-Ethics

It has become fashionable to precede any substantive ethical discussion with an extensive and apologetic methodological discussion—the assumption apparently being that the business of talking about ethics stands in need of justification. I find this practice puzzling. The only justification for talking about ethics is the belief that one has something worthwhile to say. This seems to be a perfectly adequate justification. If one has anything worthwhile to say, then it is superfluous to preface it with an elaborate defence of the claim that there might possibly be some worthwhile things to be said about ethics. Better, surely, simply to present one's substantive claims or arguments and hope that others find them persuasive or helpful. As Derek Parfit puts it, the only convincing way to demonstrate that it is possible to make progress in ethical discussion is to make such progress.[41]

Accordingly, I aim to say as little as possible by way of methodological introduction. I shall confine myself to a few brief general comments, before discussing three particular issues. As far as possible, I seek to avoid any specific meta-ethical commitments. My methodology is similar to Sidgwick's 'philosophical intuitionism'.[42] I begin by considering a range of pre-existing moral theories. I then test these against certain general theoretical standards which I believe any acceptable moral theory must meet, as well as against our intuitive responses to particular cases (both actual and possible). If the standards and intuitions I use seem likely to be controversial, I attempt to justify them by appeal to less controversial assumptions, or to ground them in general considerations regarding the nature of morality, rationality, and agency. At some point, I reach assumptions I do not defend. I simply try to state these as clearly as possible, and then trust that the reader shares them to a sufficient degree to find my argument persuasive. The resulting theory should be judged comparatively and as a whole: does it provide a more plausible and satisfying account of our moral obligations than its rivals?

1.4.1. The Role of Hypothetical Examples in Ethics

Throughout this book I make extensive use of simple examples or thought experiments. These are used to clarify our intuitions, to explain various theories or distinctions, and to tease out the implications of a given theory. The assumption behind this strategy is that one test of the adequacy of a

---

[41] Parfit, *Reasons and Persons*, p. x.
[42] Sidgwick, *The Methods of Ethics*, ch. 13. See also Scheffler, *The Rejection of Consequentialism*, pp. 68–9, and Schneewind, *Sidgwick's Ethics and Victorian Moral Philosophy*, ch. 6.

moral theory is its intuitive appeal. Furthermore, my use of hypothetical examples reflects my belief that an adequate moral theory must meet two distinct criteria. Most obviously, it must give the right moral answers in particular actual cases. A theory failing to conclude that the Holocaust was wrong would be inadequate. However, it is not enough to stumble across the right answers in real cases. We also want a moral theory to explain why those answers are right. It should give the right answers for the right reasons. The judgements of an adequate moral theory should be reliably or robustly accurate. For instance, a theory that told us that the Holocaust was wrong because all and only those actions performed by Germans were wrong would not be adequate. Hypothetical examples expose an unreliable theory. Imagine that the Holocaust had been carried out by the English. Would this make it morally acceptable? Obviously not, but the theory we are considering would say that it did. Failure to give intuitively plausible responses to hypothetical examples is thus a sign that a theory has limited explanatory power.

I am aware that the use of examples in ethics is not uncontroversial. We need to be wary of placing too much weight on intuitions, especially those relating to fantastical examples. However, it is hard to see how ethics could be pursued at all without some reference to intuitions or examples. It is also worth noting that the examples discussed in this book are hardly fantastical, at least not by the standards of contemporary analytic philosophy. Most of the theorists whose work I discuss in this book make extensive use of intuitions and examples themselves. It thus seems entirely fair to test their theories against new hypothetical examples.

1.4.2. Metaphysical Assumptions

I seek to keep my metaphysical assumptions to a minimum. In particular, I try not to rely upon controversial theses regarding human nature, personal identity, or the concept of the person. As a result, I put to one side various metaphysical defences of Consequentialism. Two such defences are especially prominent in the literature. Both seek to defend Consequentialism against the charge that it ignores the separateness of persons, by denying the metaphysical significance of that separateness. The first such argument is based on Derek Parfit's Reductionist account of personal identity.[43] The Reductionist claims that there are no persons, at least not in any metaphysically significant sense. There are only experiences standing in various relations to one another. Parfit argues that, if Reductionism is true, then the boundaries between one

---

[43] Parfit, *Reasons and Persons*, pp. 321–47.

life and another are much less morally significant than we commonly suppose. The fact that it glosses over those boundaries thus constitutes a point in favour of Consequentialism, rather than an objection to it.

The second metaphysical argument in favour of Consequentialism is provided by what David Brink dubs Metaphysical Egoism. This view 'insists that we ought to modify our pre-theoretic understanding of self-interest on metaphysical grounds'.[44] Instead of seeing the interests of different agents as separate and conflicting, we need to recognize that they are interrelated. Brink identifies this view with both the Greek Eudaimonists and the late-nineteenth-century British Idealists.[45] According to T. H. Green, whom Brink identifies as a leading historical proponent of the view, 'the proper conception of self-realization involves the good of others as a constituent part'.[46] In other words, 'when each is engaged in proper self-realization, there can be no conflict or competition of interests'.[47] Like Parfit, Brink argues that the difference between intrapersonal continuity and interpersonal continuity is a difference of degree not one of kind. It follows that 'the separateness or diversity of persons is not so fundamental'.[48]

I agree that there is much to be said in favour of these forms of argument. In Part Four of this book I utilize a number of observations drawn from the broad tradition Brink identifies. However, it is not advisable for Consequentialists to place too much weight on these metaphysical arguments, as they rest on controversial claims of two sorts. The first controversy surrounds the metaphysical claims themselves. Opponents of Consequentialism may simply deny that, for instance, Reductionism is an acceptable account of personal identity. Indeed, they may argue that only someone with the impoverished world view of a Utilitarian could find such an account metaphysically plausible.[49]

The second area of controversy is the relationship between metaphysics and morality. Philosophers disagree about the significance of metaphysical debates for moral theory. Parfit argues that moral theory builds on metaphysics. Changing our metaphysical views thus affects our evaluation of competing moral theories. Others, notably John Rawls, defend the view that moral theory is independent of metaphysics.[50]

---

[44] Brink, 'Self-Love and Altruism', p. 124.   [45] Ibid. 124–52.

[46] Paraphrased in ibid. 133. See also Green, *Prolegomena to Ethics*.

[47] Paraphrased in ibid. 135.   [48] Ibid. 142.

[49] For a summary of the range of contemporary views on personal identity, see Baillie, 'Recent Work on Personal Identity'.

[50] See, in particular, Rawls, 'Justice as Fairness: Political not Metaphysical', esp. p. 233, and Rawls, 'The Idea of an Overlapping Consensus', esp. pp. 6–7. For discussions of the difference between Parfit and Rawls on this issue, see Stern, 'The Relation between Moral Theory and Metaphysics', and Scheffler, 'Ethics, Personal Identity, and Ideals of the Person'.

A prominent example of the Rawlsian approach is Christine Korsgaard's reply to Parfit.[51] Korsgaard grants the Reductionist claim for the sake of argument, but denies that it is inconsistent with Kantian ethics. The foundation of her argument is a distinction between two perspectives.

The Perspective of Theoretical Reason. This is the appropriate standpoint from which to embark on enquiries into what there is, such as metaphysics. In such an enquiry, we seek necessary preconditions for the possibility of experience. In other words, we ask: what would need to be the case for there to be any experiences at all, and what presuppositions are required for scientific, empirical inquiry?

The Perspective of Practical Reason. This is the appropriate standpoint from which to embark on enquiries into how we should act, such as moral philosophy. In such an enquiry, we seek necessary preconditions for the possibility of action. In other words, we ask: what would need to be the case for there to be any morally assessable choices at all, and what presuppositions are required for rational deliberation?

Korsgaard claims that some concepts are relevant to both perspectives, as they are used in both metaphysics and moral philosophy. The concept of personhood is a classic example. However, this concept plays different roles at the different levels. In particular, persons may be dispensable at one level and indispensable at the other. Parfit's metaphysical Reductionism establishes, at best, only that we can do metaphysics without granting the existence of persons. It does not follow that we can do moral philosophy without positing their existence. In fact, Korsgaard claims, we cannot. The business of deliberation requires the presupposition that one is an agent capable of making choices and carrying out plans. This presupposition commits one to the existence of persons. Reductionism is not an option from the standpoint of practical reason. It is, therefore, no objection to Kantian ethics that it requires us to posit the existence of persons, as such a commitment is an inevitable part of any acceptable moral theory.

This debate is complicated and controversial. It also tends to track disagreement about moral theory. For instance, Utilitarians such as Parfit tend to argue that metaphysics and morality are closely related, whereas Kantians side with Rawls and Korsgaard. A defence of Consequentialism based on Parfitian claims regarding the relationship between morality and metaphysics is thus unlikely to convert Non-Consequentialists.

---

[51] Korsgaard, 'Personal Identity and the Unity of Agency'.

Accordingly, I propose for the sake of argument to grant the following claims: (1) there are persons; (2) persons are distinct in a metaphysically significant way; (3) the interests of persons, while interrelated, are separate, and often come into conflict; and (4) all these features of persons are morally significant. The questions I wish to address in this book are: can Consequentialism accommodate these common claims about persons, and if so, what will the resulting Consequentialist moral theory be like?

1.4.3. Some Remarks on Well-Being

Consequentialism, as I have formulated it thus far, tells us to produce as much as possible of whatever is valuable. It tells us to promote value, but leaves open the question of what is valuable. A full Consequentialist moral theory would combine a Consequentialist account of how to respond to value, with some specific account of what makes outcomes valuable. The former is usually known as our theory of the right, whereas the latter will be our theory of the good.

Discussions of Consequentialism often treat these two components as entirely separable. In other words, we determine the form of Consequentialism independently of determining its content. We then plug our preferred theory of the good into our preferred theory of the right. Recently, some Consequentialists have questioned this assumption of separability, arguing that, even within Consequentialist moral theory, the appropriate response to a value may depend upon its particular nature.[52]

In this book I seek to be as neutral as possible with respect to theories of the good. For the sake of simplicity, I concentrate on human goods—those aspects of human lives that make outcomes valuable. I do not assume that these are the only valuable features of outcomes, but other possible sources of value are placed to one side. However, at certain points in the argument, it becomes necessary to distinguish different categories of human good. (We have already seen some hint of this in our discussion of the Integrity Objection in Section 1.3.1.) In particular, we will find that we must distinguish the basic necessities of life from more complex goals and projects. Even if there is no clear boundary between the two, we can usually find clear examples of each type. The underlying assumption is that some aspects of human well-being are more morally significant, more urgent, or more meaningful than others; and that these differences should affect our considered response to those components of well-being. This assumption seems extremely plausible in general terms, and Chapter 7 provides an extended

---

[52] See esp. Griffin, 'On the Winding Road from Good to Right', and Griffin, *Value Judgement*.

elaboration and defence of it. Indeed, I cannot imagine how we could ever hope to construct an adequate moral theory without attending to these differences.

1.5. Conclusion

Having spent enough time on preliminaries and scene setting, we are now ready to embark on our main task—the evaluation of attempts to construct a reasonable Consequentialist morality. We have seen that this task should be of interest to all moral theorists. The next chapter begins our exploration, by outlining the various possible Consequentialist responses to the Demandingness Objection. These include various departures from the Simple Consequentialism we have considered thus far. Perhaps none of those responses will prove entirely satisfactory. However, when a theory is as prominent as Consequentialism, it is a worthwhile exercise to examine all its theoretical resources, especially those that have been hitherto neglected, even if we cannot as yet find conclusive reasons to use those particular resources. At the very least, a thorough examination of an option we finally reject will deepen our understanding of those we endorse.

2

Options for Consequentialism

There are many ways Consequentialists might respond to the Demandingness Objection. We can introduce these by breaking the objection down into
a cluster of separate arguments of the following form:

1. Consequentialism makes demand D;
2. D is an unreasonable demand for a moral theory to make; therefore,
3. Consequentialism makes unreasonable demands.

For any argument of this form, Consequentialists can deny either premiss.
Faced with any alleged demand, they can either deny that Consequentialism
makes that demand, or deny that this is unreasonable. As we shall see, most
Consequentialist responses to the Demandingness Objection combine these
two moves.

The first Consequentialist solution is to deny that a given demand is
unreasonable. Following Shelly Kagan, I call this the Extremist solution.[1] At
its most extreme, this move rejects the claim that *any* demand could be unreasonable. However demanding morality turns out to be, we cannot reject its
demands simply because we find them unpalatable. Somewhat more moder-
ately, we might define the notion of a reasonable demand in Consequentialist
terms. An unreasonable demand would be one where the sacrifice required
of the agent is greater than her contribution to the welfare of others. By definition, the demands of Consequentialism would never be unreasonable.

There is a separate form of Extremism for each allegedly unreasonable
demand. For instance, one might argue that in certain circumstances it is not
unreasonable to require agents to distance, detach, or even alienate themselves from the central projects of their lives. One could even argue that it is
not unreasonable for a theory to make impossible demands on some occasions. However, these forms of Extremism are not popular. Most Extremists
argue that it is reasonable to require agents to devote virtually all of their time
and material possessions to the task of promoting the overall good. This
Extremist response to the material demands of Consequentialism can then
be combined with a denial of the claim that Consequentialism also involves

---

[1] For a definition of Extremism, see Kagan, *The Limits of Morality*, pp. 1–2, 6–10.

alienation. By revising both our notion of a reasonable demand and our account of what Consequentialism demands, we might hope to demonstrate that all of its demands are reasonable.

Non-Extremists have two responses to the Demandingness Objection. The first is the Strategy of Denial, whereby we deny that Consequentialism makes extreme demands. In particular, Non-Extremists deny that Consequentialism requires agents to make great financial or personal sacrifices, or that the theory demands alienation. The precise demands of any moral theory are a function of both the structure of the theory and the state of the world. To deny that a given theory makes some particular demand, we clearly have two options. The first is to deny the factual claims that allegedly generate that demand. In the case of the Demandingness Objection, these concern the amount of unmet need in the world and our ability to meet that need. If there were no unmet need in the world, then Consequentialism would not require great sacrifices to meet such need. One common move is to deny that large donations to international charities are an efficient way of promoting the good.

The second Non-Extremist option is to restructure Consequentialism. We might accept that a theory requiring agents always to maximize the good would be very demanding, but deny that Consequentialism need be such a theory. We must then construct a recognizably Consequentialist moral theory that does not always require the best consequences.

Many Non-Extremists opt for a combination of these two responses. They seek to solve the Demandingness Objection by a mix of empirical revision and theoretical restructuring. Indeed, many Consequentialist responses combine all three solutions. A typical Consequentialist will revise our notion of a reasonable demand, redefine the way Consequentialism calculates its demands, and then re-evaluate what the resulting theory would demand in the actual world.

In this book, I focus on the restructuring option. In Section 2.3, I outline the various forms such restructuring can take. In the next two sections, I seek to explain why I reject the other two solutions to the Demandingness Objection.

2.1. Extremism

Several philosophers argue that an extremely demanding moral theory need not be unreasonable. Prominent recent examples are Peter Singer, Shelly Kagan, and Peter Unger.[2] Despite their many differences, all three argue in a similar way. Each begins with a presumption in favour of a Consequentialist

---

[2] Singer, 'Famine, Affluence and Morality'; Kagan, *The Limits of Morality*; Kagan, 'Does Consequentialism Demand too Much?'; Kagan, 'Defending Options'; and Unger, *Living High and Letting Die*.

view of morality, and then seeks to rebut arguments or principles designed to motivate departures from that starting point.

The Extremist begins with an allegedly uncontroversial moral principle. This might be one of the following:

The Reason to Promote the Good.   The fact that an action will produce a valuable outcome provides a reason to perform that action. If two actions will each produce a valuable outcome, then our reasons to perform them are proportional to the value of those outcomes. If we choose actions solely on the basis of the Reason to Promote the Good, we will thus always opt for the action with the best consequences. This is Kagan's starting point.[3]

The Principle of Harm Prevention.   'If it is in our power to prevent something bad from happening, without thereby sacrificing anything of comparable moral importance, we ought, morally, to do it.' This is Singer's starting point.[4]

The Principle of Aid to Innocents.   If we are able to provide assistance to an innocent person in great need, at negligible cost to ourselves, then we ought to do so. This is Unger's starting point.[5]

These starting points are justified in a number of ways. Their proponents appeal to their intuitive plausibility, sketch arguments in their favour, point out that the principle is endorsed in some form by most Non-Consequentialist moral theories, or produce simple cases or thought experiments where the principle clearly applies. For instance, Kagan motivates the Reason to Promote the Good by suggesting that only an extreme Anti-Consequentialist would deny that valuable consequences provide some reason for action. The Reason to Promote the Good is thus common ground between the Consequentialists and their more moderate opponents, who seek to combine it with other moral principles.[6] The best-known example of the use of a thought experiment to motivate a Consequentialist starting point is Peter Singer's tale of a person walking to work in the morning who passes a small child drowning in a pond. The person can save the child, at the cost of a wet suit and the loss of a few minutes. Singer argues that they have a clear obligation to save the child.[7] He concludes that there is a general duty to prevent harm.

The next stage of the Extremist argument involves the examination and rejection of all intuitions, principles, and arguments motivating departures

---

[3] Kagan, *The Limits of Morality*, pp. 16–19, 47–60.
[4] Singer, 'Famine, Affluence and Morality', p. 231.
[5] Unger, *Living High and Letting Die*, p. 7.   [6] Kagan, *The Limits of Morality*, pp. 4–5, 47–80.
[7] Singer, 'Famine, Affluence and Morality', p. 231.

from the Consequentialist starting point in some cases. If no such departures are justified, then the starting point represents the whole of morality. As the starting point, if left unconstrained, will be very demanding, morality is thus very demanding. The fact that it makes great demands thus constitutes no objection to Consequentialism.

At this final stage, Extremists typically rely on a combination of three strategies. The first aims to undermine intuitions offered in support of departures from the starting point. Two prominent examples here are Peter Singer's Consciousness Raising Strategy and Peter Unger's Method of Several Options.

Singer argues that, if people (1) were better informed, (2) reasoned more clearly, and (3) were better able to imagine what life is like for the starving, then they would no longer regard the demands of Consequentialism as unreasonable. (Elsewhere Singer employs an analogous strategy to motivate the claim that conventional morality unjustly ignores the interests of non-human animals.[8]) Consciousness Raising is not just a practical strategy. It also has a theoretical dimension. Consequentialists who adopt this strategy argue that a moral theory should cohere, not with peoples' actual intuitions, but with their ideal hypothetical intuitions: the intuitions they would have if their consciousness were raised appropriately. The intuition that Consequentialism is too demanding constitutes an objection to Consequentialism only if it survives the idealization process.

Unger's Method of Several Options is a variation on the thought-experiment approach.[9] The basic idea is simple. Begin with a short tale involving two moral options, where the Non-Consequentialist option is intuitively preferable. An example might be the hackneyed case of hanging the innocent person to avoid a race riot. Then retell the story, progressively introducing a range of intermediate options, each with some features in common with each of the original options. Eventually, we reach a tale where an agent must choose from a continuum of different options, with the two original options at opposite ends of that continuum. When applied to this new tale, our intuitions tell us that the Consequentialist option is morally acceptable. Or so Unger argues in each of the particular cases he discusses.

The purpose of this method is to make us wary of taking our moral intuitions at face value. In particular, Unger seeks to undermine intuitions supporting a strong distinction between acts and omissions. As he puts it, his strategy is to 'liberate' our Common-Sense Morality from certain inconsistencies and misconceptions.

---

[8] Singer, *Practical Ethics*, pp. 48–54, and Singer, *Animal Liberation*.

[9] Unger, *Living High and Letting Die*, esp. the elaborate tale introduced at pp. 88–90. See also Haslett, 'Values, Obligations, and Saving Lives'; Hooker, 'Sacrificing for the Good of Strangers—Repeatedly'; and Mulgan, Review of Unger's *Living High and Letting Die*.

A second Extremist strategy rejects outright any moral intuition that cannot be supported by a sound argument. Singer bluntly states that 'the way people do in fact judge has nothing to do with the validity of [his] conclusion'.[10] Kagan argues that there is no place in moral philosophy for intuitions that lack an adequate rationale.[11] The rejection of intuitions is often backed up by a deflationary explanation of their origins. If our moral intuitions are the products of evolution, culture, or self-interest, then they are unreliable.

Non-Consequentialists do not merely appeal to intuition. They also offer rationales for moral principles that motivate departures from the Consequentialist starting point. The third Extremist strategy is to undermine those rationales. The best recent example is Shelly Kagan's discussion in *The Limits of Morality*.

Kagan argues that intuitions should be taken seriously only if they are supported by reasons. He sees Common-Sense Morality as a moderate position, situated between Extremism (Consequentialism) and Minimalism (Egoism). In common with Consequentialism, Common-Sense Morality accepts that we are sometimes required to sacrifice our own interests in order to promote the good. Common-Sense Moralists must explain why we are not always required to promote the good.

To provide such reasons Common-Sense Morality must include *options*, permitting agents to pursue their own projects at the expense of the overall good. Kagan then argues that, if Common-Sense Morality includes options, then it must also include *constraints*, prohibiting certain actions, such as killing or lying. Kagan's argument here is directed at Samuel Scheffler's Hybrid View, which includes options without constraints.[12] Kagan's debate with Scheffler is discussed at length in Chapters 6 and 9 below. Kagan considers two possible rationales for constraints: the distinction between doing and allowing, and the distinction between intending and foreseeing. He argues that the former can only be defended if the latter is presupposed. He then rejects the latter. Kagan's general aim is to show that, far from being self-evident, the intuition that morality should not be very demanding is based on a very unstable foundation.

For several reasons, I doubt that Extremism can solve the Demandingness Objection. The arguments of Extremists often seem unfair. Their opponents are always on the back foot. Extremists claim that no rationale for departures from the Consequentialist starting point meets a reasonable standard of proof. The question naturally arises whether the starting point itself would

[10] Singer, 'Famine, Affluence and Morality', p. 236.
[11] Kagan, *The Limits of Morality*, pp. 11–15.
[12] Scheffler's original presentation of the Hybrid View is in his *The Rejection of Consequentialism*. For further references, see below, Ch. 6 n. 1.

fare any better. Could Extremists provide arguments in favour of the positive element of their theory that meet the standards they set for others?

Extremists cannot consistently appeal to the intuitive plausibility of their various starting points, as they reject such appeals on behalf of departures from Consequentialism. Yet, as Garret Cullity notes, 'to most people, it is about as obvious that there is a moral difference between our relations to a child drowning in front of us and a child starving in another country as it is that failing to save a drowning child is wrong'.[13] In other words, the intuitions that support Non-Consequentialist principles are at least as strong as those behind the Extremist's Consequentialist starting point.

Shelly Kagan sets a particularly high standard for Non-Consequentialist rationales. Yet he provides no sustained defence of the Reason to Promote the Good. Kagan acknowledges the need for a positive justification, but leaves this task for another time, as his immediate target is the moderate, who accepts the Reason to Promote the Good. However, many moderate moral theorists deny this.[14] They argue that moderation does not require a general Reason to Promote the Good, although it may include a number of more specific principles deriving reasons for action from features of possible outcomes. If some plausible moderate theories reject the Extremist's starting point, then the case for Extremism is only as strong as the case for that starting point itself. If they wish us to adopt their theory, Extremists must provide such a case. They must also demonstrate that it meets the standards of justification they set for others.

A crucial issue here is the relationship between particular cases and general principles. Like many moral philosophers, Extremists often begin with a moral judgement relating to a simple story, and then generalize to a principle of which the initial judgement is said to be an instance. Unfortunately, in ethics as in science, the data underdetermine the theory. Even if we agree with the Extremist's judgement about a particular case, we may disagree with the general lesson he draws from that case. Especially when drawing up their starting principles, Extremists often seem to operate with a very controversial and distinctly Consequentialist account of what constitutes legitimate generalization in ethics. For instance, Singer's example of the drowning child might generate a very limited duty, rather than a general duty to prevent harm *per se*.

Similar points apply when Extremists deal with conflicting intuitions. Unger's Method of Several Options is a good example. Having claimed that

[13] Cullity, 'International Aid and the Scope of Kindness', p. 104.
[14] For a classic presentation of the case against the existence of a general Reason to Promote the Good, see Foot, 'Utilitarianism and the Virtues', p. 227. See also Dancy, 'Non-Consequentialist Reasons', and Scheffler, 'Agent-Centred Restrictions, Rationality and the Virtues', pp. 409–13.

our intuitive response to multiple option tales is different from our response to simpler stories, Unger uses this result to discredit the latter. Someone with less Consequentialist sympathies might draw the opposite lesson. Perhaps the presence of too many options clouds our intuitive responses. Also, others may simply not share Unger's intuitions. My own attempts to replicate his results using undergraduate classes have been singularly unsuccessful.

The crucial question is whether Extremists could sell the Reason to Promote the Good to someone who was as sceptical about Consequentialism as they themselves are about departures from Consequentialism. Extremists will claim that they could convince such a person, but the recent history of moral philosophy suggests otherwise.

A further problem with Extremism, as a universal solution to the Demandingness Objection, is that we need to clarify which of the alleged demands of Consequentialism the Extremist seeks to legitimate. It seems fairly clear that an Extremist will defend the severe financial demands of Consequentialism. It is not unreasonable for a moral theory to require me to give virtually all my money to the poor. However, do Extremists also want to defend alienating, dislocating, or impossible demands? Some Extremists might be tempted to go this far. After all, they might point out that morality sometimes requires agents to lay down their lives. If this ultimate sacrifice can be required, then there may be no limits to what morality can reasonably demand. On the other hand, many people will be very suspicious of the suggestion that a moral theory can legitimately require ordinary people systematically to undermine their own integrity on a daily basis. At the very least, an Extremist who wished to defend these more extreme demands would need to provide an especially strong argument for his starting point. In practice, Extremists usually want to deny that Consequentialism makes these more extreme demands. Even Extremists tend to go into denial at some point.

2.2. The Strategy of Denial

We turn now to the Strategy of Denial. One response to the Demandingness Objection is to argue that Consequentialism does not make great demands in practice. We begin with the simplest alleged demand of Consequentialism: the extreme financial and personal sacrifice it seems to require from affluent people living in a world with a great deal of unmet need. Some deny that Consequentialism requires such sacrifices, as we would actually produce better results by spending our time and money on ourselves and those close to us. Several arguments have been advanced in favour of this claim. Unfortunately, none of them is convincing. We examine each in turn.

THE ARGUMENT FROM IGNORANCE REGARDING THE GOOD

We know a great deal about ourselves and our friends. We are very well placed to know what our own needs are, and to know what would add value to our lives. By contrast, we know very little about people on the other side of the world, especially those whose socio-economic situation is very different from our own. We cannot know what would be good for those people. Therefore, it is pointless for us to try meeting their needs. We will achieve better results if we focus on meeting the needs of those we know.

It is certainly true that our knowledge of what is good for other people is less than perfect, and varies greatly according to our degree of acquaintance with those people. However, there are two points to be made. The first is that, while we may not know very much about the more sophisticated interests of distant strangers, we surely do know that they need clean water, freedom from curable diseases, adequate food and shelter, and some element of peace and stability. To deny that needs as basic as these are cross-cultural is to embrace a cultural relativism of the most absurd sort. The second crucial point is that, while we may not know precisely what distant strangers need, we can always donate our money to charitable organizations who do possess such knowledge. To argue that our own ignorance prevents us from effectively rendering assistance is analogous to claiming that it is pointless for medically ignorant taxpayers to fund hospitals.[15]

THE ARGUMENT FROM IGNORANCE REGARDING THE CONSEQUENCES

Grant that we know what results would be desirable in a distant country. Unfortunately, owing to the complexity of the causal processes involved, we cannot ever be certain what results our actions will have in some far distant place. The consequences of our actions can be much more reliably ascertained if we focus on achieving results closer to home, especially within our homes and families.[16]

Of course, we can never be certain of the consequences of our actions. Like everyone else, Consequentialists must deal with uncertainty. The most

---

[15] Another striking analogy is the case of generations who will live in the far future. Some have argued that, as we have no idea what these people will be like, we cannot know what will be good or bad for them. We can thus ignore them when deciding how to act, and we have no obligations to them. However, even though our detailed knowledge may be quite limited, our ignorance of the needs of future people is far from total. We can be fairly sure that they will not prefer polluted air, malnutrition, or radiation poisoning. (See Barry, 'Justice between Generations', pp. 274–5.)

[16] For defences of this view, see Jackson, 'Decision-Theoretic Consequentialism and the Nearest and Dearest Objection', pp. 473–80, and Sidgwick, *The Methods of Ethics*, pp. 256–9, 430–9. For a rejection of the argument, see Singer, 'Famine, Affluence and Morality', pp. 239–42.

popular solution is that a Consequentialist agent should seek to maximize the expected value of her actions. The value of each possible outcome is multiplied by the probability that that outcome will result if the action is performed. The sum of these weighted values is the expected value of that action. The agent should then choose the action with the highest expected value.[17]

This argument from ignorance was much more credible when advanced by Sidgwick than it is today. In the late nineteenth century, the expected value of trying to send money to aid the distant poor was very low, as the chances of success were not great. It was also very difficult to determine accurately the likelihood of various possible outcomes. Nowadays, however, we are able to place our money in the hands of much more reliable aid agencies, who can generally provide comparatively accurate estimates of the expected value of a given donation.

Before going any further we should note a number of complexities and distinctions which often arise in discussions of Consequentialism. The first is the distinction between actual results and probable results. For instance, assume that A must press one of two buttons (X and Y). Independently, a random number between 1 and 100 is generated by a computer. If A presses button X and the number is 100, then an innocent person is electrocuted. If she presses X and the number is not 100, then no one is hurt. If A presses Y and the number is 100, then no one is hurt. On the other hand, if A presses Y and the number is not 100, then an innocent person is electrocuted. Assume that A does press button X and the number selected is 100. Consequentialism based on actual results would say that A has acted wrongly, as things would have turned out better if she had pressed the other button instead. By contrast, a Consequentialism based on probable results would say that A has acted rightly, as pressing button X was far more likely to lead to good results than pressing button Y.

A second distinction is between objective and subjective probabilities. Returning to our previous example, assume that A is misinformed about the machine. She believes that if she presses button X there is a 99 per cent chance of an innocent person being electrocuted. She also believes that if she presses button Y there is only a 1 per cent chance of someone being electrocuted. Assume that A presses button Y. Consequentialism based on objective probabilities would say that she has acted wrongly, as pressing button Y is actually 99 per cent likely to lead to electrocution. On the other hand, a Consequentialism based on subjective probabilities would say that A has acted rightly, as she has performed the action with the lowest subjective probability of harm.

---

[17] See e.g. Jackson, 'Decision-Theoretic Consequentialism and the Nearest and Dearest Objection', pp. 462–72, and Pettit, 'Decision Theory and Folk Psychology'.

Many objections to Consequentialism, and many confusions within Consequentialism, can be removed by careful attention to these and other related distinctions. For the purposes of this book, however, I wish to avoid these complexities as far as possible. Accordingly, unless otherwise stated, all examples should be interpreted so that actual results, objective probabilities, and subjective probabilities coincide.

THE ARGUMENT FROM IMPOTENCE

Another common argument is that we are unable to assist people who are starving in distant countries. At best, we might be able to keep them alive for a few days in a very bad state. But we are not able to do anything to enhance the quality of their lives significantly.

Such worries are greatly exaggerated. We are often able to render assistance to those in need in distant countries. Our donations can provide water, food, and medicine to enable people to lead worthwhile lives. Furthermore, the cost of meeting their needs is far less than the cost of meeting comparable needs in our own country, including our own needs. Because of international exchange rates our dollars go much further in poor countries. We can thus be fairly sure that our next dollar would produce a much more valuable result if we donated it to charity rather than spending it on ourselves. For instance, in 1990 the World Bank argued 'that the principal elements of an effective strategy are well understood and that the external resources needed to support it could be made available at little cost to the industrial countries'. They concluded that 'a substantial increase in the resources for fighting poverty in the poorest countries appears entirely affordable. It is a matter of political commitment and the reassessment of donors' priorities.'[18]

THE MALTHUSIAN ARGUMENT

This very common argument grants the premiss that we are able to improve and safeguard the lives of those who are currently starving. It then draws the conclusion that this would be an undesirable result. If we aid those who are starving, then more of them will live to maturity. As the birth rate in poor countries is often very high, this will lead to a population explosion. Unpleasant as it may seem, a high rate of infant mortality is necessary in the long term.

The simplest response to this argument is that all the empirical evidence to date suggests that Malthus was completely wrong. Increases in the standard of living tend to be followed by decreases in the birth rate, with the

---

[18] World Bank, *World Development Report 1990*, pp. 5–6, 136.

overall result that population growth is reduced. Furthermore, even where population has expanded rapidly, both life expectancy and average material standard of living have tended to rise rather than fall.[19]

THE ARGUMENT FROM LIMITED HUMAN SYMPATHY

In defending traditional family arrangements against Plato's system of communal living, Aristotle argued that human beings are able to feel genuine affection for only a small number of people. If we ask them to feel equal affection for all, then they are unlikely to feel strong affection for anyone. Some philosophers have applied Aristotle's thought to Consequentialism, concluding that Consequentialism does not require agents to try to meet the needs of many strangers, as it will be better if they display strong affection towards their friends and families. Of course, it would best if we could display strong affection for strangers as well, but this is not psychologically feasible.[20]

There is certainly much truth in Aristotle's argument. We probably can feel genuine, deep affection for only a small number of people. However, we can render assistance to others without becoming their friends. In many cases, we may be able to produce more good overall by meeting the basic needs of a large number of strangers than by providing affection to a much smaller number of already very well-off friends.

THE ARGUMENT FROM OPTIMAL GLOBAL RESPONSE

Some philosophers suggest that, to find the demands of Consequentialism, we should imagine a course of action being pursued not just by one individual but by everyone. If everyone in the world were to devote all their time and resources to famine relief, then the result would not be nearly as good as if everyone adopted a more moderate strategy combining charitable work with participation in the productive economy and ordinary family and social life. Viewed from this perspective, the demands of Consequentialism do not seem too great.[21]

If everyone were to donate all their money to aid agencies, then the result would almost certainly be an economic disaster. Perhaps the optimal global response would involve a moderate level of sacrifice from individuals. However, it is not obvious how these observations relate to the assessment of

[19] For an account of the evidence regarding this argument, see Sen, 'Population: Delusion and Reality'; Sen, 'Legal Rights and Moral Rights', pp. 163–6; and Hooker, *Ideal Code, Real World*, pp. 147–8.

[20] See Brink, 'Self-Love and Altruism' for an account of this debate.

[21] Jackson, 'Decision-Theoretic Consequentialism and the Nearest and Dearest Objection', pp. 478–81. See also Hooker, *Ideal Code, Real World*.

Simple Consequentialism. After all, the theory we are currently considering tells each individual how to act, given that others will continue to behave as they presently do. From the perspective of Consequentialism, the behaviour of other agents enters into my calculations in the same way as any natural phenomenon, such as the weather. I need to take account of the actual or likely behaviour of others, but possible variations in their behaviour are only relevant if I am able to influence them by my actions. If I am very well placed to influence others, then perhaps Consequentialism will advise me to spend my time and resources lobbying for greater government expenditure on foreign aid. The potential benefits of this action are enormous. However, this would hardly reduce the sacrifices required of me, as I would still be devoting all my financial and other resources to the task of maximizing the extent to which the needs of others are met.

If our discussion of the optimal collective response moves beyond consideration of the possible consequences of the various courses of action open to me as an individual, then we have moved beyond Simple Consequentialism. In particular, we would be in the realms of Collective Consequentialism, the subject of Part Two of this book.

This argument does bring out a significant feature of Simple Consequentialism. The theory requires more of me if other people do less. I must meet as many needs as I can, even though the demands on each of us would be quite moderate if everyone pitched in. Consequentialism demands great financial sacrifices in a world where few people do their share.

Before leaving the Strategy of Denial, let us see how it applies to the more extreme alleged demands of Consequentialism. This will serve to introduce a number of themes to be explored in later chapters. We focus on the Alienation Objection. It may seem obvious that, if Consequentialism requires me to devote all my resources to charity, then Consequentialism will be a very alienating moral theory, asking me to abandon most of the projects around which I presently structure my life.

Proponents of the Strategy of Denial may wish to distinguish two separate objections. The first is that Consequentialism requires me to detach myself from the projects and commitments in which I am currently involved. The second, more serious, objection is that Consequentialism demands that I never be attached in any deep way to any project at all. Defenders of Simple Consequentialism might agree with the first claim, but deny the second. They would then argue that Consequentialism is not really an alienating moral theory, as it permits a life of engagement and attachment. I should detach myself from my present projects and then attach myself to a new set of projects. Perhaps I should structure my life around charity work or political activism, as this would produce the best possible results. Consequentialism does attach some value to my happiness. Faced with a choice between a miserable life of charitable service and an equally effective happy life, I should obviously choose the latter.

Consequentialists may thus argue that, while the theory requires great sacrifices, it need not lead to total alienation. Their opponents, however, will remain unconvinced. They will reply that Consequentialism does indeed prevent me from identifying with any project at all. If I follow Consequentialism, then I will pursue a given project only when doing so best promotes the overall good. On any occasion where my project does not maximize the good, I will be obliged to abandon or undermine it. The motivation for my actions always comes directly from Simple Consequentialism, not from my attachment to my project. My commitment to my projects is thus motivationally inert. Many philosophers conclude that no Consequentialist agent can ever really be attached to or engaged in any project. This claim is often linked to the Integrity Objection (see Section 1.3.1).

It seems to me that this objection is a very powerful one. So long as we stick with a simple version of Consequentialism the spectre of alienation will be hard to avoid. If Consequentialism really does tell me always to be ready to abandon my loved ones, my projects, and all other commitments in my life, in order to produce a little more impersonal value, then it will demand an alienating life. Indeed, Consequentialism seems set to destroy the integrity of my life along with my capacity for agency, just as its opponents allege.

At this point in the argument, those following the Strategy of Denial tend to introduce distinctions and complexities into their theory, so that Consequentialism no longer requires every agent always to act on each occasion so as to maximize the impersonal value of her actions. The Strategy of Denial thus gives way to that of restructuring Consequentialism, just as the Extremist strategy earlier gave way to denial. If we are successfully to rebut the Demandingness Objection, then it seems that we need to combine the three strategies.

2.3. Restructuring Consequentialism

Simple Consequentialism does require great financial and personal sacrifices. We saw earlier that this stringent requirement is hard to defend. The strategies of Extremism and Denial, on their own, cannot defeat the Demandingness Objection. Simple Consequentialism is not an acceptable moral theory. We need to explore alternative formulations of Consequentialism.

We now turn, finally, to the real subject of this book: the restructuring of Consequentialism. In this section I outline the various ways Consequentialism might be restructured. The exploration of these options will occupy the remainder of this book. To see how Consequentialism might be amended, we must first examine the structure of the theory. Simple Consequentialism has five principle features.

Impartiality.   Consequentialism assesses the value of an outcome from an impersonal point of view, rather than from the perspective of the agent. To illustrate this feature, we will employ a distinction popularized by Amartya Sen, who distinguishes two types of value.[22] The first is *agent-neutral value*—the value of an outcome from an impersonal standpoint or perspective, giving equal weight to the values, commitments, and interests of different agents. This contrasts with *agent-relative value*—the value of the outcome from the perspective of an individual agent. This may accord some features of an outcome a weight disproportionate to their impersonal value. We must distinguish the agent-relative value of an outcome from the question of how well the agent fares in that outcome. The former does not ignore the interests of other agents, it merely weighs them in the light of one agent's own values. For instance, the interests of my family and friends may contribute significantly to my agent-relative valuations. Consequentialists seek to promote agent-neutral value, as opposed to agent-relative value.

Maximization.   Consequentialism tells agents to perform the action that will produce the best possible outcome, or that has the highest expected value. Agents should optimize the good, not merely promote it to some lesser degree.

Individualism.   Consequentialism assesses an action by looking at the consequences of that action being performed on a particular occasion by a particular agent. The focus is on individual actions rather than on collective patterns of behaviour.

Directness.   Consequentialism assesses actions directly. The best action is the one with the best consequences, not the action prescribed by some optimal rule.

Act Focus.   Consequentialism focuses on assessing acts, as opposed to rules, dispositions, or motives. The principal aim of the theory is to find the best action on any occasion.

---

[22] Sen, 'Evaluator Relativity and Consequential Evaluation'; also Nagel, *The View from Nowhere*, pp. 152–3; Parfit, *Reasons and Persons*, p. 104; and Pettit, 'Universalisability without Utilitarianism', p. 75.

We can depart from Simple Consequentialism by varying one or more of these five basic features. We now briefly address each of the five resulting variations.

Much of the stringency of Consequentialism stems from its commitment to impartiality. We can depart from this commitment by allowing agents to give particular weight to their own interests or values. We might express this by replacing the agent-neutral values in the Consequentialist formula with agent-relative values. This formulation is suggested by Sen.[23] Alternatively, we might combine the impersonal perspective of Simple Consequentialism with elements derived from the agent's own personal perspective. This variation is pursued by Samuel Scheffler.[24] Departures from impartiality are explored in Chapter 6, and help to lay the foundation for the new version of Consequentialism presented in Part Four.

Another reason why Consequentialism is so demanding is that it always requires the best possible result. It is not enough for agents to produce good consequences, they must maximize. It may seem that the easiest way to make Consequentialism less demanding will be to abandon maximization. We might dub the result *Sub-Maximizing Consequentialism*. The best-known example is Michael Slote's Satisficing Consequentialism, which requires agents to produce a good enough outcome, without demanding the best.[25] Sub-maximizing forms of Consequentialism are discussed in Chapter 5. I conclude that they are inadequate, but provide some useful lessons for the general strategy of restructuring Consequentialism.

As we saw in the previous section, one of the problems with Consequentialism is that it requires me to do more if others do less. This is because Consequentialism asks what will happen if I perform some action, rather than asking what would happen if everyone behaved that way. Perhaps the latter question will produce a less demanding and more reasonable moral theory. We might call the result *Collective Consequentialism*. The best example is Rule Consequentialism, which tells agents to obey the set of rules whose internalization by everyone would produce the best consequences.[26] Rule Consequentialism is explored at some length in Chapter 3, while other forms of Collective Consequentialism are discussed in Chapter 4. I conclude that Collective Consequentialism is not satisfactory on its own, but that it will play a useful role in the broader Consequentialist theory developed in Part Four.

---

[23] Sen, 'Evaluator Relativity and Consequential Evaluation'.

[24] Scheffler, *The Rejection of Consequentialism*. For further references, see below, Ch. 6 n. 1.

[25] Slote, 'Satisficing Consequentialism'. For further references, see below, Ch. 5 n. 1.

[26] See e.g. Hooker, *Ideal Code, Real World*, and the various works cited below, Ch. 3 n. 1.

Rule Consequentialism also introduces us to the possibility of varying the fourth feature of Consequentialism, as it replaces the direct assessment of acts with the assessment of acts in terms of rules. An act is now evaluated in terms of the consequences of the rules that produce it rather than those of the act itself. Rule Consequentialism thus departs from Simple Consequentialism in two separate ways: it is collective as opposed to individual, and it is indirect as opposed to direct. We could have either of these departures without the other. For instance, in Chapter 4 we will examine forms of Collective Consequentialism where acts are evaluated directly using the consequences of universal performance of each act. Alternatively, we might construct an indirect form of Individual Consequentialism. For instance, we might say that the right act follows from a rule, where the consequences of the individual agent adopting that rule over the course of her life are better than the consequences of her adopting any other rule.

The rejection of Direct Consequentialism is often combined with the rejection of an exclusive focus on acts. Other possible objects of Consequentialist assessment include rules, motives, dispositions, or virtues. Each of these can be evaluated directly. For instance, we could evaluate motives by looking at the consequences of an agent having one motive rather than another. This might lead us to Multiple Object Consequentialism.[27]

It is important to distinguish Multiple Object Consequentialism from Indirect Consequentialism. The former still assesses acts directly in terms of their consequences, but it also assesses motives directly in terms of their consequences. By contrast, Indirect Consequentialism first assesses rules directly and then assesses acts in terms of those rules. For the Multiple Object Consequentialist, the different objects of assessment are separate and equal. For the Indirect Consequentialist, one object takes precedence over another.

In the next two sections I examine these last two departures from Simple Consequentialism. Can Consequentialism avoid the Demandingness Objection simply by widening its focus, or by shifting to indirect assessment of acts? I shall conclude that it cannot. This conclusion motivates the examination of more fundamental restructurings, such as the first three types listed above. This examination occupies the remainder of the book. However, the examination of multiple object and indirect forms of Consequentialism is valuable, as it introduces a number of useful themes and distinctions.

---

[27] Kagan, 'Evaluative Focal Points', and Pettit and Smith, 'Global Consequentialism'.

2.4. The Distinction between Criteria and Procedures

If Consequentialism is to avoid the Demandingness Objection, then it should not tell me to give all my money to charity. The objection arises because the Consequentialist guide to action seems to demand the option with the best consequences. If we are to avoid an extremely demanding theory, then we must change the advice Consequentialism offers to agents. All of the restructuring options discussed in the rest of this book substantially revise the Consequentialist view of right action, thereby offering different advice from Simple Consequentialism. However, some philosophers argue that Consequentialism can offer less demanding advice without abandoning its central claim that the right action produces the best consequences. In this section we ask whether this claim is correct.

The basis of this modified Consequentialist solution is a distinction between a criterion of rightness and a decision procedure. The resulting theory is similar to Multiple Object Consequentialism and also to Indirect Consequentialism. It might best be seen as a combination of the two.

A central question for any moral theory is the following: how should an agent decide what to do? The obvious answer is: by following the best moral decision procedure. Different moral theories offer different decision procedures. It may seem obvious that the decision procedure recommended by Consequentialism will be one where the agent always seeks to perform the action with the best consequences. However, many Consequentialists deny that this is the best procedure, even from a Consequentialist point of view. They argue that Consequentialists should evaluate decision procedures the same way they evaluate anything else. The best decision procedure will be the procedure that produces the best results. This may be the simple procedure of seeking to maximize the good, but it may not be. If some other procedure would produce better results, then Consequentialism will advise agents to follow it instead. Yet, from a Consequentialist point of view, the right *action* remains that which produces the best consequences. Sometimes, this criterion of right action is not the best way to decide what to do.[28]

The consequences in question are usually taken to be those of the individual agent following that particular procedure throughout her life. The best procedure may sometimes lead an agent not to choose the act that

[28] For discussions of the distinction, see Bales, 'Act Utilitarianism'; Griffin, 'The Distinction between Criterion and Decision Procedure'; Griffin, 'Modern Utilitarianism', p. 347; Hare, *Moral Thinking*, pp. 35–40; Jackson, 'Decision-Theoretic Consequentialism and the Nearest and Dearest Objection'; Lyons, *The Forms and Limits of Utilitarianism*, p. 149; Pettit and Brennan, 'Restrictive Consequentialism'; Railton, 'Alienation, Consequentialism and Morality'; Sidgwick, *The Methods of Ethics*, p. 413; and Smart and Williams, *Utilitarianism: For and Against*, pp. 42–57.

would produce the best results. However, the overall result of following the procedure on a number of occasions outweighs the resulting losses in utility.

Peter Railton explains the difference between a criterion of rightness and a decision procedure in terms of another distinction, between Objective and Subjective forms of Consequentialism.[29] Objective Consequentialism deals with the actual (or objectively probable) results of actions. The objectively right action is always what would have produced the best consequences. This provides the Consequentialist criterion of right action. Subjective Consequentialism deals with moral decisions from the agent's point of view. It advises agents how best to make decisions, in the light of their limited knowledge, time, and psychological capacity. The subjectively right action is what seems to the agent to have the greatest expected value. Naive Consequentialism will tell agents always to opt for the subjectively right action, on the grounds that this will maximize their chances of performing the objectively right action. Railton argues that sophisticated Consequentialists can depart from the subjectively right course of action, whenever they realize that another decision procedure offers a greater chance of arriving at the objectively right result.

This important Consequentialist distinction raises three basic questions. In the first place, under what circumstances might the Consequentialist criterion of rightness and the best Consequentialist decision procedure come apart? In other words, is the distinction purely theoretical, or is it likely to be of practical significance? Secondly, is the resulting dislocation desirable? Opponents of Consequentialism often argue that, in cases where the criterion and the procedure come apart, Consequentialist agents will become dislocated or alienated. They also argue that, if the two really do come apart, then the Consequentialist criterion of rightness is morally irrelevant. The final question is whether the distinction can solve the Demandingness Objection. Our primary interest is in this third question, which I shall answer in the negative.

Whenever some valuable result is not available to conscious maximizers, it will be unwise for a Consequentialist to seek to maximize directly. Such results are sometimes referred to as 'calculatively elusive'.[30] If the agent calculates too precisely, or aims too directly at the result, it will not occur. For instance, it is sometimes desirable to behave in a spontaneous or unselfconscious way. Perhaps the agent is engaged in an artistic endeavour that is most valuable if performed spontaneously. This result cannot be attained by agents who set out to be spontaneous. Alternatively, the agent might be performing some dangerous task, and risk losing her nerve if she thinks too much about the danger.

---

[29] Railton, 'Alienation, Consequentialism and Morality', p. 113.
[30] Pettit and Brennan, 'Restrictive Consequentialism', p. 442.

A second form of calculative elusiveness arises when an agent needs to make a decision very quickly. When deciding where to run to escape an oncoming truck, for instance, agents should not seek to calculate precisely the expected value of each available option. An agent's life will go better overall if she adopts the general policy of picking the first non-disastrous option that comes to mind. More generally, some philosophers have argued that an agent following a satisficing strategy, whereby she always chose the first good enough option that came to mind, would produce better results over the course of her life than one who consciously sought to maximize on every separate occasion.[31] This strategic satisficing retains the maximizing criterion of rightness. We must distinguish it from Satisficing Consequentialism, which adopts a satisficing criterion of rightness. For more on this distinction, and on the relative merits of the two approaches, see Chapter 5.

Elusive results also arise in relation to friendship. Someone generally disposed to pursue the interests of her friends rather than seeking to maximize the good will have more valuable friendships, and make a greater contribution to the well-being of her friends. This will be especially true if the friends are able to discern her motivations. Knowing that one's friend spends time with one only as a way of maximizing the good, and would abandon one immediately in order to produce a better overall result, is not conducive to the realization of the goods of friendship.[32]

The Integrity Objection helps motivate the distinction between criteria of rightness and decision procedures. Consequentialists should depart from a maximizing procedure when it threatens the integrity of their lives, or when it is inconsistent with their limitations as finite human agents. This brings us to our second question. Does the fact that its criterion and procedure come apart in many familiar situations demonstrate that Consequentialism is unacceptable? Bernard Williams argues that it does. On his view, 'there is no distinctive place for *direct* utilitarianism unless it is . . . a doctrine about how one should decide what to do'.[33] James Griffin also criticizes the relevance of a criterion of rightness that, owing to the limitations of our knowledge and psychology, could never be applied by human beings. He asks whether 'a "criterion" that cannot be applied [is] really a criterion'.[34] Defenders of the distinction reply that the Consequentialist criterion can generate useful ethical advice even if we could never apply it perfectly ourselves. My own

---

[31] On the advantages of a satisficing strategy, see ibid. 444–6; and Pettit, 'Satisficing Consequentialism'.

[32] See e.g. Pettit and Brennan, 'Restrictive Consequentialism', pp. 450–1; Stocker, 'The Schizophrenia of Modern Ethical Theories'; and Mason, 'Can an Indirect Consequentialist be a Real Friend?'.

[33] Smart and Williams, *Utilitarianism: For and Against*, p. 128.

[34] Griffin, 'The Distinction between Criterion and Decision Procedure', pp. 180–1.

view is that the distinction is certainly useful, though we must be wary of any moral theory whose criterion of rightness and decision procedure diverge too greatly.

Fortunately, we can put this controversial issue to one side. Our primary interest in the distinction between criteria and decision procedures is as a solution to the Demandingness Objection. If the distinction cannot significantly reduce the demands of the theory, then we need not examine it further. It seems clear that, on its own, this distinction cannot defeat the objection. Even if we grant that the best Consequentialist decision procedure is not relentless maximization, it hardly follows that it is not a very demanding one. Perhaps the appropriate decision procedure is not as alienating as direct maximization.[35] However, it does seem certain to involve great financial and personal sacrifices. For instance, the result of always following the simple procedure of donating most of one's time and resources to charity will generally be better than the result of following a more self-directed strategy, at least for most ordinary agents. The best Consequentialist decision procedure still makes unreasonably strong demands.

I conclude that, whatever else it may do, the distinction between criteria of rightness and decision procedures cannot solve the Demandingness Objection. Indeed, those who favour the distinction seldom argue explicitly that the best decision procedure is comparatively undemanding. Instead, they rely on other, more radical, departures from Simple Consequentialism, such as those addressed in the remaining chapters of this book.[36]

2.5. Blameless Wrongdoing

In this section I focus on the following claim.

The Parfit Suggestion. Consequentialists can reduce the force of the Demandingness Objection by appealing to the notion of blameless wrongdoing, without resorting to indirect or collective assessment of either acts of any other unit of assessment.[37]

---

[35] Even this claim is controversial. There may be times when the best results *from an impersonal perspective* do require an alienating procedure.

[36] A classic recent example is Frank Jackson's argument in 'Decision-Theoretic Consequentialism and the Nearest and Dearest Objection', which is plausible only if glossed in collective terms.

[37] I call this the Parfit Suggestion because it was suggested to me by Derek Parfit, not because it is to be found explicitly in any of his writings. The argument of this section is abridged from Mulgan, 'Two Moral Counterfactuals'.

Parfit illustrates the notion of blameless wrongdoing by means of the following tale.

Clare's Case. Judged in Direct Consequentialist terms the best possible sets of motives all include strong love for our children. Clare has one of these sets of motives. She can either give her child some benefit, or give a much greater benefit to an unfortunate stranger. Her love for her child leads her to benefit him rather than the stranger.[38]

Consequentialists adopting the Parfit Suggestion will make three claims about this story.

1. Clare performs the wrong act. Faced with a choice between two options, she fails to choose the one that would maximize the good.
2. Clare should not be blamed for her action. This is because she acts from a desirable set of motives. The only way Clare could have acted otherwise would be if she had had different (less desirable) motives.[39]
3. Clare is not to be blamed for her failure to alter her motives at some previous time. This is because, overall, things would have gone worse if Clare had taken such steps than if she had not.

The distinction between blameworthiness and wrongdoing is analogous to the distinction between criteria of rightness and decision procedures. Both distinctions contrast the Consequentialist criterion of rightness (or wrongness) with some other feature of moral deliberation. Both distinctions rely upon the fact that human agents are not perfect calculating machines, nor would it be desirable for us to aspire to be such machines. However, the two distinctions are not necessarily identical, as an agent's motives are not the same as her decision procedure. In particular, we might think of Clare's motives as being beyond her direct control at the time of action, whereas her decision procedure may be consciously chosen.

Parfit's position has been much discussed.[40] I shall not enter into this debate here. For the sake of the present argument, I propose to accept that there are times when the best motives produce a wrong action. I shall also accept that Clare's story is such a case. We must then ask if these admissions are sufficient to dissolve the Demandingness Objection.

[38] Parfit, *Reasons and Persons*, p. 32.
[39] It turns out that a great deal depends on how we gloss this last sentence. See Dancy, 'Parfit and Indirectly Self-Defeating Theories', and Mulgan, 'Two Moral Counterfactuals'.
[40] See e.g. Dancy, 'Parfit and Indirectly Self-Defeating Theories'; Darwall, 'Rational Agent, Rational Act'; Mendola, 'Parfit on Directly Collectively Self-Defeating Moral Theories'; Moser, 'Consequentialism and Self-Defeat'; Mulgan, 'Two Moral Counterfactuals'; Rabinowicz, 'Act-Utilitarian Prisoner's Dilemmas'; and Tannsjo, 'Blameless Wrongdoing'.

If the Parfit Suggestion is to work, then we must show that Affluent's situation is analogous to Clare's. We are assessing acts directly. Affluent knowingly and deliberately fails to maximize the good. She has taken account of the possible effect of her present choice on the future strength of her desirable parental motives. Any negative effect of a charitable donation is more than outweighed by the benefit the donation would bring. On balance, the donation is the better act. Her act is thus clearly wrong. Affluent will claim that she is still blameless, as she acts in accordance with the best possible set of motives.

On the face of it, this seems rather implausible. It is relatively easy to imagine other sets of motives with better consequences. For instance, if Affluent had completely impartial motives, she would donate large amounts to charity on a regular basis. Affluent and her friends would no doubt suffer as a result, but this would be greatly outweighed by the good produced by her donations. Affluent does not have the best possible motives.

Affluent and her supporters have three options at this point. First, they might argue that, although Affluent's case is not analogous to the first of Parfit's Clare cases, it is analogous to the second.[41]

Clare Two's Case.   Clare Two can save either her child, or several strangers. Because she loves her child, she saves him, and the strangers all die.

Parfit concedes that, if at some time in the past Clare Two had given herself more impartial motives, then things would have gone better overall. However, she didn't know then that her present situation would arise. The probability that Clare Two would end up in this type of life-or-death situation was sufficiently low that the expected value of parental motives exceeded the expected value of impartial motives. This is enough to absolve Clare Two from blame.

Fortunately, we need not assess Clare Two's defence, as her case is not analogous to Affluent's. Unlike Clare Two, Affluent cannot plausibly claim that she did not know that her present situation would arise. A letter from a charitable organization is hardly a bolt from the blue. Affluent has known for some time that she would face such choices. She must have known that, given her current motives, she would act very wrongly. She could have taken steps to change her motives. She did not. She can thus be blamed for acting on her present motives, as they never looked like the best possible set.

Affluent's first reply fails. She cannot admit that her current motives are not the best, and then attempt to excuse herself. She must claim that she has

---

[41]   Parfit, *Reasons and Persons*, p. 33.

the best possible motives. Her two remaining options represent two different forms this claim might take. The first amends our story as follows. Affluent is not an inhabitant of the world as it is now. Rather, she lives in an improved world of the (possible) future, where there is far less poverty, and people are much more generous. In that society, the best set of motives for Affluent are her actual parental ones.

As it stands, this reply is inadequate. We are interested in Affluent precisely because her situation is so similar to our own. To escape the Demandingness Objection, Consequentialists must deal with a real-world Affluent, not one who lives in some idealized never-never land. Affluent might reply that the best motives for her to have in our actual world are those that would produce the best consequences in that ideal society. In other words, Affluent could replace her individual assessment of acts with a collective one. Unfortunately, such a move constitutes an abandonment of the Parfit Suggestion, which aims to avoid collective assessments. Whatever the merits of Collective Consequentialism, it is not an option for Affluent at this point.

I discuss the merits and demerits of Collective Consequentialism at length in Part Two. Collective assessments are likely to be less demanding than individualistic ones, but they face other objections that the latter avoid. In addition to general worries regarding Collective Consequentialism, we would also have to ask whether a direct collective assessment of motives is compatible with a direct individualistic assessment of acts. This question has both a practical and a theoretical dimension, though these overlap. The practical problem is that, although we want some divergence between the best act and the best motive—otherwise we would not have been attracted to the Parfit Suggestion in the first place—this present combination may produce too much divergence. Blameless wrongdoing may become too common. The theoretical problem is that there may be a tension between our rationale for a collective assessment of motives, and our rationale for assessing acts individually. We must justify assessing the two features in such radically different ways. This would lead us to another issue, the possibility of combining our direct collective assessment of motives with a direct collective assessment of acts. This would take us still further from the original intention of the Parfit Suggestion.

Affluent's final option is to claim that she could not have given herself more impartial motives without the benefits of those impartial motives being outweighed by the negative effects of the inculcation process itself. Perhaps a more impartial Affluent would be a listless and morose figure who was not much good to anyone. To test this new claim, we must imagine a set of motives containing the highest degree of impartiality Affluent could have successfully inculcated in herself without any negative side effects. Affluent would then have to demonstrate that this set of motives is not unduly demanding.

The question of psychological possibility is extremely complicated, and I do not hope to address it adequately here. However, Affluent's claim does seem rather dubious. In general, people do seem capable of having very demandingly impartial motives. Affluent is already more impartial than most, as she gives a significant amount to charity. Yet it seems likely that she could have trained herself to give more, if she had chosen to do so. (See Section 3.4.2 for further discussion of the limits of psychological possibility.)

Even if we grant Affluent's claim, her approach leaves us too much at the mercy of empirical facts. We certainly want the demands of morality to be sensitive to the limits of psychology. Morality should not demand what is psychologically impossible. However, should it demand *all* that is psychologically possible? Perhaps those who are capable of greater impartiality should be more impartial than others, but are we all required to be as impartial as we possibly can? (The only limit on our impartiality would be the proviso, noted above, that the benefits of more impartial motives must be weighed against the cost of inculcation.) This seems too demanding. An adequate response to the Demandingness Objection should leave us with some breathing space between the demands of morality and the limits of psychology. We should not always be blamed (or blame ourselves) for failing to be the best we possibly could.

We must distinguish two claims proponents of the Parfit Suggestion might make:

1. Affluent was right not to take steps in the past to give herself different motives;
2. Affluent is right not to take steps now to give herself different motives.

These two claims are distinct. In particular, (2) seems more plausible than (1). Affluent might claim that she has the best motives for her present situation, but she cannot deny that she should have given herself different motives that would have landed her in a different situation. If she could establish (2) without (1), then we might say that Affluent was partially blameless. There would probably be no point in our castigating her, as we do not want her to change her motives now, but we would still judge that her present lack of impartiality was blameworthy.

However, this partial blamelessness would not be enough. Even if Consequentialism did not make great demands in Affluent's present situation, it would still be very demanding in what we may call the pre-Affluent situation, as no affluent person would ever be allowed to develop a taste for theatre or any other suboptimal pursuit. Most of us would regard such a demand as excessive. Affluent has no compelling reply to the charge that her motives are not the best. The notion of blameless wrongdoing cannot solve the Demandingness Objection.

2.6. Conclusion

We have seen that the strategies of Extremism and Denial are unconvincing, while neither the distinction between criteria of rightness and decision procedures nor the notion of blameless wrongdoing is sufficient to defeat the Demandingness Objection. Consequentialists must abandon the claim that the right act on any occasion produces the best consequences. The remainder of the book explores Consequentialist moral theories that depart from this claim. Part Two deals with Collective Consequentialist theories, Part Three examines restructured forms of Individual Consequentialism, while Part Four presents a new Consequentialist theory, combining elements from each of the theories discussed in earlier chapters. It is hoped that this new theory will have the resources to dissolve the Demandingness Objection.

PART TWO

Collective Consequentialism

3

Rule Consequentialism

Consequentialism derives much of its initial appeal from its apparent simplicity: it gives me the single moral project of making the world a better place. Complexities multiply as soon as I ask what this project involves. The division between Parts Two and Three of this book turns on a prior question: in what sense does Consequentialism give this project *to me*? In the Consequentialist tradition, two standard answers are interwoven. On the one hand, the Consequentialist project is seen as an individual project given to me as a single moral agent. Alternatively, Consequentialism may be a group project, which is mine only because (and in so far as) I belong to some particular group (which may be the set of all moral agents, or some subset of them). For generality, I shall refer to these approaches as Individual Consequentialism and Collective Consequentialism respectively.

Historically, the principal Consequentialist alternative to Simple Consequentialism has been Rule Consequentialism, which can be initially characterized as follows: an act is morally right if and only if it is called for by a set of rules the following of which by everyone would result in at least as good consequences judged impartially as any other.[1]

Rule Consequentialism exemplifies the collective approach, and is often presented as a less demanding alternative to Simple Consequentialism. More generally, Collective Consequentialist theories are seen as less demanding

---

[1] For a representative statement of Rule Consequentialism, see Hooker, *Ideal Code, Real World*. For further elaborations of Hooker's theory, see his 'Rule Consequentialism'; 'Rule-Consequentialism and Demandingness'; 'Rule-Consequentialism, Incoherence, Fairness'; 'Compromising with Convention'; 'Rule-Consequentialism and Obligations toward the Needy'; 'Ross-Style Pluralism versus Rule-Consequentialism'; and 'Reply to Stratton-Lake'. For discussions of Hooker's theory, see R. Carson, 'A Note on Hooker's Rule Consequentialism'; Miller, 'Hooker's Use and Abuse of Reflective Equilibrium'; Mulgan, 'Ruling Out Rule Consequentialism'; Mulgan, 'Rule Consequentialism and Famine'; Mulgan, 'One False Virtue of Rule Consequentialism'; and Stratton-Lake, 'Can Hooker's Rule-Consequentialist Principle Justify Ross's Prima Facie Duties?'. For other discussions of Rule Consequentialism, see Brandt, 'Some Merits of One Form of Rule-Utilitarianism'; Brandt, 'Fairness to Indirect Optimific Theories in Ethics'; Gibbard, 'Rule Utilitarianism'; Hooker (ed.), *Rationality, Rules and Utility*; Hooker, Mason, and Miller (eds.), *Morality, Rules, and Consequences*; Lucas, 'African Famine'; Lyons, *The Forms and Limits of Utilitarianism*; Moore, 'The Utilitarian Ethics of R. B. Brandt'; Schaller, 'A Problem for Brandt's Utilitarianism'; and Decew, 'Brandt's New Defense of Rule Utilitarianism'.

than Individual Consequentialist theories. In Part Two, I evaluate Collective Consequentialism. Chapter 3 focuses on Rule Consequentialism, while other collective approaches are addressed in Chapter 4.

Rule Consequentialism has considerable intuitive appeal. A relatively small percentage of the combined income of the well off should be enough to feed the world. Rule Consequentialism would thus place reasonable demands on Affluent. It is also natural to see moral philosophy as the search for the optimal set of moral rules, and to expect those rules to produce the best consequences. Rule Consequentialism also seems fairer than Simple Consequentialism, as it does not require an agent to do more than her 'fair share' in promoting the good, even if others fail to do theirs.

Given its initial plausibility, it is worth asking whether Rule Consequentialism really does provide an adequate response to famine. More generally, is it a plausible moral theory? In this chapter, I present a number of new objections to Rule Consequentialism. These fall into three basic categories: (1) objections to the actual results given by Rule Consequentialism (Section 3.4); (2) objections to the results Rule Consequentialism would give in certain plausible hypothetical cases (Sections 3.5 and 3.6); and (3) theoretical problems in the formulation of Rule Consequentialism (Section 3.7). I conclude that Rule Consequentialism is an undesirable alternative to Simple Consequentialism.

The basic idea of Rule Consequentialism is quite simple. We begin by looking for the optimal set of rules. We assess each possible set of rules collectively, asking what would happen if everyone followed that set of rules. The optimal rule set is the set of rules such that the consequences of everyone following them would be better than the consequences of everyone following any other set of rules. We then assess acts indirectly. The right act in any situation is the act dictated by the optimal set of rules. I shall sometimes speak of the possible world where everyone follows the optimal set of rules as 'the ideal society'. This phrase should always be interpreted in the light of Rule Consequentialism.

Variations on this simple Rule Consequentialist theory are usually motivated by particular objections. We will concentrate on a recent version of the theory developed by Brad Hooker. However, my aim is to develop a general critique of Rule Consequentialism, not just a critique of Hooker's particular version.

3.1. Arguments in Favour of Rule Consequentialism

We will now examine the various arguments put forward in support of Rule Consequentialism. The force of various objections to Rule Consequentialism often depends upon what the theory is trying to achieve, and how it is justified. In particular, many objections to Rule Consequentialism focus on difficulties surrounding attempts to discover what the theory requires of us in the real world. If Rule Consequentialism is an abstract criterion of rightness defended on purely theoretical grounds, then objections of this form may not be fatal to the theory. On the other hand, if Rule Consequentialism is defended on the basis of the intuitive appeal of its judgements regarding particular cases, then the inability to discover those judgements will be a fatal blow.

There are three main types of argument in favour of Rule Consequentialism. These are as follows.

Consequentialist Arguments.   Rule Consequentialism is the best account of the central Consequentialist principle that morality is about promoting value.

Theoretical Arguments.   Rule Consequentialism is the best account of some general moral ideal such as fairness, impartiality, or equality.

Practical Arguments.   Rule Consequentialism fits our everyday moral judgements better than competing moral theories.

Strictly speaking, the first type of argument is a subset of the second. However, it is convenient to separate the two, as Consequentialist defences of Rule Consequentialism raise a number of specific issues. Many defenders of Rule Consequentialism run several of these arguments together. They also often argue for Rule Consequentialism by comparing it with various rival moral theories across a range of criteria.

In the recent literature, arguments of the first type are considerably less prominent. Rule Consequentialists such as Hooker are now more likely to offer Non-Consequentialist justifications for their theory. Nonetheless, Consequentialist justifications provide a useful introduction to Rule Consequentialism.

3.1.1.   *Consequentialist Defences of Rule Consequentialism*

This argument claims that Rule Consequentialism is superior to Individual Consequentialism, purely on Consequentialist grounds. Someone solely interested in maximally promoting value would prefer Rule Consequentialism to any form of Individual Consequentialism. One common claim is that the world would be a better place if everyone followed the optimal rule set than if everyone followed Individual Direct Consequentialism. The latter is thus 'collectively self-defeating'.[2]

This argument is analogous to arguments supporting a move from Individual Direct Consequentialism to Individual Indirect Consequentialism (see Section 2.4). Rule Consequentialism departs from Simple Consequentialism in two ways: it is indirect and it is collective. Discussions of Rule Consequentialism often run together these two separate elements of the theory. For instance, Rule Consequentialism is often compared with 'Act Consequentialism', where the latter is both direct and individualistic.

This is a mistake. These two elements are distinct and must be justified separately. If Rule Consequentialism is the best form of Consequentialism, then it must be superior not only to Direct Individual Consequentialism but also to *Indirect* Individual Consequentialism. The collective element of the theory must earn its keep independently of the indirect element.

The two elements of Rule Consequentialism might be justified in different ways. In particular, the indirect element of the theory often emerges in response to objections to Rule Consequentialism. This suggests that, while the main argument in favour of the collective component of Rule Consequentialism may be largely theoretical, the purpose of the indirect component is to soften the edges of the theory and generate more intuitively plausible judgements about particular cases.

Rule Consequentialism can be defended either as a criterion of rightness or as a decision procedure. We saw in Chapter 2 that this distinction is central to any discussion of Individual Indirect Consequentialism. Most Rule Consequentialists offer their theory as a distinct criterion of rightness, not simply as an efficient strategy for Individual Consequentialists. They argue that what makes an action morally right is the fact that it follows from the optimal set of rules.

We will discuss Consequentialist justifications of Rule Consequentialism in more detail when we consider objections to the theory, as a number of objections are aimed primarily at these justifications. (See especially the Incoherence Objection and the Homogeneity Objection: Sections 3.2 and 3.7 respectively.)

---

[2] Parfit, *Reasons and Persons*, pp. 24–9.

3.1.2. Theoretical (Non-Consequentialist) Defences of Rule Consequentialism

There are a number of options here, each based on a different moral ideal. One very common defence of Rule Consequentialism sees it as the most natural way to develop the moral ideas underlying the common accusation: 'What if everyone did that?'[3] These include universalizability and fairness. This idea of fairness relates to a fair distribution of the demands of morality, not to a fair distribution of goods or opportunities. The thought is that it is unfair for a moral theory to require some to do more because others are doing less (see Chapter 4 and Section 8.2). This argument is comparative. Other moral theories provide competing accounts of these moral ideals. Rule Consequentialists claim theirs is the most plausible.

There are two ways Rule Consequentialism and another moral theory might be related with respect to a given ideal. The first is *competition*, whereby two theories offer conflicting and mutually exclusive accounts of the same ideal. For instance, a Rule Consequentialist criterion of rightness and a Simple Consequentialist criterion offer competing accounts of how to respond to values, or how to be impartial. To cite another example, a Rule Consequentialist set of moral rules might compete with a Kantian set of maxims passing the Categorical Imperative test. Each is presented as an account of the ideal of universalizability.

The second possible relationship between theories is *complementarity*. Two theories dealing with the same ideal might be compatible, as one offers a more precise specification of the general account provided by the other. The first theory thus completes or fills out the second. For instance, Rule Consequentialism might provide a more detailed answer to general questions posed by Contractualist or Kantian moral theories. Such theories seek rules that cannot be reasonably rejected, or rules chosen in the Original Position, or rules passing the Categorical Imperative test. These might be the rules whose general acceptance produces the best consequences. (The classic example of this strategy is John Harsanyi's attempt to derive a Rule Consequentialist set of rules from a Rawlsian Original Position.[4]) Analogously, Individual Indirect Consequentialism might offer its own set of rules. Rule Consequentialism would then compete with Individual Indirect Consequentialism as a complement to the original Contractualist or Kantian theory.

---

[3] As Hooker notes, a more relevant question is often: 'What if everyone felt free to do that?' For instance, a rule permitting everyone to use a public park may have good consequences, even though it would be disastrous if everyone actually used the park at the same time (Hooker, *Ideal Code, Real World*, p. 5).

[4] Harsanyi, 'Can the Maximin Principle Serve as a Basis for Morality?'.

Rule Consequentialists might use both relationships. They might argue as follows. As it is usually formulated, Contractualism (for instance) is inferior to Rule Consequentialism. If we revise Contractualism to make it a plausible rival for Rule Consequentialism, then the resulting theory will choose the same rules as Rule Consequentialism. For instance, Brad Hooker objects to Contractualism that it gives no moral status to animals.[5] If a Contractualist responded by grounding morality in the capacity for suffering rather than the capacity for reasonable rejection, then the difference between Contractualism and Rule Consequentialism would be greatly reduced. The two theories might recommend the same rules.[6]

Theoretical defences of any theory often go together with practical arguments. One test of an account of a general moral ideal is whether it enables us to make plausible judgements in particular cases. A moral theory generating absurd particular result is unlikely to have accurately captured the essence of our general moral ideals.

3.1.3. Practical Justifications of Rule Consequentialism

Those who defend Rule Consequentialism often place great weight on its intuitive plausibility. Hooker, for instance, goes so far as to say that 'the best argument for rule-consequentialism is that it does a better job than its rivals of matching and tying together our moral convictions'.[7]

These convictions operate at various levels. They might relate to general moral ideals, general moral rules, or particular moral judgements. We focus on particular cases, concentrating on the demands of Rule Consequentialism, especially the obligations of affluent people to relieve the sufferings of distant strangers.

We will address the following questions. What does Rule Consequentialism require me to give to famine relief? What rules regarding famine (and other disaster) relief would Rule Consequentialism regard as optimal? How demanding will Rule Consequentialism be for someone in my position? Are

[5] Hooker, *Ideal Code, Real World*, pp. 66–70, and Hooker, 'Rule-Consequentialism, Incoherence, Fairness', p. 23. However, some Contractualists do seek to take account of animals. See e.g. Singer, 'An Extension of Rawls's Theory of Justice to Environmental Ethics'; Elliot, 'Rawlsian Justice and Non-Human Animals'; and VanDeveer, 'Of Beasts, Persons and the Original Position'.

[6] Similarly, as we shall see in Chapter 4, Liam Murphy argues that no acceptable moral theory can violate his Compliance Condition. The revisions necessary to bring any competing moral theory into line with that condition would greatly reduce its distance from Collective Consequentialism.

[7] Hooker, *Ideal Code, Real World*, p. 101. See also Hooker, 'Rule-Consequentialism, Incoherence, Fairness', p. 29.

the resulting demands reasonable? To answer these questions, we examine several theoretical problems facing contemporary Rule Consequentialism.

Hooker has recently argued that Rule Consequentialism requires each of us to donate approximately 10 per cent of our income to charity.[8] Is the optimal rule 'Donate 10 per cent', or some other rule that happens to require a donation of 10 per cent in the actual world? This question looms large when we come to ask what Rule Consequentialism would demand if things were different.

It is important to realize that the defenders of Rule Consequentialism do not see their theory as merely providing a list of plausible moral judgements. They also present it as explaining, underpinning, and justifying those particular judgements. Rule Consequentialism aims to offer a principled rationale for plausible moral rules. Hooker explicitly acknowledges this when arguing for the superiority of Rule Consequentialism over Ross-style pluralism.[9] It is thus legitimate to test Rule Consequentialism against hypothetical examples as well as actual cases. (For a general justification of this approach, see the discussion of hypothetical examples in Section 1.4.1.)

For the sake of argument, I propose to grant that it is not unreasonable for a moral theory to require one to donate 10 per cent of one's income. This leaves two questions. (1) Does Rule Consequentialism really demand only about 10 per cent? (2) Does Rule Consequentialism generate this result for the right reasons? Before addressing these issues, however, we must examine some old objections to Rule Consequentialism, as these provide the motivation for contemporary formulations of the theory.

3.2. Three Old Objections to Rule Consequentialism

Opponents of Rule Consequentialism have long argued that the theory is absurdly unrealistic in practice, that it collapses into Simple Consequentialism, and that it is theoretically incoherent. These three objections are all related, as later objections respond to Rule Consequentialist replies to earlier ones. Let us look at each objection in turn.

Perhaps the most obvious objection to Rule Consequentialism is the following.

The Partial Compliance Objection. Because it chooses moral rules on the basis of what would happen if everybody complied with them, Rule

---

[8] Hooker, 'Rule-Consequentialism', and Hooker, 'Rule-Consequentialism and Demandingness'.
[9] Hooker, *Ideal Code, Real World*, pp. 105–7, and Hooker, 'Ross-Style Pluralism versus Rule-Consequentialism', pp. 543–6.

Consequentialism gives undesirable results in situations of partial compliance, where not everyone conforms with the rule in question. For instance, assume I am living in Sweden prior to 1967. I decide it would be best if everyone drove on the right-hand side of the road. As a Rule Consequentialist, I begin to drive on the right-hand side, even though everyone else drives on the left. The results are not pleasant.[10]

To avoid this objection, Rule Consequentialists usually say that the optimal rules include clauses of the following form: do x, unless doing x will lead to great disaster because everyone else is not doing x, in which case do y (where y avoids disaster). The rule for Sweden would be: drive on the right unless driving on the right will have disastrous consequences because everyone else is driving on the left, in which case drive on the left.
   This move leads directly to another objection, due to David Lyons.[11]

The Co-Extensionality (or Collapse) Objection.   Rule Consequentialism collapses into Individual Consequentialism. It will be best for everyone to obey rules of infinite complexity telling people to maximize utility in each particular situation. This is an extension of the disaster-avoidance clause, where any failure to maximize the good counts as a disaster.

There are two ways one theory might collapse into another. The first is *extensional equivalence*. The two theories generate different sets of moral rules, but these happen to produce exactly the same particular moral judgements. For instance, if Rule Consequentialism adds a disaster-avoidance clause every time one of its rules produces a suboptimal result, then we will end up with a very complicated set of rules with the same practical results as Direct Individual Consequentialism. The second, and more complete, form of collapse leads to *intensional equivalence*. Not only do the two theories produce the same judgements, but they also recommend exactly the same moral rules. On this version of the Collapse Objection, the rule set chosen by Rule Consequentialism will consist of a single rule, 'Always choose the act with the best consequences'.[12]

---

[10] Gibbard, 'Rule Utilitarianism', p. 217, and Hooker, 'Rule-Consequentialism', p. 74.

[11] Lyons, *The Forms and Limits of Utilitarianism*, p. 133. For critical discussion, see Feldman, 'On the Extensional Equivalence of Simple and General Utilitarianism'; Goldman, 'David Lyons on Utilitarian Generalization'; and Horwich, 'On Calculating the Utility of Acts'.

[12] In his discussion, Hooker mentions three possible forms of collapse. However, as he himself observes, the first two are effectively equivalent. They correspond to my intensional equivalence. Hooker's third form of collapse is my extensional equivalence. (Hooker, *Ideal Code, Real World*, pp. 93–9.)

To avoid these two objections, Rule Consequentialists seek a middle ground between overly simplistic rules and infinitely complex ones. Many contemporary formulations of Rule Consequentialism are driven by the need to differentiate the theory from Individual Consequentialism. One common response is to distinguish between 'following a rule' and 'accepting a rule'. The Co-extensionality Objection is said to apply only if Rule Consequentialism is built on the former notion, as there are limits on the complexity of the rules a community can accept. For instance, Brad Hooker introduces a distinction between two forms of Rule Consequentialism.[13]

Compliance Rule Consequentialism. To find the optimal rule set we ask what would happen if a given set of rules were always *complied with* by everyone.

Acceptance Rule Consequentialism. To find the optimal rule set we ask what would happen if a given set of rules were *accepted* by everyone. For Hooker, to accept a set of rules involves

not just the disposition to comply with these rules. . . . [but] also . . . the disposition to encourage others to comply with them, dispositions to form favourable attitudes toward others who comply with them, dispositions to feel guilt or shame when one breaks them and to condemn and resent others' breaking them, all of which dispositions and attitudes being supported by a belief that they are justified.[14]

Hooker focuses on the cost of inculcating the set of rules in the next generation. The costs of acceptance include both transitional costs of moving from our present code to the ideal code and ongoing costs once the code has been internalized.

Hooker argues that these two forms of Rule Consequentialism will recommend different sets of rules. The main reason is that the acceptance of a rule by a population has consequences over and above compliance with that rule. Also, some people might accept a rule even though they do not always comply with it; while others might comply perfectly with a rule they do not accept.

---

[13] Hooker, *Ideal Code, Real World*, pp. 75–80; Hooker, 'Rule-Consequentialism, Incoherence, Fairness', p. 21; and Hooker, 'Rule-Consequentialism', p. 67. Derek Parfit has suggested (in conversation) that Moral Realists will regard compliance as more relevant than acceptance, whereas Constructivists will be more interested in acceptance. This is because the Moral Realist is less likely to expect a close link between the precise details of human motivation (such as the consequences of the acceptance of rules) and the content of the correct moral rules. For the Moral Constructivist, by contrast, it is natural to expect a close connection. If we associate Moral Realism with those who offer Consequentialist justifications of Rule Consequentialism, whereas Constructivists highlight the intuitive appeal of the theory, then this suggestion appears to be confirmed. However, as the argument of this chapter is designed to demonstrate the inadequacy of both forms of Rule Consequentialism, it should not rely upon either of these meta-ethical positions.

[14] Hooker, *Ideal Code, Real World*, p. 76. See also Brandt, 'Some Merits of One Form of Rule-Utilitarianism'.

Hooker argues that Acceptance Rule Consequentialism is superior to the compliance-based theory. He offers two basic arguments. The first is based on the connection between moral motivation and acceptance. Hooker argues that for the Rule Consequentialist 'compliance is not the only thing of importance. We also care about people's having *moral concerns*. So we had better consider the costs of securing not only compliance but also adequate moral motivation. From a rule-consequentialist point of view, "moral motivation" means acceptance of the right rules.'[15]

This argument also helps to explain why Rule Consequentialists are especially interested in rules. The acceptance of rules is closely linked to disposition and moral character. In Hooker's theory, 'accepting rules is a matter of having certain associated motivations and beliefs, indeed of having a certain character and conscience'.[16] On this view, Rule Consequentialism is similar to a Consequentialism whose prime focus is on dispositions, motives, or character. Some might question this account of what it is to accept a rule. For our purposes, the more significant question is whether the resulting Rule Consequentialism fares better or worse than a theory founded on any alternative account of rule following.

Hooker's second argument is that Acceptance Rule Consequentialism produces better judgements about particular cases than the compliance form of the theory. In particular, the move from compliance to acceptance is designed to solve the Demandingness Objection as well as the Collapse Objection. These two objections are clearly related. If Rule Consequentialism does deliver the same results as Individual Consequentialism, then the two theories will obviously be equally demanding. If Individual Consequentialism is unreasonably demanding, then so is Rule Consequentialism.

If Acceptance Rule Consequentialism does not collapse into Individual Consequentialism, then this must be because widespread acceptance of Individual Consequentialism would not produce the best consequences. We must look at the costs and benefits of getting different sets of rules accepted within a population. In the present context, we are particularly interested in two sets of rules. The first is the simple Individual Consequentialist rule: 'Always act so as to maximally promote value'. The second contains complex rules extensionally equivalent to Individual Consequentialism.

Let us begin with this second set of rules. It seems clear that the costs of inculcating such complicated rules in an entire population would be very high. Indeed, it is not clear that rules complicated enough to be genuinely coextensive with Individual Consequentialism could ever even be fully

---

[15] Hooker, *Ideal Code, Real World*, p. 76.
[16] Hooker, 'Rule-Consequentialism, Incoherence, Fairness', p. 21.

formulated. Rules that cannot be formulated can hardly be accepted by everyone. Furthermore, even if this set of 'endlessly complicated and qualified rules'[17] could be successfully taught to everyone, it is very unlikely that this would be a cost-effective thing to do. A less complicated set of rules would be much easier to apply, and would produce greater net benefit. If the Rule Consequentialist set of rules contains detailed exception clauses, it must diverge from Individual Consequentialism in some particular cases. (We return to these issues in Section 3.4, when we explore the demands of Rule Consequentialism.)

Let us turn now to the single Individual Consequentialist Rule. On the face of it, this seems a very plausible candidate. How could the consequences not be best if everyone always sought the best? At this point, we need to distinguish two questions. (1) Does Rule Consequentialism collapse into Direct Individual Consequentialism? (2) Does Rule Consequentialism pick out the same decision procedure as Indirect Individual Consequentialism? Many of the replies to the Collapse Objection address only the first of these questions. For instance, Rule Consequentialists argue that, if everyone actively sought to promote the good, the consequences would be suboptimal. The same argument is used to show that the best decision procedure for Individual Consequentialism does not always seek to maximize value. This motivates a move to Indirect Consequentialism, not the move to Collective Consequentialism.

If Rule Consequentialism and Individual Consequentialism both select the same decision procedure, then the two theories will be coextensive in practice. In particular, if they nominate identical decision procedures, then they will make identical demands. To escape the Demandingness Objection, Rule Consequentialism must differentiate its decision procedure from that of Individual Consequentialism.

Hooker argues that Simple Consequentialism and Rule Consequentialism 'by and large agree about how people should do their day to day moral thinking', as both theories recommend that agents apply rules of thumb rather than seeking to calculate the consequences of actions.[18] Even if both theories advocate the use of rules of thumb, it would be odd if they came up with exactly the same set. If they did, then the move from individual to collective assessment of rules would make no practical difference, and Rule Consequentialism could not be any less demanding than Simple Consequentialism. The two theories sometimes appear to recommend the same rules of thumb. However, this is because they both specify their rules very generally, and thus greatly over-estimate their resemblance to Common-Sense Morality (see Section 3.4).

---

[17] Ibid. 27.   [18] Hooker, *Ideal Code, Real World*, p. 144.

In Section 2.4, I argued that Simple Consequentialism recommends an unreasonably demanding decision procedure. The best way for me to live my life, in terms of promoting impersonal value, would involve a great deal of personal sacrifice. Will Rule Consequentialism recommend a less demanding decision procedure? We return to the precise demands of Rule Consequentialism below. At this stage, we are concerned only to establish that they differ from those of Simple Consequentialism.

Hooker's attempt to differentiate Rule Consequentialism centres on the costs of internalizing the Simple Consequentialist decision procedure. He notes that 'the costs of getting such a demanding rule internalized would be extremely high'. Many of these costs will be transitional costs, as we move from a society where partiality is the norm to one governed by Simple Consequentialism. However, 'one of the [main] internalization costs may be not just a recurring transition cost but an ever-present one. . . . [namely] the suppression of strong affections and partiality'. Hooker 'follow[s] Sidgwick in assuming that the combination of *strong* concern for some and *equal* concern for all is psychologically impossible (for human beings, short of genetic engineering)'. In a world where everyone accepted the Simple Consequentialist decision procedure, no one would feel strong concern for anyone else.[19]

Similar concerns motivate Individual Consequentialists to reject Simple Consequentialism as a decision procedure. However, the costs are greater under Rule Consequentialism. For the Individual Consequentialist, the cost is merely the loss of my capacity for partiality or agency. For the Rule Consequentialist, it is the loss of *everyone's* capacity for partiality and agency. The latter cost is higher for two reasons. The first is simply that the loss is borne by everyone rather than by a single agent. A second reason is that a lone alienated person living in a conventional human society would benefit from economic and social structures produced by the partiality of others. Such parasitic benefit is clearly not available in a world of universal alienation. The cost per person of alienation will thus be higher in the world where Simple Consequentialism is internalized by all.[20]

On the other hand, the benefit per person of internalizing an extremely demanding rule is likely to be less under Rule Consequentialism. Under Individual Consequentialism, the alienating rule enables me to do a great deal of good, as there is a vast amount of need to be met. By contrast, in a world where even a modestly demanding rule is internalized by all, there will be far less unmet need. The amount of good each individual can do is thus much less.

[19] Hooker, 'Rule-Consequentialism and Obligations toward the Needy', p. 24.
[20] See also Cottingham's discussion of the parasitism of impartialism, in his 'Partiality, Favouritism and Morality', p. 366.

Compared with less demanding alternatives, the decision procedure of Simple Consequentialism thus produces greater cost per person and less benefit per person when internalized universally than when internalized by a single agent. Rule Consequentialism will choose a different decision procedure from Simple Consequentialism, the main difference being that the former is less demanding.

It thus appears that Rule Consequentialism can avoid the Collapse Objection. Unfortunately, its method of doing so brings us to the last of our trio of old objections to Rule Consequentialism: the Incoherence Objection. This objection is usually put forward by Individual Consequentialists, once Rule Consequentialists have attempted to differentiate the two theories. Individual Consequentialists argue that Rule Consequentialism is incoherent, as it begins with the standard Consequentialist commitment to maximize the good, and ends up telling us to follow certain rules, even where this will obviously not produce the best possible consequences. 'What sort of Consequentialists are you?' Individual Consequentialists say to Rule Consequentialists, accusing them of irrational 'rule worship'. Instead of using their rules as strategies, decision procedures, or rules of thumb, they turn them into criteria of rightness, abandoning the underlying Consequentialist goal of maximizing the good.[21] In Section 3.7, I present a new objection to Rule Consequentialism, designed to strengthen the Incoherence Objection.

The Incoherence Objection has been very influential. As a result of it, many contemporary Rule Consequentialists have abandoned the claim that Rule Consequentialism is derived primarily from an over-arching commitment to maximize the good. Obviously, if Rule Consequentialism is not derived from the basic Consequentialist principle, then it does not matter whether it conflicts with it. Rule Consequentialists then seek alternative defences of their theory, along the lines discussed in Section 3.1. In particular, Rule Consequentialism is now often defended primarily by reference to the intuitive appeal of its particular judgements and of the general moral rules it recommends.

3.3. Contemporary Rule Consequentialism

Having distinguished Rule Consequentialism from individual forms of Consequentialism, let us now examine its demands. Even if these are less than the demands of Simple Consequentialism, it remains to be seen whether they are reasonable.

---

[21] Lyons, *The Forms and Limits of Utilitarianism*, p. 144; and Hooker, 'Rule-Consequentialism, Incoherence, Fairness', p. 28.

We will focus on Brad Hooker's most recent formulation.

Hooker's Rule Consequentialism.   An act is wrong if and only if it is forbidden by the code of rules whose internalization by an overwhelming majority in each new generation has maximum expected value.

Expected value is calculated in terms of well-being, with some priority for the worst off. All costs of getting the code internalized are included. If two or more codes tie for first place in terms of expected value, we should follow the one closest to conventional morality.[22] The key feature of this account is the shift from compliance to acceptance, or 'internalization'. Several aspects of Hooker's use of this notion are worth noting.

1. We are interested, not in what would happen if a set of rules were internalized by everyone, but rather in the results of internalization by an *overwhelming majority*. Hooker explains and justifies this move as follows:

we should not imagine that the code's internalization extends to young children, to the mentally impaired, and even to every 'normal' adult. A moral code should be suited to the real world, where there is likely to be, at best, only partial social acceptance of, and compliance with, any moral code. An adequate ethic must provide for situations created by people who are malevolent, dishonest, unfair, or simply misguided. . . . a moral code needs provisions for dealing with non-compliance.[23]

While admitting that it is difficult to specify precisely what an overwhelming majority is, Hooker stipulates internalization by 90 per cent of the population.[24]

2. When assessing the costs and benefits of internalizing a code of rules, we are to imagine that 'moral rules are inculcated pretty much as they are now— that is, by family, teachers, and the broader culture'.[25] We are not to imagine any centrally coordinated mass indoctrination.

3. The costs of inculcation are those associated with teaching a code to a *new* generation, and maintaining their allegiance to that code. We do not ask what would happen if we tried to teach the new code to a generation of adults who had already internalized a different moral code. We put such transition costs to one side.

Two other broad features of Hooker's Rule Consequentialism will be significant later on. The first is the focus on expected value, rather than the actual consequences of internalizing a code. One motivation for this move is to preserve the close tie between wrongness and blameworthiness. Another motivation is to avoid some recent objections to Rule Consequentialism. In Section 3.4.2, we ask whether this move succeeds.

---

[22] Hooker, *Ideal Code, Real World*, p. 32.   [23] Ibid. 80.   [24] Ibid. 84.   [25] Ibid. 79.

The final feature of Hooker's theory is the adoption of what he dubs 'wary rule consequentialism'—the use of closeness to conventional morality as a tie-breaker.[26] This move obviously increases the probability that the recommendations of Rule Consequentialism will be in tune with conventional morality. We address the plausibility of this limited conventionalism in Section 3.4.2.[27]

3.4. The Demands of Rule Consequentialism

In defence of Rule Consequentialism, Brad Hooker has recently argued that, in a society where everyone follows the optimal code of rules, poverty would be eliminated by every affluent person in the developed world giving 10 per cent of their income to charity.[28] Let us grant, for the sake of argument, that a rule requiring donations of 10 per cent would not be unduly demanding. The crucial question remains: is this what Rule Consequentialism will demand?

When discussing the demands of Rule Consequentialism, we need to separate several questions. (1) What will Rule Consequentialism demand under full compliance (or, in Hooker's version, under near universal internalization)? What sacrifices do people make in the ideal society? (2) What is the rule those people accept? What is the ideal rule regarding famine? (3) What would that rule require under partial compliance? In particular, if the optimal rule differs significantly from the general practice in our own society, what would the rule require of us? How would someone who had internalized that rule respond to Affluent's choice? (4) What will the rule require in various hypothetical situations?

These questions are all interrelated. I begin with the first set, trying to tease out what life would be like in the Rule Consequentialist ideal society

---

[26] Ibid. 114–17.

[27] What do we do when two codes are equally close to conventional morality? Hooker dismisses this possibility as remote (ibid. 115). This may be unduly optimistic. Imagine a case where a deficiency (in Consequentialist terms) in conventional morality can be removed by altering either of two moral rules. Consider the two moral codes resulting from each of these alterations. We can imagine that both codes are superior to conventional morality, without either being superior to the other. Alternatively, if we admit the possibility of widespread incommensurabilities, then we may often be faced with a situation where neither of two codes is closer to conventional morality. This may become significant, as we shall see in Chapter 8 below that Rule Consequentialism is most plausible in situations where incommensurability occurs. (For an introduction to incommensurability, see Raz, *The Morality of Freedom*, 321–66. See also below, Sections 7.5 and 7.6.)

[28] Hooker, 'Rule-Consequentialism', p. 72. Hooker has since abandoned this formulation. However, he seems to retain the assumption that Rule Consequentialism demands approximately 10% from the affluent.

(Sections 3.4.1 and 3.4.2). I then move on to Hooker's attempts to characterize the optimal rule regarding famine (Sections 3.4.3–3.4.6). Sections 3.5 and
3.6 discuss some hypothetical situations.

3.4.1. Famine Relief under Full Compliance

The ideal society is very different from the actual world. This increases the possibility that the ideal code will be quite demanding, even when it is almost universally internalized. It also increases the difficulty of applying the ideal code to
the real world, and reduces the likelihood that the result is intuitively plausible.

Recall the situation of Affluent, sitting at her desk with her cheque book.
Affluent knows that others will not act optimally. However, under Rule
Consequentialism, the degree of sacrifice required of her is whatever would be
optimal under full compliance. The demands morality places on Affluent will
thus depend upon the following question: what would be the optimal response
to famine from the developed world as a whole, if everyone did their bit?

Unfortunately, this is a terribly difficult question, which cannot be answered
without a credible and comprehensive account of the causes of famine and
poverty. There are three traditional analyses: Developmentalist or Supply-Side
(famine is caused by a sudden decline in the food supply); Neo-Malthusian or
Demand-Side (overpopulation causes famine); and Microeconomic (famine is
caused by the collapse of direct or exchange-entitlement economic relationships in the local situation). Our interest is in the philosophical significance of
this economic debate, rather than in the details of its resolution.

Jean Dreze and Amartya Sen argue for the third analysis of the causes of
famine.[29] They argue that the severity of famine depends largely upon local
conditions and institutions, especially political institutions and public relief
programmes. It is less dependent on the availability of food or on population
size. In their analysis, the behaviour of developing countries where famine is
a real possibility is in many ways far more important than the behaviour of
the developed world.

George Lucas has argued that, if we accept this Microeconomic analysis,
our response to famine should be as follows:

1. local governments should provide 'an elaborate economic safety net';
2. developed countries should provide monetary assistance to those local
   governments;
3. developed countries should establish safety nets in the affected countries.[30]

---

[29] Dreze and Sen, *Hunger and Public Action*. See also Sen, 'Population: Delusion and Reality', and
Dasgupta, *Well-Being and Destitution*.

[30] Lucas, 'African Famine'.

How much individual sacrifice would this involve? At first glance, it looks as if dispositions such as 'vote for governments that will institute fair and effective aid programmes' and 'pay your taxes' will be sufficient. Yet such dispositions require hardly any sacrifice at all. So Rule Consequentialism might not be demanding enough.

The lesson here is that Rule Consequentialism's approach to famine relief cannot be considered in isolation from the whole optimal code of rules. Even in a world without famine, there will still be some unmet needs to attend to. So the theory's demands are not too limited. Once we broaden our scope in this way, however, we open the possibility that the optimal code will be very demanding.

3.4.2. Optimal Redistribution

In his original discussion, Hooker considers only the amount of money required to lift everyone in the world above the poverty line. He implicitly assumes that further redistribution would not yield further improvements in welfare. This seems unwarranted. Assume, for the sake of argument, that 10 per cent of the wealth of the developed world would be just enough to raise everyone in the world above the poverty line. This redistribution would leave millions of people in almost poverty, while a few remain almost affluent. A further redistribution bringing the almost poor further above the poverty line, while still leaving them worse off than the more affluent, would increase aggregate welfare.

In response to this argument, Hooker argues that, in fact, 10 per cent of the income of the developed world is enough to do far more than merely alleviate extreme poverty.[31] This response is not sufficient. However much good it does, a transfer of 10 per cent would still leave a very unequal distribution of resources. Hooker needs to show that further redistribution is unnecessary.

If we assume that there are enough resources in the world to provide at least an adequate life for everyone, and we also assume that, other things being equal, any given sum of money provides a greater amount of welfare for a poorer person than for a wealthier one, then we might conclude that, in the ideal society, the developed nations would aim for perfect redistribution of the world's resources. It is difficult to estimate the overall effect of perfect redistribution. However, it would clearly require a much greater sacrifice from well-off people in affluent societies than Hooker's token 10 per cent.

---

[31] A version of this argument is presented in R. Carson, 'A Note on Hooker's Rule-Consequentialism'. For Hooker's reply, see Hooker, 'Rule-Consequentialism and Demandingness'.

The most common objection to this line of argument is that perfect redistribution would be extremely inefficient. This is an analogue of the familiar argument that extensive tax-benefit programmes reduce people's incentive to work, as the comparative benefits of working are greatly reduced. Perfect redistribution is an extreme form of tax-benefit programme, where everyone receives exactly the same standard of living, irrespective of how hard (or even whether) they work. It is argued that, in such a system, entrepreneurs, producers, and workers would not take the risks or make the sacrifices necessary for economic production. The amount of wealth available to be distributed would fall so far that perfect redistribution reduces aggregate welfare.[32]

There is certainly something to this objection. Perfect redistribution is unrealistic. However, it is important to tease out the precise nature of this unrealism. Rule Consequentialism determines what is right by asking what would be the case in the hypothetical situation of full compliance (or, more accurately, full acceptance). Any such theory is built around unrealistic situations. The ideal society is not the actual world. The fact that a particular scenario is 'unrealistic' does not necessarily rule it out as a potential ideal world. The crucial question is whether or not it is unrealistic in the wrong way.

The usual presentation of the 'taxes-reduce-incentives' argument presents perfect redistribution as 'economically impossible'. The relationships between effective marginal tax rates, overall tax burden, and productivity are said to be governed by 'economic laws', much as the relationships between mass, acceleration, and force are governed by physical laws. In morality, we do not usually decide what to do on the basis of what we might have been able to do if the laws of physics had been radically different. Similarly, we should not decide what to do by considering radical alterations to the laws of economics.

The analogy between economic laws and physical laws is not sound. Economic laws come in two types: those dealing with physical relationships, such as laws of increasing returns to scale or diminishing marginal productivity of capital, and those dealing with human behaviour, such as laws describing people's response to certain incentive structures. The former laws should not be varied in moral deliberation, any more than the laws of physics, except in so far as appropriate research might alter even the physical laws of production. However, not all psychological 'laws' concerning human behaviour should necessarily be held constant within a counterfactual moral theory such as Rule Consequentialism. Such a theory is primarily concerned with human behaviour. If we are not allowed to vary any generalization regarding such behaviour, then the inhabitants of the ideal society will be

---

[32] Hooker, *Ideal Code, Real World*, pp. 55–6, 64–5.

carbon copies of ourselves. Our theory will not offer any suggestions for improvement. It will never be able to say that we have done the wrong thing. This seems unreasonably restrictive.

Economic laws regarding the disincentive effects of perfect redistribution are, at least partially, psychological. It is thus reasonable to ask whether or not these laws should remain fixed in our search for the ideal society. The following fantasy may prove instructive in discussing this question.[33]

The Centralized Charity. Shareland is a world with resources, population, and technology approximately equal to our own. The economy of Shareland is capitalist: resources are allocated by market forces rather than by centralized planning. Firms and means of production are privately owned and operated. Initially, everyone receives only his market income. At the end of each month, each inhabitant of Shareland fills out a form saying how much market income he received that month. Everyone fills out his form honestly and accurately. These forms are then sent to a central organization, which calculates the average market income over all inhabitants. This average is then published. People who received more than the average pay their 'extra' income into a central account, which is then used to top up the incomes of those with below average incomes. There is no negative effect on production, as the system is entirely voluntary and Sharelanders are motivated by a desire to equalize resources.

This story is certainly unrealistic. But it is not unrealistic in the way that, for instance, a story about edible rocks would be unrealistic. The Centralized Charity makes no unrealistic assumptions regarding the physical limits of various factors of production, or the efficiency of technological processes. Its unrealism is purely psychological: the Shareland system would not work, not because it could not work, but because people would not let it work. People would fill out false returns, claim more than their 'fair' (in Shareland terms) share, misuse the centralized store of information required to set up the system, and so on. (Of course, in a society where it was established, the Shareland system would not be so easy to subvert. If everyone had exactly the same wealth, it would be very difficult to utilize any ill-gotten gains. Any conspicuous wealth would be suspicious. The main problem with the Shareland system is that it could not get off the ground in the first place.)

The Shareland system is unrealistic primarily because people would not behave in the totally selfless and scrupulously honest manner it requires.

---

[33] A similar tale is discussed in Carens, *Equality, Moral Incentives, and the Market.* See also the discussion of related issues in G. Cohen, 'Incentives, Inequality and Community'.

However, one of the central questions for Rule Consequentialists is how selfless we can reasonably expect people to be. Obviously, if we rule out any possible world where people are more selfless than they would ordinarily be, we will inevitably conclude that we cannot reasonably expect people to be any less selfless than they are. This may be the right answer, but surely we should not arrive at it quite so easily. We must allow for the possibility that people in the ideal society are more selfless than we would be in similar circumstances.

We cannot ignore Shareland simply because its inhabitants are more selfless than we would ever be. However, we might rule it out using a stronger claim. For instance, we might suggest, not just that we would not be as selfless as the Sharelanders, but also that we could not. We might even go so far as to claim that no human beings could ever be completely unselfish, irrespective of how they were brought up. Alternatively, we might claim that people could never be free of 'self-referential attitudes'. These might be directed either towards oneself or towards one's nearest and dearest, one's projects, one's commitments, and so on. Even if it is possible to imagine a completely unselfish life, it may well be impossible to imagine a life with no attitudes of this kind, as this suggests an agent with no perspective of her own.[34] The Sharelanders are not ideal people, because they are not people at all. A less extreme claim would be that, although people could be made as selfless as Sharelanders, the costs of doing so (in psychological or other terms) would outweigh the benefits. While the Centralized Charity is possible, it is not the option with maximum utility.

This line of argument is more promising. If a certain way of life is really impossible for human beings, or if the costs of getting people to lead that life are prohibitive, then we may reject it as a standpoint for assessing our moral behaviour. Unfortunately, it is obviously very difficult to say exactly which logically possible societies are humanly possible. We need a precise account of the boundaries of human nature, which we do not have.

Even if we reject the original version of our story as unrealistic, we can still use the Centralized Charity as a conceptual tool. We can progressively water it down until we reach a plausible story: the redistribution need not be total, safeguards might prevent false returns and abuse of information, and so on. Eventually, we would end up with something akin to the tax-benefit systems currently operating in modern welfare states. The fact that these systems exist suggests that they are humanly possible. We can conclude that, at some point, the Centralized Charity becomes a plausible story.

---

[34] I owe this suggestion to Derek Parfit.

Of course, we may not be able to specify exactly how much redistribution is involved in the most redistributive plausible version of the Centralized Charity. Also, unlike the original system, the redistributive mechanisms in watered-down stories may involve inefficiencies: if people are no longer perfectly selfless, redistribution may affect their incentives. So we can no longer assume that the best plausible version of the Centralized Charity has the greatest degree of redistribution.

In theory, we could rank all possible versions of the Centralized Charity along two scales: degree of redistribution and degree of inefficiency. Using these two measures, we could generate a single measure of aggregate welfare. In the plausible versions of our story, an increase in redistribution will tend to be accompanied by an increase in inefficiency. The net effect on aggregate welfare of a given change in redistribution cannot be determined a priori.

Hooker's claim, in effect, is that, among the plausible versions of the Centralized Charity, aggregate welfare is maximized when redistribution removes only 10 per cent of the income of well-off people in affluent societies. This claim, as we have seen, will be very difficult to assess. Of course, no moral theory could be expected to give perfectly precise answers in our complex world. However, we do expect a reasonable amount of guidance. The foregoing discussion suggests that Rule Consequentialism raises such complex issues that it is unlikely to provide enough precision to be helpful. Furthermore, Hooker's figure does, on the face of it, seem rather low. After all, 10 per cent is a far lower figure than the rate of taxation in many developed nations, where redistribution does not seem to have crippling disincentive effects. Hooker may reply, of course, that his 10 per cent is on top of current taxation, but even then the total disincentive effect need not be crippling. In practice, there is no good reason to believe that Rule Consequentialism will not be unreasonably demanding.

Indeed, several factors suggest that, even under full compliance, the optimal code will be more demanding than Hooker's discussion suggests.

1. In the ideal society, cooperation is likely to be far more widespread than in the actual world. It is hard to deny either that more cooperation would produce good results, or that people could be somewhat more cooperative. As a result, people may well see their interests as interdependent to a far greater degree than we do. Other things being equal, the consequences are better overall if, in seeking to further my own interests, I also further yours. Those who had internalized the ideal rules might not see the abandonment of cherished self-directed projects as a great cost, especially if they were replaced by other-directed projects. The negative effects of redistribution would thus be less in the ideal society. (See also Sections 1.4.2 and 7.9.)

2. Relatedly, it is difficult, if not impossible, fully to separate judgements about the right from judgements about the good. The optimal code tells us how we ought to balance our own good against the goods of others. Those who have grown up internalizing the ideal code may have a conception of the good markedly different from ours. In particular, they may attach less value to self-directed goods and more value to collective (or interdependent) goods. Some demands we regard as unreasonable may strike them as perfectly reasonable.

Human societies have differed enormously in their views on the relationship between individuals and communities, the balance between individual and collective goods, the relationship between metaphysics and morality, and so on. These differences render different moral theories more or less plausible. In particular, many contemporary Consequentialist philosophers have argued that changing our views about personal identity, the relationship between thought and community, and the nature of collective goods, will lead us to adopt a much more impartial morality.

Derek Parfit argues that adopting a Reductionist account of personal identity leads to Consequentialist moral theory, and undermines the moral legitimacy of self-interest.[35] David Brink argues that, as self-concern cannot be clearly separated from our relations with others, Consequentialism's other-regardingness need not demand extreme self-sacrifice.[36] Philip Pettit argues that a holistic account of social psychology supports a Republican interpretation of liberalism as against the more traditional libertarian alternatives.[37] In Chapter 9, I adapt Pettit's argument to enlist holism in support of my own favoured form of Consequentialism. Such arguments do not establish decisive links between metaphysical doctrine and moral theory. At most they alter the balance of reasons. Yet moral theory largely is the balancing of reasons and reasoned intuitions. We cannot reliably predict the moral beliefs and dispositions of any group of people without some knowledge of their metaphysical beliefs. These are not idle philosophical debates. Comparisons with the Indian tradition raise the possibility that the metaphysical theories favoured by contemporary Consequentialists could be inculcated within a wider population.[38] Similarly, different industrialized nations, with different political and social traditions, seem to sustain very different levels of redistribution.

The cost of inculcating a given principle of aid may thus depend on background metaphysical beliefs. In the absence of a good account of the limits of the plasticity of human nature, we cannot accurately identify the constraints

[35] Parfit, *Reasons and Persons*, ch. 15.   [36] Brink, 'Self-Love and Altruism', pp. 124–52.
[37] Pettit, *The Common Mind*, pp. 302–22.
[38] See e.g. Perrett, 'Egoism, Altruism, and Intentionalism in Buddhist Ethics', and Perrett, 'Personal Identity, Minimalism and Madhyamaka'.

on inculcation. Yet we have no accurate account of those limits.[39] Therefore, we have no clear idea how difficult (or, conversely, how easy) it would actually be to bring up people much more impartial then ourselves.

3. One of the main motivations for the shift from compliance to acceptance is to render Rule Consequentialism less demanding. Unfortunately, it may have precisely the opposite effect. The ideal society is usually discussed as if it were free from moral tension, conflict, or guilt. However, the literature on the problem of demandingness suggests that the tension between self-interest and other regarding obligation is an irreducible feature of moral life. Perhaps even those who have internalized the optimal moral code will feel some unease about the amount of their own resources they devote to themselves. They may aspire to a moral code they do not live up to.

There is no obvious reason to assume in advance that people in the ideal society generally regard their own behaviour as morally correct. The optimal moral code may thus be more demanding than the code that those who accept it comply with. By accepting a more demanding theory and striving towards it, people may make their world a better place than if they rested on their laurels.

Hooker rejects this idea. He argues that Rule Consequentialism should not select rules by looking at a world where they are hardly ever followed. Let us introduce a distinction between two types of moral rules: *Aspirational Rules* presenting ideals for people to strive towards, and *Absolute Rules* laying down absolute prohibitions. Hooker argues that rules are not primarily aspirational. This may well be true for moral prohibitions. The optimal effect of rules such as 'do not murder', 'keep promises' and so on will presumably result from their being (more or less) universally complied with. For the so-called imperfect duties matters are less clear. Aspirational rules might be more effective than rules everyone follows. People will fall short of the ideal to varying degrees. If the acknowledged moral requirements were set at a level most people actually met, then the psychological push towards supererogative behaviour might be less than the corresponding push towards an ideal regarded as (in some sense) obligatory. The result will be less charity, and hence less good done overall. Consider the contrast between a society where the accumulation of wealth is regarded as somehow morally suspect, and one where it is regarded as morally neutral. The former might be a place of stagnation and underproduction, but it need not be. For instance, in Renaissance Italy official antipathy to usury coincided with the rise of rich banking houses. To salve their consciences, bankers often made significant contributions to public and charitable works.[40] Of course there are costs in

---

[39] For an introduction to the complexities involved here, see Daniels, 'Moral Theory and Plasticity of Persons'.

[40] Hibbert, *The Rise and Fall of the House of Medici*, esp. ch. 1.

terms of guilt and the risk of widespread hypocrisy regarding 'accepted' moral norms. However, there is no a priori reason to believe that these costs would not be outweighed by the benefits of additional charity.

If these speculations are accurate, then a society might internalize a moral code with some purely aspirational aspects. It is not clear what Rule Consequentialism will say in such a case. Of course, the foregoing speculations are very speculative. Yet if Rule Consequentialism cannot rule them out, then it will be very difficult to discover what it demands.

At this point, Hooker might be tempted to appeal to his tie-breaker rule. If two or more sets of rules are equal in terms of the expected value of the consequences of their universal acceptance, then Rule Consequentialism will select the one 'closest to conventional morality'.[41] Once this clause is in place, it may seem that indeterminacy is a good thing for Rule Consequentialism, as it increases the likelihood of intuitively appealing results. If complexity prevents our having any reasonable expectations at all, then Rule Consequentialism coincides with Common-Sense Morality.

I would reply that Rule Consequentialism contains too much indeterminacy. There are a vast array of (very different) codes the consequences of whose universal acceptance cannot be accurately compared. If we use any tie-breaker to choose between these codes, then the tie-breaker does virtually all of the real work in our moral theory. Rule Consequentialism would thus have collapsed into conventional morality. This might be acceptable to some defenders of Rule Consequentialism. They might argue that Rule Consequentialism also provides a justification for conventional morality: we would be justified in departing from convention only if we could reasonably expect that the code we were shifting to would produce better consequences if it were universally accepted. Unfortunately, we can never reasonably have such expectations, as the world is too complex. Therefore, we are never justified in departing from conventional morality.

However, this response renders Rule Consequentialism considerably less influential in determining our moral rules than most of its proponents seem to wish. It also raises two further questions. (1) Is the conventional moral code intuitively acceptable? (2) In particular, does that code itself make reasonable demands? Unless conventional morality is perfect, we need a moral theory to offer some practical guidance as to its reform. If Rule Consequentialism is completely indeterminate, then it cannot play this role.

---

[41] Hooker, 'Rule-Consequentialism and Obligations toward the Needy', p. 4.

3.4.3. Moving to the Real World

I conclude that we cannot share Hooker's confidence that Rule Consequentialism will make reasonable demands, even under full compliance. For the remainder of our discussion, however, let us grant that, under full compliance, the ideal code requires the affluent to sacrifice approximately 10 per cent of their income. Unfortunately, internalization of any such rule is not widespread in our world. We must ask what the ideal code requires under partial compliance.

For a taste of the complexities involved here, consider four possible rules producing identical patterns of behaviour under full compliance.

Rule A. Give 10 per cent of your income to the best available charity, irrespective of what other people do.

Rule B. Give 10 per cent of your income to the best available charity if most other people will do so; otherwise give nothing, as any contribution you made would not be sufficient to alleviate poverty.

Rule C. Give 10 per cent of your income to charity if enough others will do so; otherwise give more on the grounds that there is more suffering to alleviate. There are many possible variations of Rule C, depending on precisely how much more I should give if others fail to follow this rule.

Rule D. Give 10 per cent of your income to charity if enough others will do so; otherwise maximize utility.

Hooker's initial discussion suggests Rule A. Even in our world of almost total non-compliance, a follower of this rule will donate only 10 per cent of her income. The ideal rule is unlikely to be that rigid. As Hooker himself notes, 'Rule-consequentialism is implausible if it holds that how much I should contribute is completely insensitive to how much others are actually contributing.'[42] Once we admit the need for flexibility, the Rule Consequentialist is on a slippery slope leading to Rule D, and the Collapse Objection. We must stop between A and D. Presumably we want a moderate form of Rule C.[43]

[42] Hooker, *Ideal Code, Real World*, p. 164.

[43] Another solution to the problem of partial compliance is provided by Donald Regan's Cooperative Consequentialism (see Regan, *Utilitarianism and Cooperation*). Regan's view is fairly complicated, but it consists essentially of recommending the following decision procedure to moral agents.

Step 1: identify all potential cooperators.
Step 2: predict the likely responses of non-cooperators to various patterns of behaviour by potential cooperators. Treat those responses as given.
Step 3: play your role in the optimum cooperative strategy.

Under widespread non-compliance, Cooperative Consequentialism is not much less demanding than Simple Consequentialism. Consider the case of famine relief in the actual world. The amount

In his recent book, Hooker offers two formulations of the optimal rule regarding famine relief:

1. 'A rule requiring contributions of at least 1 per cent to 10 per cent of annual income from those who are relatively well off by world standards.'[44]
2. 'Over time agents should help those in greater need, especially the worst off, even if the personal sacrifices involved in helping them add up to a significant cost to the agents. The cost to the agents is to be assessed aggregately, not iteratively.'[45]

The reason for focusing on aggregative cost is that 'Small sacrifices, repeated indefinitely, can add up to a huge sacrifice'.[46] For instance, a rule requiring a one-off donation of 100 dollars is not demanding, whereas a rule requiring such a donation every day could be extremely demanding.

Hooker seems to regard these two formulations as equivalent, or at least compatible. I shall distinguish them, as they represent two different ways of formulating moral rules regarding famine. (1) is a *Mechanical Rule*, specifying a more or less precise level of required donation. (2) is a *Subtle Rule*, characterizing the requirements of beneficence in general terms. The two rules raise different theoretical issues, even though they recommend the same course of action. Our primary interest is in Rule Consequentialism in general, not just Hooker's particular version. Mechanical and subtle rules are two general ways to develop Rule Consequentialism. If we are adequately to assess the theory, we must look at both.

3.4.4. *Mechanical Rules*

Mechanical rules specify a precise level of required donation. Hooker himself has offered two different mechanical rules regarding aid:

1. 'a rule requiring contributions of at least 1 per cent to 10 per cent of annual income from those who are relatively well off by world standards';[47]
1a. a rule requiring affluent citizens of the developed world to contribute 10 per cent of their annual income.[48]

of good to be done is very great, whereas the number of people willing to cooperate is pretty small. Each person's share will be substantial, and Cooperative Consequentialism makes significant demands. If Rule Consequentialists seek a theory without great demands in the actual world, then they will not be satisfied with Regan's solution.

[44] Hooker, *Ideal Code, Real World*, p. 163.   [45] Ibid. 166.
[46] Ibid. 167. See also Cullity, 'Moral Character and the Iteration Problem'.
[47] Hooker, *Ideal Code, Real World*, p. 163.   [48] Hooker, 'Rule-Consequentialism', p. 72.

For simplicity, I shall read (1) as requiring the maximum contribution of 10 per cent from the affluent citizens of the developed world. The two rules thus coincide with respect to those people. The main remaining difference is that (1) requires some sacrifice from those who are well off by world standards but not affluent by the standards of developed countries, whereas (1a) does not. This group will include both some in developed countries who are comparatively poor, and many of those in poorer countries who are comparatively well off. As we shall see, this feature of Hooker's new rule plays a crucial role in his argument. In particular, he uses it to show why more demanding analogues of (1) would not be optimal. If he is correct, then more demanding versions of (1a) may be easier to inculcate than analogous versions of (1).

One might object that rules such as (1a) cannot be part of the optimal code, since they explicitly apply only to a minority, and thus cannot be internalized by an overwhelming majority. This objection is misconceived. The optimal code includes many rules telling agents how to act in specific circumstances: when to keep promises, how to react to immanent natural disasters, how to discharge public office, and so on. We can imagine everyone internalizing these rules, even if they never actively comply with them. Similarly, the optimal code may include instructions on how to deal with wealth, even if most agents never need to act on them.

For the moment, let us focus on the affluent citizens of the developed world. Under full compliance (or, more accurately, under near universal internalization), both mechanical rules require such people to donate 10 per cent of their income.

Mechanical rules are comparatively easy to evaluate. Their advantages are obvious: simplicity and comparative ease of application to the real world. Unfortunately, the disadvantages are prohibitive. Given the richness and complexity of moral life, it is extremely unlikely that the ideal code will consist of mechanical rules. Any plausible moral code will be based on general, subtle rules using vague moral predicates rather than precise empirical descriptions. If the ideal code does include mechanical rules, these are most likely to be rules of thumb, telling those in the ideal society which situations in their world fall under which subtle rules. Such mechanical rules will be highly adapted to the particularities of the ideal society. For instance, if the ideal code contains the mechanical rule 'donate 10 per cent of your income to charity', this will only be because that is the appropriate way to discharge a duty of beneficence characterized in more general terms. If our donations are to be guided by the underlying morality of those in the ideal society, we should ask what mechanical rules that general duty might generate for us, rather than slavishly following the mechanical rule it generates for them. Finally, even if we did wish to follow the mechanical rules of the ideal society, the very fact that these are tailored to the particular circumstances of that society will make it virtually impossible for us to calculate them with any precision.

3.4.5. Subtle Rules and the Poor

In *Ideal Code, Real World*, in response to various objections to Rule Consequentialism (including those in the previous section), Brad Hooker shifts from mechanical to subtle rules. Subtle rules offer generic descriptions, rather than precise specifications. For instance, a subtle rule might be 'Keep promises' rather than the more mechanical 'If you have uttered the words 'I promise to do x', then you should do x'.[49] Subtle rules seek to avoid the problems of mechanical rules. For instance, Rule Consequentialism will recommend different mechanical rules in different circumstances, leading to an unacceptable degree of variation in our obligations. Subtle rules appear to avoid this charge. The same subtle rule may apply to many different situations.

Can subtle rules really do the job required of them? Recall Hooker's own subtle rule:

2. 'Over time agents should help those in greater need, especially the worst off, even if the personal sacrifices involved in helping them add up to a significant cost to the agents. The cost to the agents is to be assessed aggregately, not iteratively.'[50]

Those who have internalized the optimal code will sometimes be confronted by great need. The ideal set of rules will include some rule such as (2). This rule raises two main questions. (1) Would Rule Consequentialism really recommend it? (2) Is it relatively undemanding in the actual world? We need to consider these two questions together. There are interpretations of Hooker's rule on which it is not unreasonably demanding. There are also interpretations under which it would be chosen by Rule Consequentialism. Unfortunately, no single interpretation meets both desiderata. The optimal form of the rule is unreasonably demanding in the actual world.

We must focus on the vague comparative terms used in the rule. In particular, how are we to interpret the phrase 'significant (aggregate) cost'? In his recent article 'Ross-Style Pluralism versus Rule-Consequentialism', Hooker

[49] The real subtle rule underlying the practice of promise keeping may be even more general, perhaps relating to the general moral significance of behaviour creating expectations in others. See Scanlon, *What We Owe to Each Other*, pp. 295–327.
[50] Hooker, *Ideal Code, Real World*, p. 166.

stresses the need for moral judgement in the application of Rule Consequentialist rules to particular cases.[51] To interpret Hooker's rule about aid, we must ask what judgements of relative cost would be made by someone who had internalized the ideal code. How would she interpret the phrase 'significant cost'? Unfortunately, we will find this question particularly difficult to answer.

We might begin with a perfectly impartial version of the subtle rule. Perhaps a cost to the agent is 'significant' if and only if it is greater than the amount of need the agent is able to meet. This rule is clearly very demanding. The cost to the agent will almost never be significant, owing to diminishing marginal returns. If both cost and need are assessed aggregatively, then this rule is the decision procedure of Individual Consequentialism. Hooker's first task is to convince us that the optimal code will not include this interpretation of his rule.

Recall our general discussion of redistribution in Section 3.4.2. Hooker relies on the cost of inculcating a very demanding rule in the whole population. He asks us to consider the costs of inculcating the rule in the poor as well as in the rich. He argues that a completely impartial rule would be very costly to inculcate in everyone.

We have three questions to address. (1) Should we follow Hooker in including the cost of inculcating rules in the poor? I shall argue that we should not. (2) When applying the optimal code, whose judgements should we use? In other words, how are we to apply the optimal code? I shall argue that we should focus on how the optimal code would be applied by those who had internalized it. This brings us to our final question. (3) How would those in the ideal society apply their code to our situation?

The cost of inculcating a rule in the poor seems unlikely to assist Rule Consequentialism. The very poor and the more affluent will make very different judgements concerning relative cost. To someone in great need, most of the material components of affluent life will seem trivial luxuries. A destitute person would not regard the sacrifice of such luxuries as a great cost. The very poor might well internalize an interpretation of Hooker's rule that would be very demanding for the affluent. For instance, a poor person might interpret 'significant aggregate cost' to mean 'cost that brings one down to the average level in affluent societies, but no further'. This would be very demanding for affluent people. If Hooker wishes the demands of his rule to be congruent with common sense, then presumably he wishes to rule out this interpretation. He cannot do so by appealing to the cost of inculcating the rule in the poor.

[51] Ibid. 88, and Hooker, 'Ross-Style Pluralism versus Rule-Consequentialism', pp. 543–6.

Hooker himself argues that the difficulty of inculcating a rule will be a function, not of the benefits the agent would derive from others following the rule, but rather of the cost to the agent of complying with it.[52] However, a progressive rule requiring large sacrifices from the wealthy might demand nothing from the poor. Accordingly, by Hooker's own reckoning, it should be comparatively easy to inculcate such a rule. Recall Hooker's two mechanical rules. Either of those could be offered as a gloss on Hooker's subtle rule. It is not obvious that interpretation (1) should be preferred to interpretation (1a). Yet the latter will obviously be easy to inculcate in the poor, as it requires nothing of them.

As Hooker notes, in another context, this is too swift. The ideal code of rules is likely to leave open the possibility that some who start out poor may later become affluent. Accordingly, it will not be possible to get the poor genuinely to internalize an extremely demanding version of rule (1a). They would not accept a rule requiring all wealthy people to become living heart donors. However, we might reasonably expect their reluctance to be less than that of the affluent, especially as those who are poor may have a clearer idea of the positive benefits of charity.

A further complication concerns the relationship between Rule Consequentialism and national boundaries. Consider a rule telling people in affluent countries how to respond to the plight of the distant starving. Do we count the costs of inculcating such rules in the poor *of those distant countries*? Rule Consequentialists divide on this question. Some say we seek rules for our own society only; others that national boundaries should themselves be objects of the Rule Consequentialist evaluation, rather than constraints upon it.[53] If we take the latter option, then our first problem will be exacerbated. The starving millions are unlikely to interpret 'significant aggregative cost' in anything like the way that we would. Much of what strikes us as significant cost might well strike them as trivial. On the other hand, if we restrict ourselves to our own society, then the question of what it would cost to inculcate a rule in all of the world's poor is obviously redundant. (As we shall see in Section 3.6, this would also undermine Hooker's favoured response to the Wrong Facts Objection.)

I conclude that we should focus on the cost of inculcating a code of rules in affluent people in developed societies—not because there are no costs associated with inculcation in the poor, but because those costs are not sufficient to rule out demanding rules.

---

[52] Hooker, *Ideal Code, Real World*, pp. 171–2.
[53] Hooker's own view is that Rule Consequentialists seek the rules it would be best for everyone throughout the world to accept (see Hooker, *Ideal Code, Real World*, pp. 173–4).

3.4.6. Subtle Rules and the Affluent

How much should Affluent give to Oxfam? In order to assess this particular case, we need both a set of rules and a judgement applying those rules to that case. Our set of rules is the Rule Consequentialist optimal code. Whose judgement should we use to apply that code? It may seem obvious that we can use only our own judgement. However, things are not so simple. Should we apply the rules in the optimal code as we ourselves would apply them? Or should we seek to apply those rules as they would be applied by someone who had been brought up in a society where they were commonly accepted? These two procedures may produce quite different results. Recall that Rule Consequentialism is designed to provide a criterion of rightness and not merely a decision procedure. As a criterion of rightness the theory might well refer to the judgements of those who had internalized the optimal rules, even if those judgements were inaccessible to us.

I shall now argue that Rule Consequentialism must refer to the judgements of those living in the world of the optimal code, as well as to their rules. One simple reason is that the distinction between rules and judgements is (at best) vague. Given any complete description of the beliefs, actions, and judgements of the inhabitants of any society, there will be many different ways to categorize their moral system in terms of abstract rules and particular judgements. Some of these categorizations will be more natural than others, but there may be no unique set of rules and judgements capturing their morality. If we keep rules and judgements together, then this indeterminacy does not matter very much. However, if we seek to separate the rules of a society from judgements applying those rules, and then replace the latter with our own judgements, then we must make an arbitrary choice.

The consequences of widespread acceptance of a set of rules depend crucially upon how they are applied. A given set of rules will be optimal only because it is applied in a certain way. It thus seems odd for a moral theory to select a set of rules because of the consequences of one method of application, and then instruct us to apply those rules in a completely different way. Such a theory would be very *ad hoc*.

I conclude that the Rule Consequentialist criterion of rightness should be as follows: an act is right if and only if it would be judged to follow from the optimal set of rules by someone who had internalized those rules and had grown up in a society where such internalization was the norm.

Therefore, we must ask how someone who had internalized Hooker's rule would interpret the phrase 'significant cost to themselves'. We saw earlier that the judgements of those in the ideal society will differ from our own. In particular, their interpretation of 'significant (aggregate) cost' is likely to be significantly more demanding.

Furthermore, if cooperation is more widespread in the ideal society, then opportunities for applying the subtle rule may be fewer than in the actual world, or of a different type. Therefore, the judgements of those in the ideal society may not shed much light on how we ought to act. As Hooker points out, there is a limit to the complexity of a moral code that can be inculcated in a population, and there are limits to the sensitivity of any individual agent's judgement.[54] The optimal code will be most sensitive to common situations, and provide much less detailed guidance for uncommon ones. Natural disasters will still occur, whereas disasters caused by widespread human moral failing will be less common. The optimal code will be more sensitive where suffering results from natural disaster than where it is caused by the moral failings of others. (See Section 3.5 for Rule Consequentialist attempts to avoid this conclusion.)

This is significant for two reasons. The first is that the optimal code will produce more demanding judgements than we might like. Our own common-sense judgements regarding obligations to aid others are more demanding regarding natural disaster than human-caused disasters. If the optimal code applies the subtle rule primarily in cases of natural disaster, then its general application of that rule may well be very demanding.

This assumes that the divergence between human-caused famine and natural disaster carries over to the ideal code. A Rule Consequentialist might reply that the real underlying moral distinction is between rare situations and everyday ones. Hooker argues, for instance, that the ideal code is more demanding with respect to the former than the latter. A rule requiring significant sacrifice in comparatively rare cases is easier to inculcate. Overall, however, it is not clear that human-caused catastrophes are more common than natural disasters. It is unlikely that I will ever be directly confronted with a natural disaster. However, I am regularly confronted with appeals from temporary aid agencies set up in the wake of natural disasters. Hooker's distinction between the rare and the everyday cannot assist us here. (In Part Four, I offer an alternative account of this divergence in common-sense intuitions.)

A more general problem is why we should be interested in the moral judgements of people whose sensitivities are ill equipped for our moral world. When we ask how someone who had internalized the optimal code (and who lived in a society in which this was the norm) would act in

<hr>

[54] Hooker, 'Rule-Consequentialism, Incoherence, Fairness', and Hooker, 'Rule-Consequentialism and Obligations toward the Needy', pp. 6–8.

Affluent's case, we are asking how she would act in a situation that people with her background and disposition would never encounter, and for which they would be totally unprepared. Even if we could answer this question, why should we want to? What guidance can the (hypothetical) response of an ideal agent to a situation completely alien to her experience provide for those of us for whom that situation is an everyday reality?

For instance, Utopians (as we might christen the inhabitants of the ideal society) might be particularly sensitive to the sufferings to others. They might also be disposed to feel extreme moral outrage when confronted by needless sufferings resulting from the moral failings of third parties. These sensitivities might be very useful in the Utopians' natural environment, where such sufferings are minimized. However, in our real-life situation, such dispositions might produce paralysing despair. While some degree of remorse or regret may well be appropriate when one is confronted with moral dilemmas, despair does not seem to be morally desirable.

This point is not confined to the case of famine relief. Many (if not most) of our difficult moral choices concern situations totally foreign to a Utopian, arising from the moral or organizational imperfections of individuals (sometimes ourselves) and institutions. The ideal subtle rules will offer no reliable guidance here.

Inhabitants of developed countries with underdeveloped welfare states are regularly confronted with people living in poverty. Giving aid to such people whenever one encountered them would crowd out all other personal projects. However, Utopians are unlikely to encounter beggars, so they may be disposed to help them as much as they can. In Utopia, such a disposition would save the small number of Utopian beggars, and would have no significant negative effects. Yet it would be very demanding in the actual world.

We can imagine the Utopian's predicament by extrapolating from a common experience in our own world. Consider the case of a tourist from a civilized country with a well-developed welfare system who visits a distant nation where homeless people beg on the streets. To capture the confusion of a Utopian, imagine this tourist has lead a sheltered life, and was not even aware that such places existed. If he applies his domestic morality to this alien situation, the result might be very demanding. He may feel on obligation to do everything he can to find each homeless person a home.

Our own Common-Sense Morality often does make quite demanding judgements about how others, especially the affluent, should behave in societies we regard as extremely unjust. For instance, many people feel that affluent whites living in South Africa in the 1980s were obliged to do what they could to change the political system of the country. Those who did nothing are often judged harshly. A Utopian might well make exactly the same judgements about contemporary nations in the developed world. To them, the fact that people in the USA are homeless might demonstrate that the USA was an unjust society whose citizens were obliged to take radical and demanding political action.

We might question whether it even makes sense to ask what a Utopian would do in my situation. How much of what is essential for the description of my situation is tied to my being the particular person I am, to my having my particular relationships? Could another person, specifically a Utopian, be in precisely that situation? A complete answer to these questions would take us well into the realms of complicated metaphysical questions of personal identity and the description of situations and events. Yet, without a more detailed specification, it is difficult to see how we can answer the central moral question: 'How should I behave in my situation?'[55]

In extreme cases, it may be impossible for a Utopian to be in my situation. For instance, I may have done something very wrong, perhaps because I acted in ignorance of the optimal code of rules. But no Utopian would have acted this way. No Utopian could find herself in my situation. If Rule Consequentialism says I should do what a Utopian would do in my situation, it lapses into incoherence.

Similarly, what if the action a Utopian would choose in my situation is not available to me? For instance, the Utopian's action might be something I cannot imagine, something psychologically impossible for me, or something I lack the skills, techniques, or knowledge to perform accurately. We could, of course, rule out this possibility by our definition of 'my situation'. Perhaps being in my situation requires the availability of only those options I can understand. However, this response threatens to undermine the whole Rule Consequentialist approach, as it may produce a theory in which what I should do is always whatever I will do anyway. This is particularly true if we rule out options I find psychologically difficult. This response also greatly increases the chance that it is impossible for a Utopian to be in my situation. If being in my situation means recognizing only the options I can recognize, and if a Utopian's moral perception is greater than my own, then, by definition, she cannot ever be in my situation.

Rule Consequentialism must accept the possibility that what a Utopian would do in my situation is not a genuine option for me. However, this raises the possibility of my being under an effectively impossible obligation. If x is what I should do, and x is not a genuine option for me, then I should do something I cannot do.

Rule Consequentialists may reply that Utopians are not perfect. They will occasionally do the wrong thing. Accepting the ideal code does not mean

---

[55] For a discussion of related difficulties, see Pettit and Smith, 'Brandt on Self-Control'.

always complying with it. Utopians thus need rules to deal with their own imperfections and wrongdoing. While it might avoid the present objection, this reply places us on the slippery slope outlined in the next section.

Subtle rules are harder to assess than mechanical rules. Our conclusions must be more tentative. At the very least, we cannot be confident that Rule Consequentialism is not very demanding in practice. It is anyone's guess what the optimal rule regarding famine relief would actually tell Affluent to do.

3.5. Against Brandtian Exception Clauses

Rule Consequentialism is implausible because the ideal world is so different from our own. Rule Consequentialists attempt to reduce this divergence, by adding some of the imperfections of our own world to the ideal world. In this section, I argue that this leads the theory to collapse back into a demanding version of Simple Consequentialism.

Recall Hooker's definition of Rule Consequentialism: 'An act is wrong if and only if it is forbidden by the code of rules whose internalization by the overwhelming majority of everyone everywhere in each new generation has maximum expected value. . . .'.[56] He then goes on to say that: 'We should not imagine that the code's internalization extends to young children, to the mentally impaired, and even to every 'normal' adult. . . . An adequate ethic must provide for situations created by people who are malevolent, dishonest, unfair, or simply misguided. . . . a moral code needs provisions for dealing with non-compliance.'[57]

The last clause is adapted from Richard Brandt.[58] As Hooker explains, 'we need rules for dealing with problems created by the non-compliance of adults.'[59] We exclude from the set of cooperative agents those whose behaviour causes the initial problem. For instance, if we wish to discover the optimal rules for dealing with theft, we take as given the fact that a small proportion of the population will be thieves (or, at least, potential thieves) and ask what would be the optimal response from the rest of us.

I shall now argue that Brandt's exception clause is unacceptable, as it causes Rule Consequentialism to collapse into Individual Consequentialism in cases where famine results from (near) universal failures to act. Consider five simple hypothetical cases.

---

[56] Hooker, *Ideal Code, Real World*, p. 32.   [57] Ibid. 80.
[58] Brandt, 'Some Merits of One Form of Rule-Utilitarianism', and Brandt, 'Fairness to Indirect Optimific Theories in Ethics'.
[59] Hooker, 'Rule-Consequentialism, Incoherence, Fairness', p. 20.

Famine Just Happens.   Through no fault of any person, some people face starvation or famine. For instance, a large and adequate store of grain may have been destroyed by an unpreventable or unforeseeable act of God.

The Brigands' Famine.   There is plenty of grain in the country, but the soldiers of one side in a civil war burn all the crops in the territory of the other side.

The Hoarders' Famine.   Famine arises because those who own the grain decide to hoard it. They refuse to give it to those who require it, or to sell it at an affordable price.

The Ignorers' Famine.   Famine results (in part) from the collective inaction of developed countries.

The Capitalist Famine.   In a regime of pure international capitalism, a famine results from the mysterious interactions of the global market.

In Famine Just Happens, we do not have to exclude anyone from the domain of collective acceptance, as no one's wrongdoing or action causes the problem. In the Brigands' Famine, we must exclude those responsible for destroying the grain. Their acceptance of desirable moral rules is inconsistent with the existence of the problem. In the Hoarders' Famine, the problem under discussion would not arise without the behaviour of the grain hoarders. Therefore, collective acceptance now includes everyone except grain hoarders. Note that the grain hoarders cause the famine through inaction. The grain is not destroyed. Indeed, nothing is done to it. It is just not delivered to those who need it. We are now excluding people from the domain of collective acceptance on the basis of what they do not do, as well as what they do.

Our penultimate tale, the Ignorers' Famine, is the situation faced by Affluent, and by ourselves. An appropriate response from developed countries would remove the famine. The behaviour of ordinary citizens in the developed West is necessary for the continued existence of the problem under discussion. Therefore, they must be excluded from the domain of collective acceptance.

In our final tale, the Capitalist Famine, it is hard to see how we can avoid excluding everyone in the world from the domain of collective acceptance, as we are all participants (to some degree) in the global capitalist system. It will be almost impossible to isolate some subset of market participants whose behaviour can be said to have caused the famine in question. Rule Consequentialism asks us to seek out a tribe untouched by global capitalism, and ask what their optimal response might be.

By now our Rule Consequentialism is hardly collective at all. To decide what I should do, I must look at all possible sets of rules and examine their collective acceptance by everybody except brigands, grain hoarders, citizens of the developed West, and participants in the global economy. Our universal acceptance is now a (near) universal rejection.[60]

Excluding virtually everyone in the developed West greatly reduces the appeal of Rule Consequentialism. In particular, it weakens Hooker's claim that his theory is less demanding than Individual Consequentialism. When deciding how much money I should give to Oxfam, I should ask how much would be sufficient if given by all those people in the West who already give significant amounts to charity. Clearly, my share of the burden of relieving famine is now far greater than in Hooker's original version.

Rule Consequentialists may seek to avoid this objection by drawing a distinction between action and inaction. However reasonable it may seem, this move is not really available to the Consequentialist. A major plank of the Consequentialist position has traditionally been the claim that there is no basic moral difference between doing and allowing. A version of Rule Consequentialism that survives only by smuggling such a distinction into a Brandtian exception clause would be unacceptably *ad hoc*. Building a distinction between doing and allowing into the foundations of Rule Consequentialism in this way is very different from the claim that the optimal rule set includes a distinction between doing and allowing. (This latter claim is explored in Sections 9.2.3 and 10.6.) This move would also be unable to deal with the Capitalist Famine, where it is very hard to draw a line between market participants who have contributed to the disaster by their actions and those who have contributed through inaction.

An over-exclusionary Brandtian exception clause would also require different sets of moral rules for almost every particular problem situation. Many current problems exist or persist only because of the inaction of some group of people. For instance, environmental problems are often exacerbated by the inaction or ignorance of the majority of people in the developed West. So those people would need to be excluded from the domain of collective acceptance. Similarly, if our problem were poverty in the USA, we might need to exclude from the domain of collective acceptance all those people (whether affluent or not) who are in the habit of voting for the current political parties, as the combination of their action in electing a Government

---

[60] If we exclude all those whose inaction is a necessary part of describing the problem situation, then we come very close to Regan's Cooperative Consequentialism (see Regan, *Utilitarianism and Cooperation*, and n. 43 above). Regan's procedure is almost identical to a Rule Consequentialism factoring out the behaviour of non-cooperators whose actions contribute to disaster. In practice, it also seems perilously close to Individual Consequentialism. A full discussion of Regan's theory is beyond the scope of this chapter. However, the possible collapse from Hooker's Rule Consequentialism through Regan's Cooperative Consequentialism to Individual Consequentialism highlights the precarious nature of the Rule Consequentialist search for an acceptable response to non-compliance.

unwilling to use public funds adequately to relieve poverty, combined with their collective inaction in not providing sufficient charitable donations, may be a significant cause of the existing poverty.

We thus face a dilemma. Either we exclude everyone from the domain of collective acceptance for the optimal code, or we treat different moral problems in isolation, in each case excluding only those whose behaviour causes the problem. Neither option seems very appealing.

Rule Consequentialists may reply using the distinction between following a rule and accepting a rule. Perhaps in the Ignorers' Famine, the majority of people accept a moral rule that, if everyone followed it, would alleviate the problem. They simply do not follow that rule. However, this move strains the notion of 'accepting' a moral rule. As I acknowledged above, we certainly should allow that people can accept a rule they do not quite live up to. But can a rule be accepted in a community where almost no one makes any serious attempt to follow it?[61] Also, this response would be incompatible with Hooker's overall strategy in two key ways. First, if a rule can be accepted without being followed at all, then we will have little reason to accept Hooker's claim that very demanding rules cannot be accepted. If acceptance requires little more than lip service, then such rules will be demanding to follow, but not to accept. Secondly, Hooker's theory gives great weight to the consequences of a rule's being accepted. If a rule can be accepted without anyone attempting to follow it, then it is not clear either what the consequences of acceptance will be, or why we should be particularly interested in them. The significance of the acceptance of a rule presumably lies in the existence of some close connection between rule acceptance and behaviour. Even aspirational rules are valued only when they have a significant effect on people's behaviour.

3.6. The Wrong Facts Objection

In this section, I demonstrate that Rule Consequentialism, in addition to probably giving unacceptable results in actual cases, definitely gives unacceptable results in a wide range of plausible hypothetical cases.

We saw earlier that it is very difficult to determine (even very roughly) what Rule Consequentialism requires of us in the actual world. Rule Consequentialism requires us to be experts in global political economy to an extraordinary degree to decide how much, or indeed whether, we should

---

[61] Hooker distances himself from this loose notion of 'acceptance'. Hooker, *Ideal Code, Real World*, p. 77.

donate to Oxfam. In situations where compliance with the best global response will be extremely partial, it is hard to see why such questions should be so relevant. Hooker makes the answer to the question 'What should we do here and now?' depend on the wrong empirical questions.

We can see this by discussing some variations on Affluent's Tale. In the first set of thought experiments, we vary the number of starving people. Consider three possible variations on Affluent's Tale, each exactly like the original except where stated.

Few Poor.   There are only 1 million people starving in an affluent world.

Medium Poor.   There are 50 million people starving or facing famine.

Many Poor.   Famine has broken out across Asia. There are 2,500 million people starving.

In all three cases, the eradication of famine lies far beyond Affluent's means. All she can do is make a very small dent on the overall problem.

Under Rule Consequentialism, the answer to the question 'How much should Affluent donate to Oxfam?' will be radically different in each of the three cases. Let us assume that, in Medium Poor, the optimal global response to poverty would be a donation equivalent to 10 per cent of the income of all inhabitants of the developed world. So Affluent should donate 10 per cent in Medium Poor. In Few Poor, the appropriate sacrifice will be one-fiftieth of 10 per cent of Affluent's income. If 10 per cent of the incomes of all the affluent people will save 50 million people from starvation, then roughly one-fiftieth of that amount will be required to save 1 million people from starvation. At the other extreme, if 10 per cent of the income of the affluent will save 50 million people from starvation, then saving 2,500 million people would require virtually all, if not all, of the income of those in developed countries. In Many Poor, Affluent would be required to denote virtually all of her income to Oxfam.

These extreme differences seem unreasonable. In Few Poor, it seems ridiculous for Affluent to donate only one-fifth of 1 per cent of her income, simply because there are *only* 1 million people starving, rather than 50 million. Similarly, it seems unreasonable to demand that the Many Poor Affluent give up all of her income simply because there are 2,500 million people starving rather than *only* 50 million. The difference between the situations does not seem sufficient to justify the vastly different sacrifices required of the three Affluents. To further illustrate this, we can unite the three cases in a single thought experiment.

Affluent's First Ignorance.   Affluent does not know how many people are starving. Indeed, she is so radically misinformed that all she knows is that she is in one of the three situations described (Few Poor, Medium Poor, or Many Poor). As she sits down at her desk, Affluent is able to resolve her ignorance, by ploughing laboriously through the fine print of the latest World Bank report.

Does Affluent really need to do this before deciding how much money to give to Oxfam? Rule Consequentialism says that she does. Until she has resolved her ignorance, Affluent does not know whether to donate 0.2 per cent, 10 per cent, or (nearly) all of her income. Yet this seems implausible. If a donation of 10 per cent is the appropriate sacrifice if there are 50 million people starving, then giving something like 10 per cent seems to be the right response, whether there are actually 50 million or only 1 million or as many as 2,500 million. Once we know that millions of people are starving, the exact number of millions does not seem to bear the weight accorded it by Rule Consequentialism.

My objection here is not merely that Rule Consequentialism makes Affluent's obligations dependent on specific empirical facts. After all, Individual Consequentialism requires similarly detailed information, as what an agent should do depends on the precise consequences of her actions. Indeed, any moral theory must link obligations to facts in some way. However, unlike Individual Consequentialism, Rule Consequentialism requires extensive knowledge of facts that have no effect on the consequences of our actions. Affluent knows that her most efficient aid-contribution method is to write a cheque to Oxfam. She also knows (roughly) how much good would be produced by any given level of donation. She also knows that, whatever she does, millions of people will be left in poverty by the inaction of others. Does she really need to know how many millions will be left in poverty before she can have any idea how much she ought to donate?

In our second thought experiment, we vary not the number of starving people, but rather the number of people in the developed world. This produces the following tale.

Affluent's Second Ignorance.   Affluent, as she sits at her desk, is drastically misinformed about the size of the developed world. She knows that the number of people in the developed world is very large, but she does not know exactly how large. She only knows that she is in one of the following three situations.

Few Rich.   The developed world is very small, containing only 1 million people.

Medium Rich.   The developed world includes 50 million people.

Many Rich.   Owing to rapid economic progress in China, the developed world contains 2,500 million people.

Under Rule Consequentialism, Affluent must resolve her ignorance before she has any idea at all how much she should give to Oxfam. Assume that in Medium Rich Affluent should donate 10 per cent of her income. If 10 per cent of the income of 50 million people is enough to remove poverty, then one-fifth of 1 per cent of the income of 2,500 million people should also be sufficient. Therefore, in Many Rich Affluent is required to donate only one-fifth of 1 per cent of her income. By contrast, if there are only 1 million people in the developed world, they will have to sacrifice all of their income and resources. In Few Rich the sacrifice required of Affluent is extreme.

This seems unreasonable. If 10 per cent is enough if there are 50 million people in the developed world, why should it not also be enough if there turn out to be only 1 million, and not too much even if there turn out to be 2,500 million people? Affluent knows there are millions of people in the developed world, and that the vast majority of them will not do what they should. Does she really need to know the precise number of millions who are not doing their share, before she has any idea how much she should sacrifice?

Rule Consequentialism falls into these mistakes because it presupposes a rigid relationship between the sacrifice required of any particular individual and certain features of their global situation. Crudely, the sacrifice Rule Consequentialism requires of an individual is equal to the total sacrifice required of all moral agents in that situation divided by the number of agents able to make the appropriate sacrifice.

In our third set of stories, we vary not the number of people facing starvation, nor the number of people in the developed world, but rather the nature of political economy: in particular, the nature of the laws governing famine. Consider the following tale.

Affluent's Third Ignorance.   Affluent is completely ignorant of political economy. She knows only that one of the following is an accurate description of the nature of her world.

Developmentland.   The Developmentalist account holds true. Famine is caused by a sudden decline in the food supply.

Malthusia.   The Neo-Malthusian view is correct. Overpopulation is the primary cause of famine.

Senland.   Sen's Microeconomic analysis is correct. Famine is caused largely by the collapse of direct or exchange-entitlement economic conditions.

As Lucas has argued, the appropriate global response to famine depends crucially on which of these three is the actual world. Sacrifices under full compliance vary greatly between the three worlds. Under Rule Consequentialism, Affluent must resolve her doubt before she acts. Before she knows how much to donate, Affluent must become an expert on global political economy.

This seems unreasonable. Affluent's behaviour has little chance of bringing about the optimal global response, whatever it may happen to be. Her questions should be only: 'Will giving money to Oxfam do good as things are? How much good will it do? Therefore, how much am I required to give, given other considerations?' The nature of the precise optimal global response does not seem to be one of those other considerations Affluent must address. If 10 per cent is about right on one economic account, why should it not be right on other accounts? The amount of good that particular donation will do is more or less the same in each case. I do not claim that these empirical differences should have no effect at all on Affluent's obligations. I claim only that they should not affect her obligations to the extreme extent that Rule Consequentialism implies.

The Wrong Facts Objection brings together three separate problems for Rule Consequentialism. The first is that the theory makes the wrong judgements about particular cases, both actual and hypothetical. The second is that the theory bases its judgements on the wrong facts, which explains why its particular judgements are mistaken.

There are two dimensions to this second component of the Wrong Facts Objection. The first is the epistemic claim that Affluent should not need to acquire such detailed empirical knowledge before she decides how much to give to charity. The second claim is that the morally acceptability of a given level of donation should not depend upon such complex empirical details. We might call these two claims the 'subjective' and 'objective' sides of the Wrong Facts Objection. In the foregoing discussion (and in previous papers), I have tended, for simplicity's sake, to run the two claims together. They are obviously mutually supporting. One explanation for the claim that Affluent does not need to plough through the World Bank report before acting is that the facts in question would not affect the objective rightness or wrongness of her actions. On the other hand, the very fact that the suggestion that Affluent should plough through the World Bank report strikes us as odd should lead us to see that those facts cannot be morally relevant. Despite their intimate connection, the subjective and objective claims are distinct, as someone who distinguished between objective and subjective rightness could make one without making the other. Such a person would accept only one side of the Wrong Facts Objection.

The third problem is that, in many cases, the facts on which Rule Consequentialism relies are not even epistemically available to the agent whose actions are being assessed, often because they are not epistemically available to any human agent. For instance, what Affluent ought to do depends upon details concerning the optimal global response to famine. Such facts lie beyond her ken.

Some moral philosophers will respond to this last objection by separating the objective and subjective dimensions, and then denying that the objective element is a problem. For instance, a Moral Realist might accept that the rightness of actions is determined by facts beyond our ken. Rule Consequentialism might be an impractical decision procedure, as it is hardly practical to instruct Affluent to seek such complicated information. However, it could still be the correct criterion of rightness.

This move is not available to those, like Hooker, who defend a Rule Consequentialist criterion of rightness on the basis of the intuitive appeal of its particular judgements. A theory defended in this way simply cannot render rightness epistemically inaccessible to human agents. If we are to compare the judgements of the theory to our own judgements, then we must be able to determine the former. Accordingly, Rule Consequentialists such as Hooker must soften the Wrong Facts Objection. Rule Consequentialism must direct us to facts we can hope to discover.

Another possible defence of Rule Consequentialism is to assess rules, not in terms of their actual consequences, but in terms of the consequences it would be reasonable to expect them to produce. (Indeed, the desire to avoid the Wrong Facts Objection is one motivation for this move, at least in Hooker's theory.) This move seems to make it true by definition that Rule Consequentialism depends upon accessible facts. After all, we can easily form reasonable expectations regarding matters we cannot fully discover.

This solution is inadequate. It does not seem reasonable to expect agents to acquire the detailed empirical information they would need in order reasonably to estimate and compare the expected value of competing patterns of global response. The reason for this is not that we believe, as a general rule, that agents are never obliged to discover relevant information that may affect their moral obligations. We often do think agents are so obliged. The reason we do not blame Affluent, or ourselves, for failing to acquire detailed counterfactual economic expertise is that we do not regard such expertise as relevant to the determination of her obligations.

The Wrong Facts Objection relates especially to mechanical rules, which usually proceed by calculating the amount of good to be done and then dividing the result by the number of potential do-gooders to generate the requirement on each individual. How does the objection affect subtle rules? Rule Consequentialists may claim that, owing to inculcation costs, the same subtle rule will be chosen in different situations. The variations the Wrong Facts Objection objects to will thus not arise for subtle rules.

A common Rule Consequentialist response to objections of this type is to impose various constraints on the complexity of the optimal code of rules, especially by appeal to the notion of 'teaching costs'.[62] Our choice of moral rules is limited to those we could teach to a human population at non-prohibitive social cost. A rule requiring Affluent to donate virtually all her income to charity could not be effectively taught. Therefore, Rule Consequentialism cannot demand so much. Its demands will not be subject to the wild fluctuations alleged in the Wrong Facts Objection.

I have discussed such Complexity Constraints at length elsewhere.[63] Whatever their fate overall, they cannot dissolve the Wrong Facts Objection. For one thing, it is by no means obvious that, in certain circumstances, a significantly demanding morality could not be taught. In particular, consider a case such as Many Poor. The benefits of inculcating a demanding morality among the developed world of Many Poor would be immense. If it were possible to do so, any social or psychological costs could well be outweighed by those benefits. Perhaps the resulting morality would not tell Affluent to donate all of her income. However, it probably would tell her to donate far more than 10 per cent. The donation required in Many Poor would thus be far greater than that required in Medium Poor. The discrepancy to which the Wrong Facts Objection objects would still remain.

Rule Consequentialists might appeal at this point to the costs of inculcating a very demanding morality in the poor people of Many Poor, who are much more numerous than the rich people of that world. Indeed, this is Hooker's response.[64] I do not believe that it can save Rule Consequentialism. In the first place, as we saw earlier, it is not clear that Rule Consequentialism even applies to the poor of Many Poor (see Section 3.4.5). It would be too costly to inculcate a rule as demanding as Individual Consequentialism among the poor of Many Poor. However, it does not follow that it would not be cost-effective to teach them a rule placing significant demands on the rich. For reasons suggested earlier, the best rule to teach everyone in Many Poor is considerably more demanding (especially for the rich) than Hooker predicts.

A final problem with this response is that it seeks to defeat the Wrong Facts Objection by showing that Rule Consequentialism is not too demanding. Yet the Wrong Facts Objection claims that, in some cases, Rule Consequentialism does not demand enough. The present reply leaves this half of the objection untouched. Take the case of Few Poor, where we objected that Affluent would have to donate only 0.2 per cent of her income. A rule requiring such donations could clearly be taught without prohibitive costs. The

---

[62] Hooker, 'Rule-Consequentialism, Incoherence, Fairness', pp. 24–7.
[63] Mulgan, 'Ruling out Rule Consequentialism'.
[64] Hooker, *Ideal Code, Real World*, pp. 85–8.

appeal to inculcation costs cannot rule out this side of the Wrong Facts Objection.

Rule Consequentialists might reply that the optimal set of rules will always include a certain basic level of benevolence, which can be inculcated at negligible cost. However, they would then face a dilemma. Either this basic level of benevolence translates to a donation of approximately 10 per cent in Affluent's original situation, or it does not. If it does not, then the disparity alleged by the Wrong Facts Objection remains. If it does, then Rule Consequentialists are asking us to believe that there is little significant difference between the demands of a principle of benevolence teachable at negligible cost, and those of a principle that is too demanding to be taught at all. This would be a very contentious claim.

In any event, even if this response enables Rule Consequentialism to get the right answer in a particular case, it will do so for the wrong reasons. The Wrong Facts Objection alleges that Rule Consequentialism takes too much account of morally irrelevant facts. The present reply is not that the theory does not take account of such facts, but merely that they do not greatly affect Affluent's obligations. This is not enough. The fact remains that, if a significant range of principles of benevolence were teachable, then Rule Consequentialism would place vastly different demands on Affluent in different situations. This is enough to show that the theory is misguided.

Hooker's most recent response to the Wrong Facts Objection is as follows:

the fact that how much rule-consequentialism demands of us can increase as the number of people starving increases does not necessarily count against rule-consequentialism. . . . rule consequentialism's opponents must not merely describe a world in which rule consequentialism is extremely demanding. . . .[they] must . . . describe a possible case in which the theory's rule about aid is counterintuitively severe.[65]

Hooker argues that proponents of the Wrong Facts Objection fail to discharge their burden of proof. For instance, even if the demands of Rule Consequentialism are extreme in Many Poor, this accords with common sense. In response, one must ask whether such demands really are accepted by Common-Sense Morality. The intuitions behind the Wrong Facts Objection suggest that they are not. The differences between the cases do not strike us as morally significant, in anything like the way that Rule Consequentialism requires them to be. For instance, when we ask why extreme demands are not reasonable in *this world*, the verdict of Common-Sense Morality does not appeal to the relative numbers of starving and

---

[65] Ibid. 172–3.

affluent people. (For discussion of what it *does* appeal to, see Chapter 6 and Part Four.) The force of the objection is perhaps clearest in Affluent's Third Ignorance, where many of us are actually in Affluent's situation. We do not know the optimal global response to famine. Resolving our ignorance does not seem a necessary prerequisite to the discovery of how much we ought to donate to charity.

Rule Consequentialists can reduce the bite of the Wrong Facts Objection in some cases, but they cannot dissolve it. I conclude that the objection remains a serious problem for any form of Rule Consequentialism, whether based on mechanical or on subtle rules.

3.7. The Homogeneity of the Ideal Society

We have seen that it is very difficult to tell what Rule Consequentialism demands. Furthermore, however the theory is formulated, it seems to produce intuitively unattractive demands, both in actual cases and in hypothetical ones. The significance of these results depends in part upon how Rule Consequentialism is defended. For those like Hooker whose defence of Rule Consequentialism is founded on its intuitive appeal, indeterminacy and counter-intuitiveness are fatal. This may tempt some Rule Consequentialists to return to a purely Consequentialist defence of their theory. After all, Consequentialists in general are no strangers to complexity or counter-intuitiveness.

Those taking this path would need to overcome the Incoherence Objection, and demonstrate that Rule Consequentialism is a plausible interpretation of the central Consequentialist ideal. The problem of indeterminacy is also serious for Consequentialist defenders of Rule Consequentialism. If we cannot tell what the results of internalizing any particular code of rules would be, how can we evaluate that code on consequentialist grounds?

In this section, I present a new problem for Consequentialist justifications of Rule Consequentialism, which reinforces the Incoherence Objection. I then ask whether this objection can also be levelled against Hooker's intuition-based theory.

Rule Consequentialists generally assume that everyone in the ideal society has the same moral character and follows the same moral rules. Let us call this assumption the 'Homogeneity Thesis'. It is usually left unnoticed and undiscussed, and renders it comparatively easy to discover what Rule Consequentialism requires of us. We need only locate the ideal society, and then proceed to emulate any one of its inhabitants. In this section, I shall argue that the Homogeneity Thesis is unwarranted. Without it, Rule

Consequentialism is much less appealing than its adherents would have us believe. Our discussion of the thesis will focus on the following story.

Dictator's Education.   Dictator, a benevolent ruler, is responsible for education in a large nation state. Dictator is a Consequentialist, so she wishes her education system to maximize the good. In general, Dictator thinks it would be best if people were kind, well-meaning Non-Consequentialists. However, there are two small classes of people who should be different: politicians and soldiers. Politicians allocate resources within society. Dictator reasons that these people should make their decisions solely on the basis of impersonal cost-benefit analyses. Soldiers protect the society from hostile invasion. Dictator believes that violent, specialized mercenaries make the best soldiers. Dictator thus wants three types of moral character: citizen, politician, and soldier. The total population in each generation is n. Dictator decides that, when the next generation graduates, society will need p politicians and s soldiers. Three schools are established: Calculator College (with p pupils), Warrior College (with s pupils), and Ordinary College (with $n - p - s$ pupils). Each school produces a different moral outlook. Graduates of Calculator College are hard-nosed Simple Consequentialists, making decisions on the basis of impersonal cost-benefit analyses. Graduates of Warrior College are vicious, highly disciplined, order-obeying killers. Graduates of Ordinary College believe that morality is largely a matter of personal, one-to-one relationships with people one knows individually. Calculators are thus ideally suited to the politician role in Dictator's society, Warriors are fitted for the soldier role, while Ordinaries are the sort of people you generally want in your society. By creating three groups with radically different moral views, Dictator creates a better system (from a Consequentialist perspective) than would have been possible if everyone had the same moral character.

Defenders of the Homogeneity Thesis must argue that Dictator is wrong. A single moral character would be, at least, no worse than Dictator's non-homogenous solution. Likely options include the following:

Universal Calculators.   Everyone attends Calculator College. Everyone is an Act Utilitarian.

Universal Warriors.   Everyone attends Warrior College. Everyone is a trained and obedient killer.

Universal Ordinaries.   Everyone attends Ordinary College. Everyone gives moral priority to their nearest and dearest.

Universal Flexibles.   A Flexible is a versatile moral character. She is able to modify her behaviour according to her social role. Flexibles believe that social policy should be based on cost-benefit analyses. So they will be well suited to the role of politician. On the other hand, Flexibles believe that cost-benefit analysis is inappropriate in ordinary life. In everyday life, Flexibles thus behave exactly like Ordinaries. Finally, Flexibles believe that ordinary standards of decency are inappropriate in a state of war. So they are capable of behaving like Warriors if the need arises. In effect, a population of Flexibles will behave exactly like Dictator's own population, with the additional advantage of improved flexibility, as Flexibles can switch roles in a way that Calculators, Warriors, and Ordinaries cannot. If a society consisting exclusively of Flexible characters is feasible, it must be preferable to Dictator's non-homogenous combination.

In other aspects of their theory, Rule Consequentialists are very concerned with the limitations and particularities of the human condition. One of their principal objections to Simple Consequentialism is that it ignores these real-world features. Rule Consequentialists do not imagine the best society that is logically possible for rational agents. Rather, they ask which characters are possible in a human society. In order to remain true to this tradition of psychological realism, proponents of the Homogeneity Thesis must argue that human beings could be Flexibles.

Our discussion of Dictator's Education shows that the issues surrounding the Homogeneity Thesis are very complicated, even in this simplified situation. Introducing the complexity of the real world would muddy the waters still further. The combined effect of all these complications is hard to predict. At the very least, we cannot be confident that introducing real-life complexity would vindicate the Homogeneity Thesis.

Assume, for the sake of argument, that the Homogeneity Thesis is false. That is, not everyone in the best possible society has the same moral character, or follows the same moral rules. Let us focus on Perfect, an inhabitant of this ideal society, who finds herself in a situation where she has two choices: the c-act (what someone would do if they had the character such that, if everyone had that character, things would go better than if everyone had some other particular character) and the p-act (what someone with Perfect's actual character would do). What is the right thing for Perfect to do? Proponents of conventional homogeneous Rule Consequentialism must argue that Perfect should do the c-act. Perfect should act as if she possessed a certain moral character, even though her actually possessing that moral character would have made the overall outcome worse in moral terms, given the characters of others. This claim is by no means absurd. Many Non-Consequentialists hold similar views. But what surely *is* absurd is to base this claim on an argument from the moral value of outcomes. Consequentialists cannot hold this view.

Rule Consequentialists must accept that Perfect should do the *p*-act rather than the *c*-act. However, this introduces an unwelcome complexity into their theory. If we are to emulate the behaviour of the inhabitants of the ideal society, and if we accept that different inhabitants of that society will behave differently, then we must ask which of them we should emulate. Rule Consequentialism already contains more than its fair share of indeterminacies. The introduction of another dimension of complexity is not desirable

Rule Consequentialists will probably want to defend the Homogeneity Thesis. They might distinguish three interpretations of that thesis.

The Same Beliefs Interpretation. Everyone in the ideal society has the same moral beliefs.

The Same Rules Interpretation. Everyone in the ideal society accepts the same moral rules.

The Same Character Interpretation. Everyone in the ideal society has the same moral character.

My discussion has focused on the Same Character Interpretation. Defenders of the Homogeneity Thesis might argue that I have attacked a straw position. While the Same Character Interpretation has been defeated, the Same Beliefs and Same Rules Interpretations remain intact, and these are more relevant to the assessment of Rule Consequentialism. Perhaps these other interpretations survive the attack on the Same Character Interpretation. For instance, we could retell the Dictator's Education story so that, although different people had different moral characters, everyone shared the same moral beliefs. Similarly, if we cast our moral rules as hypothetical statements concerning how individuals ought to behave in certain tightly defined situations, then we might imagine a society of people with different moral characters who all accept, and perhaps even follow, exactly the same moral rules.

While I admit that the Same Beliefs and Same Rules Interpretations do seem more plausible than the Same Character Interpretation, I have two principal objections to this response. Recall that, under Rule Consequentialism, we are primarily interested in discovering what an inhabitant of the ideal society would do in certain circumstances. We are not just interested in moral beliefs. If we are told that the inhabitants of the ideal society have different moral characters, although they all have the same moral beliefs, then we must assume that in some situations different inhabitants of the ideal society would act differently. Otherwise, it is not clear what is meant by admitting that they had different moral characters. The indeterminacy problems facing the Same Character Interpretation of the Homogeneity Thesis thus recur under the Same Beliefs Interpretation. The real problem for Rule Consequentialism is the presence of indeterminacy and not the Homogeneity Thesis *per se*.

My second reservation is related to the first. Even under the Same Beliefs Interpretation, the Homogeneity Thesis is by no means obvious. For the moral beliefs of the inhabitants of the ideal society to be of any relevance to us, those beliefs must be linked to their behaviour. How can we be sure that the ideal society will not be a place where different people have different beliefs? Assume that the behaviour described in Dictator's Education is the optimum pattern of behaviour. The ideal society is the closest possible world where this pattern of behaviour is present. In other words, our description of the ideal society is the most plausible story we can tell about why the people of Dictator's Education behave as they do. The conceptual links between behaviour, moral character, and moral beliefs place limits on the range of explanatory stories we can tell. In particular, many possible stories where people with identical moral beliefs have significantly different moral characters will be psychologically implausible. Perhaps the best explanation of the behaviour in Dictator's Education is that different people have different moral beliefs. Yet, if this is so, then the falsity of the Same Character Interpretation implies the falsity of the Same Beliefs Interpretation. The Homogeneity Thesis would then be defeated under any interpretation. For another example, consider the different and conflicting moral codes accepted by doctors, nurses, hospital managers, and public servants. It may be that the best possible health system would not be one where all these different people had the same moral beliefs.

To remove my reservations, defenders of the Homogeneity Thesis would need to tell a plausible story where homogeneous moral beliefs coexisted with very different moral characters, even though moral beliefs were strongly connected to behaviour. I doubt that such a story could be told. I conclude both that the Homogeneity Thesis is dubious, and that, unless it can be established, Rule Consequentialism contains far more indeterminacy than its proponents have hitherto admitted.

An alternative for Rule Consequentialism is to reject the Homogeneity Thesis, but deny that this affects Rule Consequentialism. If we judge possible worlds purely on the amount of value they contain, then the optimal world will not be homogenous. However, Rule Consequentialism still picks out the best homogenous world, even though it is not optimal. This is Hooker's response.[66] As the foregoing discussion makes clear, this response is not available to those who derive Rule Consequentialism from purely Consequentialist premisses. It seems incoherent for such a theory to fail to select the optimal set of rules, whether it is homogeneous or not. However, this

---

[66] Hooker, *Ideal Code, Real World*, and Hooker, 'Rule-Consequentialism and Obligations toward the Needy', pp. 27–9.

response is not so implausible for those like Hooker who defend their Rule Consequentialism on the basis of intuitive appeal. Homogeneous Rule Consequentialism may well be more intuitively appealing than optimal Rule Consequentialism, if we are indeed forced to choose between the two. On the other hand, the fact that it departs from the optimal set of rules might make Hooker's Rule Consequentialism seem even more *ad hoc*.

3.8. Conclusion

We have just seen that the problems raised by the Homogeneity Thesis are especially worrying for those who base their Rule Consequentialism on a purely Consequentialist foundation. However, we saw in previous sections that other defences of Rule Consequentialism are also inadequate. In particular, Rule Consequentialism cannot be defended on the basis of its intuitive plausibility, as it generates unacceptable results in both actual and hypothetical cases. It is also far from clear that Rule Consequentialism places moderate demands on actual human agents. We must conclude that Rule Consequentialism is not a plausible moral theory. If we are to defeat the Demandingness Objection, we must look elsewhere. The next chapter asks whether other forms of Collective Consequentialism fare any better.

4

Other Forms of Collective Consequentialism

In this chapter, I discuss a recent alternative to the Rule Consequentialism discussed in the previous chapter—namely, the theory of Liam Murphy.[1] I also attempt to draw some conclusions concerning the viability of Collective Consequentialism in general.

Many of the problems faced by Rule Consequentialism were caused either by the shift from compliance to acceptance or by the need to discover exactly what action would follow from the ideal code of rules in a particular situation. As we shall see, Murphy's theory avoids such problems, as it lacks these troublesome features. However, I shall conclude that Murphy's approach is not ultimately acceptable, and that no form of Collective Consequentialism can avoid the fate of either Rule Consequentialism or Murphy's view.

4.1. Murphy's Account

Murphy explains his broad conception as follows:

Beneficence can be understood in terms of a *shared cooperative aim*. . . . if we both have a cooperative aim to promote the good . . . we do not see ourselves as engaged in separate solitary enterprises. . . . Each of us does not, strictly speaking, aim to promote the good. Each sees himself as *working with others* to promote the good. Thus the best way to describe the aim of each might be: 'to promote the good together with others.'   (emphasis in original)[2]

Such a conception of benevolence is certainly appealing in public good cases. As Murphy notes: 'insofar as beneficence is . . . a mutually beneficial project, it is natural to resist taking on the shares of people who could contribute to the project but do not.'[3]

---

[1] Murphy, 'The Demands of Beneficence'; Mulgan, 'Two Conceptions of Benevolence'; and Murphy, 'A Relatively Plausible Principle of Beneficence'. Murphy defends his theory at greater length in his *Moral Demands in Nonideal Theory*.

[2] Murphy, 'The Demands of Beneficence', pp. 285–6.

[3] Ibid. 288. It is important to note that Murphy also defends the cooperative principle in cases where beneficence is not mutually advantageous. (See below, Section 4.5, for a fuller discussion of Murphy's defence.)

Proceeding from this Collective Consequentialist perspective, Murphy suggests the following condition on principles of beneficence.

Compliance Condition.   An acceptable principle of beneficence will not increase its demands on agents when expected compliance by other agents decreases.[4]

The Compliance Condition (or something like it) does seem to be a central feature of the collectivist approach. For instance, Rule Consequentialists often defend their theory on the grounds of 'fairness', in the following manner: Assume (for the sake of argument) that a donation of 10 per cent of the income of all affluent citizens of the developed world would be sufficient to eliminate poverty and deprivation. By giving 10 per cent, I do my share. My giving another 5 per cent would improve aggregate welfare only because other people are not doing their share. Why should I be made to donate more just because other people are avoiding their moral responsibilities? That would be unfair. It is only reasonable to require me to do my share. Otherwise, other people can exploit me by not doing theirs. This line of argument is clearly based on some analogue of the Compliance Condition: no acceptable principle would require more of me simply because others are doing less. (The relationship between the Compliance Condition and Collective Consequentialism is explored more fully in Section 4.7. For more on fairness and Collective Consequentialism, see Chapter 8.)

Rule Consequentialism faces many problems. However, it is by no means the only possible form of Collective Consequentialism. Murphy aims to develop a principle of benevolence that satisfies the Compliance Condition while avoiding the pitfalls of Rule Consequentialism. He suggests the following.

Cooperative Principle of Beneficence.   An agent is required to act optimally— to perform the action that makes the outcome best—except in situations of partial compliance with this principle. It is always permissible to act optimally, but the sacrifice required of the agent is limited to the level of sacrifice that would be optimal under full compliance. Of the actions requiring no more than this level of sacrifice, the agent may choose only the one with the best outcome. The agent must then perform either that action, or some other action that makes the outcome just as good.[5]

---

[4] Ibid. 278.
[5] Ibid. 280. I have reworded Murphy's published formulation, to correct a slight inaccuracy. The version given in the text corresponds to Murphy's own use of the principle. (Murphy himself has confirmed this in correspondence.)

It is easy to see that Murphy's principle satisfies the Compliance Condition. However, I shall argue that the principle is unacceptable. In Sections 4.3 and 4.4, I present two sets of cases where Murphy's principle generates unacceptable results. Murphy's responses are explored in Section 4.5. I then seek to show that the failings of Murphy's principle do not result from any special features of that principle, as no principle satisfying the Compliance Condition could possibly be acceptable (Section 4.6). I then argue that Collective Consequentialism can dispense with the Compliance Condition only by lapsing into the various errors discussed in the previous chapter (Section 4.7). If these two claims are correct, then there cannot be an acceptable form of Collective Consequentialism.

4.2. Murphy and Rule Consequentialism

Murphy's position has obvious similarities with Rule Consequentialism. To see this, we can split Murphy's theory into two halves:

1. determining the ideal situation or society;
2. using the behaviour of someone from that situation or society to determine what actual agents should do in the real world.

Murphy's account of step (1) is analogous to Rule Consequentialism. The ideal situation is an idealized world of full compliance, where everyone acts optimally. The principal difference lies at step (2). Murphy uses the ideal situation, not directly to determine what an agent should do in any given situation, but rather to determine how much sacrifice she should bear. This enables Murphy to avoid objections to Rule Consequentialism based on the odd results it generates in situations of partial compliance.

A second difference between the two theories is that, unlike many contemporary Rule Consequentialists, Murphy does not appeal to any distinction between following a rule and accepting a rule. Murphy's ideal society is a world where everyone acts optimally, not one where everyone accepts the same rules. This will save Murphy from those objections to Rule Consequentialism that attacked that distinction. However, it will also deprive him of defences of Rule Consequentialism utilizing the distinction.

Despite these differences, Murphy's principle is subject to a number of the same objections as Rule Consequentialism, particularly the Wrong Facts Objection and the Exception Clause Objection. (For the original objections, see Sections 3.6 and 3.5 respectively.)

4.3. The Wrong Facts Objection

This objection to Murphy's account is analogous to the corresponding objection to Rule Consequentialism. Recall our first tale.

Affluent's First Ignorance. Affluent does not know how many people are starving. She knows only that she is in one of the following three situations.

Few Poor. There are only 1 million people starving.

Medium Poor. There are 50 million people starving.

Many Poor. There are 2,500 million people starving.

In all three cases, the eradication of famine lies far beyond Affluent's means. She can make only a very small dent on the overall problem. Affluent can find out exactly what situation she is in by ploughing laboriously through the fine print of the latest World Bank report.

Murphy is committed to the view that the sacrifice required of each individual is equal to the total good to be done divided by the number of agents available to produce that good.[6] For the sake of argument, let us assume that, in the actual world, full compliance with a rule requiring a donation of 10 per cent of one's income would produce the best possible results. In the actual world Affluent should follow this rule and donate 10 per cent. If this is the appropriate individual sacrifice, that must be because the total sacrifice required to alleviate poverty and starvation, divided by the number of people who could make such donations, would equal 10 per cent of the income of the latter. Changing the number of people facing starvation by a factor of fifty leads to a proportionate change in the amount of good to be done, and hence to a fifty-fold increase in the sacrifice required under full compliance.

These extreme differences seem unreasonable. In Few Poor, it seems ridiculous for Affluent to be allowed to donate only one-fifth of 1 per cent of her income, simply because there are *only* 1 million people starving rather than 50 million. Similarly, it seems unreasonable to demand of Affluent in Many Poor that she sacrifice all her income simply because there are 2,500 million people starving rather than *only* 50 million. The difference between the situations does not seem sufficient to justify the enormously different sacrifices required of Affluent.

As with Rule Consequentialism, my objection here is not merely that Murphy's principle makes Affluent's obligations dependent upon specific

---

[6] This claim requires a simplifying assumption, which I trust does not affect the substance of my argument. Murphy is committed to the view outlined in the text only where the amount of good produced by each contribution is independent of the number of actual contributors. It seems not unreasonable to make this assumption in Affluent's case.

empirical facts. After all, Simple Consequentialism requires similarly detailed information, as what an agent should do depends on the precise consequences of her actions. However, unlike Simple Consequentialism, Murphy's principle requires extensive knowledge of facts with no effect on the consequences of our actions. Affluent knows that her most efficient aid-contribution method is to write a cheque to Oxfam. She also knows (roughly) how much good would be produced by any given level of donation. She also knows that, whatever she does, millions of people will be left in poverty by the inaction of others. Does she really need to know how many millions will be left in poverty before she has any idea how much she ought to donate?

Next, recall our second tale.

Affluent's Second Ignorance.   Affluent is drastically misinformed about the size of the developed world. She knows that the number of people in the developed world is very large, but she does not know exactly how large. She knows only that she is in one of the following three situations.

Few Rich.   The developed world contains only 1 million people.

Medium Rich.   The developed world contains 50 million people.

Many Rich.   The developed world contains 2,500 million people.

Once again, under Murphy's principle, Affluent must resolve her ignorance before she has any idea at all how much to give to Oxfam. Assume that, in Medium Rich, Affluent should donate 10 per cent of her income. If 10 per cent of the income of 50 million people is enough to remove poverty, then one-fifth of 1 per cent of the income of 2,500 million people should also be sufficient. Therefore, in Many Rich, Affluent is required to donate only one-fifth of 1 per cent of her income. By contrast, if there are only 1 million people in the developed world, they will have to sacrifice virtually all of their resources. The sacrifice required of Affluent in Few Rich will be extreme.

This seems unreasonable. If a sacrifice equivalent to 10 per cent of Affluent's income is enough if there are 50 million people in the developed world, why should it not also be enough if there turn out to be only 1 million, and not too much even if there turn out to be 2,500 million people? Affluent knows that there are millions of people in the developed world, and that the vast majority of them will not behave as they should. Does she really need to know the precise number of millions who are not doing their share, before she has any idea how much she must sacrifice?

Finally, recall our third tale.

Affluent's Third Ignorance.   Affluent is completely ignorant of political economy. She knows only that one of the following is an accurate description of
the nature of her world.

> *Developmentland.*   The Developmentalist account holds true. Famine is
> caused by a sudden decline in the food supply.

> *Malthusia.*   The Neo-Malthusian view is correct. Overpopulation is the
> primary cause of famine.

> *Senland.*   Sen's Microeconomic analysis is correct. Famine is caused
> largely by the collapse of direct or exchange-entitlement economic condi-
> tions.

As we saw in Chapter 3, sacrifices under full compliance vary greatly between
the three scenarios. The appropriate global response to famine depends crucially on which of these is the actual world. Under Murphy's principle,
Affluent must resolve her doubt before she acts. Before she knows how much
to donate, Affluent must become an expert on global political economy.

Again, this seems unreasonable. Affluent's behaviour has little chance of
bringing about the optimal global response, whatever it may happen to be.
Her questions should only be: 'Will giving money to Oxfam do good? How
much good will it do? How much am I required to give, given other considerations?' The nature of the precise optimal global response does not seem to
be one of the considerations Affluent must address. If 10 per cent is about
right on one economic account, why should it not be right on other economic accounts, as any particular donation will do more or less the same
amount of good in each of the three cases?

As before, I do not claim that these empirical differences should have no
effect at all on Affluent's obligations. I claim only that they should not affect
her obligations to the extent that Murphy's principle requires.

Murphy discusses a very similar objection in his original paper: 'A way of test-
ing this is to think of the case of an extremely well-off minority in an extremely
badly off country, isolated from the rest of the world. . . . the Cooperative
Principle would impose great sacrifice on this minority even under full compliance.'[7] Murphy responds to this objection as follows: 'But would we feel that
the extreme demands in these cases were objectionable, in just the same way
that the demands made on us every day by the Simple Principle [which corresponds to Simple Consequentialism] seem objectionable?'[8]

I have suggested that, in cases such as the various Affluent stories, we
would regard the extreme demands of the Cooperative Principle as objectionable. Indeed, I would argue that those demands are, in a sense, more

---

[7] Murphy, 'The Demands of Beneficence', p. 289.   [8] Ibid. 289.

objectionable than the extreme demands of Simple Consequentialism. The latter makes the same demands of Affluent in each of our stories. By contrast, the Cooperative Principle makes extreme demands in some cases but not in others. It is this variation to which the Wrong Facts Objection objects.

We should also note that this tentative response of Murphy's seems far better suited to one side of the Wrong Facts Objection than to the other. Murphy mentions the over-demanding cases, where fluctuating numbers lead the Cooperative Principle to make extreme demands. This leaves out the under-demanding cases (Few Poor and Many Rich), where fluctuating numbers produce very light demands. Surely we do find it objectionable that a principle requires so little of agents, even when there is still so much to be done.

In combating the under-demanding case, Murphy is on much weaker ground than traditional Rule Consequentialists, such as Richard Brandt or Brad Hooker. They focus on rules, whereas Murphy deals merely with levels of sacrifice. In sophisticated forms of Rule Consequentialism, the flexibility of rules does a lot of work. For instance, Rule Consequentialists may respond to the Wrong Facts Objection by claiming that a rule which demands little under full compliance can still be very demanding under partial compliance (see Section 3.6). Such moves are unavailable to Murphy. If the sacrifice under full compliance would only be one dollar, then no acceptable moral theory can ask Affluent to donate more than one dollar. I argued in the previous chapter that the Wrong Facts Objection is a serious problem for Rule Consequentialism. It is an even more serious problem for Murphy. (Of course, we also saw earlier that the flexibility of rules creates other problems for Rule Consequentialism.)

4.4. Natural versus Artificial Disasters

We now turn to a different problem for Murphy's principle, directly analogous to the problems created for Rule Consequentialism by Brandtian Exception Clauses (see Section 3.5). Recall our set of famine tales.

Famine Just Happens.   Through no fault of any person, some people face starvation or famine.

The Brigands' Famine.   There is plenty of grain in the country, but the soldiers of one side in a civil war burn all the crops in the territory of the other side.

The Hoarders' Famine.   Famine arises because those who own the grain decide to hoard it. They refuse to give it to those who require it, or to sell it at an affordable price.

The Ignorers' Famine.   Famine results (in part) from the collective inaction of developed countries.

The Capitalist Famine.   In a regime of pure international capitalism, a famine results from the mysterious interactions of the global market.

Murphy says that our obligations depend upon what would happen under full compliance with his principle. In Famine Just Happens, full compliance would produce a worldwide disaster-relief programme. The sacrifice required of us is thus equal to that involved in our share of that ideal relief effort. In each of the other four famines, full compliance would have eliminated the famine before it began, as it results from peoples' failure to act optimally. In those cases, Murphy's principle would thus require no sacrifice from us at all.

The demands of Murphy's principle would thus vary enormously depending upon whether or not the disaster we face is caused by natural forces or human actions. This seems unreasonable. When faced with a disaster, surely my first questions should be 'How can I help?' and (perhaps) 'How much will it cost me?' not 'Is this the result of an act of God?' (followed by 'If it is not, then I'm not obliged to help at all.')

However, things are not quite so straightforward. Murphy's principle deals only with full compliance *from now on*. We are to idealize away expected failures of beneficence in the future, but not actual failures in the past. If famine already exists, even as a result of past failures of beneficence, Murphy's principle will still require agents to take steps, from now on, to alleviate it. It would seem, then, that Murphy can avoid allowing agents in our last four famines to do nothing at all.

There are two problems with Murphy's restriction to full compliance from now on. The first is that, in certain cases, it appears unacceptably arbitrary. For instance, consider the following tale.

Oxfam's Future Famine Fund.   Oxfam are tired of endlessly raising funds on an *ad hoc* basis to deal with particular disasters as they arise. They decide to solicit donations to establish a fund to deal with any famines that might arise in the future. They ask Affluent to make a donation towards this fund, at a time when no current famine requires her attention. Affluent has read a report by a reliable agency predicting that, in the future, virtually all famines will be of one particular type. Sadly, she cannot remember which type it was. All she remembers is that one of the following is an accurate account of the likely future of her world.

Famines Just Happen.   Future famines will arise through no fault of any person.

Brigands Cause Famine.   Future famines will arise because soldiers in civil wars regularly burn all the crops in the territory of the other side.

Hoarders Cause Famine.   Future famines will arise because those who own the grain decide to hoard it.

Ignorers Cause Famine.   Future famines will arise because of the collective inaction of developed countries.

Capitalism Causes Famine.   All future famine will result from the mysterious interactions of the global market.

On Murphy's principle, Affluent must resolve her ignorance before she has any idea whether or not (let alone how much) she should donate to Oxfam's fund. If any of the last four descriptions is an accurate account of the future course of her world, idealization to full compliance *from now on* would result in there being no future famines at all. If future famines result only from failures of beneficence, then Affluent is not required to make any sacrifice at all to alleviate them. On the other hand, if future famines just happen, then Affluent will be required to make a possibly considerable donation to Oxfam's fund.

Murphy's principle thus makes radically different demands on Affluent in the various possible situations. This seems unacceptable. Furthermore, because it idealizes away only *future* failures of beneficence, the demands of Murphy's principle regarding Oxfam's future famine fund differ significantly from its demands regarding current famines. Given that, in both cases, the failures of beneficence lie outside Affluent's control, should the mere fact that some of them lie in the future rather than the past carry that much weight?

A second problem with the appeal to the future-looking nature of Murphy's principle is that, even in our original set of tales, the principle will make significantly different demands in the different cases. For instance, assume that a current famine results from the past activities of grain hoarders. Those hoarders could probably do a great deal to alleviate the famine they have caused. As Murphy's principle does not idealize away their failure to do so in the future, it may well demand less of Affluent that it would have required if the famine had resulted from an act of God. Though they are less significant than they first appeared, such differences do seem somewhat arbitrary.

In a footnote to his paper, Murphy seeks to avoid a similar conclusion by suggesting that 'the Cooperative Principle is accompanied by deontological constraints against violence, thieving, and the like. For . . . we would not characterize the actions of wrongdoers like those in the former Yugoslavia and in Somalia as failures in beneficence.'[9]

[9] Murphy, 'The Demands of Beneficence', 280–1 n. 27.

This move might remove the anomaly of the Brigands' Famine, but it cannot help us in the Hoarders' Famine, the Ignorers' Famine, or the Capitalist Famine, unless we include deontological constraints against failing to give discounts to starving customers, or failing to make adequate donations to Oxfam. The introduction of such constraints would crowd out the original principle of benevolence. If our deontological constraints rule out all human behaviour that leads, either actively or through omission, to the existence of unmet needs, then there will be no room left for benevolence.[10]

4.5. Murphy's Responses

In a reply published in *Philosophy and Public Affairs* in 1997, Murphy replies to the objections raised in Sections 4.3 and 4.4. Murphy has three principal responses. The first is to appeal to the distinction between criteria of rightness and decision procedures (see Section 2.4). Murphy argues that this distinction can defeat many of the claims underlying the Wrong Facts Objection. The Cooperative Principle is not 'offered as a guide to be consulted in everyday life'.[11] Referring to my 'Two Conceptions of Benevolence', he notes:

Mulgan has said nothing to call the strategy [of appealing to the distinction between criteria of rightness and decision procedures] into question, or to suggest that while it might work for the Simple Principle [which corresponds to Simple Consequentialism] it breaks down in the face of the new kinds of information made relevant by the Cooperative Principle.[12]

Accordingly, we can safely ignore the question of whether agents are required to acquire all the information involved in Affluent's various ignorances, as the Cooperative Principle does not require them to do so. We should focus instead on whether or not the information in question is, in principle, morally relevant.

Murphy's second response is that his defence of the Cooperative Principle is based on its comparative intuitive appeal: 'The issue of what is required of us in respect of beneficence is one where none of the familiar positions is immediately attractive. Even more so than elsewhere in moral theory, progress can be made only by offering judgements of overall relative plausibility.'[13] Therefore, we cannot rule out the Cooperative Principle simply because it has some intuitively odd results. In particular, 'any principle short

---

[10] Murphy concedes a similar point in Murphy, 'A Relatively Plausible Principle of Beneficence', at p. 28 (see his n. 12).

[11] Ibid. 25.   [12] Ibid. 26.   [13] Ibid.

of the Simple Principle will in some cases seem too lenient'.[14] So we cannot rule out the Cooperative Principle simply because it is allegedly too lenient in Few Poor or Many Rich.

Murphy's third response is that my objections are based on rejecting the claim that the number of potential cooperators is morally relevant. Murphy complains that I fail to engage with his arguments in defence of this claim, relying instead on its intuitive failings: 'Since the main part of my article is an attempt to say why the existence of other potential contributors does matter, and since Mulgan does not address my arguments, it is a little hard to know what to add here.'[15]

Let us now examine these three responses. We discussed the distinction between criteria of rightness and decision procedures at some length, both in Chapter 2 and in the context of the Wrong Facts Objection to Rule Consequentialism in Chapter 3. There are two questions to address. (1) How well do my earlier remarks relate to the Cooperative Principle? (2) Is this strategy as plausible for Murphy as for Individual Consequentialism?

It may seem inconsistent for Murphy to invoke the distinction between criteria of rightness and decision procedures while also relying on the intuitive appeal of the Cooperative Principle. If we cannot tell what judgements of right and wrong the theory actually makes, how can we evaluate the intuitive appeal of those judgements? We should note, however, that Murphy's defence of the Co-operative Principle is not based entirely on the intuitive plausibility of its particular results, as he also relies on the intuitive appeal of the underlying cooperative conception of benevolence. He may thus be able to afford a larger gap between his criterion of rightness and his decision procedure than an intuitive Rule Consequentialist such as Hooker. On the other hand, Murphy does give significant weight to the intuitive appeal of the Cooperative Principle. This suggests that we should be able to determine roughly what moral judgements the principle yields.

It is difficult adequately to evaluate Murphy's first response unless we know what decision procedure his Cooperative Principle would recommend. This question, which Murphy himself does not seem to address, is harder to answer than the corresponding question for Individual Consequentialism. Under Individual Consequentialism, we merely seek the decision procedure that would best promote value if pursued by an individual agent over the course of her life. The Cooperative Principle, by contrast, suggests several distinct criteria against which we might measure prospective decision

---

[14] Murphy concedes a similar point in Murphy, 'A Relatively Plausible Principle of Beneficence', 27. Hooker makes a similar point in terms of meanness (see Hooker, 'Rule-Consequentialism and Obligations toward the Needy', p. 10).

[15] Murphy, 'A Relatively Plausible Principle of Beneficence', p. 27.

procedures. We could rank them according to the value of their consequences, or the frequency with which they yield actions that do not involve
more sacrifice than under full compliance, or the frequency with which they
yield actions that do not involve less sacrifice than under full compliance, or
according to some aggregate measure of net degree of sacrifice. Different criteria may well rank competing decision procedures differently. We must
decide between them.

There are two problems here for the Cooperative Principle. The first is
that, unlike Individual Consequentialism, the Cooperative Principle offers
two distinct desiderata for acts: that they have valuable consequences, and
that the degree of sacrifice involved be no greater than that required under
full compliance. It must balance those desiderata. The second problem is
that, whereas Consequentialism seeks to maximize its sole desideratum, the
Cooperative Principle does not seek to maximize either of its desiderata. We
thus cannot balance them simply by asking how close competing decision
procedures come to maximizing some aggregate measure of value and sacrifice. Accordingly, it is much harder to know what sort of decision procedure
will be recommended by the Cooperative Principle.

The resulting decision procedure might actually be very simple. If there is
a correct level of sacrifice (equivalent, say, to x dollars), then there must be a
decision procedure of the following form: Donate at least x dollars to charity.
Perhaps this would be the decision procedure recommended by the
Cooperative Principle. However, if we cannot ourselves discover the correct
level of sacrifice, then we could never know which decision procedure the
Cooperative Principle recommends. We would thus be unable to assess the
intuitive appeal of that principle. In particular, we would have no reason to
believe that the Cooperative Principle was not unreasonably demanding.

The Wrong Facts Objection is designed, in part, to show that these problems
are more significant for Collective Consequentialism than for Individual
Consequentialism. While we can have some idea which procedure would produce the best consequences, we often have very little idea what level of sacrifice
would be optimal under full compliance. Or at least, this is what the Wrong
Facts Objection claims. The distinction between criteria and procedure thus cannot enable the Cooperative Principle to avoid Affluent's epistemic problems.

We turn now to Murphy's other two responses. These are best considered
together. The best reply to Murphy's challenge would be to provide a more
intuitively appealing principle of beneficence, and to offer a principled rationale for that principle, explaining where Murphy's cooperative conception
goes wrong. In Part Four of this book, I seek to construct and motivate such
a principle. I also seek to diagnose the failings of Murphy's Cooperative
Conception, in order to motivate my departure from it. In the present

section, I outline Murphy's argument in support of his conception of benevolence, and raise some general objections to it.

It is necessary to begin our discussion of Murphy's responses by attending to the structure of Murphy's conception of benevolence. Perhaps the most significant point is that Murphy's notion of cooperation is very different from that offered by mutual-advantage, fair-reciprocity, or Contractualist accounts of morality as a cooperative venture. These other views 'involve an idea of cooperation among people with different [self-concerned] aims'.[16] Murphy's conception, by contrast, regards benevolence as a *shared* cooperative aim. Cooperation is thus intrinsic to each agent's aim, not merely instrumental. Under a mutual advantage view, for instance, if agents could achieve their separate aims more efficiently by not cooperating, then they would go their separate ways. By contrast, agents with Murphy's cooperative aim cannot pursue it alone.

While Murphy acknowledges 'concern about free riding on a mutually beneficial practice as an independent source of support for the Compliance Condition',[17] the principal defence of the Compliance Condition is that it flows from the Cooperative Conception of Beneficence.

There are two basic problems with Murphy's defence of his principle. The first is that it is not clear that someone who adopted the Cooperative Conception of Benevolence would, in fact, also endorse the Cooperative Principle (even if he did endorse the Compliance Condition, which is not obvious either). After all, the Cooperative Principle looks like another standard individualist principle of beneficence. It tells me, as an individual, what I ought to do. We might expect a Cooperative Principle to make more explicit reference to active co-operation with others. This is especially significant in the light of the distinction between criteria of rightness and decision procedures, which Murphy wishes to introduce. Presumably a cooperative decision procedure would explicitly direct each agent to seek to engage in active co-operation with others. If the Compliance Condition really is justified in terms of the Cooperative Conception of Benevolence, then this ought to affect the types of principle Murphy considers. Genuinely cooperative principles satisfying the Compliance Condition should be preferable to the Cooperative Principle itself.[18]

Secondly, Murphy himself admits that morality is not entirely a cooperative venture. He rejects the cooperative conception as a full account of morality. Through the inclusion of options, permissions, and special obligations,

---

[16] Murphy, 'The Demands of Beneficence', p. 285.

[17] Murphy, 'A Relatively Plausible Principle of Beneficence', p. 27.

[18] One possible rival for Murphy in this regard might be Regan's Cooperative Consequentialism. (See Regan, *Utilitarianism and Cooperation*, and above, Ch. 3 n. 43.)

morality acknowledges many personal ventures.[19] My principle claim in this chapter is that the cooperative conception is not an appropriate model for the whole of benevolence either. In particular, it is not appropriate for our relations with distant impoverished strangers. This is because, even though they are distinct from mutually advantageous cooperation, Murphy's cooperative aims are appropriate only in the relation to such cooperation. Cooperative aims arise most naturally between (comparative) equals, and apply most naturally to relations between those equals. They are not as applicable to our relations with non-equals. (This line of thought is developed further in Part Four.)

4.6. Rejecting the Compliance Condition

As I acknowledged at the outset, Murphy's Cooperative Principle seems sensible for cases where beneficence is mutually advantageous. However, as Murphy admits, many potentially benevolent activities are not mutually advantageous. In such cases, Murphy's conception seems, on the face of it, rather odd. My aim in donating to Oxfam is to promote the good, or, more accurately, to relieve some particular suffering. Certainly, I would like all my fellow citizens to cooperate with me in this aim, but only because such cooperation would further my own individual aim.[20] Unfortunately, the demands of beneficence arise most starkly in the very situations to which Murphy's conception seems least well suited, such as when many distant people are starving.

Friends of Collective Consequentialism may be tempted to respond to my criticisms of Murphy's principle in the way Murphy himself responds to the failure of Rule Consequentialism: 'Even if your objections stand, they only tell against one particular collective account of benevolence. You may have shown that some principles that satisfy the Compliance Condition are unacceptable. You have not shown that no acceptable principle satisfies the Compliance Condition. For all you have said thus far, there may be such a principle.'

---

[19] Murphy, 'The Demands of Beneficence', p. 288.

[20] Also, their cooperation might further other aims I have, such as the fostering of community spirit. However, such aims are clearly secondary. We might note, in passing, that many actions performed for 'moral' reasons also proceed from non-moral motives. For instance, my desire to promote the good may be combined with a non-moral desire to be part of a group that shares that aim. If no such group is available, then the sacrifice involved in making a given contribution to the good will be far greater, as I will not be compensated by the benefits of belonging to a group of like-minded do-gooders. In such a situation, I might well be morally required to make a greater contribution in a cooperative setting than in a non-cooperative one, because the overall level of sacrifice involved is the same. (Similar issues are discussed at length in Chapters 7 and 10.)

It is, of course, much easier to show that a particular principle is problematic than to demonstrate conclusively that all members of a potentially infinite class of principles (namely, those satisfying the Compliance Condition) are unacceptable. However, I do believe that this general conclusion can be rendered at least probable. To see this, let P be any principle of benevolence satisfying the Compliance Condition, and consider yet another variant of Affluent's Tale.

Affluent's New Ignorance. Affluent, as she sits at her desk, is drastically misinformed about the moral state of the developed world. She has heard a rumour that the number of people willing to contribute to famine relief has changed significantly, but she does not know what the change has been. As usual, she does not even know if the rumour is true. All she knows is that she is in one of the following three situations.

> *Few Carers.* A new religion, based on Hobbesian principles, has produced a nation of Egoists. Only 2 per cent of those who were previously willing to contribute to famine relief are still willing to do so.

> *Medium Carers.* The rumour is false. The number of people willing to contribute to famine relief is unchanged.

> *Many Carers.* A new religious movement, based on sound Collective Consequentialist principles, has swept the land. Suddenly, virtually everyone is willing to make a substantial contribution to famine relief.

If P satisfies the Compliance Condition, then P must hold that, whatever else she may need to know, Affluent does *not* need to resolve her new ignorance before she can determine precisely how much she is required to give to Oxfam. I shall now present two challenges to this claim.

The first challenge is that defenders of P must ensure that it delivers the result that Affluent's New Ignorance is totally morally irrelevant, *without* suffering the fate of Murphy's principle. Recall that Murphy gave unacceptable results regarding Affluent's Second Ignorance, where Affluent is misinformed about the size of the developed world, because he made Affluent's obligations too dependent upon the number of potential cooperators. To give the right result in that case, P must not give too much weight to how many *potential* cooperators there are. Yet, to give the right result in Affluent's New Ignorance, P must give no weight at all to how many *actual* cooperators there are. This would suggest that P is not really much interested in cooperators at all. But in that case, how can P claim to be a version of Collective Consequentialism? What is the point of saying that my Consequentialist project of making the world a better place is a group project, rather than an individual one, and then saying that it does not much matter how many other folk belong to that group, or whether or not any of them will cooperate?

The point here is simple. The Compliance Condition may look very general, but it is actually very restrictive. It is by no means obvious that there are (even in principle) any principles satisfying it that are sufficiently different from Murphy's to avoid the very same problems he faces. In the relevant respects, Murphy's principle may be the only possible one that can meet the Compliance Condition, and still claim to be a plausible version of Collective Consequentialism.

At the very least, I would suggest that these considerations place the burden of proof firmly on the defenders of the Compliance Condition. They must give us some idea of how a principle might be constructed that (1) meets the Compliance Condition; (2) avoids the objections raised in Sections 4.3 and 4.4 against Murphy's Cooperative Principle; and also (3) represents a distinctively collective form of Consequentialism.

My second objection is more straightforward, though perhaps more contentious. Taken in itself, the claim that Affluent's new ignorance is totally morally irrelevant, irrespective of whatever else may be true of her situation, seems implausibly strong. Surely we can imagine at least *some* circumstances where Affluent should resolve her ignorance before deciding how much she should give to Oxfam. So far, all my tales have dealt with heavily populated worlds, where both cooperators and beneficiaries are numbered in the millions. Presumably, however, P is also meant to cover less populated worlds. For simplicity's sake, consider a version of Affluent's New Ignorance with only twenty inhabitants in Affluent's world: nineteen potential cooperators, and one potential beneficiary. Principle P claims that, even in such a world, Affluent can, in principle, precisely determine how much beneficence requires of her, without having any idea how any of her well-off fellows will behave. It follows that beneficence cannot ever demand any more of Affluent than it does in the situation where all eighteen of her well-off fellows join with her in the Consequentialist project. The sacrifice required of Affluent in that case will presumably be minimal. Therefore, Affluent is only ever required to make a minimal sacrifice, even if, because others are not doing their share, the result is that the potential beneficiary starves.

If this particular result does not seem absurd, then retell the story such that there are a hundred potential cooperators, rather than twenty. (And still a single potential beneficiary.) As the number of potential cooperators increases, the sacrifice P requires of Affluent dwindles to nothing. At some point, Affluent will be allowed to leave the sole potential beneficiary to starve rather than lift her own finger to save him, simply because even that insignificant sacrifice is more than she would be required to bear if all the potential cooperators played their part. This result looks to me like a *reductio ad absurdum* of Principle P.

We could compare this example with a tale discussed, in relation to Murphy's own theory, by both Murphy and Hooker. Two adults pass two children drowning in a pond. If both adults do their share of saving, then each is required to save only one child. However, one of the adults fails to save either child. We are inclined to say that the other adult is then obliged to save both, assuming she can do so at little cost to herself. Murphy suggests that, when the object of need confronts me directly, it is not unreasonable to expect me to do more as others do less. Our previous example suggests that the operative feature is the small number of people involved, rather than any issue of proximity or directness. (For further discussion of this example, see Section 8.3).[21]

Taken together, the considerations presented in this section add considerable support to the conclusion that P will not, in the end, prove to be an acceptable principle of benevolence. Yet we have assumed nothing about P except that it satisfies the Compliance Condition. It follows that there can be no acceptable principle that meets that condition. The Compliance Condition cannot provide a satisfactory account of benevolence. In the next section, I discuss the relevance of this failure for Collective Consequentialism in general.

4.7. Collective Consequentialism and the Compliance Condition

I said earlier that the Compliance Condition or something like it is an integral part of the Collective Consequentialist approach. Yet Rule Consequentialism itself does not meet the Compliance Condition, for two reasons. The first is that the optimal rules may demand significantly more under partial compliance than under full compliance. Indeed, its ability to make different demands under partial compliance is often presented as a virtue of Rule Consequentialism (see Section 3.2). Furthermore, many versions of Rule Consequentialism study the acceptance of a set of rules, not merely compliance with those rules. Such theories are thus not even indirectly concerned with what any set of rules would demand under full *compliance*. A theory's demands under partial acceptance may not match its demands under full

---

[21] Murphy, 'The Demands of Beneficence' pp. 291–3, and Hooker, *Ideal Code, Real World*, p. 164. The example is originally due to Singer (see his 'Famine, Affluence and Morality', pp. 231–3). It might also be instructive to consider the examples in the text in the light of the literature on the moral significance of numbers (see e.g. Taurek, 'Should the Numbers Count?'). I leave this comparison for another day.

compliance. We also saw earlier that forms of Rule Consequentialism based on full acceptance may be more demanding than full compliance versions. If this is correct, then, even when the optimal rules are fully accepted, Rule Consequentialism may demand more than would be required by mere compliance with those rules.

The rejection of the Compliance Condition does not entail the wholesale rejection of Collective Consequentialism, as many versions of the latter reject the former. Furthermore, as Murphy himself notes, 'for any theory that merely happens to satisfy the Compliance Condition, it may be possible to avoid Mulgan's complaints by making revisions'.[22] This option is not available to Murphy, as his principle is explicitly designed to meet the Compliance Condition.

However, as we saw in Chapter 3, forms of Collective Consequentialism that avoid the Compliance Condition face many problems of their own. Nor does this seem to be a coincidence. Many problems for Rule Consequentialism are caused by the very features of the theory that distinguish it from the Compliance Condition, such as Brandt's exception clauses and Hooker's emphasis on the flexibility of rules. Rejection of the Compliance Condition thus poses the following dilemma for Collective Consequentialism.

Let T be any Collective Consequentialist theory. Either T complies with the Compliance Condition, or it does not. If T does comply with the condition, then T will be unacceptable, as demonstrated in Section 4.6. If T does not comply with the condition, then T will be subject to objections analogous to those raised in Chapter 3 of this book. In either case, T will be unacceptable.

To resolve this dilemma, Collective Consequentialists must construct a new theory (T*) such that (1) T* does not comply with the Compliance Condition; (2) T* is radically different from contemporary Rule Consequentialism; and (3) T* is a form of Collective Consequentialism. It is very hard to prove that no such theory exists, principally because it is virtually impossible to specify a set of necessary conditions a theory must satisfy to count as a form of Collective Consequentialism. However, we can tentatively conclude, from the extensive discussion in Chapter 3, that T* will be very difficult to find. At the very least, if T* does exist, then it will be very different from any extant moral theory.

---

[22] Murphy, 'A Relatively Plausible Principle of Beneficence', p. 24.

4.8. Towards a Consequentialist Pluralism

We have seen that, when presented as a full account of benevolence, Collective Consequentialism fails. The natural reaction would be to jettison it altogether. In this final section, I shall suggest some reasons for resisting this temptation.

I began Part Two of this book by noting the appealing simplicity of Consequentialism: the whole of morality is reduced to the single project of making the world a better place. It has become something of a commonplace in moral philosophy to regard this simplicity as more of a vice than a virtue. Morality is not a simple business, and so much the worse for any theory that says that it is. One Consequentialist response is to restrict the ambitions of the theory: we are no longer providing a full account of morality, but merely an account of one part of it—namely, the part called 'benevolence'. Our Consequentialist account of benevolence can then be combined with Non-Consequentialist elements in a pluralistic moral theory. This, indeed, is the context in which Murphy places his own principle.[23]

One response to our discussion of Collective Consequentialism is to further limit the theory's ambitions. Individual Consequentialism and Collective Consequentialism present themselves as rivals, each striving to provide a full account of benevolence. I have argued that Collective Consequentialism is unequal to this task. However, the Compliance Condition is not without its intuitive appeal. It does seem to delineate and characterize an important set of moral projects. Perhaps the best solution is to see the two conceptions of benevolence, not as competitors, but as collaborators, each describing an important but distinct form of moral project. On this new account, we have a pluralist story, not just about morality, but also about benevolence. Just as benevolence is not the whole of morality, so the cooperative projects falling under the Compliance Condition are not the whole of benevolence. More ambitiously, I suggest in Part Four that this new pluralist account of benevolence enables us to resurrect the claim that benevolence *is* the whole of morality.

Deflating the exclusive question 'A or B?' with the inclusive answer 'Let us have both!' is apt to look like a cop-out. And it is certainly true that moving from monism to pluralism invariably raises more questions than it answers. If benevolence is not a single project, but a whole cluster of projects, some individual and some collective, what is the relationship between these components? Are all of them compulsory projects (that is, projects that no benevolent agent would omit)? Or do moral agents have some legitimate moral

---

[23] Murphy, 'The Demands of Beneficence', p. 281, see n. 27.

discretion over which types of benevolent project they will undertake? Does the move from a monistic account of benevolence (either individual or collective) to a beneficent pluralism render Consequentialism more or less demanding?

I address these questions in Part Four of this book. At this point I claim only that, in the light of the difficulties faced by Rule Consequentialism and by Murphy's Cooperative Principle, Collective Consequentialists would be better advised to pursue a pluralistic benevolence than to continue along the high road of monism. The war with Individual Consequentialism is one that Collectivists cannot win. Perhaps it is time to negotiate a truce, and divide the disputed territory accordingly.

As we saw in Chapter 2, Simple Consequentialism itself is unreasonably demanding. This may suggest that, if we abandon Collective Consequentialism, we cannot construct a plausible Consequentialist moral theory. My response is that if we are to limit the demands of Consequentialism, then we should first seek such limits within Individual Consequentialism, rather than within Collective Consequentialism.

I said at the outset that I would be developing a compromise between Individual Consequentialism and Collective Consequentialism. It may seem that the theory I am developing is not really a compromise at all, as it appears to reject Collective Consequentialism altogether. However, this is not necessarily the case. Let us assume that Individual Consequentialists have found a solution to the problem posed by the extreme demands of Consequentialism. (I discuss several such solutions in Part Three of this book.) They have thus developed a theory that does not require me to devote all my energies and resources to promoting the good. The question arises as to how I should use the resulting morally sanctioned discretion. Perhaps Collective Consequentialism can assist in addressing this question.

The simplest constrained Individual Consequentialist theory contains only a Reason to Promote the Good and a constraint on that reason. All actions within the limits of the Reason to Promote the Good would be permitted. As we shall see in Part Three of this book, such theories are insufficiently discriminating. We must supplement our limited Individual Consequentialist principle with other moral principles. These may be either Collective Consequentialist principles or Non-Consequentialist ones. There is considerable scope for Collective Consequentialist principles to constrain, require, forbid, and encourage within the boundaries of an Individual Consequentialist principle governing our obligations to meet the needs of others. Paradoxically, by limiting Individual Consequentialism, we may thus make room for Collective Consequentialism. In Part Four of this book, I develop such a Combined Consequentialist moral theory.

PART THREE

Individual Consequentialism

5

Sub-Maximizing Consequentialism

Having rejected Collective Consequentialism, we must now examine the resources of the Individual Consequentialist tradition. Individual Consequentialism begins with a demanding principle of impartial maximization. We can soften it in two ways: either by limiting that principle from within, or by constraining it from without. The former option leads to Sub-Maximizing Consequentialism, where we are no longer required to bring about the best possible outcome. The latter option leads to a Hybrid Moral theory, where a Maximizing Consequentialist principle is combined with other moral principles to produce a less demanding overall theory. Part Three examines these softer forms of Individual Consequentialism.

In this chapter, I discuss a prominent moral theory that responds to the Demandingness Objection by incorporating an explicit departure from Consequentialism within a broadly Consequentialist framework—namely, Michael Slote's *Satisficing Consequentialism*.[1] Most of my comments are directed at Slote's theory, but analogous criticisms apply equally well to any other Sub-Maximizing Consequentialist theory where a single moral principle tells us to produce good results without requiring the best. I shall conclude that Sub-Maximizing Consequentialism is unacceptable. However, by examining its failings, we discover how Consequentialist restructuring should proceed.

5.1. Slote's Argument

Slote's Satisficing Consequentialism is based on the economic notion of satisficing: (rational) economic agents may sometimes seek less than the best, may sometimes choose what is good enough (in terms of the agent's own

---

[1] In Slote, 'Satisficing Consequentialism'; Slote, *Commonsense Morality and Consequentialism*; and Slote, *Beyond Optimizing*. For critiques of Slote's position, see Mintoff, 'Slote on Rational Dilemmas and Rational Supererogation'; Mulgan, 'Slote's Satisficing Consequentialism'; Mulgan, 'How Satisficers Get away with Murder'; Pettit, 'Satisficing Consequentialism'; and Pettit, 'Slote on Consequentialism'. Other good discussions of satisficing include Hurka, 'Consequentialism and Content'; Hurka, 'Two Kinds of Satisficing'; Hurka, *Perfectionism*, pp. 55–60; and Swanton, 'Satisficing and Virtue'. Slote himself has since abandoned Satisficing Consequentialism, in favour of a form of virtue ethics. (See esp. Slote, *From Morality to Virtue*.)

interests), without regard for whether what they have chosen is the best thing (outcome) available in the circumstances.

Call this behaviour 'economic satisficing'. Similarly, moral satisficers claim that moral agents may sometimes seek less than the best, may sometimes choose what is good enough (in terms of moral value), without regard for whether what they have chosen is the best thing (outcome) available in the circumstances.

The most familiar form of moral satisficing is the following.

Strategic Moral Satisficing.   Maximizing agents should adopt satisficing procedures because these will produce better results than maximizing procedures. For instance, if time is short, it may be best just to take the first 'good-enough' option that turns up, rather than laboriously calculating the exact value of each option.

Many Consequentialists accept some form of Strategic Moral Satisficing.[2] In Chapter 2, I argued that strategic satisficing alone is not sufficient to enable Consequentialists to defeat the Demandingness Objection. Any satisficing procedure adopted as the most efficient way to optimize value will still be very demanding.

Slote, however, goes beyond Strategic Moral Satisficing. He also accepts the following.

Blatant Moral Satisficing.   Even when the agent already knows which particular act is best from a Consequentialist perspective, she is still perfectly justified in selecting any other act which is good enough.

Slote thus supports satisficing even when it is not a strategy for maximizing. In other words, Slote advocates satisficing as a criterion of the moral rightness of acts, not just as a decision procedure that might be recommended by those who adopt a maximizing criterion of rightness.

Slote begins with the general suggestion that Consequentialist morality should be analogous to economic rationality. This leads him to the following two theses.[3]

The Analogy Thesis.   If blatant economic satisficing is a rational way for economic agents to pursue their goals in certain circumstances, then Consequentialism should accept blatant moral satisficing in similar circumstances.

---

[2] See e.g. Pettit and Brennan, 'Restrictive Consequentialism', pp. 444–6.
[3] The formulations and names of all theses and principles are my own.

The Economic Thesis.   Blatant economic satisficing is often a rational way for economic agents to act.

These theses combine to produce the following further claim.

The Satisficing Thesis.   Consequentialists must accept some blatant moral satisficing.

This thesis in turn allows Slote to reply to the Demandingness Objection. Slote would agree that the objection defeats a theory based on a Maximizing Consequentialist criterion of rightness, even if that theory incorporates Strategic Moral Satisficing within its decision procedure. However, he claims that Satisficing Consequentialists can defeat the objection. By employing an appropriate notion of the 'morally good enough', Consequentialists can use blatant moral satisficing to avoid unreasonable demands. The remainder of this chapter is an evaluation of this claim.

5.2. Common Objections to Slote

One common response to Slote's argument is to reject the Economic Thesis, to deny that blatant economic satisficing is ever rational. Most economists advocate only Strategic Satisficing, and not Blatant Satisficing. For instance, in his discussion of rational institutional behaviour, Herbert Simon concludes that it is not always rational to seek to maximize and that institutions should instead be satisfied with attaining a certain 'aspiration level'. However, he explicitly says that 'when a firm has alternatives open to it that are at or above its aspiration level, it will choose the best of those known to be available'.[4]

Simon thus rejects Blatant Satisficing. Following Simon, Philip Pettit suggests that Slote's position is incoherent, as 'it is not clear what it can mean to rank A above B if when other things are equal one insists on choosing B'.[5]

At this point, we should note an ambiguity in the notion of Satisficing. This is the distinction between the strong claim that an agent can have a reason to *choose* B over A (when A is better than B), and the weaker claim that, although the agent can give no reason for choosing B over A, she is still (rationally) permitted to *pick* B instead of A. As originally formulated, Pettit's argument tells only against the stronger claim, as proponents of the weaker claim can accept that the agent has no reason to choose B rather than A. However, Slote often

---

[4] Simon, 'Theories of Decision Making', p. 264.
[5] Pettit, 'Satisficing Consequentialism', p. 173. For a defence of Slote against Pettit's charge of irrationality, see Swanton, 'Satisficing and Virtue'.

speaks as if he intends the stronger claim, especially as some of his examples appear to turn on the idea that moderation is a virtue (and, hence, a source of reasons for action). More importantly, Pettit's argument can be modified to deal with the weaker claim as well. If we accept that A's being better than B gives the agent a reason for choosing A over B, then proponents of the weaker view must give us some reason why, in the absence of a counter-vailing reason to choose B over A, the agent is allowed to pick B. Pettit's argument would then be that no such reason can be given, as the idea of picking A over B without reason only makes sense if A and B are effectively identical (as, for instance, when I pick one of two identical cans of soup). As the same reasons are likely to be suggested in either case, it is convenient to retain Pettit's original formulation.

Pettit supports his attack on Blatant Satisficing as follows:

Suppose that an agent ranks A above B . . . whereas he could have given a reason for choosing A . . . he can give no reason for choosing B. It will not do for him to say simply that B is good enough. That might be a reason for him to go for B, if he were unaware of the nature or value of alternatives. It is not a reason for him to choose B rather than A.[6]

In response, Slote argues that we *can* find reasons to support blatant economic satisficing.[7] He offers two candidate reasons:

1. the agent does not need more; and
2. the agent is perfectly satisfied with her present state.

Slote argues that either of these could provide an agent with a reason to choose B rather than A, even when the only salient difference between the two options is that A is 'better' (for the agent) than B.

I propose not to discuss Slote's reasons at this point. Rather, I shall later use them to impale him on the horns of a dilemma. If Slote uses his two reasons to defend the claim that blatant economic satisficing is sometimes rational, then he can no longer claim that Consequentialist morality is analogous to economic rationality. This is because, whatever the fate of Slote's reasons in their original context, they have no acceptable moral analogues. Slote will be forced to reject either the Analogy Thesis or the Economic Thesis. Either way, his arguments in favour of the claim that Satisficing Consequentialism is not unreasonably demanding will be dissolved.

[6] Pettit, 'Satisficing Consequentialism', p. 172.
[7] These are given in Slote, *Beyond Optimizing*, pp. 21–2.

5.3. A Moral Counter-Example

Slote's claim is that blatant moral satisficing can be used to rebut the Demandingness Objection. This objection arises because there are times when agents can leave room for their own projects only by producing significantly less good than they could if they concentrated on promoting the good. Maximizing Consequentialism cannot permit this. Slote replies that Satisficing Consequentialism leaves room for personal interests and projects. To show this, he must first establish that it is sometimes acceptable to do much less good than one could, simply on the grounds that one has produced enough good already. I shall argue that we cannot accept this.

Consider the following story.

The Magic Game. Achilles is locked in a room, with a single door. In front of him is a computer screen, with a number on it (call it n), and a numerical keypad. Achilles knows that n is the number of people who are living below the poverty line. He also knows that, as soon as he enters a number into the computer, that number of people will be raised above the poverty line (at no cost to Achilles) and the door will open. There is no other way of opening the door. Because of the mechanics of the machine, any door-opening number takes as much time and effort to enter (negligible) as any other.

Achilles enters a number (p) that, although fairly large, is significantly less than n. We ask him why he opted not to raise a further $n-p$ people above the poverty line. He replies that he is a Satisficing Consequentialist who thinks that saving p people from poverty in one day is 'good enough'. He thus sees no reason to save more people, and does not think he has done anything wrong.

Achilles' choice is morally unacceptable. If he really could have saved more people from poverty at absolutely no cost to himself, then he should have done so. His justification of his choice is, on the face of it, absurd.

It may be objected that I am being unfair to Slote. My story is, of course, implausible, incomplete, and, quite possibly, impossible. However, the Magic Game is effectively identical to one of Slote's own fairy stories.[8]

The Dead Warrior. Eric, a great warrior, dies and arrives in Valhalla. The gods reward him by offering to grant any wish he makes. Eric asks that his family and their descendants be made 'fairly well off' for the rest of their lives. The gods ask him if he means as well off as possible. 'No,' Eric replies, 'I think fairly well off would be good enough.'

---

[8] Ibid. 27.

Slote endorses Eric's choice. He argues that Eric has done nothing wrong by not requesting that his family be made as well off as possible. He does enough by ensuring that they will be fairly well off.

However, Slote ignores another, more serious, dimension in which Eric satisfices. Eric requests benefits *only* for his family. This is suboptimal, as he could have considered everyone else. In particular, he could have asked that the many people who are (or will be) living in poverty or misery also be made fairly well off. Once this dimension is noted, the similarity to Achilles' story is striking. One small disanalogy between the two stories as they stand is that Eric is able to choose which people will be saved, whereas Achilles is not. However, nothing turns on this, as we can easily add an additional feature to Achilles' machine, allowing him to make that choice at no additional cost. This alteration would not render Achilles' refusal to save everyone from poverty morally acceptable.

Slote's defence of Eric's choice is based on the following principle: 'Ordinary morality permits one sometimes to do less than the most or best one can do for others as long as what one does produces a large or sufficient amount of good for others'.[9] Our discussion suggests that in the context of Slote's own example his notion of 'large or sufficient amount of good for others' is ambiguous between the following two interpretations.

The Individual Interpretation.   One does a large or sufficient amount of good for others if and only if one produces a large or sufficient amount of good *for each individual* who is in a position to benefit from one's actions.

The Total Interpretation.   One does a large or sufficient amount of good for others if and only if the total amount of good one produces *for other people in general* is above a certain threshold.

In his discussion of Eric, Slote seems to adopt the Individual Interpretation. We do not blame Eric for not requesting additional benefits *for his family*, as he has already provided enough benefit *for them*. However, Eric's family are not the only people affected by his satisficing. Everyone else loses out too. Eric fails to do the best he can for many people for whom he has not produced any benefits at all.

Under the Individual Interpretation, for any given person, Eric is permitted to do less than the best he can for that person if and only if he has already produced a large or sufficient amount of good for that particular person. There are many people for whom this is not the case. Consider a person living in poverty and misery (call her Pauper). In making his choice, Eric could request a greater benefit for Pauper than he does. He is only allowed to

---

[9] These are given in Slote, *Beyond Optimizing*, pp. 21–2.

do this if he is already providing a 'large or sufficient amount of good' for Pauper. But Eric has not done any good for Pauper at all. So Eric's action will not be permitted under the Individual Interpretation.

To satisfy the Individual Interpretation, Eric would have to produce a large or sufficient amount of good for *each* individual. The following request would suffice: please make everyone who will ever live satisfactorily well off. Unfortunately, this request would undermine the claim that Satisficing Consequentialism is not unreasonably demanding. To establish that claim, Slote must argue as follows: Eric is in a situation where he can (costlessly) do as much good as possible. In that situation, Eric acts on a satisficing maxim. That maxim is morally acceptable. Acting on that maxim would not be too demanding in our everyday lives. So morality need not be too demanding.

If Eric is to satisfy the Individual Interpretation, then he must be using the following maxim: 'You do not have to make everyone maximally well off. It is enough to make everyone who will ever live fairly well off. Once you have done that, you can get on with your own personal projects.' Given the state of our world, following this maxim would, in practice, be every bit as demanding as Maximizing Consequentialism. It would leave us no time at all for our personal projects, as there would always be someone who was not fairly well off and whom we were in a position to help.

If we want to use Eric's story to establish that Satisficing Consequentialism is not unreasonably demanding, we must turn to the Total Interpretation. Under that interpretation, I am allowed to refrain from (costlessly) providing the greatest possible benefit to a particular person even if I have not provided that particular person with any benefit at all, so long as the total amount of good I have provided to other individuals is sufficiently great.

Unfortunately, proponents of the Total Interpretation must approve of Achilles' behaviour. To see this, let G be the amount of good beyond which I am allowed to refrain from assisting people, let g be the amount of good produced by raising one person from poverty[10] and let m be the smallest whole number such that $mg > G$ (that is, raising m people from poverty would produce at least G amount of good). So long as he makes p (the number of people he saves from poverty) at least equal to m, Achilles can thus ensure that he does enough good to satisfy the Total Interpretation. He will then be absolved from providing any benefits to anyone else. m must be significantly less than n. Otherwise, it would be impossible to do enough good without saving nearly everyone from poverty, which would undermine the claim that Satisficing Consequentialism is not unreasonably demanding.

[10] This argument makes the simplifying assumption that each person's rise from poverty has the same value, but nothing of substance turns on this.

Slote must endorse Achilles' choice, for he cannot establish that Satisficing Consequentialism is not unreasonably demanding without adopting the Total Interpretation, under which that choice is acceptable. Yet it seems absurd to sanction Achilles' behaviour. Achilles refuses (costlessly) to provide a vital good to a vast number of people. Those people's needs clearly provide Achilles with a reason for providing those goods. Achilles must respond either by producing a positive argument in favour of the action he performs, or by producing a negative argument demonstrating that he is permitted to ignore such a strong reason to act otherwise. Yet Achilles cannot produce such reasons.

5.4. Slote's Moral Reasons

Perhaps we should not be so hasty. After all, in analogous cases, Slote claimed to find a reason for blatant economic satisficing. Perhaps he will be able to find similar reasons in the moral case as well. To establish that Satisficing Consequentialism is not unreasonably demanding, Slote must demonstrate that there is a certain number (q) that satisfies the following two conditions:

1. saving q people from poverty is 'morally good enough', even if one could have saved more than q people at no cost to oneself;
2. saving q people from poverty would not place an unreasonable demand on my resources.

If we can find some q which meets both these requirements, then by setting p equal to q, we can provide Achilles with a morally acceptable reason for his action.

In the economic case, Slote offered the following two reasons for blatant satisficing, which can be treated either as reasons to satisfice or as reasons why satisficing is permitted.

No Need.   The agent does not need more.

Satisfaction.   The agent is perfectly satisfied with her present state.

We must now ask if analogous reasons can be found in the case of blatant moral satisficing. We begin with the argument from No Need. This seems to have the following moral analogues.

No Agent Need.   The agent does not need more.

No Dearest Need.   The agent's nearest and dearest do not need more.

No Human Need.   No one at all needs more.

Agent Need and Dearest Need are both absent in Achilles' case. Neither he nor his family need anyone else to be saved. Unfortunately, such absence of need is not, in itself, a morally acceptable reason. Morality cannot be just a matter of considering your own needs and those of your nearest and dearest. It also requires you to take account of the needs of others. You cannot decline (costlessly) to provide a benefit for someone else simply because you do not need them to have that benefit: you must also ask if *they* need it.

I do not deny that people are often permitted to refuse to provide certain benefits. I deny only that such permissions can arise simply because the agent does not need the benefit to be conferred. Of course, there could be moral theories constructed solely out of special, personal obligations. However, as I said in Chapter 1, no plausible morality can give no weight at all to the needs of persons beyond the agent's immediate circle. Any such theory will certainly be rejected in the Consequentialist tradition.

The argument from No Human Need looks more promising. It is at least plausible to say that, once you have taken care of all the needs of everyone affected by your actions, your moral obligations are fully discharged. However, Human Need is not absent in Achilles' case. He leaves many people in poverty. People need to be saved from poverty. This argument thus cannot give Achilles a reason for not saving everyone from poverty.

Moreover, the argument from No Human Need could not provide the basis for an undemanding morality. It tells us that we can pursue our own personal projects only once every need of every person is met. In practice, this would render the Total Interpretation as demanding as the Individual Interpretation, as there will always be unmet needs we could meet. The argument from No Need cannot support an acceptable moral theory with moderate demands.

Slote's first argument cannot provide Achilles with a credible reason for his blatant moral satisficing. All possible interpretations are either morally unacceptable or not applicable to Achilles' situation. We turn now to Slote's second reason, the argument from Satisfaction. Once again, there are several moral analogues:

Agent Satisfaction.   The agent is perfectly satisfied with the present state of the world.

Dearest Satisfaction.   The agent's nearest and dearest are perfectly satisfied with the present state of the world.

Universal Satisfaction.   Everyone is perfectly satisfied with the present state of the world.

Ideal Satisfaction.   An ideal moral observer would be perfectly satisfied with the present state of the world.

The first three arguments will fare no better than the analogous arguments concerning need. Agent Satisfaction and Dearest Satisfaction are not, in themselves, morally acceptable reasons. If Achilles and his family are satisfied with the world as he leaves it, then this merely reflects badly on them. On the other hand, Universal Satisfaction will clearly not be present in Achilles' case, as those who remain in poverty will be dissatisfied with the state in which he leaves the world. None of these arguments could be used to ground an acceptable morality that was not unduly demanding.

The argument from Ideal Satisfaction looks more promising. Perhaps I am required to do only enough to satisfy an ideal moral observer. However, an ideal moral observer would presumably not be satisfied with a situation where many people were living in poverty. Such a state might be satisfactory if it were preferable to every available alternative. But Achilles' alternatives include situations with no one in poverty. Faced with such alternatives, an ideal moral observer would not be satisfied if some people remain in poverty.

Defenders of Achilles might reply that, while an ideal moral observer would not be satisfied with the way Achilles leaves the world, such an observer might nonetheless be satisfied with what Achilles has done. Whatever the plausibility of this line of argument, it is incompatible with Slote's approach, as he seeks justifications for satisficing that are grounded in features of outcomes, not in features of agents. It must be the outcome, and not the action, that is satisfactory. (As the Ideal Satisfaction Argument is unacceptable on other grounds, we need not discuss other objections to ideal observer theories in ethics.)

Neither of Slote's reasons for economic satisficing has an acceptable moral analogue. In practice, the Total Interpretation will be no less exacting than the Individual Interpretation. Slote is thus unable to produce a morality that is significantly less demanding than Maximizing Consequentialism.

5.5. Slote's Mistake

Slote may be able to find another justification for Achilles' action. However, it is hard to see what this might be. This is because Slote's position rests on a mistaken analogy between rationality and morals. In general, there are three separate domains to which the notion of 'good enough' may be applied.

Outcome. The situation that resulted once the action had been performed was 'good enough'.

Contribution. The agent's contribution (the difference she made to the outcome) was 'good enough'.

Cost or Effort. The agent expended enough energy, paid a high enough price, ran enough of a risk, and so on.

In discussions of economic rationality we usually speak of 'good enough' results: 'I was satisfied with that outcome, it was good enough.' In his ethical discussion Slote appears to be focusing on the agent's contribution, but his reasons are more relevant to the outcome itself. If the fact that certain needs have been met is sufficient to absolve me from further contributions to the good, then, in a situation where those needs are already met before I act, I do not have to make any contribution. If things are satisfactory before I start, I do not have to do any good at all.

We could rewrite Slote's reasons in terms of contributions rather than outcomes. Borrowing a distinction from Thomas Hurka,[11] we can distinguish two ways an agent's contribution might be said to be 'good enough'. On the first ('absolute') interpretation, a contribution is good enough if and only if it is above a certain absolute threshold. This threshold would be the same for all agents and in all situations. On the second ('comparative') interpretation, an agent contributes enough if and only if she produces at least a certain proportion of the maximum contribution available to her in her situation.

Unfortunately, for Slote's purposes, neither notion of 'good-enough' contribution is any more promising than the notion of 'good-enough' outcome. To see this, we need only return to Achilles' story. There is no threshold beyond which Achilles has a legitimate reason not (costlessly) to rescue more people from poverty. Similarly, there is no percentage of his maximum contribution beyond which Achilles has a legitimate reason not (costlessly) to go.

Slote's reasons fail because the notion of 'good enough' that gives his position its intuitive appeal is not one related to either outcomes or contributions. Rather, it is the notion encapsulated by such turns of phrase as: 'she should have a rest, she's done enough good for one day'; and 'we couldn't expect any greater sacrifice—it was a good enough effort'. Yet, here, the 'good enough' refers, not to the agent's contribution, nor to the outcome resulting from that contribution, but to the effort required to produce that outcome. In other words, 'good enough' is used in sense (3), not in either of senses (1) and (2). To see this, consider the following story.

Two Doctors. Speedy and Steady are two doctors working in an overstretched emergency ward. They both start work at time t when many patients require urgent treatment. Steady tires easily and is not a fast worker. At time $t+1$, Steady is exhausted and takes a rest having treated m patients, leaving many patients requiring treatment. Speedy is extremely fit and works

---

[11] Hurka, 'Two Kinds of Satisficing', p. 108.

fast. At time $t+2$, Speedy has treated $2m$ patients and is still feeling refreshed. However, Speedy takes a rest anyway, leaving behind a few patients who require treatment.

I suggest that, in this situation, Steady's decision is justified whereas Speedy's is not. Steady stops because she is exhausted and needs a rest. Speedy takes a rest without needing one, leaving vital work undone. However, if we focus on either outcomes or contributions, then we cannot reach this conclusion. The overall situation is better at $t+2$ than at $t+1$, while in absolute terms Speedy's contribution is greater than Steady's. We may also assume that, because she stops when only a few patients require treatment, Speedy's contribution is higher as a percentage of the maximum contribution available to her than is Steady's. We thus cannot approve of Steady's rest without also approving of Speedy's rest. This result is unacceptable.

When assessing Steady and Speedy, we do not think that a doctor is entitled to a rest simply because she has cured n people today or because n people have been cured today, irrespective of whether or not she needs a rest. Rather, we think that she is entitled to a rest because she has expended y amount of energy in healing people, irrespective of how many people she has healed or of how many people have been healed overall. It is the effort, not the result, that is good enough. Similarly, when someone pays a 'high-enough' price, we excuse him from further danger because it would be unreasonable to expect a greater sacrifice. The question of how much good that sacrifice achieved is of secondary importance. (Of course, the degree of effort involved cannot be the only relevant factor, as sacrifices that are not normally required may become necessary when particularly urgent consequences are at stake. For instance, a given level of sacrifice might be required to save another person's life, but not to save him from inconvenience.)

It is tempting to think that Slote can construct a Satisficing Consequentialism based on the notion of 'good-enough effort'. However, this move would undermine his reply to the Demandingness Objection. Slote seeks to show that morality does not place unreasonable demands upon moral agents. His original theory provides an explanation: morality does not make unreasonable demands, because it never requires that agents produce more than a certain amount of good. Here, the limit on the costs an agent can be asked to bear is explained by appealing to a feature of the outcome of her actions. This is both an *explanation* and a *Consequentialist* explanation. If we turn instead to the notion of 'good-enough' effort or 'high-enough' cost, our reply to the Demandingness Objection is as follows: morality does not place unreasonable demands upon agents because it never requires them to make too great a sacrifice. We might as well say that morality does not place unreasonable demands upon agents, because morality never makes un-reasonable demands. This is not an explanation. Nor is it obvious that the resulting theory will be genuinely Consequentialist, as it defines moral obligations in terms of costs to the agent, not just in terms of features of outcomes. Replacing 'good-enough outcome' with 'good-enough effort' is not a plausible move for the Satisficing Consequentialist.

5.6. Doing, Allowing, and Satisficing

In this section, I present a second objection to Satisficing Consequentialism, based on the following tale.[12]

Mary's Choice.   Mary is standing on a bridge over a railway line. A trolley car-rying ten people is travelling along the railway line, and is about to pass under the bridge. Unfortunately, heavy rain has washed away the section of railway track after the bridge. If Mary cannot stop the trolley, then it will plunge over a cliff, and all ten people will die. Fortunately, Mary is not alone on the bridge. With her are two sand bags (one heavier than the other) and Bob (an in-nocent bystander). Mary can stop the trolley only by throwing something in its path. Her options, and their results, are as follows:

1. Throw the heavier sand bag. The trolley stops. All ten people are saved.
2. Throw the lighter sand bag. The trolley teeters on the edge. Two people fall out and die. Everyone else is saved.
3. Throw Bystander Bob off the bridge. Bob attempts to evade the oncom-ing trolley. As a result, his body only half falls on the tracks. The trolley runs over Bob, killing him instantly, and then stops just as it reaches the cliff. It teeters very slightly on the edge. One person falls out and dies. The other nine are saved.
4. Throw herself off the bridge. The trolley runs over Mary, killing her instantly. Unfortunately, the trolley still plunges over the cliff, as Mary's body is too light to stop it. All ten people die.
5. Shoot Bystander Bob in the head. Bob dies instantly. His body falls in the middle of the tracks. The trolley runs over Bob, and then stops well before it reaches the cliff. All ten people aboard the trolley are saved.
6. Do nothing. The trolley plunges over the cliff, and all ten people are killed.

---

[12] This example is based on the famous 'Trolley Case'. For the original example, see Foot, 'The Problem of Abortion'. See also Thomson, 'The Trolley Problem'.

Mary is a brilliant engineer, able to predict all of the above consequences. She knows exactly what will happen if she throws each particular thing off the bridge. She also knows that, if she does not throw something off the bridge, ten people will perish.

It seems obvious that Mary ought to throw the heavier sand bag, thereby saving all ten people. However, under Satisficing Consequentialism, Mary will be permitted to throw the lighter bag instead, as this produces a good-enough outcome. (If saving eight lives is not good enough, then we can retell the story with different numbers. As the discussion of the Magic Game story demonstrates, there must be some version of Mary's Choice in which Satisficing Consequentialism permits her to throw the lighter bag.)

This result is embarrassing enough for Satisficing Consequentialism. However, things are actually even worse. If Mary is permitted to throw the lighter sand bag, on the grounds that this produces a good enough result, then she must also be permitted to perform any other action that produces at least as good a result overall. Pushing a living Bob off the bridge produces exactly as good a result, as it leads to two deaths, rather than ten. This represents a net saving of eight lives.

We can thus construct a story where pushing a living Bob off the bridge is morally acceptable under Satisficing Consequentialism. If this was not bad enough, observe that shooting Bob in the head produces an even better result than pushing the lighter sand bag, as it leaves only one person dead as opposed to two. Therefore, if Mary is permitted to throw the lighter bag, then she must also be permitted to shoot Bystander Bob.

According to Satisficing Consequentialism, Mary thus does nothing wrong if she shoots Bystander Bob in the head, rather than throwing down the heavy sand bag. Because the theory focuses entirely on the overall amount of good produced by an agent, it will sanction acts that *do* considerable harm to some particular individual(s), so long as the overall result is good enough. For the Satisficing Consequentialist, there is no moral difference between killing someone and allowing him to die. If Satisficing were recommended merely as an efficient decision procedure for maximizing Consequentialism, then this conclusion might be avoided. Satisficing would be one component of the optimal decision procedure, which might also include a rule of thumb prohibiting agents from needlessly killing innocent people.

Of course, Satisficing Consequentialism is hardly the only moral theory to have problems with the distinction between doing and allowing. Maximizing Act Consequentialism also notoriously ignores the distinction. Agents are required to kill others if this produces the best available result. Furthermore,

Shelly Kagan has argued that Samuel Scheffler's Hybrid Moral Theory fares even worse, as it permits agents to kill innocent people in pursuit of their own personal projects, even if they could produce a better outcome by not killing. (Kagan's argument is discussed in Section 6.4.1.)

However, each of these other theories can provide at least some justification for its position. Simple Consequentialism permits killing only when this will produce the optimal result. Scheffler sanctions killing only when this is necessary for the agent to pursue her own projects. We may not be ultimately convinced by these justifications, but they at least appeal to recognizably significant moral considerations. Yet Satisficing Consequentialism can offer no such justification. It permits an agent to kill innocent people even if this promotes neither the agent's own projects nor the impersonal good. Indeed, Satisficing Consequentialism permits the killing of innocents when this serves no purpose at all.

Perhaps we can sometimes allow agents to kill in order to promote the good. Perhaps we can even occasionally permit agents to kill in the pursuit of their own interests. Theories that produce these results may turn out to be unacceptable, but they are not necessarily absurd. But surely there is something absurd about a moral theory that sanctions the pointless killing of innocent people. Satisficing Consequentialism does just that. Therefore, it is an unacceptable moral theory.

Satisficers may offer the justification that killing is permitted because it produces a good-enough result. However, this justification is much weaker than those of Scheffler or the Maximizer. These other justifications point to some desirable result that can be brought about only by killing. By contrast, Satisficing Consequentialism allows an agent to kill even when she could produce a good-enough result without killing. Suppose we ask why Mary kills Bob. 'To produce a good-enough result' provides no justification, as we want to know why she chose killing over some other way of producing a good-enough result.[13]

Satisficing Consequentialists are also unable to avail themselves of a defence available to Simple Consequentialists. The latter will argue that Mary would be allowed to sacrifice Bystander Bob only if this produced the best available outcome. However, as every agent is morally obliged to seek to bring about the best possible outcome, this would mean that Bob was

---

[13] One reader notes that Maximizing Consequentialism also 'allows killings even when they are not necessary to produce optimal results. For instance, in certain cases where results are tied-best.' However, these would presumably be cases where the negative effect of killing an innocent person was balanced by other desirable features that could not have been produced without killing. Otherwise, killing could not be tied-best. By contrast, there is nothing desirable that Mary can achieve only by killing Bob.

obliged to sacrifice himself. A Simple Consequentialist Mary would thus merely be forcing Bob to do his moral duty.[14] By contrast, our original Satisficing Consequentialist Mary forces Bob to perform a suboptimal sacrifice. Bob is not obliged to jump, as he could have thrown down a sand bag instead. Forcing someone to do his moral duty is arguably far less of an outrage than forcing him to make a supererogatory sacrifice.

5.7. General Lessons about Sub-Maximization

Our discussion thus far has focused on Slote's particular theory. However, the objections presented above apply equally well to any other Sub-Maximizing Consequentialism. Each of our two thought experiments (the Magic Game and Mary's Choice) relies only on two basic features of Slote's theory: (i) the fact that it assesses acts solely in terms of the values of outcomes, and (ii) the fact that it permits any act that produces a good enough outcome overall. These two features seem to be necessary components of any Sub-Maximizing Consequentialism. The first is the general Consequentialist commitment to promote the good, which sub-maximizers retain; while the second feature represents the rejection of maximization, the sub-maximizer's sole departure from that general commitment.

If our counter-examples prove fatal for Slote's Satisficing Consequentialism, then they will also rule out any sub-maximizing theory presented as an alternative criterion of rightness. On the other hand, we saw in Chapter 2 that, if sub-maximization is merely presented as an appropriate decision procedure for maximizers, then the resulting theory cannot defeat the Demandingness Objection. Accordingly, sub-maximization cannot solve the objection.

The real lesson to be learnt from the thought experiments presented in this chapter is that moral agents are sometimes required to do what will maximally promote the good. If we believe that agents are not usually required to maximize the good, then we need a principled way of distinguishing cases such as the Magic Game and Mary's Choice from more everyday situations. The remainder of this book seeks such a principled rationale.

---

[14] This defence of Consequentialism is suggested by Joseph Raz, himself no Consequentialist. See his *The Morality of Freedom*, pp. 273–4.

5.8. Scalar Morality

Slote also suggests another departure from Maximizing Consequentialism. This is Scalar Consequentialism, which replaces traditional Consequentialist notions of right and wrong with an account of 'better' and 'worse'. Instead of saying that acts that produce certain outcomes are wrong, Scalar Consequentialism compares pairs of acts in terms of their consequences. The better act is the one that produces the more valuable outcome.[15]

Scalar Consequentialism might take two distinct forms. The first combines an account of better and worse acts with a more traditional account of wrongness. For instance, we might combine Scalar Consequentialism with Satisficing Consequentialism. All acts with good-enough outcomes are permitted, but some such acts are better than others. We might call this theory *Partial Scalar Consequentialism*. This does not appear to be Slote's suggestion. His Scalar Consequentialism dispenses with a separate account of rightness. It only tells us whether a given act is better or worse than others. It might thus be dubbed *Pure Scalar Consequentialism*.

Neither of these two versions of Scalar Consequentialism is adequate, as the two thought experiments discussed in this chapter demonstrate. Assume that Achilles fails costlessly to raise additional people above the poverty line, and that Mary shoots Bystander Bob in the head. It is surely not enough to say that these characters could have done better. They both behave wrongly. (By contrast, many people are inclined to say that, while Affluent could have done better, her actions are not wrong.) No acceptable moral theory will deny that Achilles and Mary behave wrongly. Yet both versions of Scalar Consequentialism yield this result. Therefore, neither is an acceptable moral theory.

5.9. Conclusions

Even if blatant economic satisficing is occasionally rational, an act is never acceptable simply because it is an instance of blatant moral satisficing. More generally, sub-maximization is not a satisfactory account of the connection between the morality of actions and the values of outcomes. Consequentialists seeking to rebut the Demandingness Objection must look elsewhere. Our discussion suggests that they should concentrate on features of the agent (her efforts or the costs of her actions) and not just on features of outcomes (either the outcome itself or the agent's contribution to that outcome).

---

[15] Slote, *Commonsense Morality and Consequentialism*, pp. 76–91.

However, Consequentialists must also be wary of straying too far from their roots. Their real challenge will be to do full justice to agent-centred features without effectively abandoning Consequentialism altogether. Our discussion suggests that this will not be easy. For instance, Collective Consequentialists (and others who seek to rebut the Demandingness Objection by departing from Simple Consequentialism) may face the same dilemma as Satisficing Consequentialists. Appeals to features of outcomes cannot provide an acceptable response to the objection, whereas appeals to features of the agent fit uneasily within a broadly Consequentialist theory. The idea of explicitly making room within Consequentialist moral theory for the cost to the agent is taken up in the next chapter.

6

Hybrid Moral Theories

Consequentialist principles are impartial, with no special place for the costs incurred by the agent. Our discussion of Satisficing Consequentialism suggests that, if we are to respond to the Demandingness Objection, we need to make room for such costs in our moral theory. We must move to a Hybrid Theory, supplementing a purely Consequentialist principle with other moral ideals. The most prominent recent attempt to construct such a theory is that of Samuel Scheffler, who seeks to make room for moral agents by building Agent Centred Prerogatives (which allow agents to refrain from maximizing the good) into a Consequentialist moral theory, without also embracing Agent Centred Restrictions (which would require agents sometimes to refrain from maximizing the good).[1]

In this chapter, I discuss various objections to Scheffler's account. I then sketch various ways the original Hybrid View might be improved to avoid these objections. These are developed further in Part Four.

6.1. Scheffler's Hybrid View

In *The Rejection of Consequentialism*, Samuel Scheffler outlines a 'Hybrid View' of ethics. Under Simple Consequentialism, the weight an agent is allowed to give to her own personal projects is in strict proportion to their impersonal value. For instance, I should only pursue a particular hobby or interest of my own to the extent that the well-being I receive from so doing is at least as great as the

---

[1] Scheffler's original presentation of the Hybrid View is in his *The Rejection of Consequentialism*. For further elaboration of the view, see Scheffler, 'Agent-Centred Restrictions, Rationality and the Virtues'; Scheffler, 'Morality's Demands and their Limits'; and Scheffler, 'Prerogatives without Restrictions'. For discussions of Scheffler's Hybrid View, see Alexander, 'Scheffler on the Independence of Agent-Centred Prerogatives from Agent-Centred Restrictions'; Bennett, 'Two Departures from Consequentialism'; Conee, 'On Seeking a Rationale'; Harris, 'A Paradoxical Departure from Consequentialism'; Harris, 'Integrity and Agent-Centered Restrictions'; Hooker, Review of S. Scheffler, *Human Morality*; Hurley, 'Scheffler's Argument for Deontology'; Hurley, 'Getting our Options Clear'; Kagan, 'Does Consequentialism Demand too Much?'; Mulgan, 'A Non-Proportional Hybrid Moral Theory'; Murphy, 'The Demands of Beneficence', esp. pp. 274–7; Myers, 'Prerogatives and Restrictions from the Cooperative Point of View'; and Schueler, 'Consequences and Agent-Centred Restrictions'.

total well-being I could generate for others by acting differently. The basis of the Hybrid View is the Agent Centred Prerogative, which 'has the effect of denying that one is always required to produce the best overall states of affairs'.[2] Scheffler goes on to say that 'a plausible Agent Centred Prerogative would allow each agent to assign certain proportionately greater weight to his own interests than to the interests of other people'.[3] The justification for such a prerogative is that it constitutes 'a structural feature whose incorporation into a moral conception embodies a rational strategy for taking account of personal independence, given one construal of the importance of that aspect of persons'.[4]

As Scheffler initially presents it, the notion of the Agent Centred Prerogative is somewhat vague. In a later article, he provides the following explication:

Suppose, in other words, that each agent were allowed to give M times more weight to his own interests than to the interests of anyone else. This would mean that an agent was permitted to perform his preferred act (call it P), provided that there was no alternative A open to him, such that (1) A would produce a better overall outcome than P, as judged from an impersonal standpoint which gives equal weight to everyone's interests, and (2) the total net loss to others of his doing P rather than A was more than M times as great as the net loss to him of doing A rather than P.[5]

To illustrate this prerogative, recall our original tale.

Affluent's Tale.   Affluent is a well-off member of a contemporary first world society, sitting at her desk with her cheque book. In front of her are two pamphlets: one from a reputable international aid organization, the other from her local theatre company. Affluent has three options: donate all her money to charity, donate most of her money to charity (and buy one or two tickets), or donate nothing (and buy several tickets).

The more Affluent gives away, the greater the cost to her of making a further donation, as she will be required to give up progressively more central elements of her lifestyle. The values and costs of her options are represented in Table 1.

TABLE 1. *Affluent's original choice*

Donation	Impersonal Value	Cost to Affluent
All of income	10,000	10
Most of income	9,900	1
Nothing	5,000	0

---

[2] Scheffler, *The Rejection of Consequentialism*, p. 5.   [3] Ibid. 20.   [4] Ibid. 67.
[5] Scheffler, 'Prerogatives without Restrictions', p. 378.

Let us assume that each agent is allowed to give 600 times more weight to her own interests than to the interests of distant strangers. Affluent is not permitted to donate nothing, as the extra impersonal value of donating most of her income rather than nothing is 4,900 times as great as the extra cost to Affluent of donating most of her income rather than nothing. As 4,900 is greater than 600, Affluent is not permitted to donate nothing rather than donating most of her income. Affluent has no Agent Centred Prerogative to donate nothing.

However, this does not mean that Affluent is required to donate all of her income. The extra value of donating all of her income rather than most of it is less than the extra cost to Affluent multiplied by the extra weighting she is allowed to give to her own interests. Affluent can donate most of her income rather than donating all of it. Yet donating all is the only option with better consequences than donating most. So Affluent does have an Agent Centred Prerogative to donate (only) most of her income.

The weighting of 600 may seem implausibly high. However, a much lower weighting would lead to almost all inhabitants of developed countries being overwhelmed by their obligations to distant strangers in the developing world. As one aim of the Hybrid View is to provide a less demanding alternative to traditional Simple Consequentialism, this would largely defeat its purpose. We should note, however, that this very high weighting means that, in everyday life, agents will always be allowed to sacrifice others in their own community in pursuit of their own ends.[6] (See Section 6.4.1 for a similar objection.) The best solution might be to adopt a variable account of M, such as that developed in Sections 9.2 and 10.3.

6.2. The Demands of the Hybrid View

Our central objection to Simple Consequentialism is that it leaves the agent too little room (time, resources, energy) for her own projects or interests. For instance, assume that Affluent donates only most of her income to charity, even though she knows that the extra money would have done far more good if sent to the charity as well. Simple Consequentialism must condemn Affluent, as she deliberately fails to maximize the good. This is unreasonably harsh.

One benefit of Scheffler's Hybrid View is that it seems to provide a more intuitively plausible response to famine relief. To see this, let us first make a number of simplifying assumptions. Assume that Affluent has available a set number of dollars (call it n), and that she can give Oxfam any number of dollars from zero to n.

[6] Myers, 'Prerogatives and Restrictions from the Cooperative Point of View', p. 136, and Brink, 'Self-Love and Altruism', p. 618.

Under the Hybrid View, we can prove that, unless Affluent is required to donate all her money to charity, there is some number of dollars between zero and n (call it x), such that (i) Affluent is permitted to donate x dollars to charity rather than donating more, (ii) Affluent is required to donate at least x dollars to charity, and (iii) the additional amount of good that would be produced by a donation of $x+1$ dollars rather than one of x dollars is equal to the cost to Affluent of donating her $(x+1)$th dollar multiplied by the extra weight Affluent is permitted to give to her own interests over the interests of anyone else (Scheffler's M). (For a detailed proof, see the Appendix.)

The Hybrid Theorist's reply to the Demandingness Objection should now be obvious. By altering the value of M (the weighting the agent is allowed to give to her own interests), we can change the value of x (the amount of money she is required to donate). By choosing an appropriate weighting we can thus ensure that the maximum donation required of Affluent is not unduly demanding.

The Hybrid View thus avoids the Demandingness Objection. Unfortunately, it is open to a number of other objections, largely relating to the different demands it makes in different circumstances. These objections are developed in the next two sections.

6.3. Another Wrong Facts Objection

In this section, I argue that, although the Hybrid View avoids the demands of Simple Consequentialism, its treatment of famine relief is subject to a version of the Wrong Facts Objection. To illustrate this, consider the following variant on our original story.

Affluent's Ignorance.   Affluent is sitting at her desk with her cheque book. She has heard a rumour that, owing to circumstances entirely beyond Oxfam's control, the effectiveness of its ongoing immunization programme (that is, the amount of good it can do for each dollar it receives) has been drastically altered. However, she does not know what the nature of the alteration has been. Indeed, she does not even know if the rumour is true. To simplify, let us say that Affluent knows that one of the following is an accurate description of the state of Oxfam's operations, but she does not know which.

> *Inefficient Oxfam.*   Oxfam's efficiency has declined to 10 per cent of its previous level, owing to the appearance of a mutant virus that is largely immune to existing treatments. Each dollar spent now produces only one-tenth as much good as before.

Normal Oxfam.   Oxfam's efficiency is unchanged.

Superefficient Oxfam.   The efficiency of Oxfam's famine-relief operations has increased tenfold, owing to a breakthrough in pharmaceutical technology. Each dollar spent now produces ten times as much good as before.

We now apply the Hybrid View to this story. Let us assume, for the sake of argument, that in Normal Oxfam the maximum sacrifice required of Affluent is 10 per cent of her income. That is, Affluent has given 10 per cent of her income to Oxfam when she reaches the point where the amount of additional utility she could gain by spending her next dollar on herself, when multiplied by the disproportionate weighting she is allowed to give to her own costs, is equal to the amount of additional value Oxfam could produce using that dollar.

In Superefficient Oxfam, the amount of additional value Oxfam could produce with any given dollar is ten times as great as in Normal Oxfam. Therefore, in Superefficient Oxfam, Affluent must continue donating until the amount of additional utility she would gain by spending her next dollar on herself is ten times as great as at the point where she stopped donating in Normal Oxfam. In other words, Affluent must keep donating money until the sacrifice of an extra dollar is ten times as great as the sacrifice involved in giving an extra dollar on top of a 10 per cent donation. To put it crudely, in Superefficient Oxfam Affluent is required to give up things that are ten times as valuable to her as those she must give up in Normal Oxfam.

Similarly, in Inefficient Oxfam, the amount of additional value Oxfam could produce with any given dollar is only one-tenth as great as in Normal Oxfam. Therefore, in Inefficient Oxfam, Affluent is required to continue donating only until the amount of additional utility she would gain by spending her next dollar on herself is one-tenth as great as at the point where she stopped donating in Normal Oxfam. To put it crudely, in Inefficient Oxfam the Agent Centred Prerogative allows Affluent to indulge in things that are only one-tenth as valuable to her as those she could indulge in in Normal Oxfam.

My claim here is not that Affluent is required to give ten times as much money in Superefficient Oxfam as in Normal Oxfam, nor that she must give only one-tenth as much in Inefficient Oxfam. Indeed, as a result of diminishing marginal utilities, the differences between the amounts of money she is required to sacrifice are likely to be less than factors of ten. However, the variations in what Affluent is required to donate will still be very great. Greater, I would suggest, than we can accept.

Many actions are forbidden in Superefficient Oxfam and permitted in Normal Oxfam. Many actions are permitted in Inefficient Oxfam and forbidden in Normal Oxfam. For instance, assume that, in Normal Oxfam, Affluent's most self-indulgent permissible exercise of her prerogative is a monthly trip to her local theatre. Now consider an activity providing nine times as much utility per dollar as that theatre trip. In Normal Oxfam this activity would clearly have been permitted. In Superefficient Oxfam it will be forbidden. Similarly, consider another activity providing only one-ninth of the utility per dollar that Affluent derives from her theatre trip. This activity will be permitted in Inefficient Oxfam, though it would clearly have been forbidden in Normal Oxfam.

For any possible degree of sacrifice there will be a version of Superefficient Oxfam where that degree of sacrifice is required of Affluent. For instance, we could retell the Superefficient Oxfam story so that the increase in Oxfam's efficiency was by a factor of 100 rather than by a factor of ten. In that case, Affluent would be required to continue donating until the marginal utility of an extra dollar was 100 times as great as the marginal utility per dollar of her theatre trip. In a more extreme version of Affluent's Ignorance, she would literally have no idea at all how much (or how little) she ought to give to Oxfam. It seems unreasonable for Affluent to be made so totally a hostage to fortune.

Under the Hybrid View, Affluent's obligations and prerogatives depend crucially on which of the three situations she is in. Affluent must resolve her ignorance before she can have any idea at all how much she is required to donate to charity. As with previous versions of the Wrong Facts Objection, my complaint here is not merely that the Hybrid View makes Affluent's obligations dependent on specific empirical facts. Rather, the problem is that the differences between our three cases should not affect those obligations in the extreme way they do on Scheffler's account. In each of the three stories, the amount of good that Affluent forgoes by acting suboptimally is much greater than the sacrifice she will be required to make by acting optimally. How much sacrifice she is required to make should not depend to so great an extent on precisely how much greater the amount of good forgone is than her level of sacrifice. Scheffler seems to make the wrong empirical questions count for too much. Affluent knows that her most efficient aid-contribution method is to write a cheque to Oxfam. She also knows that any given dollar will do far more good if donated to Oxfam than if spent on her theatre trips. Does she really need to know exactly how much more good it will do before she has any idea at all how much she's required to donate?

The most obvious reply to the Wrong Facts Objection would be simply to reject our attempts to formulate the Agent Centred Prerogative with any mathematical precision. Scheffler himself suggests that such formulations give the Hybrid View an implausible air of precision, and that no such formulation can be essential to the view itself.[7] However, if we are given no formulation at all, then we have little idea what the Hybrid View really amounts to. The Hybrid View must be presented in some detail, even if it lacks fully mathematical precision. The most fruitful strategy is to concentrate on alternative formulations of the Hybrid View, to see if any of these can avoid the Wrong Facts Objection. Furthermore, we should note that the objection does not depend upon assigning some particular value to M. It requires only the assumption that M has a constant value.

A more promising response to the Wrong Facts Objection might appeal to the idea that there are some sacrifices that can never be required. We could then deny that Affluent is always required to make much greater sacrifices whenever the amount of good she can produce increases greatly. Briefly, I see three main problems with this response. The first is that it is not obvious that, in fact, there are any financial or material sacrifices so great that they are never morally required. Secondly, even if there are some such sacrifices, morality could still be very demanding. For instance, it would surely be implausible to claim that no agent was ever required to sacrifice most of her wealth for the sake of some greater good. Yet the principal claim of the Wrong Facts Objection is not that there was no limit to the sacrifice potentially required of Affluent under the Hybrid View, but rather that the Hybrid View requires a much greater sacrifice of Affluent under certain circumstances than it does in the actual world. Unless we can rule out all significant sacrifices, we will be unable to respond effectively to this claim.

A final problem is that setting an upper limit to the sacrifices demanded of agents can only possibly provide a solution to one half of the Wrong Facts Objection. The objection that, if the amount of value at stake is dramatically reduced, too little will be required of Affluent, remains untouched. We could, of course, provide a parallel response, to the effect that a certain minimum sacrifice is required of every agent in every situation. Perhaps we should always 'give till it hurts'. However, this move threatens to render the Agent Centred Prerogative effectively redundant, as all the real work would be done by the maximum and minimum levels, not by the prerogative itself.

The Wrong Facts Objection arises because M (the amount of extra weight an agent is allowed to give to her own interests when compared to the interests of others) is held constant. We could thus avoid the objection by allowing M to vary with the amount of value at stake. We could even tie M to the difference between the value produced by making the best available donation, and the value produced by making a small donation. This revised

---

[7] Scheffler, 'Prerogatives without Restrictions', p. 378.

Hybrid View would then give us exactly the same answers in each of the three cases in Affluent's Ignorance, thus removing the objection.

This extreme view is not acceptable. It amounts, in effect, to saying that Affluent is never required to go beyond a certain level of sacrifice, irrespective of how much or how little value is at stake. If a vast amount of value is at stake, then Affluent need make only a moderate sacrifice. If virtually no value is at stake, Affluent must still make the same sacrifice. This reformulated Hybrid View asks no more to save the world than to save a single stranger from a mild headache. This seems implausible.

We could avoid this consequence by adopting a less extreme version of this reformulation, where the amount of extra weight an agent is allowed to give to her own interests over the interests of others increases with the amount of value of stake, but where the former does not increase as sharply as the latter. This middle road avoids both the original Wrong Facts Objection and the problems raised in the preceding paragraph. Under the original Hybrid View, the cost Affluent must bear is directly proportional to the amount of good at stake. The Wrong Facts Objection shows that this strict proportionality is unacceptable. If we wish to defeat the objection without abandoning the spirit of the Hybrid View, perhaps we should introduce an element of non-proportionality into our account of the relationship between the cost an agent is required to bear, and the amount of good at stake. Such a revision to the Hybrid View is explored more fully in Sections 9.2 and 10.3.

6.4. Do Prerogatives require Restrictions?

In this section, we examine a series of related objections, which derive intuitively unacceptable results from the fact that the Hybrid View contains prerogatives without restrictions. In each case two claims are made. The first is that the intuitive problems faced by the Hybrid View are worse than analogous problems for Simple Consequentialism. The second claim is that the justification Scheffler offers for his Agent Centred Prerogative can also be used to construct a rationale for the Agent Centred Restriction. The conclusion is that the Hybrid View is unstable. Once prerogatives are introduced, we are lead inevitably to restrictions.

There are three separate objections of this form. We first outline each objection, and then discuss various responses available to the Hybrid Theorist.

6.4.1. *Kagan's Doing/Allowing Objection*

Shelly Kagan has argued that 'an Agent Centred Prerogative not only permits agents to *allow* harm, it will also permit agents to *do* harm in the pursuit of their non-optimal projects'.[8] He cites two situations where the pursuit of my projects requires a large sum of money. In the first case, I do not have enough money myself, so I kill my uncle in order to inherit $10,000. In the second case, I already have $10,000, so I elect to spend it on my own projects rather than give it to charity to save a stranger's life. An Agent Centred Prerogative can permit acts of killing if and only if it also permits acts of letting die. If Agent Centred Prerogatives are to be any use at all, they must (at least sometimes) allow me to spend my money on myself rather than on saving the lives of others. Some acts of letting die must be allowed. So some acts of killing must also be accepted. Scheffler must permit agents to kill to advance their own personal projects at the expense of the general good.

Of course, Simple Consequentialism also allows some killing. However, Consequentialists have the defence that they only ever allow me to kill when this is necessary to bring about the best outcome. This response is unavailable to Scheffler, as he permits killing when it produces a worse outcome, judged impartially, than not killing. (An analogous objection to Satisficing Consequentialism was discussed in Section 5.6.)

Scheffler describes this alleged feature of the Hybrid View as the 'symmetry condition', which arises because

> it seems to follow [from the Hybrid View] that if it is permissible for a person to allow an n-sized harm to befall someone else in order to avoid a q-sized cost to himself, then it must, everything else equal, also be permissible for the person to inflict an n-sized harm directly in order to avoid a q-sized cost to himself.[9]

Scheffler admits that an Agent Centred Prerogative cannot, of itself, distinguish between various ways of pursuing personal projects. However, he argues that, in practice, there will be a difference. Doing harm is an act of commission rather than omission. It thus takes time and energy that cannot then be used in the pursuit of personal projects. By contrast, an act of allowing harm saves the agent time and energy, which can then be used in the pursuit of personal goals. Acts justified by Agent Centred Prerogatives will tend to be acts of allowing harm rather than doing harm.

Scheffler gives the example of a starving inner-city inhabitant. By allowing him to starve, I am able to stay at home to work on my own personal projects. So this act may be justified by an Agent Centred Prerogative. Yet taking

---

[8] Kagan, 'Does Consequentialism Demand too Much?', p. 251.
[9] Scheffler, 'Prerogatives without Restrictions', p. 380.

active steps to kill him myself would leave me with even less, rather than more, time to devote to my projects. This act will thus not be justified by an Agent Centred Prerogative.

Scheffler's argument will work in many cases. Perhaps most harmful acts justified by Agent Centred Prerogatives will involve omission rather than commission. However, as Scheffler himself admits, it is implausible to claim that they all will. Situations are bound to arise where pursuit of my personal projects is best achieved by actively doing harm. Furthermore, acts of commission need not limit an agent's options. We can imagine a case where harming another person is the only way to open up a whole range of otherwise unavailable options. Indeed, Kagan's example seems to be just such a case.

6.4.2. The Forced Supererogation Objection

Consider the following tale.[10]

Amy's Dilemma.   Amy, Bob, and Clare are sitting in their living room. A ravenous space alien enters the room and is about to devour Clare. The only way Amy can prevent this is by chopping off her own arm and throwing it to the alien. This will distract the alien long enough for Clare to escape. Amy and Bob can then pick up their weapons and vaporize the alien.

Let us assume that, under the Hybrid View, Amy is not required to sacrifice her arm in this situation. She is permitted to do so, but also permitted to refrain. However, the Hybrid View also permits Bob to perform the action with the best consequences. Bob is thus allowed to chop Amy's arm off himself, if this is the only way he can save Clare.

Indeed, Bob may still be permitted to sacrifice Amy's arm even if he could sacrifice his own arm, and even if this would produce better consequences than sacrificing Amy. If Amy is sacrificed instead of him, the benefit to Bob, when multiplied by the weight he is allowed to give to his own interests, may well outweigh the small loss in impersonal value.

Alternatively, if Bob is not able to save Clare by sacrificing his own arm, then he may be *obliged* to sacrifice Amy's arm. Bob's Agent Centred Prerogative allows him to give disproportionate weight only to the cost to

[10] This objection is presented in Alexander, 'Scheffler on the Independence of Agent-Centred Prerogatives from Agent-Centred Restrictions' pp. 279–82; Harris, 'Integrity and Agent-Centered Restrictions', pp. 440–3; Hurley, 'Scheffler's Argument for Deontology', p. 123; and Myers, 'Prerogatives and Restrictions from the Cooperative Point of View', p. 147. For Scheffler's reply, see 'Prerogatives without Restrictions', p. 392.

himself, not the cost to Amy. Bob may be upset if he sacrifices Amy, but the cost to him is obviously far less than the cost to Amy. So Bob cannot spare Amy, even though Amy was not obliged to sacrifice herself.

Under the Hybrid View, an agent may thus be permitted (or even required) to force another agent to make sacrifices that the latter is morally permitted to refrain from making. (Kagan's tale is a special case of this objection. When I kill my uncle for my own benefit, I force him to make a sacrifice he was permitted to refrain from.)

Simple Consequentialism also permits (and sometimes requires) agents to force others to make sacrifices in pursuit of the impersonal good. This is because Consequentialism contains no Agent Centred Restrictions. Indeed, some have objected that Consequentialism always obliges agents to treat others as means in this way. However, its opponents allege that the Hybrid View is worse than Simple Consequentialism, for two reasons. Under the Hybrid View, the sacrifice Bob is allowed to force upon Amy is one Amy was not required to undergo voluntarily. By contrast, under Simple Consequentialism, if Amy's sacrifice does maximize the good, then Amy will be obliged to choose it herself. So Bob would merely be forcing Amy to do her moral duty. The second difference is that the Hybrid View sometimes allows Bob to sacrifice Amy's arm even if this is not the optimal act available to him, whereas Simple Consequentialism always forbids suboptimal sacrifices.

6.4.3. The Commitments Objection

Once again, we begin with a simple tale.

The Partnership. Ant and Bee are friends, engaged in a cooperative venture that is a significant project for both of them. At time *t*, Ant's Agent Centred Prerogative permits her to embark on the project with Bee. Between *t* and *t*+1, both Ant and Bee invest a great deal of time and effort in their project, all of which will be wasted if either abandons the enterprise. At *t*+1, Ant is permitted to continue with the project, assuming she still values it. However, Ant is also allowed to abandon the project, thereby abandoning Bee, in order to pursue the impersonal good. Ant is also permitted to abandon the co-operative project to pursue some new personal project of her own, even to enter into a new cooperative project with Spider, a sworn enemy of Bee's.[11]

---

[11] This objection is presented in Harris, 'A Paradoxical Departure from Consequentialism', pp. 91–2. Scheffler himself has recently presented a similar argument in favour of obligations derived from personal relationships. (Scheffler, 'Relationships and Responsibilities'.)

In other words, under the Hybrid View, Ant has no special obligations to Bee to continue with their joint project. In the absence of Agent Centred Restrictions, Ant can never be obliged to behave suboptimally, or to favour one personal project over another.

Simple Consequentialism also lacks special obligations. Indeed, if pursuit of the cooperative project is not optimal, then Ant will be *obliged* to abandon it. However, once again, the Hybrid View fares worse than Consequentialism. In the first place, it allows Ant to embark on the cooperative project, *because* of the significance it will have in her life, and then it allows her to abandon that project, without any consideration for the significance the project has come to assume in the life of Bee. The Hybrid View thus allows agents to make commitments to others which they are then free to break, and then justifies this permission by reference to the significance of those commitments for the individual agent. By contrast, Consequentialism motivates its requirement that agents abandon personal projects solely by appeal to considerations of impersonal value.

The second difference between the two theories is that the Hybrid View permits an agent to abandon a cooperative project, not only in pursuit of the impersonal good, but also to pursue another personal project. The latter may even be less valuable to the agent than the abandoned project, so long as its impersonal value is correspondingly higher. Intuitively, breaking a promise to further one's own interests is much worse than breaking a promise in pursuit of the impersonal good.

6.5. Rationales for Restrictions

Taken together these three objections suggest that the intuitive costs of the Hybrid View are much higher than Scheffler suggests. How might proponents of the Hybrid View respond to this cluster of objections? As ever, we focus on the demands of the theory.

The most obvious solution would be to abandon the Hybrid View, and either return to Simple Consequentialism or move to a theory incorporating Agent Centred Restrictions. For our purposes in this book, the former option is not attractive, as we have already rejected Simple Consequentialism. The option of incorporating restrictions is pursued in Part Four. In the remainder of this section, we examine responses to our objections that do not depart from the original Hybrid View.

One option is to deny that the Hybrid View has the counter-intuitive implications suggested above. Scheffler himself has replied to Kagan partly along these lines.[12] As a general strategy, however, this move seems dubious. The odd results alleged against the Hybrid View are not accidental. They stem from a basic structural feature of the theory—namely, its rejection of Agent Centred Restrictions. It is thus very unlikely that the Hybrid View can avoid conflicting with the intuitions underlying those restrictions.

The most promising response, therefore, is to defend the Hybrid View in spite of its counter-intuitive results. After all, as Scheffler himself acknowledges, the intuitive appeal of Agent Centred Restrictions was never in doubt.[13] It is thus hardly surprising that a theory without restrictions has some intuitively unattractive features. The crucial question is whether we can find a rationale for Agent Centred Restrictions. Scheffler argues that we cannot, and that restrictions should thus be rejected. If restrictions have no rationale, then the power of the present objections to the Hybrid View is greatly reduced. On the other hand, those objections may themselves provide the materials to construct a rationale.

We begin by asking which particular restrictions would resolve our present objections. Some examples might be the following: (1) agents are obliged not to harm innocent persons; (2) agents are obliged to keep their promises, especially when they were permitted originally to make those promises; (3) agents are obliged to assist others with whom they are engaged in morally sanctioned cooperative ventures. Each of these restrictions will probably be non-absolute, admitting exceptions such as promise breaking to avert disaster.

Do the situations discussed above provide a rationale for these restrictions? Many of those who discuss such thought experiments have argued that they do.[14] One common form of argument is as follows.

1. Some Agent Centred Prerogatives are self-defeating without Agent Centred Restrictions.
2. A moral theory must include Agent Centred Prerogatives if it is adequately to recognize the significance of moral agency. (This is Scheffler's own rationale for the Agent Centred Prerogative.)
3. Self-defeating prerogatives are not sufficient for the recognition of agency.
4. Therefore, an acceptable moral theory must include some Agent Centred Restrictions.

[12] Scheffler, 'Prerogatives without Restrictions'.
[13] See Scheffler, *The Rejection of Consequentialism*, p. 83, and Scheffler, 'Prerogatives without Restrictions', p. 390.
[14] Harris, 'A Paradoxical Departure from Consequentialism'; Kagan, 'Does Consequentialism Demand too Much?'; Murphy, 'The Demands of Beneficence'; and Schueler, 'Consequences and Agent-Centered Restrictions'.

There are many different versions of this argument. We shall focus on its general form. Initially, this argument seems very convincing. It seems to diagnose the problem created for the Hybrid View by its lack of restrictions. Without restrictions to back them up, many Agent Centred Prerogatives are a mixed blessing. For instance, Amy's permission to refrain from sacrificing her arm may seem worthless to her if Bob is allowed to sacrifice it for her.

However, things are not so simple. We seek a rationale for restrictions, not merely a restatement of their intuitive plausibility. It is not always clear precisely what a rationale amounts to in Scheffler's terminology.[15] However, it is clear that, if we seek a rationale for departures from Simple Consequentialism, then appeals to value or disvalue are not sufficient. We cannot defend Agent Centred Restrictions merely by appealing to the value of the agency those restrictions safeguard. Such appeals cannot justify the claim that agents must refrain from performing an act of type X even when doing so would minimize the overall number of acts of type X. For instance, if murder is bad, then why should an agent refrain from murder when the result is more murders than would have occurred if she had murdered someone herself? Yet, the whole point of an Agent Centred Restriction is that it forbids agents from performing actions of a certain type even when the result is an increase in the overall number of acts of that type.[16]

We must therefore ask if the argument we are considering really is strong enough to provide a genuine rationale for Agent Centred Restrictions. Let us focus on the claim that prerogatives without restrictions are self-defeating. In what sense is it 'inconsistent', 'paradoxical', or 'self-defeating' for a moral theory to include prerogatives without restrictions?[17] The idea behind such phrases seems to be as follows. Prerogatives serve to protect or promote the agent's freedom to live her own life. Agent Centred Restrictions are necessary further to safeguard that freedom, or to lend it appropriate meaning. For instance, if you do not pursue your projects consistently with the commitments embodied in those projects, then the projects will not be significant enough to justify an Agent Centred Prerogative. Without restrictions, both the Agent Centred Prerogative and the Reason to Promote the Good permit agents to undermine and interfere with other agents' pursuit of personal projects.

---

[15]   See e.g. Conee, 'On Seeking a Rationale', pp. 605–9.

[16]   This objection to value-based rationales is emphasized by Kagan and Scheffler. Paul Hurley has recently argued that defenders of restrictions can defeat this objection by appealing to an alternative (Non-Consequentialist) account of the relationship between value and action (Hurley, 'Getting our Options Clear'). A full discussion of Hurley's solution would take us too far afield, but his approach does have some similarities with that adopted in Part Four of this book.

[17]   For these expressions, see Harris, 'A Paradoxical Departure from Consequentialism', and Kagan, 'Does Consequentialism Demand too Much?'.

Two questions arise at this point. (1) Would the absence of Agent Centred Restrictions actually undermine Agent Centred Prerogatives? (2) Why does this provide a rationale for Agent Centred Restrictions, rather than for a general obligation to assist others in the pursuit of their personal projects? After all, my failure to assist you may render your Agent Centred Prerogative practically worthless to you, just as much as any active interference with your projects.

We begin with the first question. What must be the case for my Agent Centred Prerogative to make a worthwhile contribution to my life? If I lived in a world where everyone interfered with my activities, either to promote the good or to pursue their own interests, then it would be very difficult for me to live my life. Furthermore, if I felt free to abandon my commitment to others (and my other personal projects) on a whim, then I would find it very hard to have a rich emotional life.

However, it is not obvious that these observations are sufficient to justify an Agent Centred Restriction. They both appeal to recognizably Consequentialist reasons why it is desirable for people to act in certain ways. They thus seem more likely to justify, for instance, laws against interfering with other people's projects, or deep-seated dispositions not to interfere, rather than a full-blooded moral restriction. How much security would I, or those with whom I collaborate, get from knowing that my interference with them would be *wrong*, if it is already common knowledge both that I am reliably disposed not to interfere and that the law will punish me if I do? How much security could anyone get from the knowledge that my interference would be wrong because it would violate a Non-Consequentialist Agent Centred Restriction, rather than because it would be inconsistent with the best Indirect Consequentialist decision procedure?

In other words, can we justify an Agent Centred Restriction *honouring* the value of non-interference, rather than various Consequentialist strategies designed to *promote* non-interference? It still seems quite reasonable for Scheffler to maintain that we cannot. In Sections 10.5–10.7, I explore a Collective Consequentialist rationale for admitting Agent Centred Restrictions in some circumstances. This move would soften the counter-intuitiveness of the original Hybrid View. The account I develop in Chapter 10 is somewhat similar to Myers's cooperative defence of Agent Centred Restrictions.[18] Unlike Myers, I do not regard the whole of morality, or even the whole of beneficence, as a cooperative project, for the reasons outlined in Chapter 4. Accordingly, my restrictions may be more limited then his.

---

[18] Myers, 'Prerogatives and Restrictions from the Cooperative Point of View'.

We turn now to our second question. Why does the apparent fragility of prerogatives without restrictions justify only an Agent Centred Restriction forbidding interference with other people's projects, and not also an obligation to provide others with the necessities to pursue their projects, or to assist them with that pursuit? After all, if affluent people are pursuing Agent Centred Prerogatives, then their failure radically to redistribute resources will render practically worthless the prerogatives of those who lack sufficient resources meaningfully to pursue worthwhile projects. In such a situation, Agent Centred Restrictions will only worsen the plight of the destitute, as they will be morally prevented from taking the necessary resources by force. Nagel makes a similar point when he argues that, given the present state of the world, poor people could reasonably reject any set of principles allowing the rich to avoid donating large amounts to famine relief.[19]

Recall Scheffler's general point that no acceptable rationale may appeal to the badness of being unable actively to pursue one's Agent Centred Prerogative. Any such appeal suggests that we should promote such pursuit, rather than merely honouring it. Furthermore, if we merely appeal to the badness of being unable to live a meaningful life, then we will be unable to distinguish between active interference with the lives of others and passive failure to provide them with essential resources. Therefore, if we are to justify restrictions, we need two arguments. The first will show that interference with others is morally wrong, even in situations where a failure to provide resources is morally acceptable. (If we accept that failure to assist is wrong whenever interference is wrong, then our moral theory will be extremely demanding.) A second argument would then show that interference is wrong even when it leads to fewer acts of interference overall.

Deontologists claim to provide such arguments. However, the tales we have discussed thus far do not supply them automatically. In particular, the argument from the significance of the independence of the personal point of view (the basis for Scheffler's original rationale) to the Agent Centred Restriction will require many controversial steps. To see this, let us translate the argument into another philosophical idiom: if one is to enjoy rights, then one must accept responsibilities, especially the responsibility to respect the rights of others. At this point, proponents of the Hybrid View might reply that an acceptable moral theory must include positive rights as well as negative rights. They will then argue that, once positive rights are admitted, the most appropriate moral theory will incorporate respect for the positive rights of others into its Reason to Promote the Good. That-rights-are-respected

---

[19] Nagel, *Equality and Partiality*, ch. 4, and Nagel, 'One-to-One'. See also below, Section 8.8.

would then be just another good to be promoted. Agent Centred Restrictions are thus unnecessary.

The tales discussed in the previous section certainly do demonstrate that the Hybrid View leads to a number of very odd results. However, Scheffler himself acknowledges this. Indeed, his original discussion prefigures most of the consequences brought out by these tales. In terms of our overall strategy in this book, we are thus left with a choice between the Hybrid View (a theory with a plausible rationale and many intuitive problems) and Simple Consequentialism (another theory with both rationales and problems). Overall, does the Hybrid View fare worse than Simple Consequentialism with respect to intuitive appeal? Not necessarily. In particular, if the Hybrid View enables us to solve the Demandingness Objection, then it will have a distinct advantage over Simple Consequentialism. Perhaps the overall intuitive cost of the Hybrid View is less than that of Simple Consequentialism. Before rejecting the Hybrid View, therefore, we need further to explore the structure and limits of its demands. We should also explore possible rationales for including some limited Agent Centred Restrictions within the general Hybrid View. In Part Four, I seek to construct a more complex Hybrid View, incorporating Collective Consequentialist elements. If successful, this strategy will further reduce the intuitive cost of a Hybrid Moral Theory.

6.6. Revising the Hybrid View

The objections we have discussed do not prove that the Hybrid View is inadequate. They merely bring out the counter-intuitive consequences of the theory. The remainder of this book attempts to provide a rationale for the intuitions behind the objections. Intuitive dissatisfaction with a theory is not the final word, but it is a good place to start. If a given theory has a number of theoretical virtues, as well as a few counter-intuitive consequences, then it is worthwhile searching for an alternative theory that retains the virtues while avoiding the vices. I present my own preferred solution in Chapter 9. The present section discusses a suggestion put forward by Scheffler himself, and prefigures several of the themes of Part Four.

In his 1992 article, Scheffler discusses a variety of possible responses to Kagan's objection that the Hybrid View ignores the distinction between doing and allowing. One of these is the replacement of the original 'pure-cost' Agent Centred Prerogative with a 'no-harm' Agent Centred Prerogative, allowing the agent to give disproportionate weight to her own interests only when considering an act that does not directly harm anyone else.[20] Harming others for personal gain would thus be ruled out, but agents would still be permitted to harm others in order to produce the best consequences.

Traditionally, the rejection of the distinction between doing and allowing is seen as a central feature of Consequentialism. The modified Hybrid View thus sits uneasily between Consequentialism and Non-Consequentialism. It must provide a plausible rationale for incorporating a No Harm Prerogative, without also committing us to the full distinction between doing and allowing. Can we justify forbidding all harmings for personal gain while allowing all harmings in pursuit of impersonal value? As Scheffler himself notes, 'it is hard to see how there could be considerations that supported this claim without implying that harming is in general worse than allowing harm'.[21]

Scheffler does not claim to provide a rationale for the No Harm Prerogative. However, he does seek to show that one might be available. He discusses two possible candidates. The first arises from 'adjusted consequential considerations'.[22] Perhaps harming for personal gain is more costly (both for the agent and for others) than allowing someone to be harmed for personal gain. If so, this might justify a No Harm Prerogative.

Scheffler lists two principal ways the psychological costs of killing differ from those of letting someone die.[23] The first is 'the general empirical observation that the psychological costs of surrendering a benefit one already has tend to be greater than the psychological costs of doing without a comparable benefit that one has not yet acquired'. The second is that, if the money involved is 'obtainable only by killing', then the agent will acquire the benefits conferred by the money only 'as part of a package that may, depending on the specific circumstances, include everything from fear, horror, shame, humiliation, disgust, self-loathing . . . to profound distortions of personality and of the capacity to lead a fulfilling life'.

The first thing to note is that both of Scheffler's alleged differences are based only on psychological generalizations. So we are left with the rather odd conclusion that an agent who happened to lack the relevant feelings would be permitted to kill her own uncle. In particular, someone who had been convinced that the Hybrid View was correct might well lack such feelings. So Scheffler seems forced to ground his No Harm Prerogative in the fact that his own theory runs counter to conventional human psychology.

Even for 'psychologically normal' agents, much of the force of Scheffler's distinctions can be eliminated by changing the facts of the case. We can easily tell a story where, as a result of an unforeseen change of circumstances,

---

[20] Scheffler, 'Prerogatives without Restrictions' pp. 387–92.   [21] Ibid. 388.   [22] Ibid. 380 ff.
[23] Ibid. 381.

the only way for an agent to lay her hands on an inheritance she has always counted on receiving honestly would be for her to kill her own uncle. Perhaps the laws of inheritance have changed suddenly. The psychological loss involved in forgoing the inheritance is now comparable to the cost of giving up something one already possessed. With respect to Scheffler's second distinction, many sets of circumstances might lead an agent to feel little or no remorse at killing her uncle for profit. Some of these, of course, will be cases where the killing was to some degree justified—by the extreme cruelty of the uncle, for instance. However, it is far from obvious that every set of circumstances reducing a 'normal' agent's remorse at killing a close relative simultaneously justifies that killing.

Scheffler has a reply to this last point: 'the fact that an agent had no qualms about such a killing would not suffice to show that it was really in his interest to kill, that it really advanced his good.'[24] However, it is hard to see how we can reconcile such a claim with the view, central to the original Hybrid View, that there is no general morally relevant distinction between doing and allowing. It would be odd to say that killing is forbidden more frequently than letting die because the consequences of killing are usually worse for the agent, and then to account for this difference by appealing to the intrinsic badness of killing rather than merely letting die. If killing really is intrinsically bad, then should it not be forbidden for that reason alone? Scheffler must find some way to argue that, although an act of killing is intrinsically bad for the agent, such an act is not intrinsically bad. Perhaps this can be done, but it is hard to see how.

It is thus unlikely that we could establish that harming for personal gain is always more costly (either for the agent or for others) than allowing someone to be harmed for personal gain, without illicitly appealing to the assumption that harming is undesirable. Yet, once the latter assumption is made, we can derive a ban on harming in pursuit of impersonal value as easily as a No Harm Prerogative. Also, as Scheffler himself points out on numerous occasions, a restriction cannot be justified merely by appealing to negative features of certain kinds of acts, as such features would justify an obligation to minimize the occurrence of acts of that kind, rather than a restriction forbidding their performance.

Scheffler's second suggested rationale appeals to the 'quasi-practical advantages that prohibitions against harming have in comparison with requirements to prevent harm'.[25] For instance, the former are easier to teach, to internalize, and to obey than the latter. Scheffler's presentation of these advantages is explicitly collectivist: he compares the consequences of

[24] Ibid. 384.   [25] Ibid. 389.

the general acceptance of killing for personal gain with the consequences of the general acceptance of letting someone die for personal gain. He argues that the former would probably be far worse than the latter.[26] (There are obvious parallels with Hooker's claim that Rule Consequentialism contains many of the familiar features of Common-Sense Morality. See Sections 3.3 and 3.4.)

If the Hybrid View were presented as a version of Collective Consequentialism, then this move would be appropriate. However, the Hybrid View was originally presented as a variant of Individual Consequentialism. Unless Scheffler is significantly shifting his ground, he is presumably proposing to incorporate his collectivist reasoning into the Individual Consequentialist framework of the original Hybrid View. In that case, he has to bridge the gap from a Collective Consequentialist-style claim about the dire consequences of the general acceptance of killing for personal gain, to an Individual Consequentialist-style conclusion that, in the absence of such a general acceptance, this particular act of killing for personal gain will have dire consequences. This gap is a fairly substantial one, and Scheffler has yet to demonstrate that the Hybrid View contains the resources to bridge it. (A different way to combine the Hybrid View with Collective Consequentialism is explored in Chapter 10.)

Furthermore, it is not clear that quasi-practical advantages could ever be sufficient to generate a rationale for a No Harm Prerogative. In particular, Scheffler's approach here seems too question-beggingly piecemeal. He assumes that we already have in place a general requirement to promote the good, together with a proviso that departures are permitted (and never required) only by appeals to the agent's own interests. We then seek to draw a line between permissible and impermissible types of non-optimal, self-interested behaviour. It is only at this point that quasi-practical considerations are allowed to play their part. Either such considerations are strong enough to provide a compelling rationale for the No Harm Prerogative or they are not. If they are not, then Scheffler will have failed to demonstrate that such a rationale is available. On the other hand, if quasi-practical considerations can provide a rationale for the No Harm Prerogative, then why should they not be brought into play earlier in the construction of our moral theory? Yet, if such considerations were brought into play earlier, and if they are so strong, then how can we be sure that they will not also provide a rationale for some constraint on doing harm in pursuit of impersonal value? If we cannot be sure that this will not happen, then we are not entitled to conclude that these considerations provide a rationale for the No Harm Prerogative.

---

[26] Scheffler, 'Prerogatives without Restrictions' 384–5.

Our principle interest in the Hybrid View is as a possible solution to the Demandingness Objection. It is thus significant that the modified Hybrid View seems set to increase the demands faced by agents, rather than reducing them. The only difference between the original Hybrid View and the modified version is that the latter, in addition to forbidding some suboptimal allowings of harm, forbids all suboptimal harmings. As our motivation for considering the Hybrid View was to reduce the demands morality places on agents, this would reduce the appeal of the modified Hybrid View. Another weakness of the No Harm Prerogative is that it addresses only some of the intuitive problems posed by our set of objections to the original Hybrid View. In particular, a No Harm Prerogative could not, in itself, generate special obligations to those in collaboration with whom one pursues one's personal projects.

Proponents of the No Harm Prerogative may reply that the introduction of a constraint on suboptimal harmings will allow us to make our prerogative more generous in non-harming situations. For instance, we can now permit Kagan's inheritor to allow a distant stranger to die rather than sacrificing $10,000, safe in the knowledge that this does not commit us to allowing her to kill her uncle in order to inherit a similar sum.

There is certainly something in this reply. The modified Hybrid View may be able to combine a more demanding approach to harming with a less demanding approach to allowing harm. However, unless the justification of the modified Hybrid View is much stronger than our previous discussion suggests, it is unlikely that we will be able to establish a total ban on harming for personal gain. The question of precisely how much harming is permitted will thus depend in part on the stringency of our general prerogative. If we are not to admit too much harming, we cannot afford to be too generous with respect to the permission of acts of omission.

I have not established that it would be impossible to provide a rationale for the No Harm Prerogative. It would thus be premature to abandon the modified Hybrid View out of hand. However, I have cast some doubt on Scheffler's claim to have established the possibility of such a rationale. To salvage the Hybrid View, we will need both a more general range of Agent Centred Restrictions than those provided by the No Harm Prerogative, and a principled rationale for incorporating Collective Consequentialist elements into our moral theory. Part Four seeks to provide both.

6.7. Conclusion

Scheffler's Hybrid View seems to be the most promising of all the moral theories we have discussed thus far. Its direct acknowledgement of cost to the agent makes it superior to Satisficing Consequentialism, while it also avoids the problems faced by Collective Consequentialism's inappropriate interest in full compliance. However, we have seen that the original Hybrid View faces many problems of its own. Most of these result from the rigidity of the original Agent Centred Prerogative, which displays no flexibility when dealing with different moral situations. If the Hybrid View is to become a fully acceptable moral theory, then it will need to incorporate a more structured and flexible prerogative. Part Four continues the search for an acceptable prerogative, drawing on the lessons of previous chapters, and focusing especially on the moral significance of agency and community.

PART FOUR

Combined Consequentialism

7

Two Moral Realms

The purpose of this chapter is to introduce a device that will form the foundation of the new Consequentialist moral theory developed in Chapters 8, 9, and 10. This device is a distinction between different moral realms. Moral choices are divided into distinct realms, primarily on the basis of their impact on the well-being of others. Each realm has its own characteristic features, which suggest that different moral realms may be governed by different moral principles. If we are to develop an acceptable moral theory, then we must be sensitive to the distinct realms.

The realms are first introduced informally using the notion of moral community (Section 7.1). The differences between them are then explored more fully (Sections 7.2 and 7.3). The different realms are first characterized in terms of two broad categories of components of well-being: *needs* and *goals*. Subsequent sections explore the nature of goals, focusing on the ways goals differ from needs (Sections 7.4–7.7). The purpose of this discussion is to motivate the claim that, as goals differ from needs, we should expect the moral realm dealing with goals to differ from that concerned with needs. We then return to the notion of moral community, exploring its links with the distinction between needs and goals (Sections 7.8–7.13). In the next two chapters, this discussion forms the basis for a re-evaluation of the objections to Collective Consequentialism and Individual Consequentialism discussed in Parts Two and Three.

My principal aim in this chapter is to highlight the differences between goals and needs, and the relationships between communities and individuals, and to explore the moral significance of those differences and relationships. There is, of course, a huge literature surrounding each of the central concepts discussed in this chapter: needs, goals, autonomy, community. The chapter thus covers a lot of ground rather quickly, skipping over debates and complexities peripheral to our central concerns. I often discuss a range of possible claims one might make, seeking to establish only those comparatively modest claims that are necessary to the arguments of later chapters.

7.1. Three Moral Realms

One of the conclusions of Part Two was that Collective Consequentialism is at its most plausible in situations characterized by the possibility of reciprocity and mutual advantage, and by a comparatively equal distribution of power. The parties involved have some degree of both independence and interdependence; they stand apart but can also work together, to their mutual benefit.

Not all moral situations are of this sort. Consider, for instance, our relations with future generations. In such cases, the 'circumstances of justice' clearly do not apply.[1] This creates problems for theories of justice or morality based on those circumstances (such as those of Hobbes, Hume, or Rawls).[2] I would suggest that this is because such theories are best seen as governing relationships between moral agents, whereas future generations are not at present agents of any kind. At best, they are potential moral agents. Regarding future generations, we decide whether or not to extend membership of the community of moral agents, not how to treat existing members of that community.

Simple Consequentialism tells us to maximize value. The most natural interpretation of this is that we should produce as much as possible of what makes life worth living. The various capacities associated with moral agency are among the most valuable aspects of life. Therefore, other things being equal, Simple Consequentialism tells us to maximize the number of moral agents, and to extend membership of the moral community as widely as possible.[3]

In relation to future generations, this feature of Simple Consequentialism leads to paradoxes such as the following.

---

[1] The phrase is borrowed from Rawls, *A Theory of Justice*, pp. 126–30, where the circumstances are characterized as 'the normal conditions under which human cooperation is both possible and necessary'—namely, moderate scarcity, moderate selfishness, and relative equality.

[2] For further discussion of the implications for moral theory of our obligations to future generations, see Barry, 'Circumstances of Justice and Future Generations'; Kavka, 'The Paradox of Future Individuals'; Parfit, *Reasons and Persons*, pp. 351–79; and the introductory chapters of Heyd, *Genethics*. I develop my own views in Mulgan, 'A Minimal Test for Political Theories'; Mulgan, 'What's Really Wrong with the Limited Quantity View?'; and Mulgan, 'Dissolving the Mere Addition Paradox'; and at greater length in Mulgan, *Future People*.

[3] At this point in the text, I put to one side all other possible sources of value, such as environmental values. I also gloss over the distinction between total and average versions of Utilitarianism. (For an account of this distinction and its implications, see Parfit, *Reasons and Persons*, pp. 386–7.) It is widely acknowledged that this distinction is central to an adequate analysis of our obligations to future generations. We should also note that lives that fall short of full participation in the moral community can vary enormously in value, owing to different capacities and experiences. The instruction to extend the moral community will not be Simple Consequentialism's only recommendation. It will also tell us to make as many lives as possible as valuable as possible.

The Repugnant Conclusion.   Under Simple Consequentialism, 'for any possible population of at least ten billion people, all with a very high quality of life,
there must be some much larger imaginable population whose existence, if
other things are equal, would be better, even though its members have lives
that are barely worth living'.[4]

Parfit finds this conclusion intrinsically repugnant. If it is a consequence of
Simple Consequentialism, then Simple Consequentialism is an unacceptable
moral theory. Most philosophers agree that Simple Consequentialism does
imply some version of the Repugnant Conclusion. The debate then focuses
on whether the conclusion really is repugnant.[5]

   In other situations, however, the requirement maximally to extend the
bounds of the moral community may not lead to paradox. Consider our relations with people starving in distant countries. We are dealing with existent
potential members of the moral community, whose number, identity, and
existence are all fully determinate, in direct contrast to the status of future
generations.[6] As a moral agent, my goal in such a situation should be to
extend membership of the moral community to everyone to whom it can be
extended. Or so a Simple Consequentialist would argue. As we have seen
throughout this book, this feature of the theory renders Simple Consequentialism very demanding, but it is not necessarily paradoxical.

   The description of starving people as 'potential members of the moral
community' strikes some people as outrageous. One reader responds: 'surely,
no matter how badly off people are, they are deserving of more respect than
this suggests.' I should stress that, in describing someone as a potential member of the moral community, I do not mean to imply (1) that his interests
should count for less than other people's; or (2) that he does not matter
morally; or (3) that he is subhuman. Rather, I am drawing attention to the
fact that our relations with such a person are crucially different from our relations with those with whom we are able to interact on a basis of (approxim-
ate) equality. As a result, some accounts of the basis, nature, and content of
morality that work perfectly well for relations of the latter sort may not be
well suited to the former.

---

   [4] Parfit, *Reasons and Persons*, p. 388.
   [5] For critical discussion of Parfit's Repugnant Conclusion, see Cowen, 'What do we Learn from
the Repugnant Conclusion?'; Dasgupta, 'Savings and Fertility'; Feldman, 'Justice, Desert and the
Repugnant Conclusion'; Locke, 'The Parfit Population Problem'; McMahan, 'Problems of
Population Theory'; Mulgan, 'Two Parfit Puzzles'; Ng, 'What should we Do about Future
Generations?'; Parfit, 'Repugnant Conclusion'; Ryberg, 'Is the Repugnant Conclusion Repugnant?';
and Ryberg, 'Parfit's Repugnant Conclusion'.
   [6] I borrow this account of the three types of indeterminacy involved in future generations
choices (existence, identity, and number) from Heyd, *Genethics*, p. 23.

The notion of moral community I have in mind here is of a society of comparatively equal moral agents who can interact in mutually advantageous
ways in pursuit of their goals. These agents have individual aims (both self-
directed and other directed), as well as shared cooperative aims. In order to
participate in such a community, one must possess certain capacities (such as
autonomy and rationality), have access to certain resources (such as shelter,
clothing, and means of communication), and also meet minimal requirements (such as the absence of starvation or extreme pain). When I speak of
extending membership of the moral community, I mean increasing the number of people who possess these capacities.

We can now distinguish three realms of moral choice.

The Realm of Necessity.   We, as active members of the moral community,
encounter someone who currently lacks the resources or capacities to participate fully in the moral community. Such a person has many unmet needs
and undeveloped capacities. We can add value to their life in many ways. We
decide which of their capacities to develop, and which of their needs to meet.
One decision we must make is whether to enable the person to participate
fully in the moral community.

The Realm of Reciprocity.   We, as active members of the moral community,
decide how we will interact.

The Realm of Creation.   We decide which people, if any, to bring into existence.

It may be helpful to think of the Realm of Necessity as occupying a halfway
house between the two Realms of Reciprocity and Creation. The Realm of
Necessity differs from that of Creation in that our decision relates to someone who already exists at the moment of choice. The Realm of Necessity differs from that of Reciprocity in that, at the moment of choice, the object of
our decision is not actually a fully participating member of the moral community.

In this book, I shall put the Realm of Creation to one side, though I hope
to return to it elsewhere.[7] My use of the remaining two realms will centre
around the following claims:

1. our response to the plight of the distant starving belongs to the Realm
   of Necessity, rather than Reciprocity; while
2. our everyday lives are mostly lived within the Realm of Reciprocity;
3. when dealing with the Realm of Necessity, Individual Consequentialism is to be preferred to any Collective approach; whereas

[7] Mulgan, *Future People*. In the present text I also ignore complexities at the boundaries between
the Realm of Creation and the other two realms, such as the debate over abortion.

4. when dealing with the Realm of Reciprocity, Collective Consequentialism is to be preferred to any Individual approach.

All of these claims will be controversial. The second pair of claims are discussed in the next two chapters. This chapter seeks to establish the first pair
of claims, by exploring the differences between the two moral realms. These
differences explain why different realms are governed by different moral principles. In developing my theory, I also argue that the distinction between the
two realms is more morally significant than other distinctions often regarded
as central to moral philosophy, especially the distinction between self-
concern and concern for others.

The territorial metaphor of 'realms' is, in many ways, unfortunate, as it
suggests two separate, distinct, mutually exclusive spheres. In reality, it is
invariably impossible to separate the two realms. Most morally significant
decisions involve both reciprocity and necessity. It is more accurate to see the
two realms as representing two kinds of reasons, responding to different features of moral life. Even if every actual situation belongs to both realms
(because both sets of reasons are ever present) it is still useful to consider their
characteristics separately.

7.2. Needs and Goals

The preceding discussion in terms of moral community may seem vague and
impressionistic. If we are to make use of the distinction between moral
realms, then we need a more rigorous way of distinguishing the Realms of
Necessity and Reciprocity. In this section, I present one such account, which
focuses on the impact of my actions on the well-being of others. I divide the
components of well-being into two broad categories. Following Joseph Raz,
I shall refer to these as *needs* and *goals*. Roughly speaking, needs are the biologically determined necessities of life, such as food, oxygen, or shelter.
Goals, by contrast, are our chosen pursuits, projects, and endeavours, which
give life much of its meaning and purpose. Further differences between
needs and goals will emerge as we proceed.[8]

Once this distinction is in place, there are obviously two ways one can promote the well-being of another agent. The first is to meet her needs, while
the second is to assist her in the pursuit of her goals. I shall argue that our
obligations to meet the needs of others are best explained in terms of the

---

[8] Raz, *The Morality of Freedom*, pp. 290–1. For a full discussion of the physiological and environmental basis of basic needs, see Dasgupta, *Well-Being and Destitution*, esp. ch. 1. For more on their
moral significance, see Braybrooke, *Meeting Needs*, ch. 4; Griffin, *Well-Being*, pp. 41–5.

Realm of Necessity, while the Realm of Reciprocity provides a more useful framework for discussion of our obligations to assist others in the pursuit of their goals.

The notion of a goal is related to Scheffler's notion of a project. We need to be careful in our use of either term. When Scheffler himself speaks of a human life as if it were a series of 'projects', this term may call to mind the image of solitary, self-sufficient pursuits or hobbies. This picture is inaccurate and unhelpful. It misrepresents the structure of human life. The components of a well-integrated life are far more significant than a set of hobbies. As Susan Wolf notes, most of the engagements and attachments that give life its meaning are long-term and interpersonal.[9] For instance, it is odd to speak of personal relationships, careers, religious affiliations, or community membership as 'projects' or 'goals'. In what follows, I shall retain the term 'goal', but we must bear its limitations in mind. By speaking of projects or goals, we run the risk of making the case for departures from Simple Consequentialism (such as the Agent Centred Prerogative) appear much weaker than it actually is. This way of speaking makes an Agent Centred Prerogative appear to be merely a concession to human selfishness, rather than a rational and well-motivated response to deep structural facts about the nature of human agency.[10]

My use of the distinction between needs and goals raises several questions. (1) Does it rely on questionable assumptions about the structure (or content) of human well-being? (2) Why should we expect the two realms to be governed by different moral principles? (If the two realms are governed by exactly the same principles, then there is little point in distinguishing them.) (3) How does the account of the moral realms in terms of components of well-being relate to the account in terms of the moral community? Our primary interest in this chapter will be in the latter two questions. Sections 7.4–7.7 deal with the second, while the third is examined in Sections 7.8–7.13. Section 7.3 addresses the first question.

7.3. Controversy and Well-Being

The moral theory defended over the next three chapters does not rely upon controversial claims about the human good. The distinction I appeal to is not peculiar to some specific theory of value. On any plausible theory of the human good, one can generate something like the contrast between needs

---

[9] Wolf, 'Happiness and Meaning', pp. 211–12.
[10] I am not suggesting that Scheffler himself is unaware of the points made in this paragraph, merely that his terminology can obscure them.

and goals. Furthermore, I shall argue below that the Demandingness Objection itself presupposes this distinction (see Section 9.3). In utilizing the distinction, therefore, we are simply exploring the implications of taking that objection seriously.

Let us begin with needs. It seems obvious that there are some basic needs, determined by human physiology, such that any valuable human life is all but impossible if they are not met. For instance, only an extreme ascetic could possibly argue that food is not essential to a valuable human life. It is hard to see how any view about the value of human life could fail to accord value to the meeting of basic needs. Some people in Australia believe that human beings can live indefinitely on air and sunshine alone. Yet even they admit that it would be crazy to claim that human beings have *no* basic needs. After all, no one can survive without air and sunshine.[11]

The more significant question is whether any viable theory of well-being can avoid recognizing the value and distinctness of goals. Goals are valuable in many different ways. The first is the value of what is produced, generated, or created by pursuit of a given goal. This may be a work of art, a public util-ity such as a dam, or a valuable relationship such as a friendship. This value can be either intrinsic (because the achievement is independently valuable) or instrumental (because the achievement contributes to other independently valuable outcomes, such as the pleasure or satisfaction of others). The valu-able product may even be a state of the agent herself. For instance, one of the valuable results of the pursuit of scholarship is that the agent herself acquires knowledge, thus enhancing her own life.

A second way goals might contribute to the value of a life is through the value of the realization of the good of achievement within the agent's life. As a result of a valuable achievement, the agent's well-being may be increased, at least on many contemporary accounts of the human good.[12]

A third value produced by goals is the satisfaction or pleasure the agent herself takes in her achievement. An agent who believes that her achieve-ments are valuable may derive pleasure from those achievements, even if they are not actually valuable. Therefore, even those who seek to reduce well-being to pleasure can admit that different goals have different values for the agent herself, because of the diverse pleasures involved.

These three types of value are related. An achievement is likely to add less value to the agent's life if it is not independently valuable. For instance, the

[11] Of course, some religious thinkers might adopt the view that embodied human life has no value, as valuable existence is possible only once the soul is free of the body. However, it is hard to construe this as an account of what makes *human lives* valuable.

[12] For defences of the claim that achievement is a distinct good, see Griffin, *Well-Being*, pp. 64–8; Hurka, *Perfectionism*, pp. 39–51; and Raz, *The Morality of Freedom*, pp. 288–307.

creation of a worthless painting probably adds little to the value of its creator's life, except insofar as the pursuit of painting develops the creator's capacities and provides satisfaction. Arguably, if an agent is well informed, then she will derive satisfaction only from genuinely valuable achievements. Satisfaction based on false beliefs regarding the value of one's creations may be less valuable than (introspectively identical) satisfaction based on true beliefs.[13]

The significance of a given achievement within an agent's life may also depend upon the overall structure of that life. A particular achievement may add more to the value of a life with fewer similar achievements. Alternatively, an achievement may derive additional value from the part it plays in some broader life plan.[14]

Many contemporary accounts of the human good accord intrinsic value to achievement and to the development of rational capacities. Any such account must make room for the value of goals. Furthermore, in a modern, liberal society such as ours, not even the most blinkered hedonist could avoid recognizing goals. In such societies, people gain most of their pleasure from goals they have chosen to pursue, rather than from the meeting of basic needs, or from tasks arbitrarily assigned to them. The pleasure of pursuing goals is very different from the pleasure produced when basic needs are met. As we are seeking a moral theory to guide our own deliberations and actions, we need not ask whether this is a contingent feature of modern societies, or a necessary feature of valuable human lives. Only on a very limited view of the human good would no goals be valuable, especially in a society such as ours where the pursuit of goals plays such a central role in most of our individual lives and social institutions. (For a stark illustration of what a life devoted solely to meeting one's own basic needs might be like, see Section 7.5.)

One influential account of well-being appears to avoid a sharp distinction between needs and goals. This account analyses well-being solely in terms of preference satisfaction. Indeed, many defenders of this view cite its ability to avoid controversial questions regarding the components of well-being as one of its principal virtues. Life is much simpler once everything is reduced to the common currency of preference satisfaction.

Unfortunately, no plausible preference theory of well-being can really avoid the distinction between needs and goals. On any intuitively plausible view, we all have many preferences whose satisfaction does not contribute to

---

[13] The classic counter-example to the view that well-being depends entirely upon the agent's experiences, irrespective of their correlation to reality, is Nozick's 'experience machine' (see his *Anarchy, State and Utopia*, pp. 42–5).

[14] For a full discussion of the issues involved here, see Hurka, *Perfectionism*, pp. 84–98.

our well-being. A stock example is a desire that there be life on other planets. Such a preference is entirely unrelated to the agent's own life. Other, more controversial common examples include self-destructive and rationally un-intelligible preferences, such as the desire to mutilate oneself or eat mud.[15]

Conversely, meeting a person's basic needs is good for that person, whether they prefer it or not. People usually do prefer to have their needs met, but that preference is not the source of value. Otherwise it would make no sense to say, of someone who disregards his own needs, that 'he doesn't know what's good for him'. This remark may often be inappropriate, but it is surely not unintelligible.

The language of preferences can capture some of the flavour of goals, espe-cially their connection to personal choice and autonomy. Yet it is inadequate to the complexity of goals. What makes my goal valuable to me is not merely the fact that I prefer it, but also the way my pursuit of that goal shapes my life. The rich texture of our moral life evaporates if we reduce goals to preferences.

The overall lesson is that, even if the vast majority of things that contribute to our well-being are things we prefer, their value cannot be reduced to the common language of preference. Any acceptable preference-based account of well-being must accommodate something like the distinction between needs and goals, by recognizing the different ways preferences enhance well-being. (For more on the inadequacy of preferences, see Section 7.12.)

It may be instructive to explore the relationship between the distinction between needs and goals and Sen's distinction between agent-neutral and agent-relative values.[16] The latter distinction reflects the familiar fact that each agent has her own perspective on the world. There are several connections between these two distinctions. In the first place, as I shall argue in the next chapter, most arguments offered in support of the moral significance of our per-sonal perspectives rely upon the fact that we are creatures with goals. In a world without goals, agent-relative values would lose much of their normative force. Indeed, the notion of such values might even be incoherent in such a world.

The value of goals is also relative to agents in another sense. The value of meeting a need does not depend upon what the agent thinks, believes, or val-ues. The value of needs is thus agent neutral, in the sense that one can appreciate that value without entering into the agent's own perspective. By contrast, a goal is only of value to the agent (and, hence, only of value at all) because she values it. Unless one shares or appreciates the agent's perspec-tive, one cannot tell what will be of value to her. In relation to goals, agents confer value.

---

[15] For discussions of preference-based accounts of well-being, see Griffin, *Well-Being*, pp. 10–39; Kagan, *Normative Ethics*, pp. 36–9; and Parfit, *Reasons and Persons*, pp. 494–9.

[16] Sen, 'Evaluator Relativity and Consequential Evaluation', and the discussion above, Section 2.3.

Of course, this broad slogan is an oversimplification. In many cases, at least some of the value involved in the pursuit of a goal will be independent of the agent. Suppose my goal is to produce a great work of art. If I succeed, part of the value of my accomplishment derives from the fact that the work of art is valuable. However, even here some value does flow from the fact that I have freely chosen my goal. If I become an artist unwillingly, never engaging with my work, always remaining alienated, and so on, then my life is less worthwhile than if I had wholeheartedly embraced my vocation.[17]

Further to illustrate the differences between needs and goals, consider the moral status of creatures other than human adults. The Realm of Necessity covers our relations with any creature with needs. For instance, it applies to our obligations to animals, babies, and the severely intellectually disabled. By contrast, the Realm of Reciprocity applies only to our dealings with other moral agents. Once again, we see the connection with the different notions of value. When I alleviate the suffering of an animal, this is valuable because it is good for the animal. However, it would be odd to say that my actions were valuable from the perspective of the animal, or that the animal conferred value on my actions. This is because the animal has only needs, not goals.

The debate over our treatment of the so-called higher animals can also be addressed in terms of the two moral realms. Much of the controversy concerning our treatment of dolphins, for instance, turns on the question of whether dolphins have goals as well as needs. When we deal with these creatures, are we operating solely within the Realm of Necessity or also in the Realm of Reciprocity? If the latter, could we enter into a meaningful community with dolphins? If we cannot, then we may have to recognize the possibility of distinct, non-overlapping Realms of Reciprocity. (If different human cultures were radically incommensurable, then our own Realms of Reciprocity would also be distinct. The only common moral realm would be that of necessity. See Section 7.10.)

We can now appreciate the force of two common lines of argument in moral philosophy. The first consists of objections to Contractualist accounts of morality, on the grounds that these ignore the needs and sufferings of non-rational (but sentient) beings (see Section 3.1.2). The second are those objections to Utilitarian theories accusing them of ignoring the significance of agency in well-being, and consequently treating human beings as if they were merely receptacles containing varying amounts of pleasure. The first objection is effectively the complaint that Contractualists treat the Realm of Reciprocity as if it were the whole of morality, ignoring the Realm of

---

[17] Raz, 'Duties of Well-Being', esp. pp. 3–8.

Necessity. The second objection makes the reverse complaint against Utilitarians: they privilege the morality of necessity, thus ignoring the morality of reciprocity.

One obvious solution to both objections is to combine the two theories. The result would be a Utilitarian morality of necessity combined with a Contractualist morality of reciprocity. Alternatively, we might seek a separate Consequentialist account of the Realm of Reciprocity, perhaps drawn from Collective Consequentialism. The remaining chapters of this book develop such a theory.

7.4. Goals and Choices

There are two ways to distinguish between the two moral realms. The first is that they relate to different components of well-being. The second is that one realm deals with interactions within a moral community, while the other does not. We will focus on the first source of difference, as it underlies the significance of the second source.

The next few sections explore the differences between needs and goals, and their moral significance. Most of these differences arise because the value of a goal depends upon how it is pursued, whereas the value of a need is not directly affected by the way it is met. The significance of this for moral theory is that constraints on the promotion of well-being are much more plausible in the Realm of Reciprocity (where we respond to goals) than in the Realm of Necessity (where we respond to needs). Subsequent sections discuss the relationship between goals and community, which will lead us back to the relationship between individuals and communities, and to the notion of moral community.

One obvious difference between needs and goals is that the value of pursuing a goal may depend upon who pursues it, whereas the value of meeting a need does not depend upon who meets it.

The best way to promote the good with respect to needs is directly to meet those needs. One meets the needs of others much as one meets one's own needs. By contrast, promoting the pursuit of goals depends upon whose goals they are. The best way to promote the successful pursuit of one's own goals is to pursue them. The best ways to promote the successful pursuit of goals by others are: meet their needs, remove obstacles in their path, ensure the availability of a suitable social framework, and then join their pursuit by adopting those goals for oneself.

We can simplify matters by treating the existence of an adequate social framework as a need, as it is a necessary precondition for agents to pursue any goals. (This claim is defended in Section 7.8.)[18] Once we have made this assumption, an agent can promote the pursuit of goals by others only by meeting their needs, and perhaps by joining with them in pursuing those goals. The first of these methods of promotion leads us back to the Realm of Necessity, while the second leads us directly to the Realm of Reciprocity.

One cannot pursue another person's goals for them. Until they choose their goals, there may be no way (even in principle) to determine which goals it would be best for them to have. Furthermore, a person's goals, once chosen, are often activities they seek to perform, rather than impersonal results that they seek to bring about.[19]

This last claim may seem false. After all, my goals often involve aiming at some particular result. This raises an interesting question. If I seek x, and x is brought about independently by someone else, then does my life go better? Has my goal been achieved? These are two very different questions. The crucial question is always whether my pursuit of my goal was entirely independent of the eventual achievement. Consider a simple example. I devote my life to the study of a difficult scientific problem, which I never solve. The problem is eventually solved by other researchers. Although I never collaborate with them, they learn valuable results from my failures. I can reasonably claim to have contributed to the achievement of my goal. The success of the other researchers makes my own endeavours part of a successful collective project, rather than an isolated failure. On some views at least, this affects the overall value of my life. Assume instead that my work was unconnected to that of the successful researchers, who operate in complete ignorance of my attempts. Would we still say that I have achieved my goal? Has my life gone better? Has my goal been achieved? (Even if the later researchers are unfamiliar with my particular work, I might share in the achievement by virtue of our common membership of a unified scientific tradition. To avoid this complexity, imagine the successful researchers as members of an alien culture unconnected to my own.)

We must separate two features of my relationship with the scientific discovery: my desire that this problem be solved, and my striving to solve it. More generally, an agent will often have both the desire that p, and the goal of bringing it about that p. Consider another simple case. Both Jonah Lomu and I desire that the All Blacks win the Rugby World Cup in 2007. This is also one of Jonah's goals. It is not one of mine, as I do not plan to do anything to bring it about. Suppose I make it one of my goals that the All Blacks win the World Cup in 2007. I perform a variety of astrological rituals designed to

---

[18] See also Raz, *The Morality of Freedom*, pp. 199–206, and Scheffler, *Human Morality*, pp. 138–43.
[19] Raz, *The Morality of Freedom*, pp. 306–7, and Hurka, *Perfectionism*, p. 59.

achieve my goal. Unsurprisingly, my activities have no causal impact on the Rugby World Cup. However, owing largely to the significant causal impact of Jonah, the All Blacks do in fact win. My desire has certainly been fulfilled. Is it also plausible to say that my goal has been achieved? I would say not. I may believe that I have achieved my goal, and I may feel proud as a result. Yet something is missing. There is a vital respect in which Jonah's life goes better than mine. He has achieved something, whereas I have not.[20] The real lesson here is that, while some components of my well-being do depend solely upon what happens (whether I am responsible for it or not), other components depend for their value upon my relationship to (and responsibility for) what happens. In relation to goals, the latter components of well-being are often more significant.

One reason I cannot pursue another person's goals is because of the connection between goals and autonomy. Goals derive their value in part from their having been freely chosen by the agent, whereas needs are given to the agent by her physiological make-up. The value of a need being met is not affected by whether or not the agent chose to have it met. By contrast, the value of the realization of a goal is often largely dependent upon the agent having chosen to pursue that goal.

This may seem to overestimate the significance of choice. After all, in many cases an agent's goals are given to her by her social environment, rather than freely chosen by her. However, even in such cases, the value of those goals depends upon the agent identifying herself with those goals. In a modern liberal society, such identification will almost always involve a conscious choice to retain one's existing goals rather than seeking new ones.

If goals are to be valuable, then they must reflect the agent's autonomy. If the agent is to be autonomous, then a range of options must be available to her. Various background conditions must be met if a range of suitable options is to be available. These may include the existence of a social framework and the presence of incommensurability.[21]

The various claims in the previous paragraph have stronger and weaker formulations. The next three sections explore these, and ask which formulations are essential to our overall project. My main aim is to establish that choice, autonomy, community, and incommensurability are much more

---

[20] Much of the hype surrounding contemporary sporting events is designed to blur the distinction between desires and goals, thereby giving fans a sense of achievement when their team wins. For instance, in 1995 thousands of otherwise rational New Zealanders were lead to believe that, by sitting in front of a television set wearing red socks, they were somehow participating in the achievement of winning an obscure yacht race. On any plausible account of the value of achievement, they were badly misled.

[21] For discussions of the notion of incommensurability, see Raz, *The Morality of Freedom*, pp. 321–66; Raz, *Engaging Reason*, pp. 46–66; and Griffin, *Well-Being*, pp. 75–92. See also below. Section 7.6.

significant for goals than for needs. This suggests that a moral theory emphasizing the significance of these features will offer a more plausible account of the Realm of Reciprocity than one that ignores them. Conversely, theories ignoring these features may be more plausible in the Realm of Necessity, where such features are less prominent.

Certain conditions must be met if a choice is to be morally valuable. These affect the value of an agent's pursuit and realization of her goals. In particular, we must address the following questions.

1. How does the availability of a goal affect its value (Section 7.5)?
2. How does the availability of alternatives to a goal affect its value (Section 7.6)?
3. Why is autonomy valuable (Section 7.7)?
4. What is the connection between autonomy and community (Section 7.8)?

This final question will lead us from the distinction between needs and goals back to the notion of community (Section 7.11).

7.5. The Value of Availability

A goal may be 'available' to an agent in several ways.

Moral Availability.   A goal is morally available if the agent is morally permitted to pursue it.

Legal Availability.   A goal is legally available if it is not illegal for the agent to pursue it.

Practical Availability.   A goal is practically available if the agent is (physically) able (effectively) to pursue it.

Psychological Availability.   A goal is psychologically available if the agent is able to conceive of it, and capable of seriously considering pursuing it.

Social Availability.   A goal is socially available if the agent is not prevented from pursuing it by the absence of appropriate social structures. (For instance, being a judge is not socially available in a society with no legal system.)

Realisation.   A goal is realized if the agent actually pursues it with some reasonable degree of success.

If goals were like needs, then realization would be the only form of availability that was valuable in its own right. All other forms of availability would be valuable only because they were means to realization, or because they rendered realization more likely. We can thus measure the extent to which goals differ from needs by asking whether these other forms of availability are valuable in their own right.

The different forms of availability are related in a number of ways. Let us focus on the relationship between moral availability and each of the others. Moral availability is always relative to a set of practically available alternatives. An action may cease to be morally permitted simply because a new alternative becomes practically available. For instance, many medical practices that were morally acceptable in the past would not be acceptable now, because much more efficient alternatives are now available. We might also make similar claims about psychological and social availability. Changes in what is conceivable, or changes in social structures, may produce changes in moral availability.

Claims about legal, practical, psychological, or social availability are factual claims. It is important to separate these from various normative claims about availability. The latter fall into two categories. The first category includes claims that some goal should be available in some sense. For instance, one might claim that some activity should not be illegal, or that it should be made practically available to more people. The second category consists of claims concerning moral availability. These need to be distinguished from the claims in the first category. For instance, one might argue that the proper business of the law is to prevent agents from interfering with one another. On this view, many actions should be legally available even though they are not morally available.[22] Also, we should be wary of arguing from the premiss that autonomy requires the practical availability of a given goal to the conclusion that the goal is morally available. At most, the premiss entitles us to the conclusion that the goal should be practically available. (As we shall soon see, the availability of one goal may be necessary to enhance the value of another goal. We may want a goal to be practically available even though it is morally unacceptable.)

The most desirable social arrangement may well legally permit agents to engage in morally impermissible goals. Consider the goals we engage in instead of participating more actively in famine relief. Perhaps we are morally obliged to do far more than anyone (or, at least, any state) could justifiably force us to do.

Liberal constraints on state promotion of the good may seem at odds with a Consequentialist approach. However, our discussions of Rule Consequentialism show that there are often good reasons, on purely Consequentialist

---

[22] For statements of this view, see Hart, *Law, Liberty and Morality*, and Waldron, 'A Right to Do Wrong'. For critical discussion, see Raz, *The Morality of Freedom*, pp. 412–24; and George, *Making Men Moral*, pp. 48–82.

grounds, to limit the scope of the state's ability to interfere in the lives of its citizens, especially within the Realm of Reciprocity (see Sections 3.4.2 and 8.4).

For any claim regarding the value of availability, we must specify both a scope (what type of availability is at issue?) and a strength (how valuable is such availability?). With respect to strength, there are (at least) five possible claims. We can illustrate these using the value of realization. The claims are presented in descending order of strength.

The Conceptual Necessity Claim.   Any agent must pursue and realize that goal. No one could fail to realize that goal and still be a rational agent.

The Practical Necessity Claim.   As a matter of fact, no one who fails to realize that goal can develop or preserve human agency.

The Worthwhile Life Claim.   To have a worthwhile life, an agent must realize that goal.

The Flourishing Life Claim.   While an agent can have a worthwhile life without realizing that goal, a life including such realization will be significantly more flourishing than one without.

The Desirability Claim.   Realization of the goal is desirable.

For any goal, we thus have a wide range of separate claims to assess. Fortunately, we can save time by noting some general relationships between various claims. The most straightforward are between claims of different strength. Each claim of a particular scope entails all weaker claims of the same scope. For instance, if we can establish that the practical availability of a certain goal is conceptually necessary for the possession of agency, then we need not ask how valuable such availability is for any particular agent. Conversely, if we can establish that the realization of a certain goal is not even desirable for moral agents, then we do not need to ask whether it is necessary for agency.[23]

Relations between claims of different scope are more complicated. The only general implication is that participation (and, hence, realization) requires practical availability. If a goal is not (practically) available, then obviously the agent cannot participate in it. Uncontroversial entailments between other scopes are harder to find. To illustrate this, consider different claims regarding conceptual necessity. The fact that it is necessary for every agent to pursue a given goal does not prove that such pursuit must always be morally

---

[23] I assume here that there are no necessary evils: no undesirable drives or ambitions that are necessary for the development of human agency. Some contemporary theories of human nature, especially those influenced by psychoanalysis, may dispute this. For our present purposes, we can put these complexities to one side.

permitted. Perhaps some agents cannot avoid behaving wrongly. To get from the necessity of pursuit to the necessity of moral availability, we would need to establish that all the necessities of agency are permitted. When dealing with weaker claims, such as those dealing with flourishing rather than necessity, the move from the value of pursuit to the value of availability requires analogous additional premisses, such as that a flourishing life must be morally permissible.

Similar remarks apply to the relationship between practical availability and moral availability. The usual role of claims about practical availability is to provide support for claims relating to the value of participation or moral availability. Yet we are sometimes interested in the practical availability of goals the agent does not pursue, because of the impact this may have on the value of the goal she actually does pursue. (See the next section.)

Claims of conceptual necessity relating to particular goals are likely to be very controversial. If the argument of the next three chapters required us to endorse such claims, then the resulting moral theory would rest upon controversial metaphysical foundations. Fortunately, our general purpose requires only comparatively modest claims. If our moral theory is to avoid being impossibly demanding, then any claim of either conceptual or practical necessity will be sufficient to justify an Agent Centred Prerogative. Any claim regarding the necessities of a worthwhile life will also generate an Agent Centred Prerogative, unless our moral theory is to be extremely demanding. Claims regarding the contribution of a goal to a flourishing life will not be sufficient to establish an Agent Centred Prerogative, unless we require a moral theory that permits the most flourishing possible human life. The claim that pursuit of a certain goal is desirable will be sufficient to justify a prerogative only if we expect all personally desirable activities to be permitted.

We will focus on essential availabilities: goals whose availability is necessary for the very possibility of a worthwhile human life. If there is any Agent Centred Prerogative, then it must cover such goals. At the level of moral theory, we will also be more interested in general claims of availability than in claims about particular goals. For instance, we might endorse the following two claims.

The Practical Claim. If an agent is to have a worthwhile human life, then she must have some goals practically available to her. A life consisting solely of the meeting of basic needs is not a good human life at all.

The Moral Claim. If an agent is to have a worthwhile human life, then some practically available goals must also be morally available. One cannot live a worthwhile life if forced to choose between behaving in a morally permitted way and pursuing any goals at all.

These two claims are comparatively modest. It is hard to see how any plausible moderate moral theory can fail to grant them. Raz provides two striking examples of lives falling short of the standards set by these two claims:

The Man in the Pit. A person falls down a pit and remains there for the rest of his life, unable to climb out or to summon help. There is just enough ready food to keep him alive without (after he gets used to it) any suffering. He can do nothing much, not even move much. His choices are confined to whether to eat now or a little later, whether to sleep now or a little later, whether to scratch his left ear or not.

The Hounded Woman. A person finds herself on a small desert island. She shares the island with a fierce carnivorous animal which perpetually hunts for her. Her mental stamina, her intellectual ingenuity, her will power and her physical resources are taxed to their limits by her struggle to remain alive. She never has a chance to do or even to think of anything other than how to escape from the beast.[24]

If we do grant the two claims, then we must require any adequate moral theory to take account of both needs and goals. It also follows that any adequate moral theory must take account of the practical and moral availability of a goal as well as its realization. This brings out a central feature of goals: their connection to choice. The value of a goal often depends upon the fact that the agent has chosen it. Unless other options are available, the agent's choice is meaningless. Indeed, the very nature of a goal may depend upon the way it is chosen. Furthermore, our moral evaluation of an agent's decision to pursue a goal often depends upon the details of her choice.

If our moral theory takes goals seriously, then it must consider the conditions necessary for an agent's choice of a goal to be free. To discover whether a goal was freely chosen we must look at the available alternatives. We are thus interested in the practical availability of goals the agent does not seek to pursue. The value of the pursuit and realization of a goal is affected by its alternatives. By contrast, the value of a need being met is not so affected. (Although, of course, the moral rightness of meeting a given need may depend upon what other actions one had available at the time.) This suggests that theories that emphasize the significance of alternatives and of choice will be better suited to the Realm of Reciprocity than to that of necessity. This, in turn, will lead us to the significance of autonomy, and of community.

---

[24] Raz, *The Morality of Freedom*, pp. 373–4.

7.6. The Availability of Alternatives

The moral significance of pursuing a goal often depends very much on what other goals are available to the agent at the time. Some examples of this type of dependence include the following.

1. If the value of goal A depends upon the agent's being able to choose between goal A and goal B, then the availability of goal A may have considerably less value if goal B is not also available. One might believe both that the only valuable lifestyle is matrimonial heterosexual monogamy, and that this lifestyle is more valuable when freely chosen over alternatives such as promiscuity, non-matrimonial cohabitation, homosexuality, and so on. Accordingly, one might favour the availability of promiscuous lifestyles, but only to enhance the value of matrimonial monogamy.

2. If what really matters is the availability of *some* goals of type X, then the availability of goal A will be more significant if A is the only goal of type X available. If nursing is the only profession open to women, then the availability of a career in nursing is much more significant than if many other professions are also available.

3. The availability of unchosen options may alter the *nature* of those options that are chosen, as well as their significance. Consider a society where everyone's occupation is fixed at birth. Perhaps everyone carries on the family trade. Social mobility is then introduced, enabling people to choose different careers. In a sense, the old careers are no longer available, as no one can be a wheelwright-simply-as-a-matter-of-birth. Instead, one can only be someone-who-has-chosen-to-be-a-wheelwright, which is a very different thing. More generally, as Raz suggests, the non-autonomous life ceases to be an option in a liberal society.[25]

4. The moral significance of the availability of a goal will often depend upon the social or cultural situation of the agent. Certain choices may be more life defining in some cultures than in others. For instance, the availability of a priestly career may be more significant in a theocracy than in a predominantly secular culture. This may be true even for those who do not opt for the priestly life.

The value of the availability of alternatives has several special features. The most obvious is that this type of value is generated even if the agent never embarks on the goal in question. Indeed, the availability of a goal may be very significant even though almost no one will ever choose it, as the decision not to embark on that goal may be an important, life-defining decision. This

---

[25] Ibid. 392–5.

explains why debates over the ordination of women and the role of women in armed combat assume great significance in religious and military circles, even though few women would choose these options were they available. Or consider the example of suicide. One might believe that one's life is more valuable if one chooses to stay alive, rather than simply being forcibly kept alive by social or legal pressure. This would lead one to favour the availability of suicide, even though one might hope that few people will choose that option.

What degree of availability must unchosen alternatives have for the agent's choice to be free? There are three principal possibilities.

The Practical Availability Claim.   To be freely chosen, a goal must be chosen from a range of *practically* available alternatives.

The Moral Availability Claim.   To be freely chosen, a goal must be chosen from a range of *morally* available alternatives.

The Razian Availability Claim.   To be freely chosen, a goal must be chosen from a range of morally available alternatives, and it must be the case that at least one of those alternatives was neither better than, nor worse than, nor equal to the chosen goal.[26]

Each of the latter two claims presupposes the previous claim. The argument for the Practical Availability Claim is obvious. If there is only one thing I can do, then it makes little sense to say that I have chosen it. The argument for the Moral Availability Claim is as follows. If my choice is determined by morality, then I do not genuinely exercise autonomy in making that choice. If I want to be moral, then I have no choice. The argument for the Razian Availability Claim is similar. If one option is superior to all others, then my choice is determined by the balance of reasons. Therefore, I cannot genuinely exercise autonomy. If I want to be rational, then I have no choice. On the other hand, if my choice is not determined by the balance of reasons, but only because the options are exactly equal in value, then it makes no difference what I choose. Raz argues that, in this case, one cannot *valuably* exercise autonomy. A genuine valuable choice thus occurs only when one is balancing incommensurable reasons. Autonomy can be meaningfully exercised only in the presence of incommensurability, which Raz defines as follows: 'A and B are incommensurate if it is neither true that one is better than the other nor true that they are of equal value.'[27]

---

[26] This claim is defended by Raz, along the lines sketched below, in *The Morality of Freedom*, pp. 351–6. See also Raz, *Engaging Reason*, pp. 46–66.

[27] Raz, *The Morality of Freedom*, p. 322.

The significance of the Moral and Razian Availability Claims is clear enough. Some moral theories make room for a multitude of permissible options or for genuine incommensurability, while other moral theories do not. (For instance, it is sometimes argued that Consequentialism cannot accommodate incommensurability.[28]) If we accept either the Moral Availability Claim or the Razian Availability Claim, then only theories of the former sort will be appropriate to the Realm of Reciprocity.

We would be unlikely to accept analogous claims regarding needs. Consider my need to eat enough to keep myself alive. It is clearly valuable for me to meet this need. It would be very odd to suggest that this value depends, to any degree, on my having freely chosen the option of eating in preference to incommensurable alternatives. It is also hard to imagine what those options might be. Accordingly, moral theories without genuine incommensurability may be perfectly appropriate to the Realm of Necessity.

Personally, I find it hard not to grant that incommensurability is a feature of our experience of the pursuit of goals, but not of the meeting of needs. For those who share this intuition, this establishes at least a prima facie case in favour of the Razian Availability Claim. Moral theories can then be allocated between the two realms partly on the basis of their ability to accommodate incommensurability. More modestly, the Moral Availability Claim captures a central feature of the role of goals in our lives. We can thus expect an adequate account of the Realm of Reciprocity to leave significant room for moral choice.

The Razian Availability Claim and the Moral Availability Claim are both controversial. If we seek a broad-based moral theory, then we may wish to found our arguments upon less contentious premises. Fortunately, the Practical Availability Claim is also morally significant. It shows that goals often require a social background that needs may lack, as the agent must live in a world with a variety of pursuable goals (see Section 7.8). The Practical Availability Claim also suggests that it may be difficult for me to measure the impact of my actions on someone else's pursuit of their goals. I may affect someone's well-being by removing options they would never have chosen, as I thereby alter the value of the options they choose. By contrast, it is comparatively easy to gauge how my actions are impacting on someone's basic needs. This suggests that rules of non-interference are more plausible in the Realm of Reciprocity, as the likelihood that active interference with others will have good consequences is much lower there than in the Realm of Necessity.

---

[28] For a balanced discussion, see ibid. 358–66. In subsequent chapters, I argue that a suitably restructured Consequentialism can accommodate incommensurability.

The Practical Availability Claim is thus sufficient to establish a significant role for autonomy in relation to goals. I shall rely upon this claim throughout the rest of this book. At certain points, my argument also appeals to the Moral Availability Claim and, occasionally, the stronger Razian claim. Further arguments in support of these more controversial claims will emerge as we proceed.

7.7. The Value of Autonomy

The availability of unchosen alternatives is morally significant because it is a necessary condition of autonomous choice. The value of such availability thus rests upon the value of autonomy. Why should we believe that autonomy is valuable? There are two possibilities: (1) autonomy is a valuable component of a worthwhile life; or (2) autonomy adds value to the pursuit of goals. Goals are more valuable if pursued autonomously.

Both possibilities are distinct from the claim that autonomy is merely instrumentally valuable. To see this, note that autonomy is instrumentally valuable even with respect to needs. Each agent has a strong incentive to meet her own needs, and is well placed to know what those needs are. Promoting individual autonomy is thus often the most efficient way to promote the meeting of needs. However, the fact that a need is met autonomously does not enhance the value of meeting that need.

Many contemporary accounts of the human good accord intrinsic value to autonomy.[29] Any moral theory incorporating such an account will obviously be interested in the conclusions of the previous section. If we wish our moral theory to be as general as possible, however, then we will want it to apply also to those accounts on which autonomy is not intrinsically valuable. We thus need to explore the indirect value of autonomy.

The pursuit of a morally worthwhile human goal develops certain human excellences, including capacities for deliberation, prudence, forethought, and cooperation. These capacities will be developed to different degrees by different goals, depending upon the complexity, sophistication, or difficulty of the goal. They can be developed only if the agent is able to choose how she will pursue the goal. (Pursuit of a goal may, of course, also develop other human excellences related to the content or nature of the goal, such as knowledge, mental agility, or physical prowess.)

---

[29] For overviews of the arguments here, see Raz, *The Morality of Freedom*, pp. 390–5, and Hurka, *Perfectionism*, pp. 148–52.

Some capacities are realized in a way that enhances the agent's well-being only if the goal is pursued in a morally legitimate fashion. For instance, the pursuit of a morally prohibited goal is unlikely to develop the agent's capacity for rational deliberation as fully as the pursuit of an otherwise indistinguishable permitted goal, especially if the capacity for rational deliberation is construed as including sensitivity to the interplay between moral and prudential reasons. If the value of pursuing a goal is to be fully realized, then the agent must be morally permitted to pursue that goal, and to choose it from a range of possible alternatives. (This reinforces the Moral Availability Claim discussed in the previous section.)

Much of the value resulting from the pursuit of goals is a by-product. The agent aims at a specific goal. She does not act just to develop her human excellences. However, the moral justification for a permission to pursue the goal may be grounded in its by-products rather than in either the conscious motivations of the agent or the value of the result at which she aims. Children's games provide an excellent analogy here. In the long run, the primary value of such games often lies in their development of valuable skills and character traits. From the point of view of the participants, this value is (at most) an unintended by-product. (Recall the discussion of Consequentialist decision procedures in Section 2.4.)

The same goal may realize different goods when pursued by different people (or it may realize the same good to different degrees). The following factors all affect the value of pursuing a goal.

1. *Different agents' relative ability, potential, or motivation.* Mozart's pursuit of violin playing made a more significant contribution to the overall value of his life than the violin playing of a reluctant and musically challenged child.

2. *The fit between this goal and others in the agent's life.* A goal that contributes to the balance and well-roundedness of one individual's life may have the opposite effect in the context of a life with too many similar goals already.[30]

3. *Some social contexts may be more conducive to some goals than others.* At the extreme, many goals are impossible without the appropriate social background. (See the discussions in the next section.) On the other hand, sometimes it may be more valuable for an agent to pursue a goal in adverse circumstances, and thereby develop perseverance, courage, and other related virtues. For instance, a friendship between two people from different ethnic groups might be a more valuable achievement in a racist society than an otherwise similar friendship in a more tolerant culture.

---

[30] See ibid. 84–98.

If autonomy is intrinsically valuable, then it may be one of the valuable human characteristics developed by pursuing a goal. For instance, agents often need to choose between various different ways of pursuing a given goal. Upon finishing graduate school, a philosopher must choose between a postdoctoral fellowship and a tenure-track position. Both are ways of pursuing her goal of building an academic career. By making such choices on a regular basis the agent develops her autonomy.

Autonomy may even be the direct achievement at which the goal aims. For instance, an agent may embark on the goal of enhancing her own autonomy, by refusing to conform to constricting stereotypes and social roles. Alternatively, an agent's goal may be to promote the autonomy of others. For instance, an agent who spends her spare time providing mobility assistance to people with disabilities increases their autonomy. When such goals are successfully pursued, we tend to regard the achievement involved as highly valuable. This suggests that we do consider autonomy to be valuable in its own right.

These observations confirm that meeting a person's needs furthers his well-being in a much more predictable way than trying to assist his pursuit of his goals, especially if the latter takes the form of choosing a person's goals for him. It is often difficult, if not impossible, to tell from the outside which goal would make the greatest contribution to another's well-being, as much of that contribution comes for the very process of choosing a goal. This strengthens the case for the instrumental value of autonomy. The agent herself is often the only person who can decide which goal it will be best for her to follow. Accordingly, her life will go better if she chooses her own goals.

On any plausible account of what makes human lives valuable in the modern world, autonomy is a vital component of the value of goals. By contrast, autonomy is of purely instrumental value in relation to needs. The promotion of individual autonomy may be the best way to meet needs. However, this case for autonomy is defeasible. If paternalism were more efficient then it would be superior. In the Realm of Reciprocity, autonomy is more intimately linked to value. The pursuit of goals cannot occur without autonomy. This case for autonomy is not defeasible. Autonomy is thus more significant in the Realm of Reciprocity than in the Realm of Necessity.

7.8. Autonomy and Community

Another distinguishing feature of goals is their intimate connection with human communities. This will provide a bridge between our two accounts of the distinction between the two moral realms. One way to approach this connection is via the notion of autonomy. There is a vast literature concerning autonomy and community, from which two broad claims emerge.[31]

Autonomy Requires Community.   Pursuit of goals is valuable only if it is done autonomously, and autonomy requires the existence of a human community.

Availability Requires Community.   Autonomy requires the availability of a range of goals, and a certain class of goals (or all goals) are available only within a human community.

We are speaking here of particular human communities, not the moral community *per se*. Examples of such communities include the following: a family, a married couple, a club, a religious group, a political party, an international academic community, an ethnic group, a city, a nation state. The focus of philosophical debate is usually on linguistic, cultural, ethnic, or national communities.

We begin with the direct route from autonomy to community. There are several possible claims here.

The Conceptual Necessity Claim.   Community membership is a necessary condition for the development of individual autonomy. It is only by belonging to and participating in the life of a community that a potential agent could possibly acquire the capacity to exercise rational agency. A related claim is that participation in a community of rational agents is a necessary ongoing condition for the exercise of individual autonomy. On this view, it is impossible to lead a completely solitary autonomous life.

The Practical Necessity Claim.   While perfectly solitary moral agents may be a conceptual possibility, the facts of human psychology make it impossible for human beings to become (or remain) functioning moral agents without participating in some human community.

The Evaluative Necessity Claim.   Autonomy is possible outside of a human community, but only within such a community can it enhance the value of an agent's life.

The most natural argument for the Evaluative Necessity Claim is that autonomy is valuable only if exercised in pursuit of valuable goals, while the presence of certain human communities is a necessary condition for any goal to be valuable. This would lead us to our second set of claims, concerning the relationship between community and availability. As we will return to these claims later, we shall focus for now on claims of conceptual and practical necessity.

---

[31] See e.g. Kymlicka, 'Community'; Kymlicka, *Liberalism, Community and Culture*; Mason, 'Liberalism and the Value of Community'; Pettit, *The Common Mind*, pp. 165–214; and Raz, *The Morality of Freedom*, pp. 205–7.

Proponents of these claims often argue that many human capacities can be developed only in a human community. Such capacities include nurturing, caring, cooperation, artistic achievement, and advanced theoretical knowledge. One might also include such seemingly self-regarding capacities as deliberation and self-knowledge. For instance, perhaps an agent can acquire worthwhile self-knowledge only by comparing herself with other agents with whom she interacts regularly. As we shall see in Chapter 9, some philosophers even claim that the very capacity for thought is conceptually dependent upon interpersonal relationships, and that the very idea of value itself requires community. If any of these capacities are essential conditions of autonomous agency, then community membership will be similarly essential.

If either the Conceptual or the Practical Necessity Claim can be established, and if we accept that autonomy is valuable (either intrinsically or indirectly), then any moral theory must permit the option of belonging to and participating in a range of human communities. If the pursuit of community-based goals is necessary for agency (either conceptually or practically), then only an impossibly demanding moral theory will fail to permit such goals.

The Conceptual Necessity Claim is controversial. Our moral theory will rest more securely if it is built on less contentious foundations. Fortunately, the Practical Necessity Claim is much less controversial. Few would deny that human community is, in fact, necessary for the development of the various capacities underlying human agency. There are no recorded instances of a human being developing moral agency in the absence of some community. However, the Practical Necessity Claim is very broad. A wide range of possible human communities might provide the necessary conditions for agency. The range of moral theories consistent with such communities would be even broader. The Practical Necessity Claim alone offers little guidance to moral theory.

In search of more specific constraints on our moral theory, we turn now to the relationship between human communities and the practical availability of valuable goals. In relation to any particular goal (call it G) there are several possible claims.

The Conceptual Dependence Claim.   Pursuit of G is inconceivable outside a particular class of human communities. One cannot even aspire to be a lawyer unless one has been exposed to a society built on the concept of legal system. One cannot hope to succeed in becoming a lawyer unless one lives in such a society.

The Practical Dependence Claim.   Pursuit of G would be practically impossible outside a particular class of human communities. One cannot undertake research into particle physics unless one has a trained workforce to construct and operate one's laboratory equipment.

The Strong Value Dependence Claim.   Pursuit of G is worthless unless it occurs in a human community which values the realisation of G. Excellent performance in a particular athletic activity may only be valuable in a culture where that sport is valued.

The Weak Value Dependence Claim.   Pursuit of G is considerably more valuable if it occurs within a human community that values the realization of G than if it occurs outside such a community. Even if it always has some value, athletic performance may be more valuable in a sport-worshipping culture.

Each of these claims entails all weaker claims. If any of these claims is true, we shall say that G 'depends upon community'. We might also refer to G as a 'community-based goal'. We shall see that such goals are very significant for moral theory (see Sections 8.4 and 10.7).

   In moral theory, we are likely to be more interested in claims regarding classes of goals rather than individual goals. In particular, we will be interested in the following sets of claims.

The Global Dependence Claim.   All goals depend upon community (to a specified degree).

The Worthwhile Dependence Claim.   All valuable goals depend upon community (to a specified degree).

The Essential Dependence Claim.   There is a general class of goals (call it C) such that (1) all members of C depend upon community (to a specified degree); and (2) no agent can lead a worthwhile human life unless she pursues at least one goal belonging to C.

The Global Dependence Claim entails the Worthwhile Dependence Claim, which entails the Essential Dependence Claim. The latter implication requires the (plausible) assumption that worthwhile lives require the pursuit of some worthwhile goals (see Section 7.5). We can thus focus on the last claim, asking if even this weak claim is strong enough to establish a significant role for goals. To give our theory even broader foundations, let us focus on the weak form of this claim.

The Weak Essential Dependence Claim.   There is a general class of goals (call it C) such that (1) all members of C depend upon community, but only in the weak sense that pursuit of them is considerably more valuable if it occurs within a human community that values their realization than if it occurs outside such a community; and (2) no agent can lead a worthwhile human life unless she pursues at least one goal belonging to C.

If even this weak claim can be established, and if we seek a moral theory that is not unreasonably demanding, then we must permit agents to pursue at least some community-based goals. In subsequent chapters, we will ask whether such permissions are best captured by Scheffler's Agent Centred Prerogative, by the ideal code of Rule Consequentialism, or by some other moral theory.

The Weak Essential Dependence Claim is at least very plausible, given our culture. It is extremely difficult to see how anyone born into a modern liberal democracy could live a worthwhile life without pursuing any community-based goals. The accommodation of such goals is thus a necessary feature of any acceptable account of the Realm of Reciprocity. As we saw in the previous section, autonomy requires the availability of a number of goals. The significance of community-based goals suggests that autonomous agents must choose from a range of distinct, permissible, and preferably incommensurable, community-based goals. If our moral theory values autonomy, then it will favour the establishment and maintenance of an appropriately liberal community.

7.9. The Non-Competition Thesis

The link between goals and community also brings out several other significant differences between the two moral realms. One such difference is the following.

The Non-Competition Thesis. Conflicts of well-being between different agents are less significant (less common, less severe, less intractable) in the Realm of Reciprocity than in the Realm of Necessity.[32]

To illustrate this thesis, contrast the following two tales.

The Urgent Trade-off. Doctor Bob has two patients who will both die immediately unless they are given Drug X. Drug X leads to a full recovery. Doctor Bob has only enough of Drug X to treat one patient.

The Mild Trade-off. Philanthropic Phil has decided to make a grant to assist a struggling artist. There are two applicants, each of whom has an ambitious project he will be unable to complete without a grant from Phil. Phil has only enough money to make one grant.

---

[32] For defences of claims analogous to the Non-Competition Thesis, see Hurka, *Perfectionism*, pp. 66–8, pp. 176–80; Raz, *The Morality of Freedom*, pp. 202–9, 307–20; and Scheffler, *Human Morality*, pp. 137–45.

Each of these tales deals with a conflict between the well-being of two agents. Doctor Bob and Philanthropic Phil must each decide whose interests they will advance. However, Doctor Bob's dilemma is obviously more serious than Philanthropic Phil's. The patient who does not receive Drug X will die, and no one can do anything to prevent this. By contrast, the artist who does not receive a grant will be prevented from pursuing only one particular goal. While this goal may be very important to her, there will presumably be many other (equally valuable) goals she could pursue instead. There are also many things Phil could do to assist her in finding a less expensive goal, even if he is able to provide only one grant.

In the Realm of Necessity, conflicts such as the Urgent Trade-off are a regular fact of life. When we are allocating scarce resources, we often face hard choices between competing needs. Sometimes we will be able to find ways of meeting all those needs. Often, like Doctor Bob, we must leave some needs unmet. Indeed, moral issues arise in this realm only when resources are insufficient to meet everyone's needs.

In the Realm of Reciprocity, on the other hand, even weaker dilemmas such as the Mild Trade-off are not inevitable. The most effective way to promote an agent's pursuit of her goals is often to enhance the social framework that makes those goals available. Any such enhancement will also assist other agents in the pursuit of their goals, as a valuable social framework is a public good. In particular, it is unlikely that we will be able to increase the general level of well-being, in relation to goals, by preventing any particular individual from effectively pursuing her goals.

This may seem implausible. What about an agent with vicious goals, such as Adolf Hitler? Surely, if Hitler had been prevented from effectively pursuing his goals, then the general level of well-being with respect to goals would have increased. There are several ways to respond to this challenge. Any such restriction would have left Hitler free to pursue other goals. At least some of those other goals would have been independently valuable, while Hitler's chosen goals were not. If the value of a person's life depends, to any degree, on the independent value of the goals he or she pursues, then a restriction preventing agents from pursuing vicious goals might well have made Hitler's life go better, in respect of the pursuit of goals, rather than worse. More importantly, Hitler is an extreme case. Perhaps some restrictions on the pursuit of goals do indeed increase the general level of well-being. However, most attempts at coercion will not. Within the Realm of Reciprocity, Consequentialist considerations may be sufficient to justify something like Mill's Harm Principle, but more paternalistic interventions are likely to be counterproductive.

It is easy to misunderstand the Non-Competition Thesis. It does not claim that conflict is absent in the Realm of Reciprocity. In practice, goals often come into conflict. A most striking feature of our own culture is that many goals fundamentally require competition. In recent human history, conflict regarding goals has quite possibly produced more misery than conflict regarding needs. The Non-Competition Thesis does not deny these facts. Rather, it claims that the nature and moral significance of conflict is different in the two realms.

In the Realm of Necessity, conflicting basic needs inevitably lead to unavoidable conflicts of well-being. Either we have enough resources to meet everyone's basic needs, or we do not. If we do, then there is no conflict, and thus no real need for morality. If we do not, then we must choose whose needs to meet. For those whose needs go unmet, the result is a serious loss of well-being. The morality of necessity is all about conflicts of well-being.

In the Realm of Reciprocity, by contrast, conflict is not inevitable, nor is it so intimately linked to well-being. No goal is essential to an agent's well-being. For any actual goal an agent has, there are many alternatives that could play the same role in her life. No particular goal has as close a connection with well-being as, for instance, the need for breathable air. When a conflict arises between the goals different agents happen to have, one way to dissolve that conflict is by adopting compatible goals.

From the point of view of moral theory, basic needs are treated as given. I do not mean that all questions regarding needs are obvious, that our pre-theoretic intuitions regarding needs are infallible, or that needs are discovered by factual enquiry alone. Moral theory does have a role to play in helping to determine what our basic needs are. This is a significant part of our theory of the good. However, once we have settled on our preferred account of what basic needs there are, our theory of right action takes those needs as given. It is otherwise with respect to goals. Our account of goals will tell us which goals we can have, and one task of our theory of right action is then to tell us which of those goals we *should* have.

Much debate regarding needs concerns derived needs, rather than basic ones. Consider the controversy regarding the 'need' for literacy or access to television. Opponents of these needs point out that in previous centuries, not to mention prehistoric times, no one was literate or owned a television. Therefore, they conclude, there is no basic human need for such things. The most plausible response points to some more general, underlying need. Everyone needs the ability to participate in the culture around them. In a predominantly literate culture, this need can be met only if one is literate. In a televisual culture, it requires television. (Opponents might respond with the possibility of a perfectly isolated human being, participating in no culture. However, such a person would be unable to pursue any goals. As we saw in the previous section, his quality of life would thus be very limited. As we shall see in Chapter 9, the perfectly isolated individual may in fact be a conceptual impossibility.)

Except in exceptional circumstances, the impact of societal conditions and moral rules on needs is one dimensional. Assume, for instance, that we wish to evaluate moral rules in terms of the promotion of aggregate well-being. In the Realm of Necessity, we simply ask how well each set of rules meets agents' predefined needs. By contrast, the impact of moral rules on goals is two dimensional. Rules affect not only agents' ability successfully to pursue their goals, but also what goals they have. In this realm, morality shapes our agency, rather than simply responding to our needs.

Many moral philosophers have argued that conflict regarding goals often arises because people have inappropriate or morally unworthy goals. As Hurka puts it: 'It is not normally a condition for one person's achieving excellence that others not do so, nor do his attainments often exclude theirs.'[33] Therefore, conflict between agents would not arise if we all sought genuine excellence. 'There are ways of seeking one's own perfection that harm others. . . . [But] these ways are not usually intrinsically far preferable to others. To avoid them, one need only choose something equally or almost equally good in oneself.'[34]

T. H. Green went so far as to argue that non-competition places a necessary condition on acceptable moralities. The true notion of good, Green wrote, 'implies interest in an object which is common to all men in the proper sense . . . that there can be no competition for its attainment between man and man; and the only interest that satisfies this condition is the interest . . . in the perfecting of man or the realization of the powers of the human soul'.[35] The possibility of conflicting interests is a proof, for Green, that one's theory of the human good is inadequate.

As Hurka notes, Green's claim was disputed by Sidgwick. Sidgwick argued that 'so long as the material conditions of human existence remain at all the same as they are now', the achievements of different people can conflict.[36] In terms of our present discussion, we can see Green as focusing on the Realm of Reciprocity, where appropriate moral rules can avoid competition; whereas Sidgwick, looking at the Realm of Necessity, sees that competition cannot be alleviated by a change in moral rules alone. Goals are more plastic than needs. Consequently, an ideal code of reciprocity might reasonably be expected to generate non-competitive goals, whereas only more efficient production of various natural resources can eliminate competition regarding

---

[33] Hurka, *Perfectionism*, p. 66.   [34] Ibid. 67.
[35] Green, *Prolegomena to Ethics*, sections 232, 281, quoted in Hurka, *Perfectionism*, p. 67.
[36] Sidgwick, *Lectures of the Ethics of T. H. Green, H. Spencer, and J. Martineau*, p. 67, quoted in Hurka, *Perfectionism*, p. 67.

needs. This historical debate illustrates my general claim that Consequentialists have focused on the Realm of Necessity, while non-Consequentialists have privileged the Realm of Reciprocity.

On the Hurka–Green view, one principal aim of morality is to arbitrate between conflicting goals and desires without reducing any agents' well-being, by encouraging agents to develop and pursue compatible goals. This notion of compatibility concerns both the relationship between a particular agent's own reasons and conflict between the interests of different agents.

Scheffler expresses a similar point: 'As a person acquires the capacity for moral motivation . . . one thing that happens is that the person attempts increasingly to shape his or her projects, insofar as it is possible to do so, to avoid conflict with moral requirements'.[37] Within the Realm of Reciprocity, such internal conflicts arise only when the agent's goals are in competition with the goals of others. The best way to avoid conflict with morality, therefore, is to develop non-competitive goals. On many sophisticated accounts of well-being, 'it is in one's interests to have one's interests be compatible with moral requirements'.[38] Furthermore, 'conflicts between morality and the interests of the agent will tend to be quite common in a seriously unjust society'.[39] In a just society, on the other hand, 'it is much easier to shape one's interests so as to avoid conflicts with morality'.[40]

Conflict will be more common in an unjust society for two reasons, related to the two realms. In the Realm of Necessity an unjust society leaves many basic needs unmet. This generates moral requirements on individual agents to alleviate those needs. Such requirements may conflict with their personal goals. Within the Realm of Reciprocity, an unjust society may unduly encourage competitive goals, rather than non-competitive ones. As the nature of injustice differs between the two realms, the way moral theory responds to the potential for injustice will also differ. In the Realm of Necessity, justice requires that we meet all existing needs, in so far as our productive capacity permits. In the Realm of Reciprocity, justice may require us first to purify our existing goals, before telling us how to pursue those goals. It is this difference that underlies the Non-Competition Thesis.

Properly understood, the Non-Competition Thesis is highly plausible. We shall see its full significance in Sections 8.4, 8.5, and 8.8.

7.10. Goals and Cultural Relativism

The flexibility of goals raises the spectre of cultural relativism. The existence and value of an agent's goals depend upon her community. Different

---

[37] Scheffler, *Human Morality*, pp. 128–9.   [38] Ibid. 141.   [39] Ibid. 140.   [40] Ibid.

communities give rise to different goals. If goals are a significant component of well-being, this suggests that well-being differs across cultures. In so far as morality responds to well-being, what is right and wrong will also be culturally relative.

Cultural relativism can mean many different things. In particular, there are two distinct senses in which value can depend upon culture. (1) Views about what is valuable differ across cultures. One form of cultural relativism identifies what is right within a culture with whatever that culture believes to be right. (2) Suppose instead that a culturally neutral standard determines what is valuable. Value might still depend upon culture, as culture determines which valuable things are available to a particular agent. Our interest here is in the second form of cultural relativism. If we accept that needs and goals are the basic components of well-being, does the relationship between goals and community require us to accept that the moral code appropriate to the Realm of Reciprocity will vary across cultures?

There are several reasons to think not. Our discussion of goals taught us that the best way to promote the valuable pursuit of goals is with a liberal system of non-interference. The ideal moral code for goals does not focus on the details of particular goals, as it leaves agents free to pursue whatever goals they have. Societies with very different available goals might thus have very similar moral codes. By contrast, if basic needs differed radically between cultures, then we might find very different codes of necessity.

The efficiency of non-interference is based on the connection between goals and autonomy. This feature of goals is accentuated in Western liberal democracies. But it is not peculiar to such societies. All human goals are most valuable when autonomously pursued. The best moral code for goals may not be the code a particular society associates with its own goals. Even in an illiberal society, a liberal policy of non-interference might be the most appropriate way to respond to the value of goals.

The flexibility of goals may even serve to reduce cultural relativism. Patterns of available goals are not cast in stone. If an inadequate range of goals are available, it may be appropriate to encourage the rise of new goals. Optimal patterns of goal availability may thus differ less across cultures than actual patterns.

Cultures often borrow goals from one another. Different cultures are not radically incommensurable. It is always possible (though often very difficult) for a person from one culture to understand another culture. Goals arising in one culture often become available in another. The goal of becoming an expert chess player first arose in the culture of ancient India, but has since become available in many quite distinct cultures. Borrowing from another culture is often more efficient than inventing new goals from scratch. The search for a broader range of goals thus brings cultures closer together.

The flexibility of goals does not entail cultural relativism. Some local variations are to be expected, but the general structure of the moral code of reciprocity is likely to be fairly constant. The moral code governing the Realm of Necessity is unlikely to change at all, as basic human needs do not vary significantly across cultures.

7.11. Needs, Goals, and Community

At the start of this chapter, I presented two accounts of the distinction between the two moral realms. The first is based on the distinction between needs and goals, the second on the notion of moral community. We have focused thus far on the first account. We turn now to the second. To illustrate the connections between the two accounts, consider two extreme cases.

The Need-Free Society.   Imagine a world where all the basic needs of all agents are met, including the need to be provided with the background conditions of autonomous action. What would morality look like within such a society? Which moral questions or problems would arise?

The Goalless World.   Imagine a world of creatures whose well-being consists only of needs, rather than goals. What would morality look like within such a society? Which moral questions or problems would arise?

This is the simplest version of the Goalless World. Similar moral issues arise if we imagine a world of creatures who can effortlessly pursue their own goals without any assistance from others, and without the depletion of resources necessary for the meeting of needs, bearing in mind that the agent's own time is one such resource. Or we might imagine a world where all moral reasons derived from needs were lexically prior to all moral reasons derived from goals. This last characterization of the goalless world may correspond to the views of some extreme utilitarians.

There are several things to note about these two extreme scenarios. The first is that they give rise to very different moral problems. The main decisions facing inhabitants of a Need-Free Society relate to how they should work together to pursue their various (overlapping) goals. What they need most from a moral theory, therefore, is a set of rules governing cooperative interaction. We might say that they seek a code of reciprocity, not a code of necessity. By contrast, the inhabitants of the Goalless World will be preoccupied with meeting their own basic needs. If they have any need for moral theory, they will seek a code of necessity, not one of reciprocity. If some moral theories work better for goals, and others work better for needs, then we might thus expect two different moral theories to be useful in the two situations. A related difference between the two scenarios concerns sentient non-rational beings, such as animals. Animals have only needs, not goals. Therefore, in a Need-Free Society, where we can assume that all the needs of all animals are met, moral theory need not concern itself with animals. We shall see the significance of this fact in the next chapter (see Section 8.8).

The second significant difference is that the notion of community applies much more readily to the Need-Free Society than to the Goalless World. The Goalless World is not really a community at all. Relations between people will be very limited. In the absence of goals, one's relations with other people will be purely instrumental. Others will enter into one's calculations only as a means to one's pre-existing ends. It is only once goals (and, especially, community-based goals) enter the picture that relations with others can become an end in themselves, as such relations are intrinsic to the goals one pursues. Only at this point does it make sense to speak of a genuine community.

On the other hand, the Need-Free Society is very much a community. As we saw earlier, the connections between goals, autonomy, and community are very close. In a world with only goals, the intrinsic significance of inter-personal relationships will loom large.

Theories based on the notion of community will not apply to the Goalless World. The Need-Free Society will be their natural home. On the other hand, moral theories that have difficulty accommodating the notions of community, autonomy and goals will fare better in the Goalless World than in the Need-Free Society. Once again, we see that different moral theories, and different modes of moral justification, will be required in different realms.

Consider two prominent moral idioms: the Kantian idiom of the Categorical Imperative, with its subsidiary notions of universal law, respect for autonomous persons, and the kingdom of ends; and the Utilitarian ideal of welfare maximization. The former is better suited to the refined community of the Need-Free Society, while the latter is better suited to the simple environment of the Goalless World. A central theme of the rest of this book will be that Kantian idioms work best in the Realm of Reciprocity, while Utilitarian idioms are most at home in the Realm of Necessity.

Our two extreme scenarios are both highly implausible. It is very difficult to imagine what life might be like in either of them. One is a superhuman world of angels, the other a subhuman world of animals. A Goalless World may be even harder to imagine than a Need-Free Society. The problem with the latter is that it bears little relation to the situation of any actual moral agent. However fortunate one is, someone's needs are always at stake some-where in one's world. (Utilitarians routinely accuse their opponents of over-looking this sobering fact.) The Goalless World, by contrast, may face the deeper objection that it contains no moral agents at all. Creatures whose lives contained only basic needs would hardly count as moral agents, at least on many plausible views. If the inhabitants of the Goalless World are not moral agents, then it makes little sense to seek a moral theory to govern their behaviour.

The Need-Free Society is missing many of our most urgent moral dilemmas, including those that form the starting point for this book. The Goalless World, on the other hand, lacks most of what gives meaning and purpose to our lives. Either realm, considered in isolation, captures only a very lop-sided and implausible view of moral life. This is very significant. We must not proceed as if one realm were the whole of morality. If we are to develop an adequate moral theory to cope with everyday life, then we will need accounts of both realms. We will also need a sensitive account of the boundary between the two realms. Mistakes will inevitably arise whenever we treat one realm as if it were the whole of morality. I shall argue in the remaining chapters that many of the familiar failings of contemporary moral theories arise from mistakes of this sort.

7.12. Economics in the Two Realms

As Partha Dasgupta points out, something like the Need-Free Society is implicitly assumed in much of the traditional economic theory of resource allocation. 'The standard theory . . . does not accommodate the notion of basic physiological needs.'[41] Different methods of resource allocation are compared with a baseline where all agents can survive without interaction. 'The theory in its textbook guise assumes that each household is capable of surviving in good health even were it to be autarkic. . . . Exchange in the theory allows households to improve their lot; it is not necessary for survival.'[42] Dasgupta also notes that 'much contemporary ethics assumes . . . that [basic] needs have been met'.[43] This assumption clearly brings us close to the Need-Free Society, and firmly into the Realm of Reciprocity.

This reinforces what will emerge as a central claim of this book. Moral theory and our moral intuitions are better suited to (and implicitly presuppose) the Realm of Reciprocity. An understanding of the structure of the Need-Free Society is necessary to understand contemporary moral and economic thought, however unrealistic that ideal society may be. Dasgupta's critique of traditional resource allocation theory also provides an interesting parallel to my own critique of many moral theories. We both suggest that theories go wrong in the Realm of Necessity because they are designed for

---

[41] Dasgupta, *Well-Being and Destitution*, p. 11.   [42] Ibid. 169–70.   [43] Ibid. 45.

the Realm of Reciprocity. This is especially significant for those moral theories drawing on the insights of contemporary economics, such as many Consequentialist and Contractarian theories. We call illustrate this using a prominent example.

The distinction between the realms provides a new critique of David Gauthier's Contractarian theory, from two directions.[44]

1. Gauthier ignores basic needs, as his bargaining situation implicitly assumes that individuals can survive without interacting. This failing arises because Gauthier borrows his account of the initial bargaining situation from the orthodox economic theory of resource allocation. The Realm of Necessity is thus completely ignored. I argue at length elsewhere that the Contractarian Model yields very different moral principles once it is amended to account for basic needs.[45]

2. Gauthier's account of rationality ignores the subtle complexity of goals, especially their interpersonal dimension. This leads him to see the bargaining situation in fundamentally competitive rather than cooperative terms. The Realm of Reciprocity is misconceived. Again, this is because Gauthier borrows heavily from traditional economics, in this case adopting a preference-based account of well-being and motivation.

This brief discussion of Gauthier also suggests a more general critique of all moral theories based on traditional economic theory. Such theories tend to assimilate both needs and goals to preferences. As a result, they cope adequately with neither, ignoring one realm and misconceiving the other.

7.13. Boundaries

The categorization of moral realms in terms of components of well-being is not strictly coextensive with the division in terms of the moral community. For instance, sometimes one must meet the needs of an active moral agent, in order to maintain her capacity for agency. Under the classification based on community, such actions would fall within the Realm of Reciprocity, whereas a classification based on components of well-being would place them in the Realm of Necessity.

However, the two classification schemes will generally go together. This is because most interactions between active moral agents relate to their goals rather than their needs. (This is especially true in the modern developed

---

[44] See esp. Gauthier, *Morals by Agreement*.
[45] Mulgan, *Future People*, chapter two.

world, and most especially among its more affluent inhabitants.) Most of our everyday life thus takes place within the Realm of Reciprocity. As Raz puts it: 'All except those who live in circumstances of the most severe deprivation, have aspirations, projects and preoccupations which far transcend the satisfaction of the bare biologically determined needs'.[46] On the other hand, if one is dealing with someone who is not an active moral agent, then, by definition, one can be concerned only to meet his needs, as such a person is not in a position to pursue any goals until his basic needs have been met. This explains why deciding whether or not to contribute to famine relief falls within the Realm of Necessity.

It is worth pausing to examine two cases on the boundary between the two moral realms. In the first, questions of need arise with the moral community. In the second, we consider the goals of those in dire need in distant countries. We begin with the first boundary case. Consider a situation where the needs of people in the developed world come under threat. In my view, such cases are best treated as falling within the Realm of Reciprocity. The set of moral rules governing the legitimate pursuit of goals within a moral community will include rules for dealing with disasters within that community, such as rules of mutual aid or cooperation. (Although they fall under the Realm of Reciprocity, these first boundary cases may share some features of the Realm of Necessity. They form a special region within the Realm of Reciprocity, where slightly different moral rules may apply. This possibility is explored in Section 8.6.)

Our response to a crisis within our own community is often strikingly different from our response to famine or destitution in a foreign land. This is often regarded, especially by Consequentialist moral philosophers, as evidence of morally unacceptable parochialism.[47] Perhaps, on the contrary, it reflects the fact that the crises belong to different moral realms. When a disaster strikes those with whom we interact regularly, we respond in accordance with our code of reciprocity. Our response to distant famine falls instead under the rules governing the Realm of Necessity.

We now consider a simple example of the second boundary case. I am travelling through the desert, when I come upon two starving creatures. One is a human being, the other a cow. I have enough spare food to save one creature from starvation. Obviously, I should assist the human being. This cannot be because her needs are greater, as each creature has the most urgent possible need. Each will die without food. The needs of the human being, though

---

[46] Raz, *The Morality of Freedom*, p. 340. See also Griffin, *Well-Being*, p. 67, and Hurka, *Perfectionism*, p. 150.

[47] Singer, 'Famine, Affluence and Morality', and Unger, *Living High and Letting Die*.

no greater than those of the cow, have greater moral significance. This is because they are the needs of a creature who has, or will have, goals as well as needs. A destitute person's goals may also affect how I should go about meeting his needs. I should try to leave the person best able to pursue whatever goals he will have.

Even very destitute people can have goals and aspirations. When dealing with such a person, we need to separate two classes of goals: (1) actual present goals, which the person has even while destitute, (2) hypothetical future goals, which the destitute person does not currently have, but which we can reliably infer that he will have in future once his basic needs have been met. Both classes of goals are relevant to our moral deliberations, as both give extra urgency to my reason to meet the person's needs. The difference between these two classes of goals is not too significant in extreme cases, as no goals can effectively be pursued until the person's basic needs are met.

How does this case fit into the framework of the two moral realms? Once again, I give precedence to considerations of moral community. This case belongs within the Realm of Necessity. When we are dealing with an agent whose basic needs are unmet, and who does not already belong to our community of interaction, then we are outside the bounds of our moral community. One justification for this categorization is pragmatic: proceeding in this way provides the best explanation of our moral intuitions, and the most promising foundation for a new Consequentialist moral theory. More specific justifications will emerge as we proceed.

The boundaries between the moral realms are fluid. Many (perhaps even most) significant moral dilemmas occur at those boundaries. We may thus wonder whether the division into moral realms does any significant work. I believe that it does. The distinction tracks a significant difference between two ways a situation can invite our moral attention and concern; between two sources of moral reasons; or, perhaps more accurately, between two routes from values to reasons. Different moral theories are built upon these different routes. No moral theory based on one route alone can hope to provide a full account of the relationship between values and reasons. Moral dilemmas arise precisely where, and because, different routes intersect. Any attempt to separate the two realms neatly and completely is bound to be an oversimplification. However, such attempts are also a vital preliminary to the construction of an adequate moral theory.

We live in a world where both needs and goals are morally significant, where many needs are left unmet and many goals unrealized, and where the pursuit of our goals leaves the needs of others unmet. In any such world one of the central tasks of moral philosophy is to balance the competing moral reasons generated by needs and goals. My central claim is that this balance is best achieved by combining different moral theories, rather than by seeking to apply a single Consequentialist theory to all the disparate moral realms.

7.14. Lessons for Moral Theory

There are many differences between the Realms of Reciprocity and Necessity, mostly due to the different ways in which needs and goals contribute to an agent's well-being. These differences suggest that different moral principles are appropriate to different realms. We can draw several general lessons for moral theory, to be explored in subsequent chapters.

1. Several concepts are more significant when applied to goals as opposed to needs. These include: autonomy, community, choice, incommensurability, agency, freedom. Moral theories built upon these ideas are better suited to the Realm of Reciprocity. Conversely, objections to a particular theory based on its inability to accommodate these concepts will have great force in the Realm of Reciprocity, but comparatively little force in the Realm of Necessity.

2. The impact of my actions on the well-being of others is more predictable with respect to needs than with respect to goals. My chances of successfully improving a person's well-being by interfering with his pursuit of his goals are low. Rules of non-interference are thus likely to feature more prominently in the Realm of Reciprocity. Theories sanctioning paternalistic interventions are more at home in the Realm of Necessity.

3. Many significant moral choices arise at the boundary between the two moral realms. Any adequate moral theory must account for this fact, by telling us how to balance the demands and requirements of the two realms.

4. The distinction between the moral realms cuts across the distinction between self-concern and concern for others. In so far as the former distinction is the more morally significant, this may undermine the significance of the latter. This conclusion becomes especially important when we start to design the foundations of our new Consequentialist theory, as traditional Consequentialist moral theory regards the conflict between morality and self-interest as the central moral problem.

5. Consequentialism cannot treat well-being as a place-holder. It cannot simply tell us to promote 'whatever makes life worth living'. Needs and goals generate two very different kinds of moral reasons. Consequentialism must separate the components of well-being, and respond appropriately to their respective realms.

6. Any adequate moral theory will have three components.

(A) An account of our obligations within the Realm of Reciprocity. This part of the theory must cope well with the concepts listed under (1) above. It will be moulded to the nature and moral significance of goals, and focus on the rational, interpersonal, and social aspects of human nature. This is the natural place for the idioms of Kantian moral theory and of Contractualism. Perhaps more surprisingly, this is also the right realm for Rule Consequentialism.

As we will see in subsequent chapters, most arguments offered in support of constraints on the promotion of the good appeal to concepts belonging to the Realm of Reciprocity. Constraints and restrictions are thus more likely to feature in the Realm of Reciprocity. The same is also true of arguments in support of Agent Centred Prerogatives and permissions to depart from the Reason to Promote the Good. These too belong to the Realm of Reciprocity.

(B) An account of our obligations within the Realm of Necessity. This part of our moral theory need not pay too much attention to the concepts listed under (1) above. It will be moulded to the nature and moral significance of needs, and focus on the physical side of human (and animal) life. It is less likely to include prerogatives or restrictions. This is the natural place for the idioms of Utilitarianism, and of Simple Consequentialism more generally.

(C) An account of the relationship between the two moral realms. This part of our theory balances the two component moral theories (A) and (B). It will balance goals against needs, and explore the common ground between Kantian and Consequentialist moral idioms. Unsurprisingly, this is the natural place for Hybrid Moral Theories, such as that developed by Scheffler. As we shall see, Scheffler's original theory requires considerable restructuring before it can play this new role.

8

The Morality of Reciprocity

This chapter revisits the discussions of Part Two in the light of the distinction between the two moral realms. This discussion will play three roles. It serves:

1. to illustrate the significance of the different realms;
2. to explain why Collective Consequentialism fails; and
3. to show how Collective Consequentialist theories can nonetheless be successfully incorporated into the new Consequentialist moral theory to be developed in the final chapter.

I focus on Rule Consequentialism, seeking to establish two claims. (1) Many common objections to Rule Consequentialism (such as those presented in Chapter 3 of this book) rely on features peculiar to the Realm of Necessity. We can thus reinterpret Chapter 3 as demonstrating that Rule Consequentialism is not an acceptable account of the Realm of Necessity. (2) If the Realm of Reciprocity were the whole of morality, then Rule Consequentialism would be an acceptable moral theory.

We begin with two simple objections to Rule Consequentialism, demonstrating how they apply only in the Realm of Reciprocity (Sections 8.1 and 8.2). We then revisit Murphy's Compliance Condition (Section 8.3). Although not acceptable as a constraint on either realm, the Compliance Condition emerges as a useful tool for Rule Consequentialism in some key areas of the Realm of Reciprocity. Section 8.4 explores the Rule Consequentialist code for that realm, drawing attention to its differences from the code governing the Realm of Necessity. We then revisit our remaining objections from Chapter 3, to see if they apply in the Realm of Reciprocity (Section 8.5). Remaining sections justify the choice of Rule Consequentialism over Non-Consequentialist rivals in that realm, especially Contractualism. A key claim is that Rule Consequentialism and Contractualism coincide in the Realm of Reciprocity (Section 8.8).

8.1. The Wrong Facts Objection Revisited

In this section, I demonstrate that the Wrong Facts Objection applies when a moral theory fails to distinguish the different moral realms. The central claim of the Wrong Facts Objection, as applied both to Rule Consequentialism and to Murphy's Cooperative Principle, is that Collective Consequentialism accords undue significance to certain facts (see Sections 3.6 and 4.3). In many cases, these are facts about the agent's moral community (for instance, the number of active members of that community, the strength of their disposition to cooperate, their ability to promote the good, the ratio of active moral agents to potential members of the moral community, and so on).

The two moral realms thus provide an explanation of the intuitions behind the Wrong Facts Objection. The Wrong Facts Objection rejects appeals to facts about the moral community. Those facts are not relevant within the Realm of Necessity. As famine relief belongs to that very realm, Rule Consequentialism's treatment of famine relief illicitly appeals to facts from the wrong moral realm.

There are several ways to illustrate the link between the Wrong Facts Objection and the two realms. Recall the notion of moral community, as outlined in Sections 7.1 and 7.8. The Rule Consequentialist account of the limits of morality may be acceptable when we are distributing the fruits of membership of the moral community, but not when we are deciding whether to provide the necessary preconditions for such membership. An individual agent's claim to the preconditions of agency are, morally speaking, very different from her claims to any fruits of membership. We might classify the latter as claims of 'discretionary distributive justice', relating to the distribution of non-essential goods within a community. (A full theory of distributive justice would also address the distribution of essential goods and the meeting of needs.) These are claims that the individual agent has against the moral community in the first instance. They only indirectly generate claims against other individuals. By contrast, claims to be provided with the preconditions of moral agency are not appropriate objects of communal decision-making. (Or at least, not to the same extent or in the same way as fruit claims.) Therefore, our response to such claims should not depend upon the details of our own moral community.

Recall also the distinction between needs and goals. Within the Realm of Reciprocity, our aim is to facilitate the pursuit of goals. Agents whose basic needs are met can pursue a wide variety of goals. They must be provided with some range of pursuable goals, but no particular set of goals is required. Accordingly, no particular distribution of goods and services is essential for the well-being of agents. It is thus appropriate for the community (and the

212 COMBINED CONSEQUENTIALISM

individuals within it) to determine how life should be organized within the Realm of Reciprocity.

By contrast, the Realm of Necessity deals with agents' claims to be provided with the preconditions of moral agency. These claims are derived from basic needs, and are thus not optional, discretionary, or community dependent, unlike goal-based claims. Unlike goals, the significance and urgency of an agent's basic needs are not affected by her relations with other agents. Agents cannot choose their needs. Need-based claims hold directly between one (potential) moral agent and every other agent who is in a position to satisfy the need in question.

Michael Walzer draws an analogous distinction between basic human rights (derived from our common humanity, and owed to all human beings regardless of societal norms) and culturally relative rights (derived from our cultural norms and practices, and varying from one society to another).[1] The former presumably relate primarily to our basic needs, while the notion of culturally relative rights seems ideally suited to the complexity and significance of human goals. Walzer's distinction might thus provide the basis for a Non-Consequentialist alternative to the Combined Consequentialist theory developed in this book. It would be instructive to explore this analogy further, but I shall not attempt to do so here.

In Kantian terms, we might see an individual's failure to provide another agent with the necessary conditions for the successful exercise of his agency (by failing to meet his basic needs) as a failure to respect that agent as an end-in-himself, whereas failing to assist someone in the pursuit of some particular goal would not constitute a comparable failure to respect his humanity. (See the discussion of the demands of Kantian ethics in Section 1.1.1 above.)

Ultimately, moral justification is justification *to* someone. It must be offered not to our co-agents or cooperators, but to our patients (that is, those persons affected by our actions). This feature of justification is obscured in situations where agents interact for mutual advantage, because patient and cooperator are one and the same. If justification is offered primarily to patients, then an appeal to features of the moral community will be relevant for moral justification only if the patient is a member of that community. The justificatory significance of the moral community lies not in its existence, but in our (that is, in my patient's and my) common membership of that community. In the Realm of Necessity, where I respond to needs beyond my moral community, I cannot appeal to features of that community.

My remarks here are not based on any fully worked-out theory of moral justification. Indeed, the idea that justification is offered to someone may

---

[1] Walzer, *Spheres of Justice*, esp. pp. 78–83.

seem at odds with the impersonal nature of Consequentialist moral theory. However, this concern is inappropriate. If we fail maximally to promote someone's interests, then the best justification we can offer is that our actions are in accord with a moral theory that takes appropriate account of those interests. If there is a satisfactory form of Consequentialism, then it will be such a theory. One might, of course, doubt there is a satisfactory Consequentialist theory, but that is a separate question. (The account of justification offered here is clearly analogous to Contractualism. For more on the relationship between Contractualism and Rule Consequentialism, see Section 8.8 below.)

My argument may seem overstated. After all, if our moral theory is to avoid unreasonable demands, it must sometimes permit me to pursue my own goals rather than meeting someone else's needs. To justify my actions, I must show that my pursuit of those goals is especially significant to me. Given the close relationship between community and goals, this process of justification may include reference to the moral community where those goals are pursued. This brings out the fact that famine relief occupies the boundary between the Realms of Necessity and Reciprocity, as we are balancing the needs of others against our own goals.

To dissolve this objection, recall that the Wrong Facts Objection does not reject certain facts outright. It merely claims that they are not as significant as Rule Consequentialism implies. Information about the moral community is more salient when we are justifying an action falling entirely within the Realm of Reciprocity than when we are operating at the boundary between realms. We might also speculate that only some information regarding the moral community can appropriately be cited to justify actions on that boundary. For instance, if I seek to justify my actions to those whose needs I leave unmet, then it might be appropriate for me to point to the significance of the Realm of Reciprocity within my own life, and to my own *need* to participate in the moral community; whereas detailed information regarding the precise nature of that community (and of my participation in it) might be out of place. The latter information would be quite appropriate, however, if I were justifying my decision to pursue one particular joint goal rather than another. The latter justification takes place entirely within the Realm of Reciprocity. It is offered, not to those outside the moral community, but to those within it.

Consider a concrete example. My present project is to work for an agency providing famine relief. I decide to abandon this project and enter a contemplative monastic order. My justification of this choice will have two components. (1) I must explain my decision to those with whom I am currently cooperating, especially if my decision leaves them unable to continue. (2) I must also justify myself to those I leave to starve. (I assume that joining the monastic order constitutes a withdrawal from the world, not an attempt to develop mystical causal powers to alleviate the plight of the starving.) These two justifications will take quite different forms. The former will appeal to specific details of the projects in question, the alternatives available, my shared history with my collaborators, and so on; while the latter appeals only to the general desirability of my being morally free to pursue my own goals.

We should also consider a second boundary case. We saw in the previous chapter that the Realm of Reciprocity covers situations where the needs of members of a moral community come under threat. Recall the person passing a drowning child on his way to work (see Section 4.6). Unlike its treatment of famine relief, Rule Consequentialism's account of these cases seems acceptable. For instance, Hooker concludes that the optimal code will require one to save the drowning child. This rule is not too demanding, as such cases are comparatively rare in our society. Accordingly, it could be inculcated at comparatively little cost. Here the theory appeals to features of the moral community that are clearly relevant to our moral intuitions.

The Wrong Facts Objection highlights the fact that Rule Consequentialism treats all needs as if they arise within the Realm of Reciprocity. It thus deals inappropriately with needs arising within the Realm of Necessity. Obviously enough, there is nothing wrong with treating a given need as if it fell within the realm in which it actually falls.

Proponents of the Wrong Facts Objection need not claim that the facts in question are morally irrelevant *per se*. By objecting to the relevance of certain facts within the Realm of Necessity, we say nothing about their appropriateness in other moral realms. This enables us to incorporate elements of Rule Consequentialism into our Combined Consequentialist moral theory. Over the years, Rule Consequentialists have developed a formidable array of theoretical resources. These will now be available to our new theory.

8.2. Collective Consequentialism and Fairness

To further illustrate the significance of the two realms, I now discuss a simple general objection to Collective Consequentialism. As I noted in Part Two, Collective Consequentialists often defend their theory on the grounds of fairness. It is not fair to require me to do more than my share. Otherwise, other people can exploit me by not doing theirs (see Sections 3.1 and 4.1). This familiar argument may work well within the Realm of Reciprocity. However, decisions concerning famine relief belong to the Realm of Necessity. To appeal to the fairness argument in the latter realm is to succumb to a false analogy.

The notion of 'doing my fair share' is most naturally applied to the provision of public goods, where everyone benefits, regardless of whether or not he has contributed. If I do my share of producing the good, others who fail to do their share can be said to 'free ride' on my provision. By refusing to do their share of the work, they force me to do more than my share. This is unfair.

Famine relief is clearly not a standard public good.[2] There are two crucial differences. The first is that, while the others who refuse to do their fair share do benefit from not making donations (by having more money left over to spend on themselves), they do not benefit from my doing more than my fair share. They are not free-riding on my extra work. A related difference is that, in the case of famine relief, the others who will suffer if I only do my fair share, rather than giving as much as I can, are innocent third parties: namely, the famine victims. It would be absurd to accuse *them* of free-riding if I donate a little bit extra to keep them alive.

In the famine case, then, the notion of 'fair share', if it is to be applied at all, should have a different substantive content than in the public good case. I suggest that, with famine relief, my fair share should be dependent upon two factors: the relative disadvantage to my welfare, interests, or projects of parting with various amounts of wealth, and the benefits various donations would provide for the famine victims. I think we are more inclined, in cases of this kind, to say that someone has given his fair share if he has, say, 'given 'til it hurts', than if he has given less than he could have simply on the grounds that, if everyone had given the same, the problem would have been solved. Collective Consequentialists are right to emphasize the importance of 'doing one's fair share', but wrong to see this as an argument in favour of Collective Consequentialism. Rather, this new account of fairness suggests that something like Scheffler's Hybrid View may provide the basis for a superior account of famine relief.

Those who defend Rule Consequentialism on the grounds of fairness overlook the distinction between the Realm of Reciprocity (exemplified by public-good cases) and the Realm of Necessity (exemplified by famine-relief choices). In the former realm, a group of agents collectively pursue a joint goal, whereas the latter involves one agent meeting the basic needs of another. Considerations of fairness arise in the context of social interactions and relationships. Two points follow from this. (1) Different notions of fairness will apply in the different realms, as they deal with different social contexts. The present defence of Rule Consequentialism appeals to a notion of

[2] For an argument that famine relief is a public good in some sense, see Miller, *Market, State and Community*, Ch. 4.

fairness relevant only in the Realm of Reciprocity. (2) In general, fairness will be more significant in the Realm of Reciprocity, as the related notions of interpersonal relationship, mutual interaction, and reciprocity are more significant there. Contractualism appeals to a similar notion of fairness. It will thus also be more plausible in the Realm of Reciprocity. We shall see the significance of this in Section 8.8.

8.3. Why the Compliance Condition Failed

Rule Consequentialism was not the only version of Collective Consequentialism considered in Part Two. In this section, we re-examine Murphy's Cooperative Principle of Beneficence, to see if it too might provide an adequate account of the Realm of Reciprocity. We will focus on the Compliance Condition. My aim in Chapter 4 was to demonstrate that no acceptable principle satisfies the Compliance Condition. Murphy's own principle satisfies that condition. If the Compliance Condition is rejected, this is sufficient to undermine Murphy's principle. We begin by re-evaluating the objections to the Compliance Condition presented in Chapter 4. Do these apply only within the Realm of Necessity? We then ask whether the Compliance Condition might be plausible within the Realm of Reciprocity. I shall conclude that, while not acceptable as a constraint on either realm, the Compliance Condition has a useful role to play within the Realm of Reciprocity.

Murphy suggested that any acceptable principle of benevolence should meet the following condition.

The Compliance Condition.   A principle of beneficence should not increase its demands on agents as expected compliance with the principle by other agents decreases.[3]

In Chapter 4, I argued that the Compliance Condition is appropriate only in public-good cases, and other similar situations. It is not appropriate in cases of famine relief, as these are not best modelled in terms of cooperative interaction.

It is easy to see how this claim relates to the distinction between the two realms. My objection, in effect, was that the Compliance Condition is not appropriate within the Realm of Necessity, where we are considering extending the bounds of the moral community. It belongs to the Realm of Reciprocity, where it would govern interactions within the moral community.

---

[3] Murphy, 'The Demands of Beneficence', p. 278.

The Compliance Condition appeals more or less explicitly to features of the moral community (namely, to the number of members that community contains, and their various behavioural dispositions). It will thus have justificatory significance only if all those affected by my actions are themselves members of the moral community. In other words, my patient and I must be capable of interacting on a (more or less) equal and mutually advantageous basis, in pursuit of individual or joint goals. The Compliance Condition thus applies (if at all) only within the Realm of Reciprocity.

Unfortunately, the Compliance Condition is problematic in the Realm of Reciprocity as well. A central moral question is whether the demands of a moral theory should vary according to the degree of compliance. Rule Consequentialism permits such variation, while the Compliance Condition rules it out. Even in the Realm of Reciprocity, this extreme inflexibility is undesirable.

In the Realm of Reciprocity, partial compliance arises in two ways. The first is partial compliance regarding goals. As we saw in Chapter 3, the best form of Rule Consequentialism idealizes to general compliance rather than perfect compliance. The ideal code thus includes rules dealing with non-compliers, those whose goals are not compatible with others, and not conducive to the general good. These rules place small extra demands on the majority. This seems intuitively desirable. Yet the Compliance Condition cannot accommodate any extra demands. (For more discussion of Rule Consequentialism and partial compliance in the Realm of Reciprocity, see the next section.)

More striking cases arise at the boundary between the two realms. Recall the possibility of unmet needs in the Realm of Reciprocity. Here, too, partial compliance is possible. Consider the standard problem case.

The Two Drowning Co-Workers. You and I are walking to work. We see two of our innocent co-workers drowning in a pond. Each of us can save one co-worker at slight inconvenience, or both co-workers at slightly greater inconvenience. There is no danger involved in saving any co-workers, as neither of them weighs very much. You keep walking, making it clear that you will save no one.[4]

As a result of your non-compliance, I am now obliged to save two co-workers rather than one. Any theory according with this result will violate the Compliance Condition. Using the categorization in terms of moral community,

---

[4] The example is originally due to Singer (see his 'Famine, Affluence and Morality', pp. 231–3). See also above, Section 4.6.

this case falls under the Realm of Reciprocity. The Compliance Condition seems unacceptable here. It is too restrictive to govern the whole of either realm. Even in the Realm of Reciprocity, the demands of our new Consequentialist theory should vary according to levels of compliance.

Despite its shortcomings, we should not discard Murphy's condition entirely. In relation to public goods, a moderate Compliance Condition may be plausible. It often does seem reasonable to refuse to take on extra burdens once compliance falls below a certain threshold. As we shall see in the next section, some modest version of the Compliance Condition may have a significant role to play in limiting the demands of Rule Consequentialism within the Realm of Reciprocity, especially in relation to the underlying framework for goals, which emerges as the ultimate public good.

8.4. Rule Consequentialism and the Realm of Reciprocity

In this section I develop a Rule Consequentialist account of the Realm of Reciprocity. In the next section, I use it to show that many objections to Rule Consequentialism have less force in that realm. I aim to show that Rule Consequentialism would be an acceptable moral theory if the Realm of Reciprocity were the whole of morality.

Recall the Need-Free Society: the world where all the basic needs of all agents are met. The previous chapter showed that the main decisions facing inhabitants of a Need-Free Society will relate to how they should work together to pursue their various (overlapping) goals. What they need most from a moral theory is a set of rules governing cooperative interactions. They seek a code of reciprocity, not a code of necessity. If they are Rule Consequentialists, then their ideal code will be the set of rules with the best consequences regarding goals. As is invariably the case with Rule Consequentialist theories, it is very difficult to say anything precise about this ideal code. However, we can make a few general predictions, based on the nature and moral significance of goals.

1. NON-INTERFERENCE

One of the main lessons of the previous chapter was that, when dealing with goals, one is more likely to enhance the well-being of others by assisting them in the pursuit of their goals than by attempting to pursue goals for them. Rules of non-interference will thus play a more prominent role in a code of reciprocity than rules instructing agents to interfere with others. Rules of non-interference will also be more prominent in a code of reciprocity than in the ideal code for a world of unmet needs, as interference is often an effective (and necessary) way to meet the needs of others. Non-interference is more significant in the Realm of Reciprocity than in the Realm of Necessity.

2. AUTONOMY

The only goals an agent can pursue are her own. A Need-Free Society where everyone usually pursues his own goals will contain more well-being than one where people try to promote the successful pursuit of goals by others. Rules encouraging agents to focus on the pursuit of their own goals will be prominent in the ideal code of reciprocity. Autonomy may well be instrumentally valuable for needs, as each agent is especially well placed and motivated to meet her own needs. However, for goals autonomy is intrinsically, and not merely instrumentally, valuable.

3. MODERATE DEMANDS

The ideal code of reciprocity will be significantly less demanding in the actual world than an ideal code designed for the Realm of Necessity. There are several related reasons for this. The first concerns demands under general compliance. The second concerns levels of compliance in the actual world. The third relates to the impact of partial compliance on complying agents. We take each in turn.

Recall the Non-Competition Thesis (see Section 7.9). People's goals need not be in competition with one another. The best way to maximize overall pursuit of goals is to inculcate a code whereby everyone pursues his own (compatible) goals. In a world of almost full compliance, such a rule makes very few demands. By contrast, even in a world of full compliance, situations will still arise where one must meet the needs of others, at the expense of one's own goals (or even one's needs). The ideal code of necessity thus involves some sacrifices. For most agents, neither code will be very demanding under widespread compliance, but the demands of the code of reciprocity are lighter.

4. HIGH LEVEL OF COMPLIANCE

Compliance with the ideal set of rules will be more widespread in the Need-Free Society than in either the Goalless World or the actual world. Of course, we should not expect perfect compliance, even in a Need-Free society. However, the inhabitants of the Need-Free Society are likely to find themselves much closer to full compliance than we do. Accordingly, agents are less likely to face additional demands as a result of partial compliance.

There are several reasons to expect greater compliance. The most obvious is that a less demanding rule is easier to comply with. Agents' moral motivation is thus less likely to be overwhelmed by the cost of compliance. A second reason is suggested by Section 8.8. In the actual world, one obvious reason why compliance with any particular code is only partial is that people adhere to different moral codes. These codes offer divergent moral advice. A society of people following different codes will not comply with any one code. By contrast, I argue in Section 8.8 that, in the Realm of Reciprocity, rival moral theories are very similar in practice. Imagine a Need-Free Society equally divided between adherents of Rule Consequentialism and adherents of Contractualism. If the argument of Section 8.8 is correct, then, despite the theoretical disagreements of its inhabitants, such a society might come very close to full compliance with the Rule Consequentialist ideal code, as that code will also be one no agent can reasonably reject.

We can also appeal to empirical evidence. In the actual world, compliance with commonly accepted rules governing the Realm of Reciprocity is far higher than compliance with any famine-relief rule recommended by any moral philosopher. Promises are generally kept, property is generally respected, and so on; while almost no one even lives up to Hooker's modest suggestion of a 10 per cent donation to charity. The threat of social and legal sanctions may explain some of these differences, but certainly not all. Of course, not all aspects of the ideal code of reciprocity are commonly accepted. However, the overall fit is far closer than for the corresponding code of necessity. (This evidence of differing compliance also reflects, and reinforces, the greater intuitive appeal of the code of reciprocity. See point (6) below.)

5. IMPACT OF PARTIAL COMPLIANCE

The Non-Competition Thesis suggests a second way compliance differs across realms. In the Realm of Reciprocity, partial compliance by others does not significantly affect the demands placed on those who do comply.

Within the Realm of Necessity, the ideal code is likely to include some general requirement to meet the needs of others. Under full compliance this requirement is not too demanding. Under partial compliance, however, its demands are severe. In the Realm of Reciprocity, the ideal code tells agents to develop and pursue non-competitive goals. Compliance with this aspect of the ideal code is quite partial in the actual world. Many people pursue highly competitive goals, frequently conflicting with the goals of others. Yet this does not prevent each of us from pursuing non-competitive goals if we choose to do so, so long as our basic needs are met. Nor does the fact that others pursue competitive goals make it more demanding for us to pursue non-competitive ones. Of course, many valuable goals require collaboration with others. If *no one* will cooperate with me, then I cannot pursue those goals. However, the number of actual collaborators I need is usually very small. Beyond that inner circle, the pursuit of competitive goals by others does not undermine my collaborative endeavours.

This conclusion may seem too optimistic. In one crucial respect, partial compliance can impose new demands even in the Realm of Reciprocity. Within that realm, the ideal code is designed to create a society where, as far as possible, everyone is free to pursue his own non-competitive goals. It requires agents to maintain that social fabric. Under full compliance, the demands of this requirement would be negligible. In our own world of very partial compliance, seeking to establish a non-competitive social fabric might become a full-time job. Far from leaving us free to pursue the non-competitive goals of our choosing, the ideal code may oblige us to embark on an anti-competitive crusade.

The Rule Consequentialist has several replies at this point, seeking to show that the ideal code is not unduly demanding under partial compliance. Using the Non-Competition Thesis, one might argue that conflict regarding goals would not arise under widespread compliance. It would be costly to inculcate a very demanding rule that will seldom be used. Therefore, the possibility of significant conflict need not be addressed in the ideal code. The ideal code will not include potentially demanding provisions regarding conflict regarding goals. Unfortunately, this response is very problematic. If the ideal code is to be of any use to us, then it must offer some guidance in cases of widespread non-compliance. (Recall the discussion in Section 3.4.3.)

Alternatively, Rule Consequentialists might argue that devoting my life to the provision of a public good for my own society enhances my well-being more directly than if I devoted my life to the starving millions. Because it focuses directly on my community, the former goal improves the lot of my family and friends, by increasing the range of opportunities available to them. This goal involves less disruption to my other goals, and thus less sacrifice overall.

Finally, Rule Consequentialists might appeal to something like Murphy's Compliance Condition. In Section 8.3, I argued that the Compliance Condition is not plausible as a global constraint on either realm. However, it may be acceptable in certain limited contexts within the Realm of Reciprocity. The Compliance Condition incorporates a cooperative picture of morality. While not plausible over the whole of morality, the cooperative view may be appropriate for certain moral projects, especially the maintenance of a non-competitive framework for goals. The existence of such a framework is a public good, and its maintenance a mutually beneficial collaborative project. While the ideal code is not bound by the Compliance Condition, it may include that condition as a constraint on some of its own rules, such as the requirement to maintain the non-competitive framework. Recall also the discussion of fairness in Section 8.2. The cost of widely inculcating a rule depends largely on whether people are disposed to regard it as fair. For a public good such as the background social framework, people may well reject as unfair any rule requiring significantly more from them whenever others free-ride. The cost of inculcating such a rule would thus be prohibitive.

Even here, we may find the strict Compliance Condition too strong. We might opt instead for a more moderate version. As others fail to do their bit, our responsibility for maintaining the social fabric will increase, but only slowly, and perhaps not beyond a certain threshold.

If the free-riding of others imposes extra burdens on me, then I may respond by refusing to do even my initial share. Conversely, if partial compliance has no significant impact on those who comply, then we may expect the level of compliance to be higher. Taken together, claims (4) and (5) thus suggest that the demands of Rule Consequentialism, within the Realm of Reciprocity, will not be adversely affected by partial compliance. This reinforces our earlier claim (3). A high level of compliance suggests that the ideal code of reciprocity will not be unduly demanding. Strengthening that claim provides further support for the claim that levels of compliance will be high. Claims (3), (4), and (5) are thus mutually reinforcing. The Rule Consequentialist code of reciprocity will be moderate in its demands, and be the object of a comparatively high level of compliance.

6. INTUITIVE PLAUSIBILITY

As we will soon see in some detail, the general claims above all weaken traditional objections to Rule Consequentialism. The ideal code of reciprocity is more intuitively plausible than the ideal code of necessity, or than any ideal code designed to fit both moral realms. This applies both to general moral rules, and to particular moral judgements. Within the Realm of Reciprocity, the ideal code is closer to the rules of thumb of Common-Sense Morality. Therefore, in particular cases, the judgements of the ideal code will also be closer to those of Common-Sense Morality.

7. EASE OF DISCOVERY

The ideal code of reciprocity may be easier to discover than the ideal code of necessity. Two features of the Realm of Reciprocity are especially significant here: the role of autonomy, and the presence of incommensurability (see Sections 7.6 and 7.7). Because of these features, there is often no precise answer to the question: which goal would produce the more valuable overall result? As a result, we will often be unable to choose between competing moral codes on the basis of a detailed Consequentialist evaluation of their impact on particular goals.

This may seem to make it harder to discover the ideal code. Indeed, that may seem impossible. Actually, the complexity of goals makes it easier to discover the ideal code. Most of the value of goals is conditional on their having been autonomously chosen. Therefore, we can assess rules most accurately by examining their contribution to autonomy. As each individual's degree of autonomy depends very largely upon the background social framework, the best test of a code of rules may be: does it produce a social framework enabling all agents to lead autonomous lives? This question may be difficult to answer, but it will often be easier than a detailed evaluation of the impact of diverse moral rules on the well-being of large numbers of particular individuals. (Complications threaten if some possible codes enable some agents to pursue many goals, while drastically restricting the opportunities of others. Fortunately, the Non-Competition Thesis ensures that no such code can be optimal. See Sections 7.9 and 8.8.)

Consider a simple example: should people give priority to their nearest and dearest? If we focus on needs, then we must undertake a complex series of calculations to determine the precise impact of particular rules on the well-being of different agents. If our focus is on goals, by contrast, then we can more easily evaluate rules by asking whether they generally serve to facilitate people's pursuit of their own goals.

8.5. Old Objections to Rule Consequentialism

We have outlined several broad features of the Rule Consequentialist code of reciprocity. We must now re-examine the remaining objections from Chapter 3, to see how they fare in the Realm of Reciprocity. In Chapter 3, in addition to the Wrong Facts Objection, we discussed the following specific objections.

1. *The Partial Compliance Objection.* Because it selects moral rules on the basis of what would happen if everybody complied with them, Rule Consequentialism gives undesirable results in situations of partial compliance.

2. *The Co-extensionality (or Collapse) Objection.* Rule Consequentialism collapses into Individual Consequentialism. The rules it would be best for

everyone to obey are rules of infinite complexity designed to maximize utility in any particular situation.

3. The Incoherence Objection. Rule Consequentialism begins with the standard Consequentialist commitment to promotion of the good, and ends up telling us to follow certain rules, even where this will not produce the best possible consequences. Rule Consequentialists are 'rule worshippers'. Instead of using their rules as strategies, decision procedures, or rules of thumb, they turn them into independent criteria of rightness, thereby abandoning Consequentialism.

4. The Anti-Brandtian Objection. Brandt's exception clause states that, for Rule Consequentialism, the 'universal predominance' of rules should mean 'their acceptance by everyone except young children, the mentally impaired, and a small but indeterminate proportion of "normal' adults'. This clause is unacceptable, as it causes Rule Consequentialism to collapse into Individual Consequentialism whenever a disaster results from widespread failure to act.

5. The Homogeneity Objection. The Homogeneity Thesis states that everyone in the ideal society has the same moral character. This thesis is unwarranted. The ideal code of rules may assign different tasks to different agents, rendering it difficult to determine what Rule Consequentialism requires of *me*.

In addition, we addressed two general objections to Rule Consequentialism, which often lie behind more specific complaints.

6. The Demandingness Objection. Although less demanding than Simple Consequentialism, Rule Consequentialism still makes unreasonable demands in the actual world. At the very least, we cannot rule out the possibility that the ideal code of rules would demand significant sacrifices of agents in our circumstances.

7. The Complexity Objection. Rule Consequentialism can avoid the charge of unreasonable demandingness only by leaving itself open to charges of unreasonable complexity, and of giving inappropriate weight to the wrong empirical factors. Indeed, it may be impossible to determine what Rule Consequentialism requires at all.

We begin with these more general objections. The previous section shows they have less force in the Realm of Reciprocity. The significance of rules of non-interference, the desirability of pursuing one's own goals, and the fact that goals tend to be non-competitive all suggest that things will go best in that realm if people are generally free to pursue their own goals. Accordingly, the ideal code is likely to make only moderate demands. The Demandingness Objection is largely dissolved.

The significance of freedom and incommensurability greatly reduces the complexity of the ideal code, thus rendering it easier to discover. Paradoxically, the complexity of goals ensures that the way to produce the best consequences is by following a simple code. The Complexity Objection also loses its bite in this realm. By contrast, in the conceptually simpler realm of needs, progressively more complicated codes might produce marginal improvements.

Unsurprisingly, our specific objections are also weaker in the Realm of Reciprocity. We take them in turn.

1. In the Need-Free Society, compliance with the ideal code will be significantly greater than in the actual world. Problems of partial compliance are less significant.

2. Rule Consequentialist replies to the Co-Extensionality Objection appeal to the complexity of human motivations and psychology, arguing that the inculcation of a moral code containing complex exception clauses is inefficient. Goals are more intimately connected to the complexities of human motivation than needs. Such considerations are thus more forceful within the Realm of Reciprocity. Furthermore, Rule Consequentialists will argue that, as the ideal code does not contain complex or demanding rules, Rule Consequentialism will be substantially different from Individual Consequentialism.

This last claim may seem implausible. In this realm, agents will have less room to promote good consequences by self-sacrifice. This suggests that Individual Consequentialism will also be much less demanding in the Realm of Reciprocity. The differences between the two theories will be reduced, reinforcing the Co-Extensionality Objection.

This conclusion is too hasty. A single individual can often maximize the pursuit of goals by abandoning her own goals to assist others in the pursuit of theirs. Even in the Realm of Reciprocity, Individual Consequentialism will make significant demands. The Rule Consequentialist ideal code will not require this degree of self-sacrifice. Therefore, Individual and Collective Consequentialism will diverge. The Co-Extensionality Objection does not apply in this realm. In the Realm of Necessity, by contrast, the ideal code might be very demanding, especially under partial compliance.

3. Rule Consequentialists offer several replies to the Incoherence Objection. The first is that Rule Consequentialism *is* the appropriate way to respond to certain values, as some values are best promoted collectively. This claim is highly plausible for goals, especially given their close connection with community. This reply is thus much more convincing in the Realm of Reciprocity.

A second response denies that Rule Consequentialism rests on a Consequentialist foundation. One alternative is to appeal to a general moral ideal such as the notion of 'what if everyone did that?' This idiom in particular is obviously more at home in the Realm of Reciprocity, especially given the significance of community in that realm. There are also links with the discussion of fairness in Section 8.2 above, as the present idiom has strong connotations of fairness and free-riding. A second alternative is to rest the case for Rule Consequentialism primarily on its intuitive appeal. This response will also be significantly more plausible in the Realm of Reciprocity, where the intuitive appeal of Rule Consequentialism is greater.

Both Rule Consequentialist responses are thus more plausible in the Realm of Reciprocity. Together, they suggest that the Incoherence Objection will not apply in that realm. We will return to these issues in Chapter 10, when we address an Incoherence Objection levelled at Combined Consequentialism as a whole.

4. The tales underlying the Anti-Brandtian Objection concern disasters resulting from widespread non-compliance. These cases belong to the Realm of Necessity. The analogous case in the Realm of Reciprocity would be where a disaster arises within my community owing to widespread failure to provide assistance. There are two reasons why such cases are less problematic. The first is that compliance is much higher. In the actual world, people are much more likely to offer assistance within their moral community than beyond it. Such cases will thus be comparatively rare, whereas the examples giving rise to the original Anti-Brandtian Objection are commonplace. Furthermore, when non-compliance does occur in the Realm of Reciprocity, we have already seen that it is often not counter-intuitive to require agents to bear a heavy burden (see Section 4.6). We do expect considerable sacrifices in this realm when others fail to do their share. Therefore, the Anti-Brandtian Objection is defused. The situations where it arises are less widespread, and the results it objects to are no longer objectionable.

5. Finally, the Homogeneity Thesis is also much more plausible when we confine our attention to the Realm of Reciprocity. Within the Realm of Reciprocity, the ideal code will probably respond to the desirability of having agents behave in different ways by adopting the single rule: 'Pursue your own goals'. Given the diversity of agents' goals and dispositions, this rule is likely to generate any desired heterogeneity without resorting to complex role-related rules.

All of our objections to Rule Consequentialism are considerably weaker in the Realm of Reciprocity. Of course, Rule Consequentialism may face new objections peculiar to that realm. One crucial question is whether its demands are moderate enough. The ideal code will still make some demands in the Realm of Reciprocity. Will these be intuitively acceptable? It is best to address this question in the context of the demands of a complete moral theory. Until we know how our account of the Realm of Reciprocity is balanced against other components, we cannot really tell what it will demand in practice. Accordingly, we return to this question in Chapter 10.

8.6. Balancing the Two Realms

Rule Consequentialism offers a credible account of the Realm of Reciprocity, even though Chapter 3 demonstrated that it is not a plausible account of the whole of morality. In this section, we ask whether it can balance the two realms. We briefly re-examine two of our objections to Rule Consequentialism, to see how they apply to this new task.

Recall our discussion of the Wrong Facts Objection. Which facts should we appeal to when we are balancing the two realms? I suggest that we should appeal only to generic features of each realm. For instance, when deciding how much I should give to charity, it is appropriate for me to appeal to the significance within my own life of my participation in the moral community. It is less appropriate to appeal to the precise make-up of the particular moral community to which I belong, or to its particular rules and conventions. Rule Consequentialism appeals explicitly to such features. The Wrong Facts Objection thus applies equally strongly whether we are operating entirely within the Realm of Necessity, or balancing the competing requirements of the two realms.

Consider next the complaint that Rule Consequentialism makes immoderate demands. This objection also retains its force when we are balancing the two realms. Under Rule Consequentialism, our moral obligation to meet needs may overwhelm any considerations drawn from the Realm of Reciprocity. As ever, Rule Consequentialism leaves too many hostages to fortune.

To illustrate this failing, recall the following case from our original discussion of the Wrong Facts Objection.

Many Poor.   Famine has broken out across Asia. There are 2,500 million people starving.

In this case, the ideal code will place great burdens on all members of the moral community. Rule Consequentialism is thus unable to provide a moderate way of balancing the demands of the two moral realms.

Of course, there may be occasions when the requirement to meet needs *within* the moral community also overwhelms us, leaving no room for the pursuit of our goals. However, as I have suggested before, this result does not seem intuitively problematic (unlike the claim that we should abandon our goals in order to meet the needs of those who starve in distant countries). In some cases, we *do* expect morality to make heavy demands. In the Realm of Reciprocity, Rule Consequentialism is demanding in precisely those cases. The best way to account for these different intuitions is in terms of the distinction between the two moral realms.

Considerations relating to needs arise in both realms. They must be treated differently in the two realms. Rule Consequentialism copes well when needs arise in the Realm of Reciprocity. However, because it cannot distinguish the two realms, it cannot respond appropriately to needs in the Realm of Necessity. Rule Consequentialism cannot balance the two moral realms. We seek a more satisfactory component theory to play this role. I argue in the next chapter that the Hybrid View is to be preferred.

8.7. Why Rule Consequentialism?

Competing versions of Collective Consequentialism are not the only possible accounts of the Realm of Reciprocity. The literature provides many others. In addition to Rule Consequentialism and Murphy's Cooperative Principle of Beneficence, we also find: Slote's Satisficing Consequentialism, Scheffler's Hybrid View, and Non-Consequentialist alternatives such as Contractualism, Kantian Ethics, and Virtue Ethics.

Satisficing Consequentialism and the Hybrid View are revisited in the next chapter. In this section, I seek to explain why I favour Rule Consequentialism over its Non-Consequentialist rivals. There are several reasons. The first is that, as a fully developed moral theory, Rule Consequentialism has many sophisticated defenders, whose arguments can be adapted on behalf of Combined Consequentialism. Secondly, my overall aim is to construct a plausible Consequentialist moral theory. I wish to see how far we can go towards defeating the Demandingness Objection, while remaining true to the Consequentialist tradition. I thus seek the best *Consequentialist* account of the Realm of Reciprocity. As the Compliance Condition fails, and as Individual Consequentialism fares no better, Rule Consequentialism emerges as the leading contender. The best Consequentialist theory will include a Rule Consequentialist account of the Realm of Reciprocity.

I argue in the next section that, in the Realm of Reciprocity, Rule Consequentialism is very similar to its main rivals, especially Contractualism. Our moral theory would not differ much if we replaced Rule Consequentialism with Contractualism. Theories appearing as competitors when offered as full moral theories may turn out to be compatible in some particular moral realm. This is especially interesting if that is also where they are most plausible.

8.8. Collective Consequentialism and Contractualism

One prominent Non-Consequentialist moral theory is Contractualism. As in Chapter 1, we will focus on the formulation due to T. M. Scanlon: 'an act is wrong if its performance under the circumstances would be disallowed by any system of rules for the general regulation of behaviour which no one could reasonably reject as a basis for informed, unforced general agreement'.[5]

Rule Consequentialism and Contractualism are similar, as both appeal to some notion of full compliance. Furthermore, they diverge far less in the Realm of Reciprocity than in the Realm of Necessity. One reason is that, in the former realm, we need not address the needs of sentient non-rational beings, such as animals. Animals have only needs, not goals. In a Need-Free Society, where we can assume that all the needs of all animals are met, moral theory need not concern itself with animals. This removes one conspicuous difference between the two theories, as we saw in Section 3.1.2.

The Non-Competition Thesis provides a more significant reason to expect the two theories to converge. People's interests are less likely to be in unavoidable competition when we are addressing goals rather than needs. In particular, one person's autonomy can seldom be enhanced (in a valuable way) by restricting the autonomy of another.

This last point is crucial. Rule Consequentialism and Contractualism will diverge in a given moral realm if and only if the following is true.

The Divergence Claim.   The ideal code of rules for that realm, as defined by Rule Consequentialism, is one that at least one agent can reasonably reject.

If the Divergence Claim is false, then Contractualists cannot object to the Rule Consequentialist ideal code. It does not follow that Contractualism will *require* agents to follow that code. Other moral codes may also meet the minimum Contractualist requirement that no one can reasonably reject them. Contractualists presumably do not mind which of those codes agents follow.

I do not wish to enter into a detailed discussion of the various possible interpretations of the phrase 'reasonable rejection'. However, it does seem reasonable to suggest the following generic interpretation.

---

[5] Scanlon, 'Contractualism and Utilitarianism', p. 110, and Scanlon, *What We Owe to Each Other*, p. 4. See also above, Section 1.1.2.

The Minimal Condition.   An agent (A) can reasonably reject a set of rules (R) if and only if both

1. R imposes some burden on A (call that burden B); and
2. there is an available alternative set of rules (R+) such that R+ does not impose on any agent a burden as great as B.

The justification for these two conditions is simple. The first is necessary to prevent agents from rejecting principles for moralized reasons. For instance, I cannot reasonably reject a principle simply because it permits others to engage in activities I do not approve of. Contractualism seeks to balance the burdens falling on different agents. I must show that the principle, by permitting such activities, imposes some burden on me.

The second condition is necessary for two reasons. There must be at least one set of moral rules that no one can reasonably reject. Otherwise, Contractualists would be unable to approve of any action. The second purpose of condition (2) is to provide a convenient way to assess the comparative significance of different burdens within a particular context. What it is reasonable to reject in times of plenty may not be rejectable in times of scarcity. A principle imposing a given burden on me may be appropriate if every alternative imposes a comparable burden on someone. If one alternative places lighter burdens on everyone, then that would justify my rejection of the original principle. 'There was no need for anyone to suffer so great a burden' is clearly a more respectable ground for rejection than 'Although there had to be someone who suffered so great a burden, it didn't have to be me'.

The crucial question is whether, in a Need-Free Society, the Minimal Condition is met by any agent in relation to the Rule Consequentialist ideal code of reciprocity. If it is not, then the Divergence Claim will be false. Rule Consequentialism and Contractualism will offer compatible accounts of the Realm of Reciprocity.

I shall now attempt to prove that, in a Need-Free Society, the Divergence Claim is false. The argument proceeds by *reductio ad absurdum*. Assume that the Divergence Claim is true. Let the Rule Consequentialist Code be the code of rules recommended by Rule Consequentialism. Let the Contractualist Code be a code of rules that no one can reasonably reject. *Ex hypothesi*, the Rule Consequentialist Code and the Contractualist Code are distinct. Therefore, there must be an agent (call her Unlucky) who can reasonably reject the Rule Consequentialist Code in favour of the Contractualist Code. We can thus conclude, given the Minimal Condition, that the Rule Consequentialist Code imposes a burden on Unlucky that is greater than any burden imposed on anyone by the Contractualist Code. As we are operating within a Need-Free Society, these burdens cannot consist of unmet needs. A set of rules can impose a burden only to the extent that it prevents an agent from effectively pursuing her goals. It follows that, under the Contractualist Code everyone is able to pursue his goals better than Unlucky can under the Rule Consequentialist Code. This is clearly a respect in which the consequences of the Contractualist Code being accepted are better than the consequences of the Rule Consequentialist Code being accepted. The Contractualist Code will thus have better overall consequences, *unless* there is a countervailing respect in which the Rule Consequentialist Code is better than the Contractualist Code.

In particular, if the Rule Consequentialist Code is no worse than the Contractualist Code, then the average level of well-being (for all agents apart from Unlucky) in a world in which the Rule Consequentialist Code is accepted must be greater than the average level of well-being for those agents in a world in which the Contractualist Code is accepted. In general, people living under the Rule Consequentialist Code will be better able to pursue their goals than people living under the Contractualist Code. In this way, the Rule Consequentialist Code confers a general benefit that the Contractualist Code does not. However, for some reason, Unlucky is excluded from this benefit.

Now imagine a new set of rules, which is identical to the Rule Consequentialist Code except that Unlucky is no longer excluded from the general benefit provided by the Rule Consequentialist Code. (Call this the New Code.) At the very least, under the New Code, Unlucky is brought up to the level of the worst-off person under the Contractualist Code. Because we are operating within a Need-Free Society, this alteration is not brought about by meeting the needs of Unlucky. Rather, it consists in providing Unlucky with better opportunities to pursue her goals, where a social framework to support such opportunities already existed, and was being effectively utilized by others. In the light of the Non-Competition Thesis, it is hard to see how the extension of a generally available opportunity to Unlucky could significantly reduce the extent to which others were able to pursue their own (morally worthwhile) goals. In particular, it seems very unlikely that the average quality of life of people (including Unlucky) living under the New Code would come out below the average quality of life under the Rule Consequentialist Code. However, the New Code would then be superior to the Rule Consequentialist Code in terms of consequences. The New Code would thus be the code of rules that Rule Consequentialism would prefer. Furthermore, the New Code is not a set of rules that anyone can reasonably reject. (The worst-off person under the New Code is Unlucky, who is at least as well off as the worst-off person under the Contractualist Code. Hence, if no one can reject the Contractualist Code, no one can reject the New Code either. We need not explore the precise relationship between the New Code and the Contractualist Code for the purposes of the present proof. If no one can reasonably reject the Contractualist Code, then it may be identical to the New Code.) It follows that Rule Consequentialism would recommend a code of rules that cannot reasonably be rejected. The Divergence Claim thus leads to a contradiction. Accordingly, the Divergence Claim is false. QED.

We can thus conclude that Rule Consequentialism and Contractualism will offer equivalent (or, at least, compatible) accounts of the Realm of Reciprocity. Our discussion also brings out the oddity of considering that realm in isolation. The Need-Free Society is very far removed from our own actual situation. Indeed, such a society is scarcely imaginable. Once again, we see that a full account of morality must consider both realms. (For our present purposes, we can ignore the relationship between Rule Consequentialism and Contractualism in the Realms of Necessity and Creation.)

As well as goals, the Realm of Reciprocity also includes some obligations based on needs. Do these provide a possible point of divergence between Rule Consequentialism and Contractualism? The two theories diverge if and only if (1) maximum overall well-being would result from a code that left some needs unmet, even though (2) an alternative code would have enabled all needs to be met. These two conditions will be satisfied if there are people whose needs are very expensive or difficult to meet. Consider a severely disabled person whose basic needs can be met only by a very disproportionate allocation of resources.

Such cases raise a common problem for any theory giving priority to the worst off. To avoid devoting all resources to those with extremely expensive needs, such theories must find a way to exclude them. Common responses include: focusing on the distribution of 'social primary goods' rather than practical opportunities or natural abilities; replacing the specific reasons of individuals with generic reasons common to agents in general; or placing agents behind a veil of ignorance and asking them to gamble.[6] Once Contractualists avoid giving all resources to the severely disabled, the possibility of divergence between Rule Consequentialism and Contractualism becomes very remote.

The similarity between Rule Consequentialism and Contractualism goes further. Objections to both theories arise when they seek to move beyond their natural home (the Realm of Reciprocity) into the Realm of Necessity. We examined such objections with respect to Rule Consequentialism earlier

[6] The first option is pursued by John Rawls (*A Theory of Justice*, pp. 100–8), the second by T. M. Scanlon (*What We Owe to Each Pther*, p. 204ff.), and the third by Ronald Dworkin ('What is Equality?'.)

in this chapter. In relation to Contractualism, one key argument is provided by Nagel.[7] Nagel argues that the device of reasonable rejection breaks down when confronted by the enormous inequalities of resource distribution between the developed and developing world. Surely it will be reasonable for starving people to reject any principle of beneficence allowing affluent people in the developed world to retain a significant portion of their wealth and leave others to starve.

Contractualists now face a dilemma. Either we allow affluent people to reject a principle requiring them to donate all their resources to famine relief, or we do not. If the affluent can reject such principles, then no principle is such that no one can reasonably reject it. Depending upon the precise details of our formulation of Contractualism, this will either imply (1) that everything is permitted; or (2) that nothing is permitted. Either way, Contractualism provides no guidance. On the other hand, if the affluent cannot reject such principles, then Contractualism is extremely demanding. This dilemma arises because Contractualism treats all needs as if they arose within the Realm of Reciprocity. When needs belong to the Realm of Necessity, this is a fatal move for any moderate moral theory.

A full treatment of the Realm of Reciprocity would require a detailed comparison of Rule Consequentialism with other Non-Consequentialist alternatives, such as Kantian ethics and virtue ethics. I will not undertake this task in any detail here. The features of Rule Consequentialism I have emphasized in this chapter suggest that the ideal code of reciprocity will be closer to these rivals than the ideal code of necessity. Indeed, differences between rival moral theories within a given realm may be less significant than the differences between the realms themselves. If different moral theories evolved to explain different realms, then this is what we should expect. Combined Consequentialism would look much the same, even if we replaced Rule Consequentialism with one of its Kantian or virtue-based rivals.

8.9. Conclusions

In this chapter I have sought to establish the following claims. (1) Rule Consequentialism is not plausible within the Realm of Necessity, or as a way of balancing the demands of the two realms. (2) Rule Consequentialism is an acceptable account of the Realm of Reciprocity. (Or, at least, it is the best Consequentialist account of that realm.) (3) Murphy's Cooperative Principle is not acceptable in either realm, though it is less objectionable in the Realm

---

[7] Nagel, *Equality and Partiality*, ch. 4, and Nagel, 'One-to-One'.

of Reciprocity. (4) Within the Realm of Reciprocity, Rule Consequentialism and Contractualism are equivalent in practice. (5) The best Consequentialist moral theory will incorporate a Rule Consequentialist account of the Realm of Reciprocity.

9

The Morality of Necessity

This chapter revisits the discussions of Part Three in the light of the distinction between the two moral realms. This discussion will play three roles. It serves (1) to illustrate the significance of the different realms; (2) to explain why Individual Consequentialism fails; and (3) to show how Individual Consequentialist theories can nonetheless be successfully incorporated into the new Consequentialist moral theory to be developed in the next chapter.

We begin by revisiting our earlier discussion of various forms of Individual Consequentialism. I seek to establish the following claims.

1. Our objections to Satisficing Consequentialism apply forcefully in both moral realms. Satisficing Consequentialism will thus play no role in our Combined Consequentialist theory.
2. Many common objections to the Hybrid View (such as those presented in Chapter 6 of this book) rely on features characteristic of the Realm of Reciprocity. We can thus reinterpret Chapter 6 as concluding that the Hybrid View is not acceptable in that realm.
3. Unfortunately, the familiar rationales for the Hybrid View also rely on features peculiar to the Realm of Reciprocity. Within the Realm of Necessity, departures from Simple Consequentialism are unmotivated.
4. If the Realm of Necessity were the whole of morality, then Simple Consequentialism might well be an acceptable moral theory.
5. However, Simple Consequentialism cannot balance the two realms. The Hybrid View now comes into its own.

The chapter concludes with a sketch of the structure of Combined Consequentialism, which will be fleshed out in Chapter 10.

9.1. Satisficing Consequentialism Revisited

Satisficing Consequentialism holds that even when an agent already knows which particular act is the best (from a Consequentialist perspective), she is still perfectly justified in selecting any other act which is good enough. Is this theory a suitable candidate for any of the three roles in our combined moral theory? We already have a plausible candidate for the Realm of Reciprocity (namely, Rule Consequentialism). Therefore, we are now particularly interested in the Realm of Necessity. Is Satisficing Consequentialism acceptable in that realm?

In Chapter 5, we examined two objections.

The Magic Game Objection.   Satisficing Consequentialism permits agents to decline to benefit others, even when they could do so at no cost to themselves (Section 5.3).

The Doing/Allowing Objection.   Satisficing Consequentialism produces absurd results in many everyday situations, because it cannot distinguish between actively doing x and passively allowing x to happen (Section 5.6).

If either objection relies upon features peculiar to the Realm of Reciprocity, then it will establish only that Satisficing Consequentialism is not acceptable within that realm. The theory's suitability in the Realm of Necessity will remain open.

We begin with our first objection. Recall the following tale from Chapter 5.

The Magic Game.   Achilles is locked in a room, with a single door. In front of him is a computer screen, with a number on it (call it n), and a numerical keypad. Achilles knows that n is the number of people who are living below the poverty line. He also knows that, as soon as he enters a number into the computer, that many people will be raised above the poverty line (at no cost to Achilles) and the door will open.

Achilles enters a number (p) that, although fairly large, is significantly less than n. We ask him why he opted not to raise a further $n-p$ people above the poverty line. He replies that he is a Satisficing Consequentialist who thinks that saving p people from poverty in one day is 'good enough'. He thus sees no reason to save more people, and does not think he has done anything wrong.

Satisficing Consequentialism permits Achilles to save fewer people than he could, even though any additional savings would involve no extra cost to himself. The objection is that this is morally unacceptable. Does this complaint arise only in one particular moral realm? Does our objection depend upon the nature of the costs and benefits at stake? In particular, does it apply to needs but not goals, or vice versa?

It seems clear that it does not. The argument against Satisficing Consequentialism requires only the following two claims. (1) The goods

Achilles chooses not to produce would have been valuable to those who would have received them; and (2) if he had produced those extra goods, Achilles would not have forgone anything of value to himself. The argument requires no further assumptions regarding the values involved, or the components of well-being affected. The Magic Game Objection thus applies equally well to both needs and goals. If that objection is convincing, then Satisficing Consequentialism is not an acceptable account of either moral realm.

The Magic Game Objection seems, if anything, to be stronger in the Realm of Necessity. Achilles' wrongdoing is more striking if we assume that he fails costlessly to meet the basic needs of others, than if we assume that he merely fails to assist them in the pursuit of their goals. The crucial feature is how badly off Achilles leaves people. The worse-off they are, the more unforgivable it is for Achilles to fail to assist them. The worst off are obviously those whose basic needs Achilles leaves unmet. His failing is most blameworthy in their case.

At this stage in our enquiry, what we most urgently require is an account of the Realm of Necessity. If Satisficing Consequentialism is especially unsuited to that role, then it is of no use to us. Furthermore, we shall soon see that our second objection applies particularly to the Realm of Reciprocity. Satisficing Consequentialism thus faces one decisive objection in each realm.[1]

Our first objection is sufficient to defeat Satisficing Consequentialism. Therefore, we need not revisit our second objection. Furthermore, we will shortly be considering an analogous objection to the Hybrid View. Accordingly, we now move to the latter theory.

9.2. The Hybrid View Revisited

The second form of moderate Individual Consequentialism discussed in Part Three was the Hybrid View, which adopts Agent Centred Prerogatives (allowing agents to refrain from maximizing the good) while rejecting Agent Centred Restrictions (requiring agents to refrain from maximizing the good). We concluded in Chapter 6 that the Hybrid View was the most promising form of Individual Consequentialism. What role can it play in our ideal

---

[1] We might also ask whether the Magic Game Objection has equal force in the Realm of Creation. It is not obvious that it does. Failing to create an additional worthwhile life (at no cost to oneself) is not as objectionable as failing to confer an additional benefit on an existent person (at no cost to oneself). This asymmetry creates many puzzles regarding our obligations to future generations. Perhaps some form of Satisficing Consequentialism will provide an appropriate account of the morality of creation. For my own account of the morality of creation, see Mulgan, *Future People*.

Consequentialist moral theory? In particular, is the Hybrid View plausible in the Realm of Necessity, or at the boundary between the two realms?

In Chapter 6 we looked at the following objections to the Hybrid View.

The Wrong Facts Objection.   The Hybrid View retains a strictly proportional account of the relationship between the values of outcomes and the strengths of agents' reasons to bring about those outcomes, even when it is not appropriate to do so (Section 6.3).

Kagan's Doing/Allowing Objection.   The Hybrid View produces absurd results in many everyday situations, because it cannot distinguish between actively doing x and passively allowing x to happen (Section 6.4.1).

The Commitments Objection.   The Hybrid View ignores the fact that many personal relationships are valuable only if the agent acknowledges morally binding special obligations to others (Section 6.4.3).

The Forced Supererogation Objection.   The Hybrid View permits agents to force others to make sacrifices those others are morally permitted to refrain from making for themselves (Section 6.4.2).

If any of these objections relies upon features peculiar to the Realm of Reciprocity, then it will establish only that the Hybrid View is not acceptable within that realm. The theory's suitability in the Realm of Necessity, or at the boundary between the two realms, will remain open.

9.2.1. *Another Wrong Facts Objection Revisited*

The first objection to the Hybrid View is the last of our Wrong Facts Objections. It may seem obvious that this objection cannot be based on features peculiar to the Realm of Reciprocity. After all, in the previous chapter I argued that the Wrong Facts Objection accused Rule Consequentialism of inappropriately appealing to features relevant to the Realm of Reciprocity when operating within the Realm of Necessity. The last thing we would expect is a Wrong Facts Objection applying *only* within the Realm of Reciprocity. How can it be inappropriate to appeal to features of a particular moral realm within that very realm?

This conclusion rests upon a misunderstanding of what the various Wrong Facts Objections have in common. An objection of this general form claims that a given moral theory relies upon certain facts to a degree (or in a way) that is inappropriate in certain circumstances. In the language of moral realms, a Wrong Facts Objection accuses a theory of appealing to facts peculiar to one moral realm when offering an account of moral obligations within a different moral realm. For instance, the Wrong Facts Objection to Rule Consequentialism objects that Rule Consequentialism appeals to facts relevant to the Realm of Reciprocity, even when the theory is explicitly operating within the Realm of Necessity, where those facts are not morally relevant. A different Wrong Facts Objection might make the opposite complaint. We might accuse the Hybrid View of inappropriately appealing to facts relevant to the Realm of Necessity, when operating in the Realm of Reciprocity. Perhaps the Hybrid View takes plausible claims from the Realm of Necessity, and (inappropriately) carries them over to the Realm of Reciprocity.

I shall argue that this is precisely what this particular Wrong Facts Objection does claim. We might begin by asking why it is inappropriate to adopt a strictly proportional account of the relationship between values and reasons. The original Hybrid View offers proportional accounts of two such relationships. The first is the relationship between the value of an outcome and the strength of an agent's reason to produce that outcome. The second is the relationship between the magnitude of a cost to the agent and the strength of her reason to avoid that cost. The Wrong Facts Objection centres around the claim that this combination is inappropriate. We thus need to adopt a non-proportional account of at least one of them.

For reasons that will hopefully become apparent in the next chapter, I believe that the best hope for the Hybrid View lies in combining a non-proportional account of the relationship between costs and reasons with a proportional account of the relationship between values and reasons. (See Section 10.3 for an elaboration of such a non-proportional Hybrid View.) Accordingly, we focus on the corresponding interpretation of the Wrong Facts Objection. What is wrong with a proportional account of the relationship between costs and reasons?

The most natural explanation appeals to the structure of the human good. In particular, one might argue that different components of her own good are valuable to an agent in different ways. It is thus unlikely that the strength of an agent's reason to safeguard her own interests is directly proportional to the overall cost involved. In terms of moral realms, the most natural interpretation is as follows. Different goals contribute to well-being in different ways. By contrast, different basic needs all contribute to an agent's well-being in similar ways.[2] The Realm of Reciprocity deals with goals. Therefore, full proportionality is inappropriate only within that realm. As needs and goals contribute to well-being in different ways, full proportionality is also unappealing at the boundary between the Realms of Reciprocity and Necessity. (See Section 9.4 below.)

---

[2] This explains why theories of well-being based on a single scale yielding fully commensurable judgements are more plausible when confined to measuring basic needs. It is, of course, very difficult in practice to quantify and compare the values of needs. However, the task of quantifying and comparing the values of different goals may be impossible even in principle.

The Wrong Facts Objection to the Hybrid View thus applies only in the Realm of Reciprocity. Outside that realm, a strictly proportional view may be acceptable. To illustrate this, recall the following tale from Chapter 6.

Affluent's Ignorance.   Affluent is sitting at her desk with her cheque book. She has heard a rumour that, owing to circumstances entirely beyond Oxfam's control, the effectiveness of its ongoing immunization programme (that is, the amount of good it can do for each dollar it receives) has been drastically altered. However, she does not know what the nature of the alteration has been. Indeed, she does not even know if the rumour is true. To simplify, let us say that Affluent knows that one of the following is an accurate description of the state of Oxfam's operations, but she does not know which.

Inefficient Oxfam.   Oxfam's efficiency has declined to 10 per cent of its previous level, owing to the appearance of a mutant virus that is largely immune to existing treatments. Each dollar spent now produces only one-tenth as much good as before.

Normal Oxfam.   Oxfam's efficiency is unchanged.

Superefficient Oxfam.   The efficiency of Oxfam's famine-relief operations has increased tenfold, owing to a breakthrough in pharmaceutical technology. Each dollar spent now produces ten times as much good as before.

In Superefficient Oxfam, Affluent is required to give up things that are ten times as valuable to her as the things she is required to give up in Normal Oxfam. Similarly, in Inefficient Oxfam the Agent Centred Prerogative would allow Affluent to indulge in things that are only one-tenth as valuable to her as the things she would be allowed to indulge in in Normal Oxfam. I suggested in Chapter 6 that it seems unreasonable to make Affluent so totally a hostage to fortune.

Assume, however, that the sacrifices required of Affluent are not that she abandon her goals, but rather that she allow some of her basic needs to go unmet. The claim that what Affluent is required to sacrifice is proportional to what is at stake for others seems less intuitively troubling in this case than in the real world. This is because, in the different situations, Affluent is being asked to give up different quantities of need, on the grounds that larger quantities of need are at stake for others. The sacrifices required of her differ only in degree, not in kind. She is balancing her own needs against the needs of others. In such a case, proportionality does not seem unreasonable.

This may seem obviously false. Consider a particular basic need, such as the need for food. Surely the sacrifice of a given amount of food is more significant to an agent who has enough food than to one who has no food at all. To dissolve this objection, we must distinguish two senses in which two sacrifices may be equal. (1) They may involve the same amount of need; or (2) they may involve the same quantity of what the agent needs. These two senses often come apart. One agent's need for a given quantity of food may be greater than another agent's need for the same quantity. The present claim applies only when sacrifices are equal in sense (1).

Not everyone shares this intuition. For those who do not, I suggest the following compromise. In the Combined Consequentialist theory developed in the next chapter, the Hybrid View will play the role of balancing the two moral realms. Considerations of need arise in both realms, as needs provide the necessary background to the pursuit of goals. Any theory that includes non-proportionality with respect to goals will thus allow some room for non-proportionality with respect to needs, though only when dealing with the needs of creatures with goals.

My aim at this point is simply to rebut the Wrong Facts Objection, not directly to defend the Agent Centred Prerogative. I am arguing that, when we are dealing with needs, an Agent Centred Prerogative can be proportional. I have not yet asked whether the nature of needs requires (or even permits) such a prerogative. As we shall see, it is actually hard to justify *any* departure from Simple Consequentialism solely on the basis of needs. Why is Affluent allowed to give extra weight to her own needs over the needs of others? Why is she granted an Agent Centred Prerogative at all? I return to these questions in Section 9.3. At this stage, we can conclude that the Wrong Facts Objection, on its own, does not rule out the Hybrid View in the Realm of Necessity.

9.2.2. The Commitments Objection

We now revisit our other objections to the Hybrid View. Perhaps they apply in both realms, thus ruling out the Hybrid View altogether. Our remaining objections are all related. Each claims that the Hybrid View is unstable, as the incorporation of Agent Centred Prerogatives obliges us also to include Agent Centred Restrictions. I shall now argue that all of these objections rely heavily on features peculiar to the Realm of Reciprocity. Agent Centred Restrictions are required only within that realm. The Hybrid View could thus still be plausible in the Realm of Necessity, or at the boundary between the two realms.

We begin with the Commitments Objection, as my argument is perhaps clearest in this case. This objection rests upon the following claim.

The Dependence Claim.   Some valuable components of well-being are valuable only if they are produced in certain ways. In particular, valuable personal relationships are worthwhile only when pursued in a way that recognizes the force of special obligations to other people.

The Dependence Claim applies only to (a specific range of) *goals*. An agent's needs are morally significant, and contribute to her well-being, irrespective of how they are met. An agent who meets her own needs without any regard for others does not thereby reduce the value of the contribution made to her well-being by the fulfilment of those needs. The justifications of the Agent Centred Restrictions discussed in Section 6.4 rely upon the structure of the goals being pursued, and not merely upon the value of successful pursuit. This is because direct appeals to the value of needs and goals cannot, in themselves, motivate an Agent Centred Restriction as opposed to an obligation to promote value.

The argument that takes us from Agent Centred Prerogatives to Agent Centred Restrictions relies upon features peculiar to goals. This argument thus applies only within the Realm of Reciprocity. This leaves open the possibility that prerogatives without restrictions might be the appropriate combination in some other realm. (We explore this possibility in Section 9.2.5.)

9.2.3. *Kagan's Doing/Allowing Objection*

We now turn to Kagan's objection that the Hybrid View ignores the distinction between doing and allowing. In presenting this objection, Kagan makes two claims. The first is that the Hybrid View produces intuitively undesirable results, because it cannot accommodate the distinction between doing and allowing. The second claim it that the Hybrid View fares worse here than Simple Consequentialism, as it permits agents to inflict harm upon others even in pursuit of their own suboptimal projects, as well as in pursuit of the impersonal good.

Does this objection rely upon features peculiar to the Realm of Reciprocity? It may seem obvious that it does not. After all, the distinction between doing and allowing does not appear to rest upon any claim regarding the nature of the harms and benefits involved. It merely says that it is morally worse to do harm than to allow harm to occur.

This is too swift. The claim that it is worse to do harm than to allow harm is a claim about how agents should respond to (components of) well-being, both their own well-being and that of others. This appears to be precisely the sort of claim that should, at least in principle, be responsive to the nature of the components of well-being involved.

I do not wish to embark on a full discussion of the distinction between doing and allowing.[3] However, I would tentatively suggest that most familiar arguments in support of the moral significance of such a distinction *do* rely on features of agents (and their well-being) that are noticeably more salient in the Realm of Reciprocity than in the Realm of Necessity. In what follows, I focus on broadly Kantian defences of the distinction between doing and allowing. I am confident that most non-Kantian defences rest upon similar assumptions, but I shall not seek to establish this here. One problem is that many other defences of the distinction rest largely upon appeals to intuitions regarding particular tales, often highly complex ones. It is therefore difficult to make general claims.

Many defences of the doing/allowing distinction appeal to the notion of showing *respect* for other agents. It is often argued that one disrespects an agent by actively doing x to her, even though failing to prevent x from happening to that same agent would not display a comparable lack of respect. Those who commit murder are seen as much more disrespectful of human life than those who fail to save innocent lives. The claim that respect is the appropriate way to treat agents is often defended by appeal to the moral significance of their autonomy. When one is disrespectful, one treats the other as a mere thing, rather than as an agent with her own freedom and goals. This is why the classic example of a failure of respect is interference with another person's pursuit of his goals.

The central idea underlying such arguments appears to be that active interference impacts upon another person's moral life in a different way from passive failure to assist. This central claim certainly appears more plausible if we are dealing with an agent's goals rather than her needs. An agent's autonomy, and the role of that autonomy in contributing to her well-being, is much more significantly related to her goals than to her needs. The value of needs does not depend upon autonomy, whereas much of the value of goals does (see Section 7.4). Furthermore, it makes sense to distinguish between actions that thwart an agent's goals and those that merely fail to assist her in the pursuit of those goals. By contrast, it is hard to see why we should attach corresponding moral significance to the analogous distinction in the case of needs. Either my actions produce the result that an agent's needs are met or they do not. From the recipient's point of view, it certainly makes little difference how my actions have contributed to their needs being met. On the other hand, it may be very significant to an agent

---

[3] For an extended Consequentialist attack on the distinction between doing and allowing, see Kagan, *The Limits of Morality*, pp. 83–127. For detailed defences of the distinction, see Kamm, 'Harming, not Aiding, and Positive Rights'; Kamm, 'Non-Consequentialism, the Person as an End-in-itself, and the Significance of Status'; and Quinn, *Morality and Action*, pp. 149–93.

that I actively thwarted her pursuit of her goals whereas you merely failed to assist that pursuit.

I am not claiming at this point that the distinction between doing and allowing definitely *is* acceptable within the Realm of Reciprocity. Nor that it definitely is *not* acceptable within the Realm of Necessity. The standard arguments for the moral significance of the distinction may turn out not to be ultimately convincing, even on their own ground. The distinction may have no place in either moral realm. Alternatively, there may be other arguments for the distinction, which rely upon features common to the two realms, or even on features characteristic of the Realm of Necessity. Or we might ultimately be content to endorse the distinction even without an adequate rationale, in the light of its strong intuitive appeal.

It is thus no coincidence that the dispute between Consequentialist opponents of the doing/allowing distinction (such as Shelly Kagan) and its nonconsequentialist defenders (such as Frances Kamm) tracks a disagreement over the relative significance of rationales and intuitions in moral philosophy. Kamm relies heavily on the latter, while Kagan prefers the former.[4]

All I wish to establish at this point is that the claim that the distinction between doing and allowing is morally relevant is significantly more plausible in the Realm of Reciprocity than in the Realm of Necessity. Objections to a moral theory based on its failure to accommodate that distinction are correspondingly less plausible in the latter realm. The present objection to the Hybrid View thus arises principally within the Realm of Reciprocity.

In Chapter 7 I claimed that Kantian ethical idioms are best suited to the Realm of Reciprocity, while Utilitarian and Consequentialist idioms are more at home in the Realm of Necessity. Kantian theories are notoriously based on a very strong distinction between doing and allowing. Consequentialism is equally notorious for its rejection of any such distinction. Both theories take extreme positions. Perhaps the best explanation is that the distinction between doing and allowing is highly significant, but only in one moral realm. Kantians overestimate the significance of the distinction because they focus exclusively on the realm where it applies (the Realm of Reciprocity), while Consequentialists underestimate its significance because they focus exclusively on the realm where it does not apply (the Realm of Necessity). Only a theory covering both moral realms can give appropriate attention to the distinction.

---

[4] See the references in the previous footnote.

9.2.4. Our Final Objection Revisited

The Forced Supererogation Objection raises similar issues. Forced super-erogation is objectionable because it threatens moral agency. This is espe-cially so if we follow Raz in believing that the existence of a range of morally permitted options is necessary for genuinely valuable autonomy. (Recall the various availability claims from Section 7.6.) Deciding whether or not to per-form supererogatory acts is thus a necessary feature of moral life. Any inter-ference with such decision-making violates the agent's autonomy. If we accept the Razian Availability Claim, then the agent must have several morally permitted options. If we accept the weaker Moral Availability Claim, then autonomy requires that the agent have at least one option that is psy-chologically possible and morally permissible. Autonomy can thus be viol-ated by a moral theory, such as when Simple Consequentialism demands the optimal act in every situation, or when some forms of Consequentialism make psychologically impossible demands. Even if autonomy requires only a range of practically available options, violations of autonomy are still poss-ible. Another agent can violate my autonomy, such as where a more power-ful Consequentialist agent forces someone always to perform the optimal act. The significance of supererogation, and thus of forced supererogation, derives from the link between goals and autonomy. Consequently, this objec-tion arises within the Realm of Reciprocity.

Our discussion thus brings out the common features of several objections to the Hybrid View (namely, the Commitments Objection, Kagan's Objec-tion, and the Forced Supererogation Objection). All three argue that the Hybrid View fails to constrain the behaviour of agents acting on their Agent Centred Prerogatives. They also all seek to justify such constraints by appeal-ing to the nature of human goals, agency, and autonomy. (Some possible con-straints are explored in the next chapter.)

9.2.5. The Hybrid View and the Realm of Necessity

We have seen that several of our objections to the Hybrid View have signific-antly more force in the Realm of Reciprocity than in the Realm of Necessity. We now take a step back from those particular objections, to see if the Hybrid View offers an acceptable account of the Realm of Necessity. One way to approach this question is to ask whether the Hybrid View would be an accept-able moral theory if the Realm of Necessity were the whole of morality. Recall the Goalless World from Chapter 7: the world of creatures whose well-being consists only of needs. How might the Hybrid View apply to such a world?

As our objections to the Hybrid View apply most particularly in the Realm of Reciprocity, they will have less force in a Goalless World. This suggests that Scheffler's original Hybrid View is a serious contender there. If well-being consists solely of needs, then all moral reasons must be appropriate responses to needs. Our objections to the Hybrid View rest upon the claim that different responses are appropriate for different goods in different circumstances. The justifications offered in support of this claim rely heavily upon the complexity of goals. They would thus be unavailable in a world in which the only moral language was the language of needs. For instance, special obligations and distinctions between doing and allowing both seem undermotivated in the Realm of Necessity. Also, strict proportionality seems acceptable when we are dealing only with needs.

In the Realm of Necessity, the Hybrid View is clearly superior to Satisficing Consequentialism. We saw in Chapter 8 that all forms of Collective Consequentialism are implausible in this realm. It is tempting to conclude that the Hybrid View provides the best Consequentialist account of that realm. Before doing so, however, we must consider objections from a new direction.

Our last three objections to the Hybrid View all accuse the theory of instability. If we accept Agent Centred Prerogatives, then we should also accept Agent Centred Restrictions. The rationales provided for departures from the Hybrid View, in the form of both non-proportionality and Agent Centred Restrictions, were explicitly modelled on Scheffler's own original rationale for departing from Simple Consequentialism by incorporating Agent Centred Prerogatives. If the rationales for adding Agent Centred Restrictions are without force in the Realm of Necessity, then their common ancestry suggests that the original rationales for introducing Agent Centred Prerogatives will also be unconvincing in that realm. For instance, Scheffler presents the Agent Centred Prerogative as a response to the following features of human moral life: the separateness of persons; the independence of the personal point of view; the fact that morality governs the choices of human agents; and the significance of the personal point of view *to the agent*, over and above its value from an impersonal point of view (see Section 6.1). The prerogative thus 'constitutes a structural feature whose incorporation into a moral conception embodies a rational strategy for taking account of personal independence, given one construal of the importance of that aspect of persons'.[5] Scheffler's guiding view is that an adequate moral theory should leave human beings morally free to choose, build, and pursue their own goals, projects, activities, and relationships, even at the expense of overall value. All these justifications clearly relate particularly to human goals, and hence fall squarely within the Realm of Reciprocity.

[5] Scheffler, *The Rejection of Consequentialism*, p. 67.

This explains the uneasiness that motivates many common objections to the Hybrid View. The Hybrid View seems to straddle the two moral realms, and to be at home in neither. Its rejection of Agent Centred Restrictions is plausible only within the Realm of Necessity, yet its inclusion of Agent Centred Prerogatives is compelling only in the Realm of Reciprocity.

9.3. Simple Consequentialism Returns

We thus face a complication that did not arise in our discussion of Collective Consequentialism. Forms of Individual Consequentialism were discussed (and rejected) in Chapter 2 as well as in Part Three. In particular, our traditional, very demanding Simple Consequentialism is a form of Individual Consequentialism. We thus need to ask whether Simple Consequentialism itself is plausible in the Realm of Necessity.

I argued in previous chapters that some moral arguments are less plausible in the Realm of Necessity than in the Realm of Reciprocity. In particular, basic Utilitarian ideas are stronger in the former realm, whereas Kantian objections are weaker. We have already seen that the justifications for the Agent Centred Prerogative are weak in a Goalless World. We must now ask, more generally: if needs were the only morally significant elements of well-being, would there be anything wrong with Simple Consequentialism? We must revisit the Demandingness Objection itself. Two questions arise. (1) In a Goalless World, would Simple Consequentialism still be very demanding? (2) If so, would its demands be as objectionable as in the actual world?

The first question is comparatively unproblematic. In a Goalless World, the needs of various agents will often come into conflict. It is very likely that most agents will seek to meet their own needs rather than those of others, just as they do in the actual world. This suggests that the amount of unmet need facing any given agent will be considerable. Agents in the developed countries of a Goalless World could meet the needs of others more cost effectively than their own needs.[6] At the very least, Simple Consequentialism would require any agent in a Goalless World to devote all the resources left over once she has met her own needs to the task of meeting the needs of others. If needs are the only relevant sources of value, then an agent who has met her own basic needs cannot justify devoting any further resources to herself.

---

[6] This raises a further question: does the phrase 'Agents in the developed countries of the Goalless World' make any sense? Aside from the question of whether those in the Goalless World are *agents*, we might also doubt whether their world will include anything like our own economies based largely around goals rather than needs. As ever, we need to bear in mind that the Goalless World is a theoretical construction, not a description of some possible human situation.

We turn now to our second question. In a Goalless World would it really matter if a moral theory made extreme demands? As we saw in Chapter 7, it is very difficult to imagine what life in a Goalless World might be like. Indeed, if the inhabitants of the Goalless World are not moral agents, then perhaps it makes little sense to seek a moral theory to govern their behaviour. To make progress here, let us suspend disbelief for a few moments and focus on the arguments offered in support of the claim that the demands of Simple Consequentialism are unreasonable. We must ask whether these arguments would apply with equal force in a Goalless World. We may be able to address this question even if we cannot imagine such a world in any detail.

Arguments against Simple Consequentialism are very intimately related to the rationales offered in support of specific departures from Simple Consequentialism. Recall, once again, Scheffler's rationale for the Agent Centred Prerogative. The task of motivating dissatisfaction with a theory is closely allied to the task of justifying specific alternatives. Most arguments of this type appeal to the impact of the extreme demands of Simple Consequentialism upon individual agents, focusing especially on their projects, goals, integrity, and personal relationships. Yet all of these features of agents are only morally relevant for goals. They are all peculiar to the Realm of Reciprocity. Simple Consequentialism thus remains plausible in the Realm of Necessity. Within the Goalless World, the demands of Simple Consequentialism are not unreasonable.

The Demandingness Objection loses its bite within the Realm of Necessity. We now briefly consider other common objections to Simple Consequentialism. Do these also apply only in the Realm of Reciprocity? Simple Consequentialism is often rejected because it violates the distinction between doing and allowing, requires unjust acts, and obliges us to sacrifice one innocent person to save the lives of several others. In relation to Satisficing Consequentialism and the Hybrid View, we saw that such objections rely upon intuitions and distinctions drawn from the Realm of Reciprocity. Accordingly, they lose their bite in the Realm of Necessity.

Another familiar objection is that Utilitarianism is an alien (or alienating) moral theory, because it asks us to treat everyone (including ourselves) as mere passive receptacles for pleasure and suffering; as inert needers, rather than as active choosing agents. The features of human life that Utilitarianism is alleged to ignore are those that give rise to goals, and hence to the Realm of Reciprocity. Within a Goalless world, the simple Utilitarian model may be quite appropriate.

We can also draw a more general lesson. In the final section of this chapter, I argue that our moral intuitions are more significant and reliable in the Realm of Reciprocity than in that of Necessity. The most powerful objections to Simple Consequentialism are based on its counter-intuitive consequences. The vices of Simple Consequentialism are thus less significant in the Realm of Necessity.

While Simple Consequentialism is certainly not an adequate account of the Realm of Reciprocity, it may be appropriate within the conceptually simpler Realm of Necessity. For all its faults, Simple Consequentialism may yet be a component of the most plausible composite Consequentialist moral theory.

9.4. Balancing the Two Realms

If the Realm of Necessity were the whole of morality, then Simple Consequentialism would indeed be a contender. Perhaps, in a Goalless World, it would be the most appropriate moral theory. However, we do not live in such a world. Indeed, many opponents of Consequentialism object to the theory precisely on the grounds that it proceeds as if we did. There is more to morality than the Realm of Necessity. Our overall moral theory must account for both realms, and balance their competing demands.

It is at this point that any extremely demanding form of Individual Consequentialism (such as Simple Consequentialism) falls down in comparison to either Satisficing Consequentialism or the Hybrid View. Such a theory leaves no room for any other moral realms. Given the vast amount of unmet need in our world, and the comparative cost of meeting the needs of others rather than pursuing one's own goals, the Simple Consequentialist requirement maximally to promote value yields an obligation to meet the needs of others swamping any reasons generated by goals.

More moderate forms of Individual Consequentialism, such as Satisficing Consequentialism and the Hybrid View, admit principles other than an unconstrained Reason to Promote the Good. Accordingly, they leave room for goal-based reasons to operate. Simple Consequentialism can only be presented as an account of the whole of morality. Other forms of Individual Consequentialism can be reinterpreted as accounts of parts of morality, even though they are originally presented as complete moral theories.

We can quickly dispose of Satisficing Consequentialism. The Magic Game Objection still applies at the boundary between the two moral realms. Once Achilles has passed the threshold, he need take no account whatsoever of further needs, even if no competing reasons are generated by the Realm of Reciprocity. This is an implausible account of how to balance competing moral realms.

This leaves the Hybrid View. Perhaps Scheffler's original Hybrid View is best interpreted, as an account not of either moral realm, but of the boundary between them. The Agent Centred Prerogative does not, in itself, tell agents how they should respond to either needs or goals. Rather, it tells us how to balance the competing reasons generated by needs and goals.

The Agent Centred Prerogative balances the competing force of the Reason to Promote the Good and the agent's own personal perspective. In other words, it is a response to the conflict between a strict Consequentialist account of the Realm of Necessity, and the significance of the agent's own goals. The significance of goals leads to the Realm of Reciprocity. The Hybrid View is thus designed to provide a balance between the two realms, and to resolve the tensions between Rule Consequentialism and Simple Consequentialism. Furthermore, those tensions may provide the Hybrid View with the resources it needs to avoid the objections raised in Chapter 6.

Will our earlier objections to the Hybrid View still apply when we are balancing the two realms? It may seem that the Wrong Facts Objection is even stronger, as the difference between goals and needs is at least as significant as any differences among goals. To construct a plausible moral theory, therefore, we must avoid this objection, by constructing a non-proportional version of the Hybrid View. This is one central task of Chapter 10. The Wrong Facts Objection is not fatal for the Hybrid View. (By contrast, I see no simple way to amend Rule Consequentialism to avoid its Wrong Facts Objection.)

Our other objections all rely on the fact that the Hybrid View ignores some morally relevant consideration, such as the distinction between doing and allowing. At this point, we need to remember that we are no longer considering the Hybrid View as a full moral theory. If the other realms are covered by other moral theories, and if *those* theories are sensitive to a particular moral distinction, then our overall theory will retain that sensitivity when we come to balance competing moral realms. The Hybrid View cannot do a good job of generating reasons within the Realm of Reciprocity, because it ignores the distinction between doing and allowing. However, once those reasons have been generated in a manner sensitive to that distinction (for instance, by Rule Consequentialism), the Hybrid View may be able to balance them appropriately against those generated by the Realm of Necessity. Or so I shall argue in the next chapter.

9.5. Renouncing Self-Interest

The real role of the Hybrid View is to balance the competing demands of the two realms. Scheffler's original Hybrid View balances two sets of reasons: the Reason to Promote the Good and the agent's personal reason to promote her own interests. My new Hybrid View balances two different sets of reasons:

the moral reasons generated by the Realm of Necessity, and the moral reasons generated by the Realm of Reciprocity. One side of the equation remains largely the same, as the Simple Consequentialist Reason to Promote the Good is the best available account of the moral reasons generated by the Realm of Necessity. The other side of the equation is more complex. The Realm of Reciprocity not only generates an agent's reasons to promote her own interests, live her own life autonomously, pursue her goals, and so on. It also generates reasons for the agent to respect the interests and autonomy of others, and to interact with them in certain ways. The best overall account of these reasons is provided by the Rule Consequentialist ideal code.

We now explore reasons for replacing Scheffler's two reasons with my two realms. The simplest reason is that the resulting moral theory has considerably more intuitive appeal. Combined Consequentialism is superior to the Hybrid View in dealing with the demands of morality, and the need for special obligations and responsibilities. These intuitive claims are defended at length in Chapter 10. The next two sections reinforce them with theoretical considerations, explaining why the shift is intuitively desirable.[7]

Two broad theoretical arguments support my two realms over Scheffler's two reasons. The first is a negative argument, based on the claim that the distinction between self-interest and the general good is not as significant as Scheffler's argument requires. Some philosophers defend the stronger claim that there is no such distinction. We cannot divide a state of affairs neatly into components relating to the agent's interests, and components unrelated to those interests. Accordingly, the effects of an action cannot be divided into those affecting the agent's self-interest and those that do not. Others defend the weaker claim that, while there is such a distinction, it is either of no moral significance or, at least, not as significant as many contemporary moral philosophers suppose. The concept of self-interest does not provide a good way to carve up the space of moral reasons.

The second argument against Scheffler's reasons is more positive, based on the provision of a more appropriate alternative. In particular, I shall argue that the concept of community provides a more morally significant dividing line. The two arguments are interrelated. Many arguments against the coherence or significance of the self/other dichotomy are built on the significance of community, and the way in which self-identity is constituted through relations with others. However, positive arguments go beyond the negative, often presenting community as a foundational concept in moral philosophy, not just a factor in our best account of individual interests.

[7] I explore the connections between moral theory and metaphysics at greater length elsewhere. Mulgan, 'The Place of the Dead in Liberal Political Philosophy', Mulgan 'Two Parfit Puzzles', and Mulgan, *Future People*.

Objections to the significance of self-interest have been presented by David Brink, Joseph Raz, and Philip Pettit, among others. Brink and Raz focus on the negative argument. I first outline their claims, and then sketch positive arguments in support of community. Pettit offers a positive argument for the significance of community in political theory. I adapt his argument to moral theory. This section is especially speculative, skating lightly over complex terrain peripheral to our main concerns. My aim is to sketch possible metaphysical justifications for the moral theory developed in the next chapter.

As we saw in Chapter 1, David Brink attempts to reduce the alienating demands of Consequentialism by emphasizing that my interests are largely indistinguishable from those of my intimates. I argued earlier that this move cannot solve the Demandingness Objection on its own. However, it may help us to reconfigure Consequentialism appropriately.

Brink himself does not defend an alternative way of dividing reasons into two classes. Perhaps he would not regard such a project as worthwhile. The lesson of his work might be that moral reasons cannot be fruitfully divided into distinct realms. Alternatively, given the links between self and others, one might draw the lesson that the central moral concept is that of community. Consequently, any fruitful distinction must focus on the different ways we interact with others, both within and beyond our moral community.

Like Brink, Joseph Raz also rejects the emphasis on self-interest in contemporary moral philosophy. Raz's basic argument is that the notion of 'self-interest' does not pick out a distinctive class of reasons. His starting point is that action is ultimately motivated by reasons, not desires or wants.[8] The paradigmatic reason for action is the value of options. Something is good for me because I have reason to want it, not because I want it. This helps to undermine the distinction between morality and self-interest. 'Doing the morally good thing is good for me in the same way that playing the piano . . . is good for me, that is, because it is doing something intrinsically good.'[9]

In general, I seldom do something 'because it promotes my well-being'. Rather, I do it because I believe it to be valuable. My well-being is not the source of my reasons for action.[10] We cannot usefully divide my reasons into those that are grounded in my own well-being, and those that are not. Accordingly, we cannot characterize self-sacrifice in terms of conflict between these two classes of reasons. Self-sacrifice 'is simply a special case of conflict of reasons'.[11] Raz concludes that we should reject the common idea

---

[8] Raz, *Engaging Reason*, p. 63.   [9] Ibid. 266.

[10] Raz does admit that well-being is sometimes a direct motive, but only in peculiar and derivative cases. There is nothing irrational about a person whose well-being is never a motive for their actions (Raz, *Engaging Reason*, pp. 327–9).

[11] Ibid. 319.

that 'the central question of morality is: why is it that we must conform with morality even when doing so involves significant sacrifice of our own interests?'[12] Similarly, in an earlier discussion, Raz explicitly rejects Scheffler's emphasis on the balance between self-interest and the common good.[13]

Raz makes similar points in his discussion of the Amoralist. The Amoralist presents a threat to moral philosophy: a happy, rational person who has no time for morality. Raz's Amoralist is 'a person who denies that persons are valuable in themselves'.[14] Raz argues that the Amoralist is a challenge to morality only if he can have a rich and rewarding life while denying the value of people. As a rich and rewarding life requires genuine friendship, we are concerned only with an Amoralist who is 'like us in valuing friendship and companionship'.[15] True friendship exists only if one values one's friends intrinsically and not merely instrumentally. So the Amoralist must argue that he values his friends, but does not believe that people in general are valuable.[16]

Raz now objects that the Amoralist puts the cart before the horse. One first becomes attached to something because it is valuable. This applies to people as much as to objects and activities. One's initial belief that one's friend is valuable thus cannot be based on the (subsequent) fact that he is one's friend. More generally, 'the value (to the agent) of many intrinsic goods depends on the fact that they are . . . good for people . . . it depends on the fact that people are of value in themselves'.[17] If the Amoralist is capable of genuine engagement in worthwhile projects such as friendship, then there is no special class of 'moral' reasons that the Amoralist fails to grasp. The Amoralist is often used to illustrate the conflict between self-interest and morality. If we cannot coherently imagine the Amoralist, then that conflict disappears, along with the view that self-regarding motives are a special set of reasons.

As well as a negative argument against the priority of the self/other distinction, Raz also provides a case in favour of the greater significance of a different distinction between two classes of reasons: namely, those based on needs and those based on goals. The latter distinction forms the basis for the Combined Consequentialism developed in this book. Raz himself never explicitly uses the distinction between needs and goals to replace the discarded notion of self-interest. He may well prefer to leave that role unfilled. Perhaps we should not expect morality to have any fundamental divisions. However, the last two chapters suggest that our moral intuitions and theories do divide up in several key ways. Raz's own distinction does a better job of

---

[12] Ibid. 303.   [13] Raz, *Morality of Freedom*, p. 314.   [14] Raz, *Engaging Reason*, p. 274.
[15] Ibid. 283.   [16] Ibid. 287.   [17] Ibid. 297.

making sense of those divisions than the more common distinction between self-concern and concern for others.

9.6. Lessons from Holism

Philip Pettit has recently argued that the adoption of a holistic view of social psychology has significant implications for political theory.[18] In particular, it provides a positive case for the significance of community. I first briefly outline Pettit's defence of Holism, and the implications he draws. I then ask what Holism might imply for Consequentialist moral theory, and for our present enquiry in particular.

Pettit's notion of Holism is similar to the view of Bradley: 'I am myself by sharing with others, by including in my essence relations to them, the relations of the social state.'[19] The Holist believes that the thinking capacity of human beings is dependent, at least in part, on social relations. Creatures without social relations could not think. Pettit's defence of Holism is based on his view that thinking requires the ability to follow a rule, and that rule-following in turn requires interaction with other bearers of the relevant inclination or disposition. Such interaction is necessary to fix the reference of the rule, and thereby avoid familiar paradoxes involving the indeterminate relation between finite rules and potentially infinite extensions, such as those made famous by Kripke and others. Without reference to other users, there is no fact of the matter as to which rule I am following when, for instance, I perform addition or use the word 'red'.[20] In theory, the other users might be the agent herself at other times, instead of other persons. In practice, however, human rule following always involves interaction with other people. The rules we follow in thinking are 'commonable': capable of being understood by others. This is not surprising, as 'it is extremely unlikely that the capacity for thought should have evolved on the basis of intertemporal interaction of a person with herself'.[21]

The general lesson of Holism is that, in a fundamental sense, all our concepts are social, as they are based on commonable rules. The perfectly isolated thinking individual is thus a conceptual, not merely a practical, impossibility. 'The thinker may withdraw from social life but she will still carry the voice of society within her into her place of retreat.'[22] For both social science and moral theory, accordingly, 'the proper way of understanding other people . . . is to interact on a basis of reciprocal recognition or authorisation: to succeed in sustaining a conversational stance, in dealing with those people'.[23]

[18] Pettit, *The Common Mind*, pt. three. See also Pettit, *Republicanism*.
[19] Pettit, *The Common Mind*, p. 167.
[20] Ibid. 76–106. See also Kripke, *Wittgenstein on Rules and Private Language*.
[21] Pettit, *The Common Mind*, p. 192.   [22] Ibid. 191.   [23] Ibid. 354.

Pettit draws several specific lessons for political theory. He argues that Holism 'must lead us to think ill of the contract-centred approach'.[24] The Holist's opponent (the Atomist) regards the perfectly isolated individual as a conceptual possibility. Accordingly, he must regard a world of such individuals as a relevant alternative when evaluating competing institutional arrangements, or principles of justice. If we are to compare possible societies with a world of perfect isolation, then our 'evaluative primes' must be properties individuals could possess even in perfect isolation. The Atomist's evaluative primes must be non-social values, such as physical health or freedom from non-interference. This leads to a privileging of certain values and interests over others. Holists, by contrast, are free to regard the social features of humanity as basic. For instance, Holists can attach intrinsic value to democratic participation and social relations, rather than valuing them merely for their contribution to the non-social interests of individuals. This, in turn, leads to a reinterpretation of the key liberal value of negative liberty. For the Atomist, only freedom from non-interference can be an evaluative prime, whereas the Holist can prefer a measure of positive freedom requiring a communal context.

We need not dwell on Pettit's claims here, as political theory is not our primary concern. However, the adoption of Holism may have similarly significant consequences for moral theory. Some tentative particular implications of Holism are outlined below. At a more abstract level, Holism and Atomism suggest two different pictures of morality, leading to two quite different approaches to moral theory. The atomistic picture naturally suggests a morality built up from the interests of the (potentially isolated) individual. Its central moral question will be: how should the individual balance her own interests against those of others?

Under a holistic picture, the central moral concepts are social. This suggests that moral theory must begin with the notion of a human community, giving rise to two central questions. (1) How should the members of the community relate to one another? (We might call this the Internal Question.) (2) How should the members of a community relate to outsiders? (The External Question.)

The External Question is the analogue of the single central question of atomistic moral philosophy. The Internal Question also has an analogue for the Atomist, in the debate over the content of individual prudential rationality: how is the individual to balance her own competing self-interested reasons?

Holism thus supports a shift from Scheffler's concentration on self-interest to my focus on community. Pettit himself does not explicitly endorse this

---

[24] Ibid. 285.

shift. However, he draws a similar lesson regarding the inadequacy of rational choice theory. Pettit argues that Holism renders implausible the assumption that human motivation is ultimately traceable to self-regarding motives.[25] This rejection of the explanatory priority of self-interest has obvious affinities with my own rejection of its normative priority.

Holism might also have other consequences for moral theory, each supporting a key component of Combined Consequentialism.

THE PRIORITY OF RECIPROCITY

If Holism is true, then the Realm of Reciprocity is (in a sense) more basic than the Realm of Necessity. According to Holism, if we were not creatures who lived in communities, then thought, language, and morality would be impossible. This has several consequences. The first is that the Goalless World is impossible in a deeper way than the Need-Free Society. We can imagine what a Need-Free Society would be like, and ask what morality would require of those in such a society. Once we imagine a Goalless world, we have pictured a place without thinking beings to whom the basic concept of morality might apply. Traditional objections to Utilitarianism are thus more troubling than the parallel objections to Non-Consequentialism. A moral theory ignoring the Realm of Necessity is incomplete, whereas a theory ignoring the Realm of Reciprocity is incoherent.[26]

EXPLAINING INTUITIONS

The priority of the Realm of Reciprocity also provides a possible explanation of some intuitive responses to earlier objections. Recall the Wrong Facts Objection. This objection accuses Rule Consequentialism of applying the norms of the Realm of Reciprocity within the Realm of Necessity. Conversely, it accuses the Hybrid View of appealing to the Realm of Necessity within the Realm of Reciprocity. When presenting these objections, I have found that many people regard the former as more obviously wrong than the latter. One explanation is that the Realm of Reciprocity is more salient, more obvious,

---

[25] Pettit, *The Common Mind*, 271–3.

[26] We must be wary of the familiar distinction between (1) the reference, within a particular possible world, of words in our own language; and (2) the reference of those words in the language of inhabitants of that world. We can, of course, still ask whether events in a world without thinking agents count as 'good' or 'bad', 'right' or 'wrong', even though no one in that world uses those words. (Just as we can say the world would still have contained dinosaurs, even if humans had never evolved to use the word 'dinosaur'.) However, in so far as 'right' and 'wrong' apply only to the intentional actions of thinking subjects, nothing in such a world will count as right or wrong. While we can still apply our moral concepts to such a world, we cannot consistently adopt an internal point of view when discussing it. We cannot ask what it would be like to live in such a world.

and more familiar than the Realm of Necessity. We are thus more confident of our intuitions, and more attuned to inappropriate claims in that realm.

If our moral concepts are ultimately founded on community, then our intuitions will be more reliable in the Realm of Reciprocity. When we move to the Realm of Necessity, we apply our moral concepts beyond their natural home. We are unsure how to proceed. The tried and true rules of reciprocity seem inadequate, yet what could replace them? This explains why intuitions regarding the wrongness of killing may be stronger and more reliable than intuitions regarding the appropriate level of charitable donation.[27] Our moral concepts evolved to deal with interactions within particular communities. It is not surprising that our intuitions are most secure in that environment.

JUSTIFYING RESTRICTIONS

Also, as Pettit has argued elsewhere, Holism may provide the rationale for obligations and constraints based on personal relationships. 'Given the holistic picture, it becomes necessary to acknowledge, and natural to take account of, the great difference in the way individuals are related to personal and impersonal causes.'[28] If thought in general requires community, then my thoughts would be impossible without the background of my own community. My identity as a thinking being is constituted by my relationships with others. It should be no surprise, then, if any theory sensitively moulded to my moral concepts also gives particular weight to those relationships.

RECONCILING MORAL THEORIES

Finally, the shift to Holism may lessen the distance between Consequentialism and its rivals. Most non-Consequentialist theories place great weight on the significance of personal relationships, particular social interactions, and the context of community. They often charge Consequentialists with ignoring these. The shift to Holism renders this charge even more serious. However, it also points towards the appropriate Consequentialist response. Consequentialists are especially concerned with whatever renders human lives valuable. If Holism is correct, then the very conceptual possibility of everything we regard as valuable (and even the very idea of value itself) depends upon human relationships and community. By their own lights then, Consequentialists should devote special attention to the latter. Once Consequentialism is reconfigured to take on board the insights of Holism, the result will be a theory that has much in common with Non-Consequentialism,

[27] A similar point is made in Scheffler, 'Families, Nations and Strangers'.
[28] Pettit and Goodin, 'Social Holism and Moral Theory', p. 189.

while still proceeding from a distinctively Consequentialist concern with value.

Holism itself is controversial. The claim that Holism implies any particular thesis in moral theory will be even more controversial.[29] As I do not want my moral theory to rest on controversial metaphysical claims, Holism should not be a necessary premiss in our defence of Combined Consequentialism. I merely wish to emphasize the possibility that plausible metaphysical positions provide support for certain ways of restructuring the Hybrid View, and revising Consequentialism more generally. Once Brink and Raz have convinced us that the self/other dichotomy marks no deep distinction between categories of reasons, we must seek an alternative foundation for the Hybrid View. Holism suggests that the notion of community is our best bet.

9.7. Conclusions

Our overall project is to find the most plausible Consequentialist moral theory. The distinction between the two moral realms suggests that we have three separate questions to ask. (1) What is the best Consequentialist account of the Realm of Reciprocity? (2) What is the best Consequentialist account of the Realm of Necessity? (3) What is the best Consequentialist way of balancing the competing demands of the two moral realms?

A central thesis of this book is that these three questions have different answers. Rule Consequentialism offers the best account of the Realm of Reciprocity. This is because our objections to Simple Consequentialism, Satisficing Consequentialism, and the Hybrid View apply particularly in that realm, whereas our objections to Rule Consequentialism are either weakened or inapplicable. Once we rule out Murphy's theory as a comprehensive account of the Realm of Reciprocity, Rule Consequentialism emerges as the most plausible Consequentialist account of that realm.

By contrast, Simple Consequentialism offers the best account of the Realm of Necessity. Our objections to Collective Consequentialism and Satisficing Consequentialism apply particularly in that realm, whereas our objections to Simple Consequentialism are either weakened or inapplicable. Our objections to the Hybrid View are also weakened in this realm, but so are the rationales supporting that theory in its departures from Simple Consequentialism. The Hybrid View is left under-motivated. Simple

---

[29] For critical discussion, see Christman, 'The Common Mind'; Price, 'The Common Mind'; and Tuomela, 'In Search of the Common Mind'. See also Pettit, 'In Elucidation of the Common Mind'.

Consequentialism is the most plausible Consequentialist account of the Realm of Necessity.

Finally, the Hybrid View balances the two realms. Our objections to Collective Consequentialism, Satisficing Consequentialism, and Simple Consequentialism all apply with particular force at this boundary, whereas our objections to the Hybrid View can be alleviated by drawing on the resources of the theories adopted within the two realms. The Hybrid View is the only moral theory explicitly designed to balance the two realms.

Our project is to take the Demandingness Objection seriously, and explore the implications of this move. The Demandingness Objection rests upon two claims. (1) Simple Consequentialism makes extreme demands. (2) Those demands are unreasonable. Our discussion of the Realm of Reciprocity suggests that the first of these claims would not be true in that realm. In a Need-Free Society, agents might well be able to maximize the good by pursuing their own goals, especially if those goals involved collective projects. Simple Consequentialism would thus counsel self-indulgence rather than self-sacrifice. On the other hand, our discussion of the Realm of Necessity suggests that the second of our claims may not be true in that realm. In a Goalless World, there may well be no principled objection to the extreme demands of Simple Consequentialism.

The Demandingness Objection thus arises only in a world where both needs and goals are morally significant, where many needs are left unmet and many goals unrealized, and where the only way to pursue goals is to leave the needs of others unmet. In any such world one of the central tasks of moral philosophy is to balance the competing moral reasons generated by needs and goals. My claim is that this balance is best achieved by combining different moral theories, rather than by seeking to apply a single Consequentialist theory to all the disparate moral realms. If we need accounts of both moral realms, and of their boundaries, then we must combine the two strands of the Consequentialist tradition. Such a combination will be more plausible than any possible version of either Individual or Collective Consequentialism considered alone. Consequentialists make the mistake of expecting a single answer to the question: should value be promoted individually or collectively? Some components of the good should be promoted individually, while others are most appropriately promoted collectively. In the next chapter, I sketch one possible version of this new Combined Consequentialism.

10

The New Theory

In this chapter I sketch a new moral theory, designed to deal appropriately with both moral realms. This theory consists of three basic elements: (1) a Reason to Promote the Good, governing our behaviour within the Realm of Necessity; (2) a Rule Consequentialist ideal code of rules, governing our behaviour within the Realm of Reciprocity; and (3) a device for balancing the competing reasons delivered by (1) and (2). This final role is played by a modified version of Scheffler's Agent Centred Prerogative. The overall theory, which I shall call *Combined Consequentialism*, thus takes the form of a modified Hybrid View. I argue that it offers Consequentialists their best chance of developing a plausible moral theory without unreasonable demands.

Perhaps the clearest way to develop my new theory is to begin with Scheffler's original, and progressively add additional constraints on the Agent Centred Prerogative. These gradually transform the prerogative from a rigid balance between self-interest and the general good, into a more nuanced balancer of our two realms. This way of proceeding also establishes a range of intermediate positions, which some may find more congenial than full-blown Combined Consequentialism. Accordingly, we first return to the original presentation of the Hybrid View. Beginning with Scheffler's own defence of the Agent Centred Prerogative, we explore various constraints on such a prerogative (Sections 10.1 and 10.2.). The main argument of this chapter is that, by adding additional constraints to the original Hybrid View, we can construct a credible Consequentialist moral theory. I defend two departures from Scheffler's original theory. The first is a non-proportional account of the relationship between values and reasons, designed to defeat the Wrong Facts Objection (Sections 10.3 and 10.4). The second departure is the incorporation of a Rule Consequentialist ideal code as our account of the Realm of Reciprocity. This constrains the range of goals agents are permitted to pursue and the ways they may pursue them. This departure is designed to defeat our remaining objections to the Hybrid View (Sections 10.5–10.7). I then claim that Combined Consequentialism is an adequate theory (Section 10.8), and that it is superior to its Consequentialist rivals (Section 10.9).

10.1. Three Types of Constraint

We begin our exposition of Combined Consequentialism by recalling Scheffler's own justification for the Agent Centred Prerogative. The prerogative is presented as a response to the following features of human moral life: the separateness of persons; the independence of the personal point of view; the fact that morality governs the choices of human agents; and the significance of the personal point of view *to the agent,* over and above its value from an impersonal point of view (see Section 6.1).

The prerogative thus 'constitutes a structural feature whose incorporation into a moral conception embodies a rational strategy for taking account of personal independence, given one construal of the importance of that aspect of persons'.[1] Scheffler's guiding view is that an adequate moral theory should leave human beings morally free to choose, build, and pursue their own goals, projects, activities, and relationships, even at the expense of overall value.

This leaves two crucial questions: what constrains this freedom, and what justifies this (constrained) freedom? An Egoist might argue that the agent's moral freedom to pursue her own goals is completely unconstrained, so long as she maximizes her own interests.[2] She may choose any goal, and pursue it however she wishes. The Simple Consequentialist, by contrast, contends that the agent's freedom to pursue her goals is entirely subject to the overriding goal of maximizing value. The moral moderate, such as Scheffler, seeks a freedom for moral agents that is constrained but not empty.[3]

We seek to avoid the extreme demands of Simple Consequentialism. Combined Consequentialism is thus a moderate moral theory. It will include a constrained Agent Centred Prerogative, or something analogous. Beginning with Scheffler's own model, there are three possible ways to constrain a prerogative.

Range Constraints.   These limit the range of goals agents are permitted to pursue. For instance, agents might be allowed to pursue only goals developing valuable human capacities.

Method Constraints.   These restrict the ways agents pursue their goals. A method constraint might be global, applying to the pursuit of all goals. For

---

[1] Scheffler, *The Rejection of Consequentialism,* p. 67.

[2] Actually, a theory leaving the agent's actions morally unconstrained is some form of Existentialism, where all that matters is that the agent choose her actions. A consistent Egoist, by contrast, would *require* an agent to pursue her own good.

[3] For definitions of the notion of a moderate moral theory, see Scheffler, *Human Morality,* p. 6, and Kagan, *The Limits of Morality,* pp. 4–5. For a defence, see Scheffler, *Human Morality,* pp. 98–114. For a critique, see Kagan, *The Limits of Morality,* pp. 47–80.

instance, an Agent Centred Restriction such as 'Do not kill' restricts the methods available to agents in pursuit of any goals. Alternatively, a method constraint might be particular, applying only to the pursuit of some class of goals. For instance, specific rules such as 'Only reproduce within hetero-sexual nuclear families' restrict the pursuit of a particular set of goals.

Weight Constraints. These limit the weight agents are permitted to give to their own goals, as opposed to the general good. As with method constraints, a weight constraint can be either global or particular. A moral theory might include a variety of different weight constraints, each governing a different class of goals.

In his original discussion, Scheffler focuses exclusively on the third form of constraint. He offers a simple blanket form of this constraint, with all agents permitted to give a certain weight to all their goals. (This is why the original Hybrid View is subject to the Wrong Facts Objection.) The range of goals available, and the method of pursuit, are totally unconstrained. (This is why Kagan and others are able to construct their counter-examples to Scheffler's original Hybrid View.) To avoid the problems of Scheffler's original Hybrid View, we need both range and method constraints. In particular, we will be interested in the relationship between the two. Perhaps some permissible goals can be pursued only in certain ways. If these are the only permissible goals, then those method constraints will come close to Agent Centred Restrictions.

We can borrow our account of these additional constraints from an extant moral theory. In particular, I will suggest that the best constraints are provided by an account of the Realm of Reciprocity, such as Rule Consequentialism.

10.2. Constraints and Restrictions

Before discussing various constraints in more detail, we first ask whether a combination of range and method constraints constitutes (or implies) an Agent Centred Restriction. We begin by formalizing the various constraints. (Where A is an agent, and x is an act.)

Agent Centred Prerogative. A is permitted to do x (in order to pursue her own interests) rather than maximizing impersonal value.

Weight Constraint. A is permitted to do x if and only if, for any y, if y is an act available to A, then the additional value to A of doing x rather than y, when multiplied by the weight A is allowed to give to her own interests (call it M), is greater than the additional impersonal value of A's doing y rather than x.

This is the proportional and global form of the constraint, where M is a constant. In a non-proportional, goal-indexed weight constraint, M is indexed to both the goal the agent is pursuing and her level of well-being at the time.

Range Constraint.   A is permitted to do x if and only if there exists a goal G such that (i) x is an act of pursuing G; and (ii) G is a goal of type P (where P is a class of permitted goals).

Method Constraint.   A is permitted to do x if and only if x is not an act of type T.

This is the global form of the constraint. A method constraint indexed to particular classes of goal would specify a separate restricted class of actions (Tp) for each permitted class of goals. For some sets of goals, Tp is the empty set. The range constraint is thus a special case of the method constraint. This explains our subsequent focus on method constraints.

We can now formalize a full Agent Centred Prerogative as follows:

Full Agent Centred Prerogative.   A is permitted to do x if and only if there exists a goal G such that

1. x is an act of pursuing G;
2. G is a goal of type P;
3. x is not an act of type Tp; and
4. for any y, if y is an act available to A, then the additional value to A of doing x rather than y, when multiplied by the weight A is allowed to give to her own interests when pursuing a goal of type P given her current level of well-being, is greater than the additional impersonal value of A's doing y rather than x.

This prerogative deals exclusively with the agent's goals. This is in line with the conclusions of the previous chapter, where we saw that the justification for the Agent Centred Prerogative rests upon features peculiar to goals. This may seem to ignore the agent's right to meet her own needs, even at the expense of the general good. However, this is not the case. As we saw in Chapter 7, basic needs are prerequisites for goals. One must ensure that one's basic needs are met before one can actively pursue any goals at all. The Agent Centred Prerogative will thus permit agents to meet their own needs, as any act that meets those needs also contributes to the pursuit of the agent's goals. This indirect permission to meet needs may seem artificial. However, as we saw in the previous chapter, the Agent Centred Prerogative can be justified only by appeal to the nature and significance of goals (see Section 9.3 above). Agents are only permitted to give disproportionate weight to their own needs, as against the needs of others, because of the connection between needs and goals. Creatures without goals would have no Agent Centred Prerogative at all. An agent's permission disproportionately to meet her needs is parasitic on her permission to pursue her goals. Our formulation of the prerogative reflects this fact.

Under what conditions does a full prerogative constitute an Agent Centred Restriction? We might formalize the latter as follows.

Agent Centred Restriction.   A is required not to perform acts of class C, even if this prevents A from pursuing her own interests or maximizing impersonal value.

Take any act (call it x). If x is permitted under an Agent Centred Prerogative, then there must be some goal G such that (i) G is a goal of a permitted type P; and (ii) x is an act of pursuing G; and (iii) x is not an act of type Tp. Conversely, if there is no goal such that x is an act of a type permitted in pursuit of that goal, then x is not permitted under any Agent Centred Prerogative. (For the sake of simplicity, we leave aside condition (iv) of the full formulation. This condition might rule out a whole class of acts if, as a matter of fact, their consequences were never sufficiently valuable to the agent to outweigh their lack of impersonal value.)

We can now construct the set of all acts belonging to no permitted class of acts. Call this class C. Formally, x is a member of C if and only if it is not the case that there exists a goal G such that (1) G is a member of a permitted class of goals P; (2) x is an act of pursuing G; and (3) x is an act of type Tp. Acts of class C are not permitted under any Agent Centred Prerogative. Is this equivalent to the claim that all acts of class C are forbidden?

Not necessarily. Consider a moral theory, like Scheffler's original Hybrid View, containing only Agent Centred Prerogatives and a background Reason to Promote the Good. Even if an act is permitted under no Agent Centred Prerogative, it is still permitted if (though *only* if) it maximizes impersonal value. Therefore, acts of class C maximizing impersonal value are permitted. All others are forbidden.

There is thus a conceptual gap between a fully constrained Agent Centred Prerogative and a genuine Agent Centred Restriction. However, this gap may not be very significant in practice. After all, human agents almost never seriously consider maximizing impersonal value. They invariably choose between different (impersonally suboptimal) ways of trading off their own personal interests against impersonal value. Indeed, human agents are seldom concerned with impersonal value *per se*. We usually see our moral trade-offs in more concrete terms: balancing our own goals against the needs or goals of some particular other person(s), or against some particular impersonal value. Human agents, even when they seek to behave morally, are always seeking to exercise an Agent Centred Prerogative. A fully constrained prerogative is thus likely to rule out all actions of a particular type.

Constrained prerogatives might amount to full Agent Centred Restrictions in another way. There may be some broad categories of goals that are unavoidable. Perhaps some goals are impossible to avoid, even though they are suboptimal from an impersonal point of view. If agents cannot help but live their lives within the confines of such goals, then all their actions will be subject to the constrained prerogatives governing such goals. If all acts of class C maximizing impersonal value are incompatible with those constraints, then no acts of class C will be permitted. While this is not the same as all acts of class C being forbidden, it amounts to much the same thing in practice. For instance, it may be that, in order to function as a moral agent, one must engage in goals that render one psychologically incapable of giving serious consideration to those (few) cases where torture might maximize impersonal value. If we grant that torture is never an appropriate way to pursue one's own personal goals, then this will leave no cases where torture is both psychologically and morally available to the agent. (See the discussion of different types of availability in Section 7.5.)

For a more significant example, consider the community-based projects discussed in Section 7.8. As we saw in that chapter, agents seeking worthwhile lives cannot avoid community-based goals. If there are constraints governing the pursuit of such goals, then any agent pursuing those goals is bound by those constraints. All agents are always pursuing some such goals. Therefore, all agents are always bound by such constraints. Agents who violate the constraints would, in some sense, be undermining their own continuing capacity for agency. (This result is especially significant because, as we shall see, community-based projects are likely to be governed by comparatively stringent method constraints.)

It follows that agents will always be simultaneously responding to both the Reason to Promote the Good and whatever reasons apply within the Realm of Reciprocity. We cannot separate the two realms in practice. Accordingly, the Reason to Promote the Good cannot require anything inconsistent with the code of rules governing goals. Combined Consequentialism thus requires agents to be sensitive to the fact that they are operating within the Realm of Reciprocity, even when responding to basic needs. Basic structural features of the Realm of Reciprocity permeate the whole of morality.

Analogously, Combined Consequentialism also requires agents to be evermindful of the needs of others, even when pursuing their personal goals. This awareness takes the form of balancing the conventions and rules governing the Realm of Reciprocity against an ever-present Reason to Promote the Good. It is at this point that Combined Consequentialism diverges from standard accounts of the Realm of Reciprocity, such as Rule Consequentialism. For the Rule Consequentialist, a Reason to Promote the Good must be justified in terms of its place in the ideal code of rules. Under Combined Consequentialism, by contrast, the Reason to Promote the Good has an independent justification. It stands apart from, and competes with, the ideal code. As we shall see, this difference enables our new theory to avoid many of the problems that plague Rule Consequentialism, such as the Wrong Facts Objection.

The Hybrid View always permits the optimal act because it begins with the Reason to Promote the Good and considers Agent Centred Prerogatives only as departures from that default option. Prerogatives are seen as concessions from impartial morality. This reflects the fact that Scheffler is balancing the Reason to Promote the Good against the agent's own interests, with the presupposition that morality privileges the former. Once we recast the Hybrid View as a balance between two moral realms, this privileging of the Realm of Necessity over the Realm of Reciprocity appears under-motivated. Indeed, for the reasons sketched at the end of the last chapter, it might be more natural to privilege the Realm of Reciprocity. Alternatively, we might accord equal weight to both realms. The optimal act would not be permitted when it conflicts sufficiently strongly with the code of reciprocity. Unlike a partially modified Hybrid View, full-blown Combined Consequentialism can incorporate genuine Agent Centred Restrictions. (See Section 10.8.1 below for further discussion of the moral significance of the gap between constraints and restrictions.)

10.3. Developing a Non-Proportional Hybrid View

The remainder of this chapter charts the journey from the Hybrid View to Combined Consequentialism. The former departs from the latter in two key ways. The first is the replacement of Scheffler's proportional weight constraint with a non-proportional version. The second is the introduction of range and method constraints, drawn from our Rule Consequentialist account of the Realm of Reciprocity. These amendments enable Combined Consequentialism to rebut objections to the original Hybrid View, by removing its counter-intuitive consequences.

In the next two sections, I develop a response to the Wrong Facts Objection, leading to a non-proportional Hybrid View. The result is more intuitively plausible than Scheffler's original. The main purpose of the present section is to explain the general idea of a non-proportional prerogative. The next section defends such a prerogative, and asks what form it might take.

The Agent Centred Prerogative balances two separate moral reasons: the impersonal Reason to Promote the Good (hereafter the 'value-based reason'), and the agent's personal reason to avoid costs to herself (hereafter the 'cost-based reason'). On the original Hybrid View, each of these reasons is proportional in character. The strength of the agent's value-based reason to perform a given act is directly proportional to the amount of good at stake, while her cost-based reason to perform another action instead is directly proportional to the cost she would bear.

Recall the following tale from Chapter 6.

Affluent's Ignorance.   Affluent is sitting at her desk with her cheque book. She has heard a rumour that, owing to circumstances entirely beyond Oxfam's control, the effectiveness of its ongoing immunization programme (that is, the amount of good it can do for each dollar it receives) has been drastically altered. However, she does not know what the nature of the alteration has been. Indeed, she does not even know if the rumour is true. Affluent knows only that one of the following is an accurate description of the state of Oxfam's operations.

Inefficient Oxfam.   Oxfam's efficiency has declined to 10 per cent of its previous level, owing to the appearance of a mutant virus largely immune to existing treatments. Each dollar spent now produces only one-tenth as much good as before.

Normal Oxfam.   Oxfam's efficiency is unchanged.

Superefficient Oxfam.   The efficiency of Oxfam's famine relief operations has increased tenfold, owing to a breakthrough in pharmaceutical technology. Each dollar spent now produces ten times as much good as before.

A tenfold increase in the amount of good at stake leads to a tenfold increase in the strength of Affluent's value-based reason to give money to Oxfam. As her cost-based reasons are unaffected by any alteration in Oxfam's efficiency, this leads to a tenfold increase in the cost required to generate a cost-based reason of comparable strength. This in turn leads to a tenfold increase in the cost Affluent is required to bear before she is allowed to stop donating to Oxfam. The cost Affluent must bear is thus directly proportional to the amount of good at stake.

The Wrong Facts Objection rejects this strict proportionality. To defeat the objection without abandoning the spirit of the Hybrid View, we must introduce an element of non-proportionality into our account of the relationship between the cost an agent is required to bear and the amount of good at stake. There are two places we could introduce such an element: into our account of the agent's value-based reason, or into our account of her cost-based reasons. As we saw in Chapter 9, the justification for non-proportionality is drawn from the significance to the agent of pursuing her goals. Such a justification clearly relates to the costs borne by the agent, not to the value of the impersonal good at stake. (This also provides another explanation of the failure of Satisficing Consequentialism, which focused exclusively on value-based reasons rather than cost-based reasons.) Accordingly, in the remainder of this section I focus on a revised Hybrid View combining a non-proportional appeal to cost with a proportional Reason to Promote the Good.

Let M be the disproportionate weight the Hybrid View allows the agent to give to her own interests. Under Scheffler's original, M is a constant. The amount of extra weight the agent is allowed to give to her own interests is independent of the cost involved. Under our new theory, by contrast, M will be a variable factor determined by the cost to the agent. As the cost the agent must bear to produce a given additional amount of good increases, the weight she is allowed to give to her own interests also increases.

To illustrate this view, assume that an agent (A) faces a choice between three options (x, y, and z). In Table 2, the first column represents the value of the outcome of each action. The second column represents the cost A would have to bear if she performed that action instead of performing z, the least costly option. The third column shows the weight A is allowed to give to her own interests at that level of cost. The fourth column gives us the total weight of the cost the agent would bear if she performed that option (adding each successive unit multiplied by its weight).[4] The fifth column tells us whether or not A is allowed to perform that action: x is permitted because it is the optimal act, y is permitted because the weighted cost of the only more valuable option (x) is greater than the difference in impersonal value. z is not permitted because there is an alternative whose extra value outweighs the weighted cost (namely y).

TABLE 2. *The non-proportional Hybrid View*

Act	Value	Cost	Weight	Total	Permitted?
x	100	17	5	55	Yes
y	75	10	2	20	Yes
z	50	0	0	0	No

[4] For this example, I make the simplifying assumption that each of the first 10 units of cost has a weighting of 2, while each subsequent unit has a weighting of 5. In a more realistic theory, this simple stepwise function would be replaced by a more continuous one, but this does not affect the argument of the text.

Under the original Hybrid View, the weighting at a cost of 10 must be the same as at a cost of 17. Therefore, if A is not allowed to perform z, then she will not be allowed to perform y, as the extra cost is less while the amount of additional value at stake is the same. By contrast, under our new non-proportional theory, A is allowed to do y, even though she is not allowed to do z, as the difference in cost between x and y counts for more than that between y and z. This combination of moral judgements would be impossible under any traditional Hybrid View. In the next section, I show how this enables our new theory to defeat the Wrong Facts Objection.

We can summarize our non-proportional Agent Centred Prerogative in one simple condition. Let the agent's *value-based reason* to do x rather than y be the reason generated solely by the relative values of the outcome of performing x rather than y; and let the *weighted cost* to the agent in doing x rather than y be the cost she would have borne if she had done x rather than y (multiplied by the weighting she is allowed to give to her own interests at that level of cost).

The Non-Proportional ACP.   An act (x) is permissible if and only if for any other act available to the agent (call it y) the weighted cost the agent would have borne if she had performed y instead of x is GREATER than the agent's value-based reason to do y rather than x.

10.4. Defending Non-Proportionality

So far I have only explained the non-proportional Agent Centred Prerogative. I have not defended it. I shall now present some considerations in support of non-proportionality. A first step is to distinguish it from some controversial claims about value. For instance, we might be worried that non-proportionality contradicts the following claim.

The Proportionality of Value Thesis.   Let A and B be any two possible outcomes. If B contains ten times as much of whatever makes outcomes valuable as A, then the value of B will be ten times the value of A. For instance, assume that the existence of human lives worth living makes outcomes valuable. Let A be an outcome with 40 million people whose lives each have a value of 50. Let B be another outcome where the same people all have lives worth 100. Under the Proportionality of Value Thesis, the value of outcome B will thus be twice the value of outcome A.

I shall not discuss the plausibility of the Proportionality of Value Thesis here.[5] I wish only to point out that Consequentialists who adopt this thesis need not reject our use of non-proportionality. Under our non-proportional approach, the cost the agent is required to bear is not proportional to the amount of what makes life worth living at stake. However, this is perfectly compatible with the view that the value of an outcome *is* proportional to the amount of what makes life worth living it contains, as the non-proportionality is contained in the relationship between the values of states-of-affairs and our reasons to bring them about, *not* in the relationship between the values of individual lives and the values of states-of-affairs.

One positive argument for the introduction of non-proportionality is that a version of the Hybrid View incorporating non-proportionality provides a better explanation of our reflective moral intuitions than any Consequentialist theory with only proportional relationships between reasons and values. To illustrate this, let us apply the revised Agent Centred Prerogative to Affluent's Ignorance. This not only provides a more acceptable account of Affluent's moral obligations in that particular case, but it also shows how the revised Agent Centred Prerogative works.

As before, assume that, in Normal Oxfam, Affluent is required to make a 10 per cent donation. The shift to Superefficient Oxfam increases the amount of good a given donation will produce. Affluent will be required to bear a greater cost in Superefficient Oxfam than in Normal Oxfam. However, the cost required does not increase by a factor of ten. Similarly, in Inefficient Oxfam, Affluent's value-based reasons will be weaker, so the cost she is required to bear will be reduced. However, it will not have been reduced by a factor of ten.

Let me explain why this is so. Recall that, in our earlier discussion of the Wrong Facts Objection, we granted that in Normal Oxfam Affluent had given 10 per cent of her income to Oxfam when she reached the point where the amount of additional utility she could gain by spending her next dollar on herself, when multiplied by the disproportionate weighting she was allowed to give to her own interests, was equal to the amount of additional value Oxfam could produce by spending that dollar.

Under the original (proportional) version of the Agent Centred Prerogative, Affluent must continue making donations in Superefficient Oxfam until the amount of additional utility she would gain by spending her next

⁵ The Proportionality of Value Thesis is by no means universally held. (See e.g. Hurka, 'Value and Population Size', and Ng, 'What should we Do about Future Generations?'.) I have argued elsewhere that any moral theory abandoning this thesis faces serious problems (Mulgan, 'What's Really Wrong with the Limited Quantity View?'). However, I should emphasize that the arguments of this chapter do not rely upon this thesis. I merely claim that they are not incompatible with it.

dollar on herself is ten times as great as at the point where she stopped donating in Normal Oxfam. By contrast, under our non-proportional theory, Affluent must continue making donations in Superefficient Oxfam until the amount of additional utility she would gain by spending her next dollar on herself is p times as great as at the point where she stopped donating in Normal Oxfam (where $1 < p < 10$).

As the amount of value at stake increases, the total cost Affluent must bear to produce that value certainly increases also. However, each successive unit of cost counts for more than the last. Projects ten times as valuable to Affluent as those she was required to give up in Normal Oxfam will count for more than ten times as much. Affluent will thus not be required to give them up. In Superefficient Oxfam, Affluent is only required to give up projects p times as valuable to her as those she is required to give up in Normal Oxfam.

Now recall Inefficient Oxfam. Under the original Hybrid View, Affluent was required to continue making donations only until the amount of additional utility she would gain by spending her next dollar on herself was one-tenth as great as at the point where she stopped donating in Normal Oxfam. By contrast, under our non-proportional theory, Affluent must continue making donations in Inefficient Oxfam until the amount of additional utility she would gain by spending her next dollar on herself is q times smaller than at the point where she stopped donating in Normal Oxfam (where $1 < q < 10$). In Inefficient Oxfam the Agent Centred Prerogative would allow Affluent to indulge in projects one q-th as valuable to her as those she would be allowed to indulge in in Normal Oxfam.

If we set p and q both equal to ten, then our non-proportional Agent Centred Prerogative will be identical to Scheffler's original version. At the other extreme, setting p and q both equal to one would give us a theory where the demands placed on Affluent remained exactly the same throughout our three scenarios. By setting p and q sufficiently close to one, we can ensure that Affluent's prerogatives remain similar in each of the three cases. Our initial objection was not that Scheffler's theory produced different demands in the three situations, but rather that the resulting differences were too great. The introduction of a suitable non-proportional Agent Centred Prerogative should thus be sufficient to dissolve our objection.

Our new theory may seem to face a variant of the Wrong Facts Objection, in the following way. For any level of cost to the agent, there will be *some* natural number (call it n) such that the amount of good produced by saving n people from starvation is greater than the cost to the agent multiplied by the weighting the agent is allowed to give to her own interests at that level of cost. If we set the number of people who would be saved in Superefficient Oxfam sufficiently high, we can always construct a situation where the cost required of Affluent in Superefficient Oxfam is exactly ten times that required in Normal Oxfam. We can then retell the tale of Affluent's Ignorance, replacing the original Superefficient Oxfam with this new, more populous scenario. Once again, Affluent will need to know whether or not Oxfam's efficiency has increased before she has any idea how much she is obliged to donate.

Fortunately, this new Wrong Facts Objection lacks the force of the original. The original objection did not object in principle to the notion that differences in the agent's ability to affect the world should impact on her obligations. It objected only to the claim that changes in obligations should be directly proportional to any such change in ability. Once we grant that variations in the agent's ability to affect the world should have some effect on the extent of her obligations, the Wrong Facts Objection can no longer provide a general refutation of non-proportional Hybrid Views. Assume we begin with a particular non-proportional Hybrid View specifying the precise relationship between the cost to the agent and the weight she is allowed to give to her own interests. We are then presented with a situation like Affluent's Ignorance where, on this theory, variations in the agent's abilities would produce an intuitively disproportionate change in her obligations. The existence of such a situation does indeed count against that particular revised Hybrid View. However, there will be countless other non-proportional hybrid theories that would not yield an unacceptable result in that particular situation. We would thus be free to replace our first theory with one of those. Of course, we know that there will be situations in which our new hybrid theory will lead us from variations in the agent's abilities to significant variations in the extent of her obligations. However, we have already accepted that there should be some such variations. We thus cannot conclude in advance that our new theory produces counter-intuitive variations. It may turn out that it does, but then we can replace it with another theory without those particular variations.

The discovery of counter-intuitive variations between the agent's ability to affect the world and the extent of her obligations thus provides a means of refining a particular non-proportional Hybrid View, not an objection to such theories in general. If there is an intuitively acceptable pattern of variations, then, *a fortiori*, there must be some theory that countenances those, and only those, variations. The revised Wrong Facts Objection gives us no reason to believe that this ideal theory will not be some non-proportional Hybrid View.

We can thus conclude that the revised Hybrid View is considerably more intuitively plausible than Scheffler's original. This improvement in intuitive fit also suggests a deeper rationale for the non-proportional approach. Some elements of an agent's well-being are more central to her life than others. Even where two agents are in some sense giving up the same amount of well-being, the one who was worse off to start with is making a greater sacrifice, as her cost-based reason not to give up that well-being was stronger than that of her fellow. Losses of well-being when one's level of well-being is already low have a stronger pull on the agent than identical losses when one is better off. Without a non-proportional structure, we would be unable to allow for this possibility, as any difference in the strength of reasons would have to be reducible to a difference in the amount of well-being at stake. These non-proportionalities are mostly due to the nature of goals. This helps to explain why, as we saw in Chapter 9, Affluent's Ignorance would not create intuitive problems for the original Hybrid View in a Goal-Free World. Such a world will not require a non-proportional Hybrid View, as there is no reason to expect different needs to generate reasons of different kinds.

We can explain non-proportionality in terms of a combination of range and weight constraints. Different goals attract different weight constraints, depending upon the significance of each goal to the agent's well-being. The more goals an agent is actively pursuing, the less significant each one is to her. In general, the significance of a given goal increases if the agent is made worse off in other respects. The weight the agent is permitted to give to that goal thus also increases. This provides a justification for the non-proportionality required to remove the Wrong Facts Objection.

The non-proportional structure just outlined might be fleshed out in many different ways. One option would be to break down the Reason to Promote the Good into separate component reasons to promote different goods. These component reasons might be of different weight, or be differently structured. Another option would be to adopt a set of rules for the Realm of Reciprocity based on some underlying Consequentialist rationale, although perhaps not explicitly formulated as a set of reasons to promote different goods. For instance, the rule set might be designed to promote the good overall, as in Rule Consequentialism. If different goals require different responses, then we can expect the Rule Consequentialist ideal code to have a non-proportional structure overall.

Let us focus on the rule governing donations to charity. Initially, we might expect the optimal rule to require maximum possible donations. However, as we saw in Chapter 3, we must balance the benefits of donations against the psychological cost and practical difficulty of inculcating a demanding rule in a human population. The cost to the agent of sacrificing a given unit of well-being increases as the agent's well-being decreases. The cost of inculcating a rule requiring those sacrifices thus also increases. Accordingly, the optimal rule will require the well off to sacrifice more of their well-being than the worse off.

Recall that the role of the Hybrid View within Combined Consequentialism is to balance the Reason to Promote the Good against the reasons generated by the Realm of Reciprocity. Accordingly, there are two points at which non-proportionality might enter our theory. Either (1) we might incorporate non-proportionality directly into the structure of the Hybrid View, by making the weight of the reasons from the Realm of Reciprocity a decreasing function of the agent's level of well-being; or (2), leaving the formal structure of the Hybrid View in its original proportional form, we might rely on the ideal code of reciprocity to introduce non-proportionality by allowing agents who are worse off to give extra weight to their own interests. Perhaps a suitable Rule Consequentialist ideal code will supply all the non-proportionality we need. For maximum flexibility, however, we leave open both forms of non-proportionality.

10.5. Range and Method Constraints

Our first departure from the original Hybrid View is the introduction of a non-proportional weight constraint. This move is sufficient to dissolve the Wrong Facts Objection. We now consider more radical departures—namely, the introduction of range and method constraints. In this section, we ask why such constraints might be needed.

Scheffler justifies his prerogative, as a departure from Simple Consequentialism, in terms of the role the ability to choose and pursue goals plays in human agency. This suggests that the prerogative will be easiest to defend for goals central to our agency. To deny the need for range and method constraints is to claim that all choices involving personal goals make an equal contribution to the development and flourishing of human agency. This is a very strong claim. Indeed, one of the principle lessons of Chapter 7 was that this claim is, at best, highly implausible. Different goals are morally significant in very different ways. Accordingly, we should regard range and method constraints as genuine possibilities, and examine arguments supporting them. Such arguments will be of two types: theoretical and intuitive. This section examines general theoretical reasons for adopting method and range constraints. Subsequent sections demonstrate the superior intuitive appeal of any theory incorporating such constraints.

Theoretical arguments in favour of a constraint on the range of goals agents are permitted to pursue all turn on the claim that some goals make a more significant contribution to the agent's well-being, or are more morally salient from the agent's personal point of view, than others. This claim might take several forms.

The Pursuit Claim.   The *pursuit* of goal G1 is more morally significant to the agent than the pursuit of goal G2.

The Achievement Claim.   The *achievement* involved in successfully completing goal G1 is more morally significant to the agent than the achievement involved in completing goal G2.

The Availability Claim.   The *availability* of goal G1 is more morally significant to the agent than the availability of goal G2.

Considerations of pursuit and achievement are closely interrelated, especially if we take the term 'goal' in a broad sense. When dealing, for instance, with interpersonal relationships it is virtually impossible to disentangle the positive effects of pursuing the goal from the valuable outcomes produced.

The theoretical argument for method constraints is similar. As we saw in Chapter 7, the pursuit of a goal is valuable in itself, not merely as a means to the realization of the goal. The value of a goal may thus depend upon how it is pursued. If an otherwise valuable goal is pursued in an inappropriate way, then it may not be sufficiently valuable to justify an Agent Centred Prerogative. The Agent Centred Prerogative governing this goal would thus be subject to method constraints.

It might seem that a suitable weight constraint will be able to accommodate the different values of different goals. If Goal G1 is more valuable to the agent than Goal G2, then the weight constraint will permit the agent to pursue Goal G1 to a greater extent than Goal G2. This suggests that range constraints are unnecessary. Similarly, if a goal is less valuable (or not valuable at all) if pursued in an inappropriate way, then the weight constraint will discount it accordingly. This suggests that method constraints are unnecessary.

However, things are not so simple. The arguments in the previous paragraph assume that the moral significance of a given goal is proportional to its contribution to the agent's well-being. Yet the discussion in Sections 6.3 and 7.2 suggests that strict proportionality between personal value and moral significance is not always appropriate. Perhaps some components of an agent's well-being have greater significance in certain contexts than other equally valuable components. In particular, the justification of the Agent Centred Prerogative turns on the importance of certain features of human agency. This suggests that components of well-being closely related to those features may generate stronger prerogatives than equally valuable components contributing to other features of a flourishing human life. For instance, the Agent Centred Prerogative may privilege goals developing one's autonomy over goals that merely exercise that autonomy, even though the latter may develop other valuable capacities.

In a similar vein, Raz notes that, even when my reason to do something relates to my well-being, the strength of the reason generated need not be directly proportional to the contribution to my well-being. My stronger reason may derive from something less central to my well-being. These considerations are especially significant when we move from Scheffler's original Hybrid View to a theory balancing the two realms. Even within the Realm of Reciprocity, the moral significance of a given factor need not be proportional to its contribution to the agent's own well-being.

This line of reasoning also enables moderate moral theorists to avoid an objection frequently levelled at liberal political theories. Such theories claim to be neutral with respect to competing theories of the human good. It is sometimes objected that, far from being neutral, liberal theories presuppose a distinctly liberal theory of the self. This objection is usually based on the emphasis liberals place on autonomy and freedom. It is argued that this emphasis is justified only if autonomy is assumed to be a highly valuable component of any worthwhile human life, a claim non-liberal theories of the good will reject.[6]

Unlike political liberals, Consequentialists need not seek strict neutrality with respect to competing theories of the good. However, most Consequentialists desire a theory applicable across a wide range of theories of the good. In his defence of the Hybrid View, Scheffler places considerable weight on the significance of autonomy. The appeal of his theory will be greater if this argument does not rely upon controversial claims about the value of autonomy. This is much more likely once we have learnt to separate claims regarding the moral significance of autonomy as a ground for Agent Centred Prerogatives from claims regarding the contribution of autonomy to an agent's well-being. Scheffler's argument requires strong claims of the former sort, but it may be compatible with considerably weaker claims of the latter sort.

10.6. Doing and Allowing Revisited

The nature of goals thus strongly supports the introduction of range and method constraints. We turn now to intuitive arguments supporting such constraints. These aim to show that, by incorporating them, Combined Consequentialism can avoid some of the counter-intuitive implications of the original Hybrid View. Over the next few sections, we revisit the remaining objections of Chapter 6.

Kagan claimed that the Hybrid View produces absurd result in many everyday situations because it cannot distinguish between actively doing x and passively allowing x to happen. In this section, I explore various ways Combined Consequentialism might incorporate that distinction, thereby defeating Kagan's objection.

---

[6] For an overview of this debate, see Kymlicka, *Liberalism, Community and Culture*, pp. 47–73.

In Section 9.2.3, we discovered that the distinction between doing and allowing is significantly more plausible in the Realm of Reciprocity than in the Realm of Necessity. This implies that Kagan's objection is more effective in the former realm. To escape that objection, Combined Consequentialism needs an account of the Realm of Reciprocity incorporating a doing/allowing distinction. By contrast, we saw that an adequate moral theory need not acknowledge such a distinction in the Realm of Necessity.

We should bear in mind, however, the impossibility of completely separating the two realms (see Section 7.13). Owing to the overlapping nature of the two realms, there is no place where our combined moral theory leaves us free completely to ignore the distinction between doing and allowing, as we are always responding simultaneously to the demands of both moral realms. Even where the Realm of Necessity ultimately wins the day, and the Reason to Promote the Good prevails, we may still feel the residual pull of the distinction between doing and allowing, or of some other feature of the Realm of Reciprocity (see Section 10.8.1).

In Chapter 8, I concluded that, while not acceptable as a full moral theory, Rule Consequentialism may be appropriate within the Realm of Reciprocity. This is precisely the realm where agents pursue the goals protected by their Agent Centred Prerogatives. If Rule Consequentialism offers an appropriate account of that realm, then perhaps it can provide a rationale for some amendment to the structure of the Agent Centred Prerogative, possibly along similar lines to Scheffler's own No Harm Prerogative (see Section 6.6). The result would be a more intuitively appealing moral theory, built entirely on Consequentialist foundations; just as the move to non-proportionality discussed in Sections 10.3 and 10.4 increased the intuitive appeal of the Hybrid View without abandoning its basic Consequentialist structure.

As in Chapter 8, I focus on Rule Consequentialism. There are two reasons for this. Rule Consequentialism is the most common and well-developed form of Collective Consequentialism. It thus has many resources we can utilize. Furthermore, the flexibility of Rule Consequentialism and its emphasis on the acceptance of rules (rather than mere compliance) provide the key elements of a response to Kagan's objection.

Rule Consequentialism may seem no better placed than Individual Consequentialism to accommodate a distinction between doing and allowing. After all, like other forms of Consequentialism, Rule Consequentialism is primarily interested in what happens, not in how it comes about. The optimal set of rules is selected solely on the basis of consequences. However, as its proponents are fond of pointing out, Rule Consequentialism is not so simple. The optimal set of rules is not designed to be implemented by perfect Utilitarian calculators, but to be taught to (and internalized by) fallible, finite creatures such as ourselves. The rule set is thus constrained by human psychology, and by current institutions and practices. It may be that, whatever a perfectly idealized set of rules would look like, the best set of rules we (or creatures like us) could be taught includes many of the Non-Consequentialist distinctions of Common-Sense Morality. Indeed, this closeness to Common-Sense Morality is often cited as one of the principle virtues of Rule Consequentialism, especially in comparison to Individual Consequentialism (see Section 3.1.3).

The limits of human development are almost certainly such that the costs of attempting to eradicate a tendency to distinguish morally between doing and allowing would outweigh the benefits. The strength, near universality, and resilience of intuitions supporting that distinction strongly suggest this. The ideal set of rules will differentiate between doing and allowing. If we combine a constrained Individual Consequentialist account of the Realm of Necessity with a Rule Consequentialist account of the Realm of Reciprocity, we get a theory distinguishing clearly between doing and allowing within the latter realm, even though no such distinction is made in the former realm.

We must also remember that, as we saw in Chapter 8, certain features of Rule Consequentialism are accentuated in the Realm of Reciprocity. Within that realm, Rule Consequentialism is especially likely to recommend a code of rules with a strong distinction between doing and allowing. A Need-Free Society where people refrain from interfering with one another's pursuit of goals is likely to enjoy a higher level of well-being than one whose inhabitants regard such interference as no worse than a failure to assist others in the pursuit of their goals (see Sections 8.4 and 8.5).

Rule Consequentialism thus seems able to offer us exactly what we need. If the Agent Centred Prerogative must be exercised in accordance with the rules governing the Realm of Reciprocity, and if those rules incorporate a strong distinction between doing and allowing, then agents will not be permitted to harm others in pursuit of their own goals, even when the significance of those goals would have been sufficient to permit them to fail to assist those others. To use Kagan's own example, I would not be permitted to kill my uncle in order to inherit $10,000, even though I would be justified in refusing to donate $10,000 to save a stranger's life (see Section 6.4.1). This is because the Rule Consequentialist code of reciprocity incorporates a far stronger prohibition on killing than on letting die.[7]

---

[7] The discussion in the text relates to Kagan's original comparison. In Scheffler's more symmetrical version, I face a choice between letting my uncle die and letting a stranger die. The distinction between doing and allowing is no longer relevant. To accommodate Kagan's objection, we must look elsewhere. Perhaps Combined Consequentialism will not permit me to allow my uncle to die rather than donate $10,000, as my relationship with my uncle will be governed by the special obligations included in the Rule Consequentialist ideal code. (See the next section.)

As we have often seen, it is notoriously difficult to determine the precise content of the ideal set of rules. Even if those rules include *some* distinction between doing and allowing, we are still a long way from concluding that they include precisely the same distinction as Common-Sense Morality. Indeed, this seems unlikely, as the common sense failure to censure harmful omissions can have very significant negative consequences. Similarly, there is a large gap between the claim that the demands of Rule Consequentialism are constrained by human developmental capacities, and the claim that those demands are roughly equal to the demands of Common-Sense Morality (see Sections 3.4 and 10.8.3). Yet, whatever problems it may face there, Rule Consequentialism remains considerably more plausible in the Realm of Reciprocity than in the Realm of Necessity. For instance, the common-sense failure to censure omissions occurs most often within the Realm of Necessity. While we do not blame those who fail to donate to Oxfam, we certainly would censure someone who failed to save a starving child. The gap between common sense and the Rule Consequentialist code is thus less pronounced when we are operating strictly within the bounds of the moral community.

The Combined Consequentialist incorporation of a Rule Consequentialist code of reciprocity promises a considerably more intuitively appealing overall moral theory than Scheffler's original. The detailed rules of the ideal code limit agents' pursuit of their own goals, and may even rule out some undesirable goals altogether. They thus provide both method and range constraints for the Agent Centred Prerogative.

At the very least, the burden of proof is now firmly back with the opponents of the Hybrid View. They must find a specific application of the distinction between doing and allowing that is intuitively plausible, and that our new Combined Consequentialist theory cannot accommodate.

10.7. Special Obligations Revisited

The incorporation of Rule Consequentialist elements into our Combined Consequentialist theory also enables us to respond to the complaint that the Hybrid View fails to acknowledge the significance of special obligations. We saw in Chapter 9 that this objection applies principally within the Realm of Reciprocity. Accordingly, our account of that realm must provide a solution. We thus need to ask whether the Rule Consequentialist ideal code governing the pursuit of goals includes special obligations.

The ideal code maximizes agents' ability to pursue their goals. Will general acceptance of special obligations promote the successful pursuit of goals? We focus on community-based goals, as it is here that special obligations are most often thought to arise. We first recall the nature and significance of community-based goals, to see why one might expect them to give rise to special obligations. We then look at possible Rule Consequentialist codes of rules governing the pursuit of such goals.

Recall the discussion of community-based goals from Section 7.8. We saw that, on most plausible views of the human good, a life without participation in any human community is not a valuable human life. Indeed, such a life may not even be possible. Any plausible moderate moral theory must include Agent Centred Prerogatives permitting at least some community-based goals.

Goals based on membership of (and participation in) a human community are essentially other-directed. Appropriate pursuit of such goals thus places the agent under a number of special obligations, both to other individuals within the relevant community, and to the community as a whole. An Agent Centred Prerogative covering community-based goals will be justified partly in terms of the tendency of such goals to develop the agent's other-regarding capacities, such as cooperation and empathy. (We also saw in Chapter 9 that many seemingly self-regarding capacities are ultimately other-regarding, in that their development requires interaction with others.) If these excellences are sufficiently valuable to justify an Agent Centred Prerogative, they will also generate method constraints. An agent violating such constraints is not pursuing the community-based goal in a manner consistent with the grounds on which it is permitted.

We can cast the foregoing discussion in Kantian terms. The justification of community-based goals is that they develop the agent's capacity to treat other people (and herself) as ends-in-themselves. Such goals are therefore permitted only if pursued in a way that treats others as ends-in-themselves.

This feature of community-based goals suggests that rules governing reciprocal interactions between agents will constrain the Agent Centred Prerogative. Only goals pursued in accordance with those rules are consistent with the justification of the prerogative sanctioning them. Once again, the best moral theory will incorporate an account of the morality of reciprocal interaction. By attending more closely to the structure of the Agent Centred Prerogative, we thus acquire more support for the claim that Rule Consequentialist elements should be incorporated within our new Combined Consequentialist theory.

Recall the Need-Free Society, the world where all the basic needs of all human beings are met, including the need to be provided with the background conditions of autonomous action. Suppose we are Rule Consequentialists choosing between two competing codes of rules for such a society. One of the codes includes special obligations while the other does not. (Let us call these the Restrictive Code and the Permissive Code respectively.) We must compare the consequences of accepting each code. In a world where the Permissive Code was accepted, people would find it very difficult to pursue their goals, as they would be unable to rely upon others to fulfil any promises or undertakings on which those goals relied. By contrast, people who lived under the Restrictive Code would have confidence in one another's promises. Pursuit of goals would thus be much more widespread and ambitious. This considerable advantage is sufficient to outweigh any disadvantages of the Restrictive Code. Accordingly, within the Need-Free Society, Rule Consequentialists would recommend that code over its rival (see Section 8.4). Of course, we do not live in the Need-Free Society. However, if we are adopting a Rule Consequentialist account of the Realm of Reciprocity, then similar considerations will lead us to prefer the Restrictive Code over the Permissive Code, at least within that moral realm.

Community-based goals thus suggest that our Agent Centred Prerogative is subject to method constraints, in the form of special obligations to those with whom one interacts regularly. These obligations will be incorporated into the ideal Rule Consequentialist code governing the Realm of Reciprocity. As Rule Consequentialists always argue, it is much easier to get people to internalize a moral code with obligations and permissions based on personal relationships.

Once again, we see the significance of the shift from Scheffler's original Hybrid View to a theory balancing the two moral realms. Personal relationships are central to the Realm of Reciprocity. Indeed, if Holists are right, then such relationships are conceptually necessary for the very existence of moral agents. Personal obligations thus emerge directly from the basic structure of our moral theory, rather than having to be justified as peculiar departures from a foundational Reason to Promote the Good.

Combined Consequentialism can thus avoid the objection that it leaves no room for special obligations. The precise nature and scope of the obligations incorporated into Combined Consequentialism is another matter. As ever, it is difficult to say precisely what the Rule Consequentialist code entails. Perhaps we will not end up with an intuitively plausible code of special obligations. Once again, however, the burden of proof is now firmly back with the opponents of the Hybrid View. They must find a specific special obligation that is intuitively plausible, and that our new Combined Consequentialist theory cannot accommodate.

10.8. The Adequacy of Combined Consequentialism

My aim in this book is to find a plausible Consequentialist moral theory that is not unreasonably demanding. The previous sections have argued that our new Combined Consequentialist theory is significantly more plausible than Scheffler's original Hybrid View, itself the most promising of the Consequentialist theories surveyed in the first three parts of this book. Our remaining tasks are to address possible objections to Combined Consequentialism, to explore the limits and variations of its demands, and to demonstrate its superiority over its Consequentialist rivals. It is impossible to anticipate all possible objections. However, I will now address some of the most obvious candidates.

10.8.1. Unjust Optimal Acts

We begin with the question of whether Combined Consequentialism permits the optimal act. One common objection to Simple Consequentialism is that it requires flagrantly unjust acts whenever they produce better consequences than just acts. A similar objection applies to the Hybrid View, although it merely permits unjust optimal acts without requiring them. Can Combined Consequentialism avoid this common fate of two of its components?

We should first note that Combined Consequentialism will permit unjust optimal acts only within the Realm of Necessity. In the Realm of Reciprocity, our actions are governed by a code of reciprocity provided by Rule Consequentialism. Rule Consequentialism itself does not, of course, explicitly prohibit the optimal action. Other things being equal, the ideal code will always allow agents to promote the good. However, the code does include familiar prohibitions on killing, lying, and torture. Some of these rules will include disaster avoidance clauses, allowing agents to kill or lie to avert disaster. Other rules, however, may include no such clause. For instance, it might be best on balance to inculcate an absolute prohibition on torture, rather than encouraging agents to evaluate torture on a case-by-case basis. If the optimal code includes an exceptionless rule, then the optimal act will be prohibited whenever it falls under that rule. Optimal acts of torture will be forbidden. Optimal acts falling under rules containing exception clauses will also be prohibited, unless the alternative is disastrous.

In the Realm of Reciprocity, Combined Consequentialism can use the Rule Consequentialist code to prohibit unjust optimal acts. However, the Realm of Reciprocity is not the whole of morality. Outside that realm some forms of Combined Consequentialism always permit the optimal act. For instance, the theory seems to permit agents to kill someone in order to steal his money and donate it to famine relief. This is intuitively unacceptable.

It is true that some forms of Combined Consequentialism allow agents to opt out of the Realm of Reciprocity, and focus all their attention on the Realm of Necessity, provided they can do more good there. Such agents would be permitted to perform unjust optimal acts. However, the theory also requires agents who choose not to opt out of the Realm of Reciprocity to abide by the rules governing that realm. (This follows from the method constraints under-lying the Agent Centred Prerogative.) Agents thus have only two options. They must *either* abide by the code of reciprocity when pursuing all their pro-jects, *or* opt out entirely and seek continually to maximize utility. If they take the first option, and if the code of reciprocity contains absolute prohibitions against murdering the innocent, then the agent must abide by those prohibi-tions at all times.

What of the second option: opting out of the Realm of Reciprocity alto-gether? This extreme lifestyle choice will tempt very few agents. We might even wonder it is psychologically possible for a human being. If it is not pos-sible, then, in practice, Combined Consequentialism will never permit agents to breach any absolute prohibitions contained in the code of reciprocity.

Suppose, for the sake of argument, that some agents are psychologically able to opt out altogether. What would we think of someone who made this choice? I doubt we would condemn him as strongly as someone who made use of the rules of reciprocity when it suited him, but occasionally breached those rules in pursuit of good consequences. Such a person might rightly be accused of hypocrisy, and of a certain sort of free-riding. He should decide, once and for all, whether he really wished to belong to the moral community or not. The pure Utilitarian who opts out altogether, eschewing all the bene-fits of cooperation, cannot be accused of hypocrisy. While we may not agree with it, there is a certain nobility and self-sacrifice involved in his choice. The fact that Combined Consequentialism fails to condemn this lifestyle choice is not obviously a knock-down objection to the theory. Perhaps it is part of the legacy of any truly Consequentialist theory that it find something admirable in the life of the agent who unrelentingly promotes the good.

Furthermore, as we saw earlier, my new method of balancing the two realms offers two stronger responses. We could appeal to holistic considera-tions to establish the conceptual impossibility of any agent opting out of the Realm of Reciprocity. If community-based goals are an essential foundation for agency, then opting out of that realm makes no sense for a moral agent. Alternatively, we might reject Scheffler's way of balancing the two realms. As we saw at the end of Chapter 9, Scheffler's approach privileges the Realm of Necessity. This is implausible. Indeed, if either realm is to be privileged, it should probably be the Realm of Reciprocity. Accordingly, when no compromise is possible, conflicts between the two realms should be decided in favour of the code of reciprocity. If the latter includes absolute prohibitions, then these will always outweigh the Reason to Promote the Good. An absolute prohibition on torture would carry over into the Realm of Necessity.

This last response raises a new objection. I have argued that the code of reciprocity always applies, even when we are operating within the Realm of Necessity, and that it can trump the Reason to Promote the Good. Rule Consequentialism now seems to have completely taken over Combined Consequentialism. It is important to see why this is not so. While the Rule Consequentialist code may include some (nearly) absolute prohibitions, most of its rules will leave much scope for individual discretion, choice, and permission. In all these areas, an agent following Combined Consequentialism will feel the separate pull of the Reason to Promote the Good in a way that a strict Rule Consequentialist would not. In Combined Consequentialism, the Reason to Promote the Good has independent moral force. It is not merely a component of the ideal code of rules. Most conflicts between the two realms pit the Reason to Promote the Good against elements of the Rule Consequentialist ideal code allowing for exceptions and judgement calls. Balancing and compromise are the appropriate way to resolve such conflicts. The ideal code trumps only when its requirements are exceptionless, and no compromise is possible.

10.8.2. Is Combined Consequentialism Genuinely Consequentialist?

Any new form of Consequentialism must establish its credentials. Some might object that Combined Consequentialism combines two theories (the Hybrid View and Rule Consequentialism), neither of which is a genuine form of Consequentialism.

One is tempted to reply that this is a purely verbal matter. What turns on how we classify some particular theory? Rather than take this line, however, I wish to defend the Consequentialist credentials of the new theory. Consequentialism is a tradition of reasoning about morality. A theory should count as Consequentialist if (and only if) it remains true to the central ideals of that tradition. Combined Consequentialism does just that.

The basic Consequentialist idea is that morality is concerned with the promotion of the good. The simplest response to this idea is that I should maximize the good. As we have seen, the Consequentialist tradition includes many departures from this simple response. Perhaps we should promote the good collectively; perhaps promotion does not entail maximization; perhaps there is no single Reason to Promote the Good, but rather a set of competing reasons to promote different goods; perhaps we should promote our own good as individuals, rather than the good impersonally considered, and so on.

For each of these departures, there are purists who see the abandonment of Consequentialism. I disagree. I regard as Consequentialist any theory that bases morality on the promotion of value. This still leaves room for many Non-Consequentialist theories—namely, those seeking to honour, express, or embody certain values, or those with no direct reference to values at all, such as certain absolute deontological views. In my sense, Combined Consequentialism is a form of Consequentialism, as its foundation is the promotion of value. The ultimate justification of each element of the Combined Consequentialist framework is a story about the appropriate way to promote certain values. Of course, Combined Consequentialism is not Consequentialist at the level of what it tells us to do. The theory does not say: 'always promote the good'. One could be a good Combined Consequentialist agent and very rarely, if it all, think explicitly in terms of promoting the good. Combined Consequentialism does not wear its Consequentialist credentials on its sleeve. Yet neither does any other plausible contemporary form of Consequentialism. A Consequentialist theory must have a recognizably Consequentialist criterion of rightness, not an overtly Consequentialist decision procedure.

Prima facie, the least Consequentialist element of our new theory is Rule Consequentialism. It is thus worth pausing to establish the Consequentialist credentials of this component. We can best do this while defending Rule Consequentialism from a second attack, from the opposite direction. Some might object that Rule Consequentialism cannot be an appropriate response to the Realm of Reciprocity, given my characterization of that realm. The Realm of Reciprocity is characterized by community, mutual advantage, cooperation, autonomy, and goals. Why not use a theory explicitly based on the moral significance of mutual cooperation, or mutual advantage, or community, or autonomy, rather than one based on consequences? Why not use Contractualism, Contractarianism, Communitarianism, or Kantianism, rather than a form of Consequentialism?

My first reply is that Rule Consequentialism *is* based on such values. After all, Rule Consequentialism treats morality as a cooperative venture. Why else would it focus on the *collective* consequences of our actions? Rule Consequentialism is the *Consequentialist* account of the significance of community, cooperation, and interaction. It sees morality as a collective enterprise, where the goal is to promote the good.

There are two places where Rule Consequentialism might incorporate values such as autonomy and community: in its theory of the good, or in its account of how the good is to be promoted. Some Rule Consequentialists (such as Hooker) do explicitly value outcomes partly on the basis of fairness. They also argue that a theory based on idealization to full compliance appropriately reflects the moral significance of community, cooperation, and interaction.

Those who really do not like Rule Consequentialism are free to replace it with their own favourite account of the Realm of Reciprocity, and construct alternative combined moral theories. However, as I argued in Chapter 8, Rule Consequentialism and its Non-Consequentialist rivals (most notably Contractualism) largely coincide within the Realm of Reciprocity. Once we recognize the significance of autonomy, we see that the best way to promote the good is to follow a liberal code of rules of non-interference that no one could reasonably reject. Accordingly, Combined Consequentialism would not look very different if we replaced Rule Consequentialism with some alternative account of the Realm of Reciprocity.

Rule Consequentialism is thus both an appropriate account of the Realm of Reciprocity, and a recognizably Consequentialist account. Its closeness to its Non-Consequentialist rivals should not cast doubt on Rule Consequentialism's credentials. Rather, it emphasizes the fact that the differences between the two realms are more significant than any differences between rival moral theories within a given realm.

10.8.3. The Demands of Combined Consequentialism

Our main interest is in the demands of Consequentialism. Accordingly, we must now ask whether Combined Consequentialism makes reasonable demands.

The short answer is that we can make the demands of Combined Consequentialism as reasonable as we wish. The demands of the theory depend principally upon the various weightings specified in the definition of the Agent Centred Prerogative. If we set those weightings appropriately, then Combined Consequentialism will make reasonable demands. More importantly, the structure of Combined Consequentialism also provides us with a principled way of determining whether a particular demand is reasonable. This is because it incorporates a detailed account of the Realm of Reciprocity, against which we are to balance our Reason to Promote the Good.

Unsurprisingly, this brief answer is too brief. Some possible forms of Combined Consequentialism make moderate demands. This is because the theory is based on the Hybrid View, and some forms of the latter make moderate demands. However, my aim in this chapter is not only to defend generic

Combined Consequentialism, but also to construct a particular version of the theory, designed to overcome the shortcomings of the Hybrid View. Perhaps my particular Combined Consequentialism does make unreasonable demands.

Within Combined Consequentialism, it is useful to separate two sets of demands. The first falls entirely within the Realm of Reciprocity. It includes contributions to public works, civil defence, and the requirement that one come to the aid of fellow citizens in times of crisis. For instance, should one make a small personal sacrifice to save the life of someone who has fallen into a pond? The second set of demands arises in the Realm of Necessity. It includes our obligations to relieve famine and destitution in distant countries.

The first set of demands is governed by the Rule Consequentialist code of reciprocity. The second is governed by the Hybrid View and the Agent Centred Prerogative. As we saw in Chapters 8 and 9, Rule Consequentialism copes better with the first set of demands, whereas the Hybrid View copes better with the second. This is enough to show that Combined Consequentialism copes better than either of its two component theories. This reinforces our preference for Combined Consequentialism over other Consequentialist theories.

It is not sufficient to demonstrate that Combined Consequentialism is superior to its rivals. We must still ask whether it is acceptable. We will examine each set of demands in turn. We begin with the demands of the Realm of Reciprocity. Does the Rule Consequentialist code deal adequately with these?

We focus especially on one key question. One set of puzzles for any moral theory concerns the extent to which its demands vary as compliance with the theory increases or decreases. We have encountered this issue several times. In Part Two of this book, I rejected both Rule Consequentialism (which held that the demands of morality are directly proportional to the level of compliance) and the Compliance Condition (which ruled out any variation whatsoever). On balance, therefore, my view is that the ideal moral theory will permit some variation, but not too much. We must ask whether Combined Consequentialism gets it right. How do the demands of Combined Consequentialism vary as compliance with the theory increases or decreases? In the present context, does Rule Consequentialism cope well in the Realm of Reciprocity?

The ideal code is sensitive to compliance. For instance, one should pay one's taxes, even where the level of taxation is increased to allow for some non-compliance. As a result, one pays more tax than one would under full compliance. Similarly, the ideal code of rules will require one to save the lives of two drowning strangers, even though the cost to oneself is greater than the cost of saving one, and even though other bystanders could have saved the second stranger. Such a rule clearly requires more under partial compliance than under full compliance.

I argued earlier that these are intuitively reasonable results. In particular, any other rule seems perverse in the case of the two drowning co-workers. We see once again the implausibility of Murphy's Compliance Condition, even within the Realm of Reciprocity. When Rule Consequentialism is demanding, this is to its credit.

On the other hand, we have also seen that Rule Consequentialism can limit its demands when appropriate. If a rule requiring too much when others fail to comply will seem too unfair, then it will not be efficient to attempt to inculcate it. In such cases, the ideal code will include a moderate version of Murphy's Compliance Condition. The Rule Consequentialist justification for this condition derives indirectly from people's intuitive sense of unfairness. Accordingly, Rule Consequentialism will limit its own demands under partial compliance in precisely those cases where we find additional demands most objectionable.

We turn now to our second set of demands, the demands of the Realm of Necessity. Here, the demands of Combined Consequentialism will depend upon those of the Hybrid View. How well does the Hybrid View deal with these demands?

The Hybrid View balances the Reason to Promote the Good against the Rule Consequentialist code. The demands of the Reason to Promote the Good are extreme. The crucial question is how the Hybrid View balances them against the ideal code. In particular, how much room does Combined Consequentialism allow for the agent's own goals?

To illustrate the demands of Combined Consequentialism, let us focus once again on community-based goals. Recall our original version of Affluent's Tale. We have seen that any plausible moderate moral theory will include an Agent Centred Prerogative permitting community-based goals. As we are operating within an overarching Consequentialist framework, we need to compare the moral significance of goals in the agent's life with the impersonal value the agent forgoes by engaging in those goals. Affluent's Tale reminds us that, even for comparatively modest goals, this impersonal cost is very high. If Affluent promotes the good instead of pursuing her own goals, many people will live who would otherwise die.

Community-based goals play a very significant role in the life of any agent. Such goals are needed to develop skills, capacities, and human excellences. However, many community-based goals have a significant impact on agents beyond those who pursue the goal. This will clearly be valued by Consequentialists. The more valuable the wider impact of a goal, the easier it is to justify that goal. Conversely, it is harder to justify the pursuit of a goal if some alternative would produce much more value, while still making a significant contribution to the agent's own personal flourishing. For instance, if an agent is permitted to belong to a club to develop her capacities of cooperation and deliberation, then Consequentialists would clearly prefer that she develop those capacities by participating in a club raising funds for a reputable charity, rather than by joining the local chocolate eating club. We thus cannot conclude that a goal is permissible simply because it would develop necessary capacities. We must also ask whether other available goals would achieve the same result.

Simple Consequentialists often use the above considerations to argue that agents are obliged to spend all of their time and energy on charitable goals (whether individual or community based) rather than on other goals. This course of action provides the best of both worlds: the agent receives all the personal benefits of community membership, while still maximizing well-being overall. This suggests that Combined Consequentialism will be very demanding, and make only minimal concessions to the Realm of Reciprocity.

This conclusion is too swift, for a number of reasons.

1. Some permissible community-based goals may involve participation in the wider community, such as a national political community. In such cases, an agent cannot choose her community. If the only available community is an inward-looking one, then she may not have the option of more effectively promoting the overall good.
2. Perhaps some valuable capacities can be developed or exercised only within inward-looking communities. For instance, a child raised in an overly outward-looking family might not receive the attention necessary to develop her own capacity for moral agency.
3. The agent's historical situation may leave certain key human values available to her only in inward-looking groups. For instance, it might be argued that there are some morally significant capacities a human being can develop only by participating in the family (or other community) into which she was born. This may be especially significant in a society, such as ours, attaching great significance to familial ties.
4. The moral availability of less altruistic communities may be essential for the development and continuing exercise of human autonomy. Even if it is better for the agent to opt out of such inward-looking groups, appropriate respect for her autonomy may require that the option of choosing to participate in them be morally available to her. As we saw in Chapter 7, the *moral* availability of an unchosen option may be required in order to enhance the value of the chosen option.

This feature of Combined Consequentialism can seem vaguely paradoxical. Suppose an agent is choosing between two goals (G1 and G2). Neither is better or worse for the agent herself, while G1 would produce a more desirable result overall than G2. However, the value of G1 to the agent can be fully realized only if she freely chooses it from a range of morally available options. If G1 and G2 are the only goals practically available to her, then G2 must also be morally available. The structure of the Realm of Reciprocity thus allows G2 to acquire moral permissibility because of the significance of G1. If the Agent Centred Prerogative permits G1, on the grounds that freely chosen pursuit of G1 is sufficiently valuable to the agent, then it must also permit G2.[8] If Combined Consequentialism is to respect the basic structure of the Realm of Reciprocity, then it must permit a range of distinct community-based goals. This obviously limits the demands of the theory.

Indeed, it may seem that the demands of Combined Consequentialism are now too slight, as too many undemanding goals will be permitted. We need to be wary of this conclusion as well. We must leave open the possibility that the best Consequentialist moral theory will be a strongly revisionist theory, with much of our everyday behaviour, both individually and collectively, turning out to be morally deficient. As Scheffler and others have noted, the size of the gap between one's individual goals and those actions that would maximize the overall good depends to a large extent upon how just is the society one finds oneself in.[9] In a just society, most agents will find that they are best able to promote the overall good by pursuing goals that they find personally worthwhile and fulfilling. In a very unjust society, by contrast, an agent may find herself able to avoid disaster only by making great personal sacrifices.

A just world will be one where agents can choose from a wide range of good-producing, personally enriching, morally open, community-based goals. Arguably, the actual world is, in these respects, very unjust. Therefore, the Agent Centred Prerogative may not sanction many of our most cherished community-based goals. We would need to compare those goals with more effective Consequentialist community goals, such as active participation in charity work. In most cases, the community-based goals an agent wishes to pursue will be suboptimal in terms of impersonal value. Such goals tend to produce outcomes that are not only less valuable than the best available outcome, but also distinctly less valuable than the outcome of some alternative community-based

---

[8] We might use this feature of the Realm of Reciprocity to explain one kind of supererogation. In a situation such as this, there is a clear sense in which an agent who chooses G1 behaves better than one who chooses G2, even though both goals are morally permitted. Perhaps most cases of genuine supererogation could be characterized in this way.

[9] Scheffler, *Human Morality*, pp. 137–45. See also Murphy, 'Institutions and the Demands of Justice'.

goal, which the agent finds slightly less congenial. The agent will thus need a very generous prerogative if she is to pursue all of her preferred goals.

On balance, then, while it is not extremely demanding, Combined Consequentialism may be quite demanding. It is very likely to be more demanding than our common-sense moral intuitions. Because it incorporates a Reason to Promote the Good, which is never silenced, Combined Consequentialism always requires agents to justify their failure maximally to promote the good. Such a justification must take the form of an appeal to the significance, within her own life, of the agent's pursuit of her own goals. This shows that her action falls within the scope of her Agent Centred Prerogative. The agent must then demonstrate that her action complies with the constraints governing her Agent Centred Prerogative. She must comply with the Rule Consequentialist code governing the Realm of Reciprocity. That code will impose its own demands, especially if it incorporates special obligations. On some particular occasions, those demands might be quite severe.

Overall, we can still expect Combined Consequentialism to be not unreasonably demanding. Recall the non-proportional relationship between the two realms. As the goals an agent is required to sacrifice get closer to the core of her life, their significance within the Realm of Reciprocity increases exponentially, as does the comparative moral weight of that realm as a whole. Except in exceptional circumstances, the Realm of Reciprocity will take precedence over the Reason to Promote the Good before the latter requires the agent to compromise her autonomy. In the framework of Combined Consequentialism, the Reason to Promote the Good is not unreasonably demanding. The theory's most stringent demands will arise within the Realm of Reciprocity. However, the demands of Rule Consequentialism in that realm are not unreasonable, as we have seen. The demands of Combined Consequentialism thus seem reasonable. If Combined Consequentialism is more demanding than our common-sense intuitions, then this may be because, on reflection, we cannot defend the limited demands of Common-Sense Morality.

10.9. The Superiority of Combined Consequentialism

In this chapter we have explored the structure of Combined Consequentialism, discussed its justification, examined its demands, and considered a variety of possible objections. Our final task is to compare our new moral theory to its Consequentialist rivals: Simple Consequentialism, Rule Consequentialism, and the Hybrid View. Fortunately, we can proceed quickly here, drawing on the extensive discussions of Chapters 8 and 9.

We begin with Simple Consequentialism. One main problem for this theory, of course, is that it is unreasonably demanding. As we have just seen, Combined Consequentialism is significantly less demanding. A second classic objection to Simple Consequentialism is that it requires agents to commit injustices or atrocities wherever these produce the best available result. My own preferred version of Combined Consequentialism avoids this objection altogether, as demonstrated in Section 10.8.1. The most striking problem cases for Simple Consequentialism do not trouble our new theory, as they arise primarily in the Realm of Reciprocity. In that realm, Combined Consequentialism requires us to follow the Rule Consequentialist code, whose comparatively moderate rules prohibit most common types of injustice. Unlike Simple Consequentialism, Combined Consequentialism responds appropriately to the value of autonomy, personal relationships, and particular obligations. On balance, then, we can conclude that it is the superior theory.

We now compare Combined Consequentialism and Rule Consequentialism. All our objections to Rule Consequentialism have less force in the Realm of Reciprocity. They will thus have less force when Rule Consequentialism appears as a component within Combined Consequentialism, than when it was initially presented as a complete moral theory. Furthermore, it seems clear that those objections do not apply to the other components of Combined Consequentialism. Simple Consequentialism and the Hybrid View lack the complexities of Rule Consequentialism, especially those related to the idealization to full compliance. In general, the objection to Rule Consequentialism was that it appealed to features of the Realm of Reciprocity when operating within the Realm of Necessity. Similar complaints cannot be made against Simple Consequentialism or the Hybrid View. By departing from Rule Consequentialism within the Realm of Necessity, Combined Consequentialism thus avoids the objections of Chapter 3, and is superior to Rule Consequentialism.

Our final comparison is with the Hybrid View. The problem with the original Hybrid View lay not in its demands, but in its counter-intuitive results. We found in Chapter 6 that the Hybrid View's overall level of demandingness was appropriate. Problems arose for the theory because of inappropriate variations in those demands owing to strict proportionality and its failure to recognize morally relevant distinctions and obligations. The main purpose of this chapter has been to demonstrate how the elements introduced by Combined Consequentialism enable us to avoid the main objections to the Hybrid View. If these arguments succeed, then Combined Consequentialism is superior to each of its Consequentialist rivals. This is enough to establish Combined Consequentialism as a respectable moral theory worthy of further attention.

10.10. Conclusions

It may seem that we have made little progress. The Demandingness Objection accuses Consequentialism of making unreasonable demands. How much of an answer is it to say that the appropriate Consequentialist response is to construct a theory with appropriate demands?

Fortunately, our new Combined Consequentialist theory says considerably more than this.

1. By focusing on the significance of goals, the theory provides a detailed account of the way Consequentialists should balance the demands of the good against the requirements of their own agency.
2. By incorporating an account of the Realm of Reciprocity based on a developed moral theory, Combined Consequentialism provides structure and content to the Agent Centred Prerogative, fleshing-out Scheffler's blanket permissions.
3. By linking the two moral realms, Combined Consequentialism allows Consequentialists to respond in different ways to different goods, without abandoning the central Consequentialist focus on the promotion of value.
4. Combined Consequentialism provides a theoretical justification for all of these advances, based on (comparatively) uncontroversial claims about the structure of the human good.
5. Combined Consequentialism can also be developed to offer new insights regarding other central problems in contemporary moral theory. Two obvious areas for further work present themselves. On the one hand, we need to apply Combined Consequentialism to other problems in contemporary moral theory to see what new insights it might offer. In particular, we might ask whether there are other realms beyond those of reciprocity and necessity. Elsewhere, I ask whether human reproduction and obligations to future generations represent a separate realm—the Realm of Creation—or whether we can adequately account for our obligations in these areas in terms of the two existing realms. A second, more theoretical, enquiry uses Combined Consequentialism to explore the relationship between metaphysics and morality, focusing especially on the nature of personal identity, the relationship between individuals and communities, and the structure of well-being.[10]

Of course, Combined Consequentialism does not tell Affluent exactly how much she should donate to charity. It certainly will not tell the rest of us

---

[10] Mulgan, *Future People*.

exactly how we should live our everyday lives. Nor will it guarantee that our present everyday behaviour is always morally acceptable. But no other remotely plausible general moral theory does any of these things either. Nor is it reasonable to expect a moral theory to provide such detailed and comforting guidance. Just as we ask our moral theories not to make unreasonable demands of us, we must be careful not to demand too much from them.

Appendix. Proof for Chapter 6

In Section 6.2, I claimed that, under the Hybrid View, we can prove that, unless Affluent is required to donate all her money to charity, there is some number of dollars between zero and n (call it x), such that (i) Affluent is permitted to donate x dollars to charity rather than donating more, (ii) Affluent is required to donate at least x dollars to charity, and (iii) the additional amount of good that would be produced by a donation of $x+1$ dollars rather than one of x dollars is equal to the cost to Affluent of donating her $(x+1)$th dollar multiplied by the extra weight Affluent is permitted to give to her own interests over the interests of anyone else (Scheffler's M).

The proof of all this is as follows. If Affluent is not required to donate all her money to Oxfam, then there must be at least one amount of money that meets condition (i). Let x be the smallest such amount of money; that is, the smallest amount of money such that Affluent is permitted to donate x dollars to charity rather than donating any more. It follows that, for any amount of money less than x, Affluent is not allowed to donate that amount of money rather than donating more. If Affluent is not allowed to keep all her money for herself, then x must be greater than zero. So x meets condition (ii) as well as condition (i). Now, if Affluent is permitted to donate x dollars, then she's permitted to donate x dollars rather than donating $x+1$ dollars. The marginal utility of that next dollar to Affluent, when multiplied by the extra weight Affluent is permitted to give to her own interests (call the result the weighted cost), must be at least as great as the marginal value of a dollar to Oxfam. Assume for the moment that, at x, the weighted cost is greater than the marginal value. Assume also that both the weighting and the marginal value are constant, whereas the marginal cost is increasing. Therefore, there must be some amount of money (z) less than x, such that the weighted cost to Affluent of donating z dollars is equal to the marginal value of an extra dollar. Affluent would then be permitted to donate z dollars rather than donating $z+1$. However, for each dollar we add beyond $z+1$, the marginal value remains constant, whereas the weighted cost increases. Therefore, if Affluent is permitted to donate z rather than $z+1$, she will be permitted to donate z rather than any amount greater than z. But this would contradict our assumption that x is the least amount of money such that Affluent is permitted to donate no more than that amount. So, by *reductio*, we can conclude that, at x, the weighted cost is not greater than the marginal value. Therefore, the weighted cost must be equal to the marginal value. So x meets condition (iii). QED. (For this proof, I make the simplifying assumption that money comes in discreet amounts, which I identify with dollars.)

This proof uses two assumptions, which do not seem unreasonable. Given the size of Oxfam's operations as compared to Affluent's resources, we can assume that the marginal good produced by each additional dollar is constant. In other words, the difference between the amount of good produced by a donation of x dollars and that produced by a donation of $x+1$ dollars will be the same for any value of x between zero and n. By contrast, we can assume that the marginal cost to Affluent of each additional donation of one dollar is increasing. That is, the cost to Affluent of donating an additional dollar once she has already given most of her income will be much greater than the cost to her of donating an additional dollar when she has not given anything. However, if we reject the assumption of increasing marginal cost, then it must be the case either that Affluent is permitted to donate nothing at all or that she is required to give all of her money to Oxfam. The possibility that Affluent is required to make some donation, but not required to bring about the best possible consequences, will be ruled out. (The proof of this last claim is straightforward: both marginal value and the weighting the agent is allowed to give to her own interests are constant. If the marginal cost to the agent of donating an extra dollar is also constant, then the relationship between weighted cost and marginal value will be constant. Either weighted cost is always at least as great as marginal value, in which case Affluent is permitted to donate any amount she chooses rather than donating more, or weighted cost is always less than marginal value, in which case Affluent is always required to donate more if she is able to. Either a zero donation is permitted or a total donation is required.) Yet it is precisely this possibility that proponents of the Hybrid View seek to defend. Accordingly, the assumption of increasing marginal cost must be retained.

Bibliography

Adams, R., 'Motive Utilitarianism', *Journal of Philosophy*, 73 (1976), 467–81.

Aiken, W., 'Famine and Distribution', *Journal of Philosophy*, 87 (1990), 642–3.

Alexander, L., 'Scheffler on the Independence of Agent-Centred Prerogatives from Agent-Centred Restrictions', *Journal of Philosophy*, 84 (1987), 277–83.

Baillie, J., 'Recent Work on Personal Identity', *Philosophical Books*, 34 (1993), 193–206.

Bales, R., 'Act Utilitarianism: An Account of Right-Making Characteristics or Decision-Making Procedure?', *American Philosophical Quarterly*, 8 (1971), 257–65.

Barry, B., 'Justice between Generations', in P. M. S. Hacker and J. Raz (eds.), *Law, Morality and Society: Essays in Honour of H. L. A. Hart* (Oxford: Clarendon Press, 1977), 268–84.

—— 'Circumstances of Justice and Future Generations', in R. Sikora and B. Barry (eds.), *Obligations to Future Generations* (Philadelphia: Temple University Press, 1978), 204–48.

—— *Theories of Justice* (Berkeley and Los Angeles: University of California Press, 1989).

Beitz, C., *Political Theory and International Relations* (Princeton: Princeton University Press, 1979).

Bennett, J., 'Whatever the Consequences', *Analysis*, 26 (1966), 83–102.

—— 'On Maximizing Happiness', in R. Sikora and B. Barry (eds.), *Obligations to Future Generations* (Philadelphia: Temple University Press, 1978), 61–73.

—— 'Two Departures from Consequentialism', *Ethics*, 100 (1989), 54–66.

Brandt, R. B., *Morality, Utilitarianism, and Rights* (Cambridge: Cambridge University Press, 1992).

—— 'Utilitarianism and Moral Rights', in his *Morality, Utilitarianism, and Rights* (Cambridge: Cambridge University Press, 1992), 196–212.

—— 'Morality and its Critics', in his *Morality, Utilitarianism, and Rights* (Cambridge: Cambridge University Press, 1992), 73–92.

—— 'Fairness to Indirect Optimific Theories in Ethics', in his *Morality, Utilitarianism, and Rights* (Cambridge: Cambridge University Press, 1992), 137–57.

—— 'Some Merits of One Form of Rule-Utilitarianism', in his *Morality, Utilitarianism and Rights* (Cambridge: Cambridge University Press, 1992), 111–36.

—— 'Two Concepts of Utility', in his *Morality, Utilitarianism, and Rights* (Cambridge: Cambridge University Press, 1992), 158–75.

Bratman, M. E., 'Kagan on "The Appeal to Cost"', *Ethics*, 104 (1994), 325–32.

Braybrooke, D., *Meeting Needs* (Princeton: Princeton University Press, 1987).

Brink, D., 'Utilitarian Morality and the Personal Point of View', *Journal of Philosophy*, 83 (1986), 417–38.

Brink, D., 'Sidgwick's Dualism of Practical Reason', *Australasian Journal of Philosophy*, 66 (1988), 291–307.

—— 'The Separateness of Persons, Distributive Norms and Moral Theory', in R. Frey and C. Morris (eds.), *Value, Welfare and Morality* (Cambridge: Cambridge University Press, 1993) 252–289.

—— 'A Reasonable Morality', *Ethics*, 104 (1994), 593–619.

—— 'Self-Love and Altruism', *Social Philosophy and Policy*, 14 (1997), 122–57.

Broad, C. D., 'On the Function of False Hypotheses in Ethics', *International Journal of Ethics*, 26 (1916), 377–97 (reprinted in D. R. Chevey (ed.), *Broad's Critical Essays in Moral Philosophy* (London: Allen & Unwin, 1971), 43–62).

—— *Five Types of Ethical Theory* (London: Kegan Paul, 1930).

—— 'Conscience and Conscientious Action', in D. R. Chevey (ed.), *Broad's Critical Essays in Moral Philosophy* (London: Allen & Unwin, 1971), 136–55.

—— 'Self and Others', in D. R. Chevey (ed.), *Broad's Critical Essays in Moral Philosophy* (London: Allen & Unwin, 1971), 262–82.

—— 'Some Reflections on Moral Sense Theories in Ethics', in D. R. Chevey (ed.), *Broad's Critical Essays in Moral Philosophy* (London: Allen & Unwin, 1971), 188–222.

—— 'The Doctrine of Consequences in Ethics', in D. R. Chevey (ed.), *Broad's Critical Essays in Moral Philosophy* (London: Allen & Unwin, 1971), 17–43.

Brock, G., 'Is Redistribution to Help the Needy Unjust?', *Analysis*, 55 (1995), 50–60.

Carens, J., *Equality, Moral Incentives, and the Market: An Essay in Utopian Politico-Economic Theory* (Chicago: University of Chicago Press, 1981).

Carlson, G., 'Parfit, Sidgwick, and Divided Reason', *Philosophia (Israel)*, 18 (1988), 247–52.

Carson, R., 'A Note on Hooker's Rule Consequentialism', *Mind*, 100 (1991), 117–21.

Carson, T., 'Utilitarianism and World Poverty' in H. B. Miller and W. H. Williams (eds.), *The Limits of Utilitarianism* (Minneapolis: University of Minnesota Press, 1982), 243–52.

Christman, J., 'The Common Mind', *Philosophical Books*, 37 (1996), 90–7.

Cohen, G., 'Incentives, Inequality and Community', in G. B. Peterson (ed.), *The Tanner Lectures on Human Values*, 13 (Salt Lake City: University of Utah Press, 1992).

Cohen, L. J., 'Who Is Starving Whom?', *Theoria*, 2 (1981), 67–81.

Conee, E., Review of D. Regan, *Utilitarianism and Cooperation*, in *Journal of Philosophy*, 80 (1983), 415–24.

—— 'On Seeking a Rationale', *Philosophy and Phenomenological Research*, 45 (1985), 601–9.

Cottingham, J., 'Partiality, Favouritism and Morality', *Philosophical Quarterly*, 36 (1986), 357–73.

—— 'The Ethics of Self-Concern', *Ethics*, 101 (1991), 798–817.

Cowen, T., 'What do we Learn from the Repugnant Conclusion?', *Ethics*, 106 (1996), 754–75.

Crisp, R., 'Sidgwick and Self-Interest', *Utilitas*, 2 (1990), 267–80.
——'Utilitarianism and the Life of Virtue', *Philosophical Quarterly*, 42 (1992), 139–60.
——'First among Unequals: Review of Temkin's *Inequality*', *TLS*, 24 June 1994, 13.
——'The Dualism of Practical Reason', *Proceedings of the Aristotelian Society*, 96 (1996), 53–73.
——*Mill: On Utilitarianism* (London: Routledge, 1997).
——and Slote, M., 'Introduction', in R. Crisp and M. Slote (eds.), *Virtue Ethics* (Oxford: Oxford University Press, 1997).
Cullity, G., 'International Aid and the Scope of Kindness', *Ethics*, 105 (1994), 99–127.
——'Moral Character and the Iteration Problem', *Utilitas*, 7 (1995), 289–99.
——'Moral Free Riding', *Philosophy and Public Affairs*, 24 (1995), 3–34.
——*The Moral Demands of Affluence* (Oxford: Clarendon Press, 2004).
Cummiskey, D., 'Kantian Consequentialism', *Ethics*, 100 (1995), 586–615.
Dancy, J., 'Non-Consequentialist Reasons', *Philosophical Papers*, 20 (1991), 97–112.
——(ed.), *Reading Parfit* (Oxford: Basil Blackwell, 1997).
——'Parfit and Indirectly Self-Defeating Theories', in J. Dancy (ed.), *Reading Parfit* (Oxford: Basil Blackwell, 1997).
Daniels, Norman, 'Moral Theory and Plasticity of Persons', *Monist*, 62 (1979), 265–87.
Darwall, S., Review of S. Scheffler, *The Rejection of Consequentialism*, in *Journal of Philosophy*, 81 (1984), 220–6.
——'Rational Agent, Rational Act', *Philosophical Topics*, 14 (1986), 33–57.
——'Human Morality's Authority', *Philosophy and Phenomenological Research*, 55 (1995), 941–8.
Darwell, S. L., 'Scheffler on Morality and Ideals of the Person', *Canadian Journal of Philosophy*, 12 (1982), 247–55.
——'Reply to Scheffler', *Canadian Journal of Philosophy*, 12 (1982), 263–4.
Dasgupta, P. *Well-Being and Destitution* (Oxford: Clarendon Press, 1993).
——'Savings and Fertility: Ethical Issues', *Philosophy and Public Affairs*, 23 (1994), 99–127.
Decew, J. W., 'Conditional Obligation and Counterfactuals', *Journal of Philosophical Logic*, 10 (1981), 55–72.
——'Brandt's New Defense of Rule Utilitarianism', *Philosophical Studies*, 43 (1983), 101–16.
Den Uyl, D., 'Teleology and Agent-Centredness', *Monist*, 75 (1992), 14–33.
Donagan, A., 'Sidgwick and Whewellian Intuitionism', in B. Schultz (ed.), *Essays on Henry Sidgwick* (Cambridge: Cambridge University Press, 1992), 123–42.
Dreze, J., and Sen, A. K., *Hunger and Public Action* (Oxford: Clarendon Press, 1989).
Driver, J., 'Monkeying with Motives: Agent-Basing Virtue Ethics', *Utilitas*, 7 (1995), 281–288.
——'The Virtues and Human Nature', in R. Crisp (ed), *How Should One Live?: Essays on the Virtues* (New York: Clarendon Press, 1996).

Dworkin, R., 'What is Equality? Part I: Equality of Welfare', *Philosophy and Public Affairs*, 10 (1981), 185–246.

The Economist Pocket World in Figures 2000 edition (Profile Books in association with *The Economist*, 1999).

Elliot, R., 'Rawlsian Justice and Non-Human Animals', *Journal of Applied Ethics*, 1 (1984), 95–106.

Feinberg, J., 'The Forms and Limits of Utilitarianism', *Philosophical Review*, 76 (1967), 368–81.

Feldman, F., 'On the Extensional Equivalence of Simple and General Utilitarianism', *Nous*, 8 (1974), 101–16.

—— 'Justice, Desert and the Repugnant Conclusion', *Utilitas*, 7 (1995), 189–206.

Fishkin, J., *The Limits of Obligation* (New Haven: Yale University Press, 1982).

——'Obligations beyond Borders: The Limits of Impartial Consequentialism', *Tulane Studies in Philosophy*, 33 (1985), 9–20.

Foot, P., 'The Problem of Abortion and the Doctrine of Double Effect', in her *Virtues and Vices* (Berkeley and Los Angeles: University of California Press, 1978).

—— 'Utilitarianism and the Virtues', *Mind*, 94 (1985), 196–209.

Frey, R. G., 'Act-Utilitarianism: Sidgwick or Bentham or Smart', *Mind*, 86 (1977), 95–100.

Garcia, J., 'The New Critique of Anti-Consequentialist Moral Theory', *Philosophical Studies*, 71 (1993), 1–32.

Gauthier, D., *Morals by Agreement* (Oxford: Clarendon Press, 1986).

George, R., *Making Men Moral* (Oxford: Oxford University Press, 1993).

Gibbard, A., 'Rule Utilitarianism: A Merely Illusory Alternative?', *Australasian Journal of Philosophy*, 43 (1965), 211–20.

Goldman, H. S., 'David Lyons on Utilitarian Generalization', *Philosophical Studies*, 26 (1974), 77–95.

Gomberg, P., 'Self and Others in Bentham and Sidgwick', *History of Philosophy Quarterly*, 3 (1986), 437–48.

Green, T. H., *Prolegomena to Ethics*, 5th edn. (Oxford: Oxford University Press, 1907).

Griffin, J., 'Is Unhappiness more Important than Happiness?', *Philosophical Quarterly*, 29 (1979), 47–55.

——'Modern Utilitarianism', *Revue internationale de philosophie*, 36 (1982), 331–75.

—— *Well-Being* (Oxford: Clarendon Press, 1986).

——Review of S. Kagan, *The Limits of Morality*, in *Mind*, 99 (1990), 128–31.

——'On the Winding Road from Good to Right', in R. Frey and C. Morris (eds.), *Value, Welfare, and Morality* (Cambridge: Cambridge University Press, 1993), 158–79.

——'The Distinction between Criterion and Decision Procedure: A Reply to Madison Powers', *Utilitas*, 6 (1994), 177–82.

——*Value Judgement* (Oxford: Oxford University Press, 1996).

Hampton, J., 'Should Political Philosophy be Done without Metaphysics?', *Ethics*, 99 (1989), 791–814.

Hardin, G., 'Lifeboat Ethics: The Case against Helping the Poor', in W. Aiken and H. La Follette (eds.), *Morality and World Hunger* (Englewood Cliffs, NJ: Prentice-Hall, 1977).

Hare, R. M., *Moral Thinking* (Oxford: Clarendon Press, 1981).

Harris, G., W., 'Integrity and Agent-Centered Restrictions', *Nous*, 23 (1989), 437–56.

——'A Paradoxical Departure from Consequentialism', *Journal of Philosophy*, 86 (1989), 90–102.

Harsanyi, J., 'Can the Maximin Principle Serve as a Basis for Morality? A Critique of John Rawls' Theory', *American Political Science Review*, 69 (1975), 594–606.

Hart, H., *Law, Liberty and Morality* (Oxford: Oxford University Press, 1963).

Haslett, D. W., 'Values, Obligations, and Saving Lives', in B. Hooker, E. Mason, and D. E. Miller (eds.), *Morality, Rules, and Consequences* (Edinburgh: Edinburgh University Press, 2000), 71–104.

Herman, B., *The Practice of Moral Judgment* (Cambridge, Mass.: Harvard University Press, 1993).

Heyd, D., *Genethics: Moral Issues in the Creation of People* (Berkeley and Los Angeles: University of California Press, 1992).

Hibbert, Christopher, *The Rise and Fall of the House of Medici* (London: Folio Society, 1998).

Holbrook, D., 'Consequentialism: The Philosophical Dog that does not Bark?', *Utilitas*, 3 (1991), 107–12.

Hooker, B., 'Rule-Consequentialism', *Mind*, 99 (1990), 67–77.

——'Brink, Kagan and Self-Sacrifice', *Utilitas*, 3 (1991), 263–73.

——'Rule-Consequentialism and Demandingness: A Reply to Carson', *Mind*, 100 (1991), 270–6.

——Review of S. Scheffler, *Human Morality*, in *Mind*, 102 (1993), 390–4.

——(ed.), *Rationality, Rules and Utility: New Essays on the Moral Philosophy of Richard B. Brandt* (Boulder, Colo.: Imprint, 1993).

——Review of T. Nagel, *Equality and Partiality*, in *Philosophical Quarterly*, 43 (1993), 366–72.

——'Is Rule-Consequentialism a Rubber Duck?', *Analysis*, 54 (1994), 92–7.

——'Compromising with Convention', *American Philosophical Quarterly*, 31 (1994), 311–17.

——'Rule-Consequentialism, Incoherence, Fairness', *Proceedings of the Aristotelian Society*, 95 (1994), 19–35.

——'Ross-Style Pluralism versus Rule-Consequentialism', *Mind*, 105 (1996), 531–52.

——'Reply to Stratton-Lake', *Mind*, 106 (1997), 759–60.

——'Rule-Consequentialism and Obligations toward the Needy', *Pacific Philosophical Quarterly*, 79 (1998), 19–33.

Hooker, B., 'Sacrificing for the Good of Strangers—Repeatedly' (a critical discussion of Unger, *Living High and Letting Die*), *Philosophy and Phenomenological Research*, 59 (1999), 177–81.

——*Ideal Code, Real World: A Rule-Consequentialist Theory of Morality* (Oxford: Clarendon Press, 2000).

——Mason, E., and Miller, D.E. (eds.), *Morality, Rules, and Consequences* (Edinburgh: Edinburgh University Press, 2000).

Horwich, P., 'On Calculating the Utility of Acts', *Philosophical Studies*, 25 (1974), 21–31.

Hurka, T., 'Value and Population Size', *Ethics*, 93 (1983), 496–507.

——'Two Kinds of Satisficing', *Philosophical Studies*, 59 (1990), 107–11.

——'Consequentialism and Content', *American Philosophical Quarterly*, 29 (1992), 71–8.

——*Perfectionism* (Oxford: Oxford University Press, 1993).

——'Self-Interest, Altruism and Virtue', *Social Philosophy and Public Policy*, 14 (1997), 286–307.

Hurley, P., 'The Hidden Consequentialist Assumption', *Analysis*, 52 (1992), 241–8.

——'Scheffler's Argument for Deontology', *Pacific Philosophical Quarterly*, 74 (1993), 118–34.

——'Getting our Options Clear: A Closer Look at Agent-Centered Options', *Philosophical Studies*, 78 (1995), 163–88.

Jackson, F., 'A Probabilistic Approach to Moral Responsibility', R. Bacan Marcus *et al.* (eds.), *Proceedings of the Seventh International Congress of Logic, Methodology and Philosophy of Science* (Amsterdam: Elsevier Science Publishers, 1986), 351–66.

——'Decision-Theoretic Consequentialism and the Nearest and Dearest Objection', *Ethics*, 101 (1991), 461–82.

——and Pargetter, R., 'Oughts, Options and Actualism', *Philosophical Review*, 95 (1986), 233–55.

Kagan, S., 'Does Consequentialism Demand too Much?', *Philosophy and Public Affairs*, 13 (1984), 239–54.

——'Donagan on the Sins of Consequentialism', *Canadian Journal of Philosophy*, 17 (1987), 643–54.

——'The Additive Fallacy', *Ethics*, 99 (1988), 31.

——*The Limits of Morality* (Oxford: Oxford University Press, 1989).

——'Précis of the Limits of Morality', *Philosophy and Phenomenological Research*, 51 (1991), 897–901.

——'The Limits of Well-Being', in E. F. Paul, F. D. Miller Jr., and J. Paul (eds.), *The Good Life and the Human Good* (Cambridge: Cambridge University Press, 1992), 169–89.

——'Defending Options', *Ethics*, 104 (1994), 33–351.

——*Normative Ethics* (Boulder, Colo.: Westview, 1998).

——'Evaluative Focal Points', in B. Hooker, E. Mason, and D. E. Miller (eds.), *Morality, Rules, and Consequences* (Edinburgh: Edinburgh University Press, 2000), 134–55.

Kamm, F. M., 'Supererogation and Obligation', *Journal of Philosophy*, 82 (1985), 118–38.

——'Harming, not Aiding, and Positive Rights', *Philosophy and Public Affairs*, 15 (1986), 3–32.

——'Non-Consequentialism, the Person as an End-in-Itself, and the Significance of Status', *Philosophy and Public Affairs*, 21 (1992), 354–89.

——*Death and whom to Save from it* (New York: Oxford University Press, 1993).

—— 'Rationality and Morality', *Nous*, 29 (1995), 544–55.

Kant, I., *Groundwork of the Metaphysics of Morals*, trans. by H. J. Paton (London: Hutchinson, 1948).

Kavka, G. S., 'Extensional Equivalence and Utilitarian Generalisation', *Theoria*, 41 (1975), 125–47.

——'The Numbers should Count', *Philosophical Studies*, 36 (1979), 285–94.

——'The Paradox of Future Individuals', *Philosophy and Public Affairs*, 11 (1982), 93–112.

Korsgaard, C., 'The Right to Lie: Kant on Dealing with Evil', *Philosophy and Public Affairs*, 15 (1986), 325–49.

——'Kant', in R. Cavalier, J. Gouinlock, and J. Sterba (eds.), *Ethics in the History of Western Philosophy* (New York: St Martin's Press, 1989), 201–43.

——'Personal Identity and the Unity of Agency: A Kantian Response to Parfit', *Philosophy and Public Affairs*, 18 (1989), 101–32.

Kripke, S., *Wittgenstein on Rules and Private Language* (Oxford: Basil Blackwell, 1982).

Kymlicka, W., *Liberalism, Community and Culture* (Oxford: Oxford University Press, 1989).

——*Contemporary Political Philosophy* (Oxford: Oxford University Press, 1991).

Kymlicka, W., 'Community', in R. E. Goodin and P. Pettit (eds.), *A Companion to Contemporary Political Philosophy* (Oxford: Blackwell, 1993), 366–78.

Lewis, D., 'A Subjectivist's Guide to Objective Chance', in his *Philosophical Papers: Volume Two* (Oxford: Oxford University Press, 1986), 83–132.

Locke, D., 'The Parfit Population Problem', *Philosophy*, 62 (1987), 131–57.

Lucas, G. R., 'The Political and Economic Dimensions of Hunger', in G. R. Lucas and T. Ogletree (eds.), *Lifeboat Ethics: The Moral Dilemmas of Hunger* (New York: Harper & Row, 1976), 1–28.

Lucas, G. R., 'African Famine: New Economic and Ethical Perspectives', *Journal of Philosophy*, 87 (1990), 629–41.

Lyons, D., *The Forms and Limits of Utilitarianism* (Oxford: Clarendon Press, 1965).

McCarty, R., 'The Limits of Kantian Duty, and Beyond', *American Philosophical Quarterly*, 26 (1989), 43–52.

McMahan, J., 'Problems of Population Theory', *Ethics*, 92 (1981), 96–127.

Margolis, J., 'Rule Utilitarianism', *Australasian Journal of Philosophy*, 43 (1965), 220–25.

Mason, A., 'Liberalism and the Value of Community', *Canadian Journal of Philosophy*, 23 (1993), 215–40.

Mason, E., 'Can an Indirect Consequentialist be a Real Friend?', *Ethics*, 108 (1998), 386–93.

Mellor, H., 'Objective Decision Making', *Social Theory and Practice*, 9 (1983), 289–309.

Mendola, J., 'Parfit on Directly Collectively Self-Defeating Moral Theories', *Philosophical Studies*, 50 (1986), 153–65.

Miller, D., *Market, State and Community* (Oxford: Oxford University Press, 1989).

Miller, D. E., 'Hooker's Use and Abuse of Reflective Equilibrium', in B. Hooker, E. Mason, and D. E. Miller (eds.), *Morality, Rules and Consequences* (Edinburgh: Edinburgh University Press, 2000), 156–78.

Mintoff, J., 'Slote on Rational Dilemmas and Rational Supererogation', *Erkenntnis*, 46 (1997), 111–26.

Moore, A., 'The Utilitarian Ethics of R. B. Brandt', *Utilitas*, 5 (1993), 301–10.

Moser, P. K., 'Consequentialism and Self-Defeat', *Philosophical Quarterly*, 43 (1991), 82–5.

Mulgan, T., 'Slote's Satisficing Consequentialism', *Ratio*, 6 (1993), 121–34.

——'The Unhappy Conclusion and the Life of Virtue', *Philosophical Quarterly*, 43 (1993), 357–9.

——'Rule Consequentialism and Famine', *Analysis*, 54 (1994), 187–92.

——'The Demands of Consequentialism', unpublished D.Phil. thesis (Oxford, 1994).

——'One False Virtue of Rule Consequentialism, and one New Vice', *Pacific Philosophical Quarterly*, 77 (1996), 362–73.

——'A Non-Proportional Hybrid Moral Theory', *Utilitas*, 9 (1997), 291–306.

——'Two Conceptions of Benevolence', *Philosophy and Public Affairs*, 26 (1997), 1–21.

——'Teaching Future Generations', *Teaching Philosophy*, 22(1999), 259–73.

——'The Place of the Dead in Liberal Political Philosophy', *Journal of Political Philosophy*, 7 (1999), 52–70.

——'Dissolving the Mere Addition Paradox', *American Philosophical Quarterly*, 37 (2000), 359–72.

——Review of Unger's *Living High and Letting Die*, in *Mind*, 109 (2000), 397–400.

——'Ruling out Rule Consequentialism', in B. Hooker, E. Mason, and D. E. Miller (eds.), *Morality, Rules and Consequences* (Edinburgh: Edinburgh University Press, 2000), 212–21.

——'Two Moral Counterfactuals', *Philosophical Forum*, 31 (2000), 47–55.

——'A Minimal Test for Political Theories', *Philosophia*, 28 (2001), 283–296.

——'How Satisficers Get away with Murder', *International Journal of Philosophical Studies*, 9 (2001), 41–6.

——'What's Really Wrong with the Limited Quantity View?', *Ratio*, 14 (2001), 153–64.

——'Two Parfit Puzzles', in J. Ryberg and R. Tannsjo (eds.), *The Repugnant Conclusion. Essays on Population Ethics*, (Dordrecht: Kluwer Academic Publishers, 2004), 23–45.

——*Future People* (Oxford: Clarendon Press, 2006)

Murphy, L., 'The Demands of Beneficence', *Philosophy and Public Affairs*, 22 (1993), 267–92.

——'A Relatively Plausible Principle of Beneficence: Reply to Mulgan', *Philosophy and Public Affairs*, 26 (1997), 23–9.

——'Institutions and the Demands of Justice', *Philosophy and Public Affairs*, 27 (1999), 251–91.

——*Moral Demands in Nonideal Theory* (New York: Oxford University Press, 2000).

Myers, R., 'Prerogatives and Restrictions from the Cooperative Point of View', *Ethics*, 105 (1994), 128–52.

Nagel, T., *The Possibility of Altruism* (Oxford: Oxford University Press, 1970).

——*The View from Nowhere* (Oxford: Oxford University Press, 1986).

——*Equality and Partiality* (Oxford: Oxford University Press, 1991).

——'One-to-One', *London Review of Books*, 4 February 1999.

Ng, Y.-K., 'What should we Do about Future Generations?', *Economics and Philosophy*, 5 (1989), 235–53.

Nozick, R., *Anarchy, State, and Utopia* (New York: Basic Books, 1974).

O'Neill, O., *Faces of Hunger: An Essay in Poverty, Justice and Development* (London: Unwin Hyman, 1986).

——'Kantian Ethics', in P. Singer (ed.), *Companion to Ethics* (Oxford: Blackwell, 1991), 175–85.

Parfit, D., 'Repugnant Conclusion: A Reply to McMahan', *Ethics*, 92 (1981), 128–33.

——'Future Generations: Further Problems', *Philosophy and Public Affairs*, 11 (1982), 113–72.

——*Reasons and Persons* (Oxford: Clarendon Press, 1984).

——'Comments', *Ethics* 96 (1986), 832–72.

——'Overpopulation and the Quality of Life', in P. Singer (ed.), *Applied Ethics* (Oxford: Oxford University Press, 1986), 145–64.

——'A Reply to Sterba', *Philosophy and Public Affairs*, 16 (1987), 193–4.

Perrett, R., 'Egoism, Altruism, and Intentionalism in Buddhist Ethics', *Journal of Indian Philosophy*, 15 (1987), 71–85.

——'Personal Identity, Minimalism and Madhyamaka', *Philosophy East and West*, 52 (2002), 373–385.

Persson, I., 'The Universal Basis of Egoism', *Theoria*, 51 (1985), 137–58.

Pettit, P., 'Satisficing Consequentialism', *Proceedings of the Aristotelian Society*, supplementary volume, 58 (1984), 165–76.

——'Slote on Consequentialism', *Philosophical Quarterly*, 36 (1986), 399–412.

——'Social Holism and Moral Theory: A Defence of Bradley's Thesis', *Proceedings of the Aristotelian Society*, 86 (1986), 173–97.

——'Universalisability without Utilitarianism', *Mind*, 96 (1987), 74–82.

——'Consequentialism', in P. Singer (ed.), *A Companion to Ethics* (Oxford: Basil Blackwell, 1989), 230–40.

Pettit, P., 'Decision Theory and Folk Psychology', in M. Bacharach and S. Hurley (eds.), *Essays in the Foundations of Decision Theory* (Oxford: Basil Blackwell, 1989).

——*The Common Mind: An Essay on Psychology, Society and Politics* (Oxford: Oxford University Press, 1993).

——'In Elucidation of the Common Mind: A Reply to Raimo Tuomela', *International Journal of Philosophical Studies*, 2 (1994), 322–6.

——*Republicanism* (Oxford: Clarendon Press, 1997).

——and Brennan, G., 'Restrictive Consequentialism', *Australasian Journal of Philosophy*, 64 (1986), 438–55.

——and Goodin, R., 'The Possibility of Special Duties', *Canadian Journal of Philosophy*, 16 (1986), 651–76.

——and Smith, M., 'Brandt on Self-Control', in B. Hooker (ed.), *Rationality, Rules and Utility: New Essays on the Moral Philosophy of Richard B. Brandt* (Boulder, Colo.: Imprint, 1993).

——————'Global Consequentialism', in B. Hooker, E. Mason, and D. E. Miller (eds.), *Morality, Rules, and Consequences* (Edinburgh: Edinburgh University Press, 2000), 121–33.

Price, H., 'The Common Mind: An Essay on Psychology, Society and Politics', *Philosophy and Phenomenological Research*, 55 (1995), 689–99.

Prior, A. N., 'The Consequences of Actions', in his *Papers on Time and Tense* (Oxford: Oxford University Press, 1968). 51–8.

Qizilbash, M., 'Obligation, Human Frailty, and Utilitarianism', *Utilitas*, 7 (1995), 145–56.

Quinn, W., *Morality and Action* (Cambridge University Press, 1993).

Rabinowicz, W., 'Act-Utilitarian Prisoner's Dilemmas', *Theoria*, 55 (1989), 1–44.

Railton, P., 'Alienation, Consequentialism and Morality', *Philosophy and Public Affairs*, 13 (1984), 134–71.

——'How Thinking about Character and Utilitarianism might Lead to Rethinking the Character of Utilitarianism', *Midwest Studies in Philosophy*, 13 (1986), 398–416.

Rawls, J., *A Theory of Justice* (Cambridge, Mass.: Harvard University Press, 1971).

——'Justice as Fairness: Political not Metaphysical', *Philosophy and Public Affairs*, 14 (1985), 223–51.

——'The Idea of an Overlapping Consensus', *Oxford Journal of Legal Studies*, 7 (1987), 1–27.

——*Political Liberalism* (New York: Columbia University Press, 1993).

——*The Law of Peoples: With 'The Idea of Public Reason Revisited'* (Cambridge, Mass.: Harvard University Press, 1999).

Raz, J., *The Morality of Freedom* (Oxford: Clarendon Press, 1986).

——'Duties of Well-Being', in his *Ethics in the Public Domain: Essays in the Morality of Law and Politics* (Oxford: Clarendon Press, 1994), 3–28.

——*Engaging Reason: On the Theory of Value and Action* (Oxford: Clarendon Press, 1999).

Regan, D., *Utilitarianism and Cooperation* (Oxford: Clarendon Press, 1980).

Ryberg, J., 'Parfit's Repugnant Conclusion', *Philosophical Quarterly*, 46 (1996), 202–13.

——'Is the Repugnant Conclusion Repugnant?', *Philosophical Papers*, 25 (1996), 161–77.

Scanlon, T., 'Contractualism and Utilitarianism', in A. Sen and B. Williams (eds.), *Utilitarianism and Beyond* (Cambridge: Cambridge University Press, 1982), 103–28.

——*What We Owe to Each Other* (Cambridge, Mass.: Harvard University Press, 1999).

Schaller, W., 'A Problem for Brandt's Utilitarianism', *Ratio*, 5 (1992), 74–90.

Scheffler, S., 'Moral Independence and the Original Position', *Philosophical Studies*, 35 (1978), 397–403.

——'Ethics, Personal Identity, and Ideals of the Person', *Canadian Journal of Philosophy*, 12 (1982), 229–64.

——'Reply to Darwell', *Canadian Journal of Philosophy*, 12 (1982), 260–2.

——*The Rejection of Consequentialism* (Oxford: Clarendon Press, 1982).

——'Agent-Centred Restrictions, Rationality and the Virtues', *Mind*, 94 (1985), 409–19.

——'Morality's Demands and their Limits', *Journal of Philosophy*, 83 (1986), 531–7.

——(ed.), *Consequentialism and its Critics* (Oxford: Clarendon Press, 1988).

——'Deontology and the Agent: Reply to Bennett', *Ethics*, 100 (1989), 67–76.

——*Human Morality* (Oxford: Oxford University Press, 1992).

——'Naturalism, Psychoanalysis and Moral Motivation', in J. Hopkins (ed.), *Psychoanalysis, Mind and Art* (Oxford: Basil Blackwell, 1992).

——'Prerogatives without Restrictions', *Philosophical Perspectives*, 6 (1992), 377–97.

——'Families, Nations and Strangers', The Lindley Lecture, University of Kansas, 1994.

——'Individual Responsibility in a Global Age', *Social Philosophy and Policy*, 12 (1995), 219–36.

——'Précis of Human Morality', *Philosophy and Phenomenological Research*, 55 (1995), 939–40.

——'Reply to Three Commentators', *Philosophy and Phenomenological Research*, 55 (1995), 963–75.

——'Relationships and Responsibilities', *Philosophy and Public Affairs*, 26 (1997), 189–209.

Schneewind, J. B., *Sidgwick's Ethics and Victorian Moral Philosophy* (Oxford: Clarendon Press, 1977).

——'Autonomy, Obligation, and Virtue: An Overview of Kant's Moral Philosophy', in P. Guyer (ed.), *The Cambridge Companion To Kant* (Cambridge: Cambridge University Press, 1992), 309–41.

——'Sidgwick and the Cambridge Moralists', in B. Schultz (ed), *Essays on Henry Sidgwick* (Cambridge: Cambridge University Press, 1992), 93–121.

Schueler, G., 'Consequences and Agent-Centered Restrictions', *Metaphilosophy*, 20 (1989), 77–83.

Schultz, B. (ed)., *Essays on Henry Sidgwick* (Cambridge: Cambridge University Press, 1992).

Sen, A., *Poverty and Famine: An Essay on Entitlement and Deprivation* (Oxford: Oxford University Press, 1981).

—— 'Rights and Agency', *Philosophy and Public Affairs*, 11 (1982), 3–39.

—— 'Evaluator Relativity and Consequential Evaluation', *Philosophy and Public Affairs*, 12 (1983), 113–32.

—— 'Property and Hunger', *Economics and Philosophy*, 4 (1988), 57–68.

—— 'Population: Delusion and Reality', *The New York Review of Books*, 22 September 1994, 62–71.

—— 'Legal Rights and Moral Rights: Old Questions and New Problems', *Ratio Juris*, 9 (1996), 153–67.

Sidgwick, H., *Lectures of the Ethics of T. H. Green, H. Spencer, and J. Martineau* (London: Macmillan, 1886).

—— *The Methods of Ethics*, 7th edn. (Indianapolis: Hackett Publishing Company, 1907).

Simon, H., 'Theories of Decision Making in Economics and Behavioral Science', *American Economic Review*, 49 (1959), 253–83.

—— *Administrative Behaviour*, 3rd edn. (New York: Free Press, 1976).

Simpton, P., 'Justice, Scheffler and Consequentialism', *American Catholic Philosophical Quarterly*, 65 (1991), 203–11.

Singer, B., 'An Extension of Rawls's Theory of Justice to Environmental Ethics', *Environmental Ethics*, 10 (1988), 217–32.

Singer, M. G., 'Sidgwick and Nineteenth Century British Ethical Thought', in B. Schultz (ed.), *Essays on Henry Sidgwick* (Cambridge: Cambridge University Press, 1992), 65–91.

Singer, P., 'Famine, Affluence and Morality', *Philosophy and Public Affairs*, 1 (1972), 229–43.

—— *Animal Liberation* (New York, 1975).

—— *Practical Ethics* (Cambridge: Cambridge University Press, 1979).

—— 'A Refutation of Ordinary Morality', *Ethics*, 101 (1991), 625–33.

Slote, M., 'Satisficing Consequentialism', *Proceedings of the Aristotelian Society*, supplementary volume 58 (1984), 165–76.

—— *Commonsense Morality and Consequentialism* (London: Routledge & Kegan Paul, 1985).

—— *Beyond Optimizing: A Study of Rational Choice* (London: Harvard University Press, 1991).

—— *From Morality to Virtue* (New York: Oxford University Press, 1992).

Smart, J. J. C., 'Extreme and Restricted Utilitarianism', in P. Foot (ed.), *Theories of Ethics* (Oxford: Oxford University Press, 1967).

—— 'Benevolence as an Over-Riding Attitude', *Australasian Journal of Philosophy*, 55 (1977), 127–35.

—— and Williams, B., *Utilitarianism: For and Against* (Cambridge: Cambridge University Press, 1973).

Sosa, D., 'Consequences of Consequentialism', *Mind*, 102 (1993), 101–22.

Stern, R., 'The Relation between Moral Theory and Metaphysics', *Proceedings of the Aristotelian Society*, 92 (1992), 143–59.

Stewart, R. M., 'Agent-Relativity, Reason and Value', *Monist*, 76 (1993), 66–80.

Stocker, M., 'Act and Agent Evaluations', *Review of Metaphysics*, 27 (1973), 42–61.

—— 'Rightness and Goodness: Is there a difference?', *American Philosophical Quarterly*, 10 (1973), 87–98.

—— 'The Schizophrenia of Modern Ethical Theories', *Journal of Philosophy*, 73 (1973), 453–66.

Stratton-Lake, P., 'Can Hooker's Rule-Consequentialist Principle Justify Ross's Prima Facie Duties?', *Mind*, 106 (1997), 751–8.

Swanton, C., 'Satisficing and Virtue', *Journal of Philosophy*, 90 (1993), 33–48.

Tannsjo, T., 'Blameless Wrongdoing', *Ethics*, 106 (1995), 120–7.

Taurek, J., 'Should the Numbers Count?', *Philosophy and Public Affairs*, 6 (1977), 293–316.

Thomson, J., 'The Trolley Problem', in her *Rights, Restitution and Risk* (Cambridge, Mass: Harvard University Press, 1986).

Tuomela, R., 'In Search of the Common Mind', *International Journal of Philosophy*, 2 (1994), 306–21.

Unger, P., *Living High and Letting Die: Our Illusion of Innocence* (Oxford: Oxford University Press, 1996).

VanDeveer, D., 'Of Beasts, Persons and the Original Position', *Monist*, 62 (1979), 368–77.

Waldron, J., 'A Right to Do Wrong', *Ethics*, 92 (1981), 21–39.

—— *The Right to Private Property* (Oxford: Oxford University Press, 1988).

—— 'Kagan on Requirements; Mill on Sanctions', *Ethics*, 104 (1994), 310–24.

Walzer, M., *Spheres of Justice* (Oxford: Basil Blackwell, 1983).

Williams, B., 'Consequentialism and Integrity', in A. Smart and B. Williams (eds.), *Utilitarianism: For and Against* (Cambridge: Cambridge University Press, 1973) 82–118.

—— 'Utilitarianism and Moral Self-Indulgence', in H. D. Lewis (ed.), *Contemporary British Philosophy* (London: Allen & Unwin, 1976).

—— *Ethics and the Limits of Philosophy* (Cambridge, Mass: Harvard University Press, 1985).

Wolf, S., 'Moral Saints', *Journal of Philosophy*, 79 (1982), 419–39.

—— 'Moral Judges and Human Ideals: A Discussion of *Human Morality*', *Philosophy and Phenomenological Research*, 55 (1995), 957–62.

—— 'Happiness and Meaning: Two Aspects of the Good Life', *Social Philosophy and Public Policy*, 14 (1997), 207–25.

Wolff, J., *Robert Nozick: Property, Justice, and the Minimal State* (Stanford, Calif.: Stanford University Press, 1991).

World Bank, *World Development Report 1990*.

Index